Praise for 'TIL DEATH DO US PART...

" *'Til Death Do Us Part...* tells the story of one woman's despair over the loss of her dreams—and the renewing of her spirit through her realization of the gifts that every relationship brings. Out of her own painful struggle to heal and grow, Rene Yarnell shares the comforting insight that every ending is a new beginning, and that even when relationships change form, love is a power that lasts forever."
- Mary Manin Morrissey, author, *Building Your Field of Dreams*

"This book embodies the marriage spirit; it combines spirituality and relationship and creates a whole new awareness for couples to share."
- Drs. Evelyn and Paul Moschetta, marriage counselors, authors of *The Marriage Spirit*

" *'Til Death Do Us Part...* raises the interesting questions of how long a marriage should last and must it be a lifetime? Author, business executive, and former Catholic nun Rene Reid Yarnell explores these questions and her answers in this can't-put-it-down story of her own personal experiences and her need to find the truth. *'Til Death Do Us Part...* offers a means to reduce the sadness we feel at the end of a relationship when we are forced to face a new beginning. In this best-seller, quality book, the author gives the reader an understanding of how to not only cope, but to heal and grow."
- Richard Fuller, *Metaphysical Reviews*

'TIL DEATH DO US PART...

One Woman's Story of
Facing the Reality
After Clinging to the Dream

by

Rene Reid Yarnell, M.A.

A Quantum Leap Publication

A Quantum Leap Nonfiction Book

ISBN# 1-883599-17-2

Cover design by Gilbert Leiker, On-Call Graphics, Inc.
Page design by Michael B. Kitson, On-Call Graphics, Inc.
Editing: Caroline Pincus, Book Midwife
Proofreading: Jean Stoess

Publisher's - Cataloging-in-Publication
(Provided by Quality Books Inc.)

Yarnell, Rene.
    'Til death do us part : one woman's story of facing
the reality after clinging to the dream / by Rene Reid
Yarnell. -- 1st ed.
    p.cm.
    ISBN 1-883599-17-2

    1. Marriage--United States--Psychological aspects.
2. Divorce--United States--Psychological aspects.
3. Yarnell, Rene. 4. Married people--United States--
Psychology. 5. Man-woman relationships--United States--
Psychological aspects.   I. Title.

HQ536.Y37 2001   306.81'0973
                           QBI01-700174

Quantum Leap Publications
95 Rancho Manor Dr.
Reno, NV 89509

Printed in the United States of America
10 9 8 7 6 5 4 3 2 1

DEDICATION

To Mom, Frank, and Nancy,
and to those who stood by me, called me, held me, and loved me
through this most devastating and catastrophic transition,
you know who you are and I gratefully dedicate this book to you.

To you, Mark,
for the intimate sharing of yourself with me over these years
allowing us to reach out to touch the hearts and lives of so many
others and for encouraging me to rise to my full potential
that my capacity to love has been raised to a new level,
preparing me for the next phase of my life.

And, finally, to the Prince,
who had turned into a turtle under a sorcerer's spell,
thank you for sharing so much of yourself
as you initiated me to new beginnings.

Other books by
Rene Reid Yarnell

The New Entrepreneurs:
Making a Living–Making a Life through Network Marketing
•
The New Entrepreneurs:
Audio Program
•
The Encyclopedia of Network Marketing

Co-authored with Mark Yarnell

Your First Year in Network Marketing
•
Power Multi-Level Marketing
•
Should You Quit Before You're Fired?
(with Paul Zane Pilzer)

Table of Contents

Part II: Present
June 1998 – July 1999

Epilogue-Afterword
November 1999-September 2000

FOREWORD

Strange and marvelous things will begin to happen in your life with constant regularity as you capture just a few of the many lessons that are brilliantly woven throughout each of these chapters. But, let me caution you, Rene Yarnell has done such a fine job in writing this book, you can and will get caught up in the story. It has been said that a good book is a series of pictures painted in words. As you progress from one page to the next, you will be mentally seduced into participating in a dramatic, real-life movie. You will find yourself laughing, getting excited and then frustrated, possibly angry at times, voicing advice...and then laughing at yourself as you realize there is no way the characters can hear you.

It is at this point where you stop and THINK. You will become aware of what the author is sharing with you...the most intimate details of her life. You remind yourself—this is not fiction, this is real. This book is about the life of one woman, Rene Reid Yarnell.

As I read, I found my mind moving off in many different directions. I found myself wondering WHY? Why has this author opened the door for the world to look at such personal and private situations. Then, in the same subtle manner the question surfaced in my mind, the answer appeared. However the answer did not appear the way that you might expect. I was flying from the east to the west coast, totally engrossed in the book. I came to a part where two of the characters were having a conversation and one of the characters was being very disrespectful to the other. I began to think, "Why couldn't he be more considerate?" These thoughts were immediately followed with the thought, "Why couldn't I?" The book had provoked me to face up to times when I had been inconsiderate. Without hesitation I swiped my credit card through the phone in my arm rest and called my wife. I told her about the manuscript I was reading and asked her if she would remind me, from time to time, to be a little more considerate. I explained to Linda how the part of the book that I had just read helped me see that by being more considerate I would like me more and it would obviously make her happier. We discussed this for a few minutes. I hung up the phone and began to reflect on what I had read and what I was reading. I could see how there was room in every relationship I had where I could be more considerate, more honest about what I thought and felt.

I could see why Rene had written this book. She wanted to help people and it was working, she had just helped me...a lot. At that moment, my perception of this book shifted. I began to see the hundreds of lessons that were jumping off every page. I also began to think of friends who were facing certain challenges in their lives and how this book would help them. Although Rene Yarnell's entire adult life has been one of service and helping other people, I do not think for one second that she was thinking of helping other people when she began this book many years ago. It did not, in fact, even begin as a book, it began as a journal. Rene wrote it as she lived it. Then, there must have been a point and time in her mind where her journal was almost magically transformed into a book that she had to publish. Rene recognized that the pages were full of lessons that could and would apply to almost any thinking person's life and she had to share them.

Years ago, my former employer and mentor Earl Nightingale said, "If most people said what they were thinking, they would be speechless." People trick themselves into believing that mental activity constitutes thinking; it does not. Most people are merely playing old tapes, going to old movies. They would never do what they're doing or say what they're saying if they were thinking. This book will make you think. It will make you think about aspects of your life that most people would prefer to avoid and unfortunately, to their own detriment, many do avoid. However, as we begin to think about these aspects of our lives, it becomes clear how we can become better people and enjoy a greater quality of life.

It was at least 30 years ago, I was given a copy of *The Mystic Path to Cosmic Power* by Vernon Howard. It is one of the best books on introspection I have ever come across. This book by Rene Yarnell is the same type of book. It will cause you to look at yourself in ways that are absolutely essential if you want to live a good life. The English novelist Aldous Huxley once pointed out, "the only corner of the universe we can be certain of improving is our own self." Huxley was right, however if we're going to improve ourselves, we must look at ourselves...all sides of ourselves. Rene's open and honest way of doing this will inspire you to do the same. As we begin taking this in-depth, honest evaluation of what we are doing with our lives and then ask ourselves why we are doing it, we become more alive, we begin to grow. We see how everything that happens in our lives is good. It is a lesson that prepares us for bigger, better, more interesting mind-expanding experiences.

Prior to receiving the advanced copy of this book, I had never spoken to Rene Yarnell. I knew of her and she knew of me, but we did not know one another. Through reading this book and discussing it with her, we have become very good friends. I am certain as time passes, we will become even better friends. As you begin getting involved with her book, you too are going to like Rene, you might even fall in love with her. She has a personal magnetism that shines throughout each chapter. It becomes obvious to the reader that she has character and a quiet strength that is quite admirable. When I first completed the book and laid it down, I was struck by her honesty, how she has been true to herself. Those famous lines by Shakespeare that he gave us in Hamlet came to mind,

> "This above all: to thine own self be true,
> And it must follow, as the night the day,
> Thou canst not then be false to any man."

Rene has followed Shakespeare's advice and through it she has moved closer to what God wants her to become. I am honored that she asked me to write a foreword to her book. Her words and example have inspired me to become a better me. Likewise, long before you complete this classic, you are going to like you more.

Bob Proctor,
Author of best-selling book,
You Were Born Rich

INTRODUCTION

This is the story of a fairytale romance that culminated in marital crisis. My intent in writing it is to raise consciousness that a new paradigm is needed as couples embrace marriage today. Challenges in relationships are inevitable. Given this, I propose that our objective be to emerge from our marital crises more ready than ever to make sound choices—either to renew and enhance our existing unions or to move on, transforming feelings of devastation into uplifting new beginnings without the usual sense of blame and failure. Such an outlook could open the way for giving birth to new types of relationships—primary partnerships that place more focus on each other's personal development.

Of all the people we have come to know, or will ever know, there is something extraordinarily special about those with whom we have shared the emotional and sexual intimacies of living together in marriage or an equally close commitment. These relationships not only shape our life story, but also the unfolding and expansion of us as persons. It would be most unfortunate if, at the ending of such a partnership, we found nothing to appreciate. The merit of a relationship is not necessarily in its lasting forever. Its value lies in the journey two people shared while together. The more we can appreciate our relationships and honor them for the unique contribution they made to our lives, the less devastation there will be surrounding their endings.

Of course, our human nature will always lead us to enter relationships with the belief and commitment that they will last forever. No one goes into intimate partnerships expecting serious crises, much less for them to end. Certainly I never have. But neither can we go on, as a society, burying our collective heads in the sand: More than one out of two marriages, including the second and third nuptials, ends in divorce. And the rest end in death. These aren't hypotheses. These are facts. And with the extended longevity of life, these statistics are likely to increase, not diminish. Endings are inevitable. Isn't it time that we cease being so surprised if or when our relationships reach an impasse? Isn't it time that we acknowledge this reality and find healthier, more compassionate ways for coping with these unavoidable events?

That is not to say that, for both sides, partings are not fraught with emotion, anguish, and despair. The pain of a relationship ending is unavoidable. The very roots of our soul are shaken. For those of us who have been left feeling that deep sense of abandonment, we doubt our ability to go on without our partner. It is difficult, at first, to see any future at all. We lack confidence in ourselves and in our ability to stand on our own. The only good news about these debilitating experiences is that, without them, we could not possibly create a new life for ourselves—a life founded on purpose and driven by conviction.

Some will, by necessity or choice, continue on together in a new form of relationship after the old form ends. Whether out of convenience or a mutually redefined transformation of the shared bond, fault-finding and accusation must be replaced with forgiveness and reconciling love in order to be able to go on effectively in each other's lives. If children are involved, both parties should feel compelled to put the children's good ahead of their own personal emotions. This isn't an option but should be considered mandatory for the basic human dignity of lives that otherwise cannot yet fend for themselves. If the couple decides to continue a friendship or professional association, the healing process must be respected. Once it is complete, the alliance can often become one of deep friendship and authentic sharing. If the encounter is just to fill the emptiness, a continued involvement may not be as healthy.

As we move from one relationship to the next, it is less a matter of learning from the mistakes we made and more of giving ourselves permission to absorb the good that came from the relationship and allow it to propel us to the next level of interpersonal relations. This can only happen by choice. You and I have the power within us to create any attitude we choose. Instead of focusing on the hurts and the disappointments and what has come between us, we have the choice to focus on what drew us together.

Scientists with no theistic tendencies have concluded that the human thought is more powerful than electricity, more forceful than an atomic explosion. Human thought can transcend the physical universe. It is my hope that this book will enable you to utilize various means of self-empowerment—already accessible to you and perhaps lying dormant—to take hold of the steering wheel of your life and set it on course, accelerating wherever you feel bogged down and slowing down in moments worth savoring.

I remember years ago when "process philosophy" was popularized. I studied it hungrily, and today I cannot imagine anything not in "process." It is that forward thrust that gives life its meaning, in which each conclusion is only the beginning of yet another level of personal growth, a new transition of life experience.

At whatever stage of life you find yourself at this moment, I trust you will enjoy the honest depicting of my story. It is not my intention to represent myself as an expert on relationships, but rather as someone who has been through the ending of deep relationships often enough to perhaps have something of value to share—as much by my mistakes as by those matters I handled with some maturity. Nor is it my desire to offer you cookie-cutter solutions for your own relationships. So much of life is looking inside of ourselves and discovering who we are as authentic persons. Having done this, you and you alone will know how to address your own relationship crises: when to renew the existing partnership and when to let it go and begin again to create a new spiritual bonding.

After much thought, I have chosen storytelling over the more traditional self-help book to reach readers who may be encountering marital crises, perhaps feeling trapped in a marriage or wallowing in the self-pitying stage of abandonment after a relationship has ended. I hope also to touch the souls of those who leave relationships with no tears, no sense of loss in moving on, yet find themselves troubled when the same pattern keeps repeating itself. Using the narrative art form, I feel freer to share a series of processes that helped me emerge from the depths of my despair to actually discover solutions to my own dilemma and experience the joy that follows.

The story I am about to tell is my story, told through my eyes, my feelings, and my perspective. It is as accurate a story as can be when told through one person's viewpoint. At my husband's encouragement, I began writing this book in the summer of 1996 while we were living in our second home in Gstaad, Switzerland. I had titled it "Marriage and Merger." Serious problems had not yet arisen and, therefore, my purpose in writing at that time was to share insights into the successful achievement of having both a personal relationship and a business partnership. I have the advantage of having written about many of the blissful parts of our life while I was experiencing the relationship that way.

Two years later, by the summer of 1998, I had retreated to Sunset Beach just south of Santa Cruz, California, and used writing as a means of expressing my sadness and pain. From the perspective of the value of this as a piece of literature, it is good that I also wrote this portion of my story while I was going through the despondency. The letters, poetry, and e-mails are exactly as they were because I saved them. I would often capture the dialogue shortly after it occurred, recalling it as accurately as I could. Out of respect for those in the story, I have not attempted to second-guess their attitudes. Rather, I am unfolding a story only as I experienced it.

Introduction

It is not my intention to denigrate any person in this story. I hope to share enough background and family heritage to help the reader see the patterns that inevitably form throughout the decades of family history. That is not to excuse some behavior, but it does help us understand it. If in every conversation, every human exchange, we had the ability to know each other's family lineage and deeply grooved models for living life, how much more sympathetic we might be of each other's perspective about life. I attempt to interject this into some of the dialogue as the story unfolds.

An alcoholic often chooses to be open about his disease for two reasons: hoping to help others by the honest exposure as well as to keep from falling back into old patterns. It has not been an impulsive decision on my part to tell my story. But after deep consideration, thoughtful prayer, and guidance from those upon whom I rely, I have concluded that sharing my story is akin to the alcoholic model. If I can effect change in public attitude toward marriage, divorce, and starting over after the loss of someone special in our lives, the good for the whole of society is offset by the discomfort I may cause myself and a handful of people in my life. I have shared my own shortcomings and the evolution of my personal growth with all the awareness of which I'm capable. By doing so, if I can help even one individual overcome the belief that he or she has failed, is a victim, has let the children down, is unlovable, or is unworthy of having a loving relationship, then the self-exposure has been worth it.

My purpose is not only to set forth a compelling narrative. Through this book, I hope to recount how one seemingly overpowering love affair—one that touched and transformed the lives of many people, and certainly the two of us and our children in a dramatic way—could reach the point of such devastation. By telling my story—our story—my objective is to embrace the myriad of others who have suffered their own losses and have gone through their own crises, separations, or endings. It is my hope that together we may find our exodus out of the dark cavity—

the debilitating anguish and inherent failure associated with the temporary separation or permanent ending of a relationship—into an illuminated realm of joyous inner strength.

Of all the people I know, certainly I—not only raised Catholic but one who spent several years as a nun and holds a Master's in Theology—had every reason to believe that I would grow up, get married, bear children, and live with my husband "'til death do us part." But now, having lived through more than forty years of close relationships (counting my high school sweetheart), including more than twenty years of cumulative marriages, and observing firsthand the changes in our society, I recognize the unlikelihood of that occurrence for the majority of couples today. While I remain in awe of those who achieve this phenomenon, it is my objective to open up new paradigm possibilities for those whose lives move in different directions (the etymology of the word "divorce"), perhaps more than once. When we face these crossroads, perhaps we will begin to look beyond the legal and fiscal confinements of traditional marriage and explore alternatives—life choices wherein more emphasis is placed on the personal and spiritual growth of ourselves and our partners. If something I share in this book compels you to take stock of your relationship and to clarify your direction, then this will have been a worthwhile project.

Rene Reid Yarnell
Reno, Nevada
July 2000

To My Readers

This book is for visionaries with utopian philosophies and romantics who continue to pursue the fairytale. It is for those men and women who cling to the hope that, somewhere out there, their soul mate is waiting or searching for them. It is for couples who are searching for new forms of relationships or those who choose to blend their work life and family life in this new millennium. It is for professional network marketers who share the idealistic view that ethics and business *can* coexist. It is for those in public office who share the idealistic view that ethics and politics *can* coexist. It is for dependents and co-dependents struggling to overcome alcoholism or drug addiction. This book is for self-explorers interested in probing their life's purpose and understanding the links between various events. It is for those who must inevitably face transitions in their lives, whether they are solicited or not. This book is about the struggle to overcome human weakness and the aspiration to make ourselves, our relationships, and our world just a little better. This book is about emerging from the sheltered place we may currently be lingering to enter into a world of our own creation filled with meaningful activities, loving relationships, commitment to spiritual growth, and promise for the future.

With Love,

Rene

'TIL DEATH DO US PART...

*One Woman's Story of Facing the Reality
After Clinging to the Dream*

CHAPTER 1

CLINGING TO THE DREAM

June 1998

I couldn't sleep. Sliding out of bed trying not to wake Mark, I groped my way in the dark to the walk-in closet, shut the door, and turned on the light. I slipped into a warm-up suit and made my way downstairs. Cody met me at the bottom of the stairs and lapped my face affectionately. On autopilot, I began brewing the coffee, let the dog out for his morning run, and switched on my computer. I found comfort touching the keys and staring at the screen. I clicked onto the file that contained my morning affirmations. "I am passionate as I show my love for Mark," I read as I began my list, "making our relationship my highest priority, opening up our communication, and doing little acts of kindness for him throughout the day." Reciting these was an important part of my morning ritual, keeping me focused on my vision and on track to pursue my life's purpose.

I caught myself going back over one of the affirmations, as if repeating it would somehow make it happen instantly. "I feel supported working with a team of positive business partners who share my values." *Boy, I really have to work on this one!* As I finished reading my list of positive statements, I closed my eyes and, laying my head against the back of my chair, I began praying. *Oh, God, I'm frightened. Mark and I could lose everything: our marriage, our business, our life savings. Every penny we have is going into this new company—like a voracious money-shredder—and he wants to keep borrowing more money to pour into it. Making this company a success is all that matters to him. Not to me. I could easily walk away from it. I just want him back—the old Mark, my loving, adoring, precious husband. We had a life that others only dream about. No stress, not really. No financial worries. No restrictions. Our family under one roof. We had the freedom to go anyplace in the world—and we have. We've been a role model for so many who aspired to achieve what we have, both materially and spiritually. How did we get ourselves in this mess? Dear God, I wish we'd never started this company. It is destroying us. The silence between us is piercing. Please help us. Show me what to do. I feel so powerless.*

I grabbed a tissue and blew my nose. Wiping away the tears with my fingers, I closed the file, poured myself a cup of coffee, clicked on my personal journal file, and began writing:

> With every passing day, the pressure of our business finances is putting unbearable strain on us and leading Mark to question the core values of both our personal relationship and business partnership. A "marriage and merger" he loved to call it. I remember when he had our business cards printed up with the name 'Yarnell and Yarnell.' He was so eager and proud to have me take his name. Holding public office, I was known as Rene Reid or Commissioner Reid, but it was critical to him that I go by Rene Yarnell. Not even Rene Reid Yarnell. Just Rene Yarnell, Mark Yarnell's wife.
>
> But when a crisis hits, living and working together can be double jeopardy, and in our case it is. We are at risk of losing everything at this moment: each other, our family, our business, our reputation, our finances. Even our commitment to putting God first seems to have slipped.

> Our every conversation is turning into an argument. We know how to avoid this. And yet, despite every good intention, we end up fighting. The stress is destroying us. What happened to the Mark who promised never to stop putting our love first and asked me to do the same? There was a time when we planned everything together. Now, we can't agree on much of anything—especially the way we are going through our money. And when I try to make our partners understand that we can't keep this up, they shut me out. They prefer to hear Mark's grandiose assurances rather than to listen to my voice of reality.
>
> One of the endearing qualities about my husband is that he really believes that money grows on trees and, somehow, it will never stop reproducing itself.
>
> Dear God, if only I could be all that I aspire to be...to myself, to Mark, to my partners. I am at a complete loss. What should I do? No matter what I say, I seem to alienate our partners more. I've got to do something before it is too late.

I saved the file and poured myself a second cup. I sat down at my desk but couldn't concentrate on anything in front of me. I was shivering. Not from the cold but from emotions. Leaning back in my chair, with both hands wrapped around my cup for warmth, I began reflecting on how we got ourselves in this disaster.

The catalyst for all of our arguments these days stemmed from financial pressures. We had taken on "equal" partners to begin our own network marketing company, 21st Century Global Network. American Technologies Group and Integrated Health Inc. each represented a third of the company and our own group, Global Trust, consisting of three couples, made up the last third. The joy of starting a new business didn't last long. It was quickly supplanted by the anxiety of cash flow concerns.

Mark offered all our partners equal status in the company. And yet there was not equal investment. That's Mark. Generous to a fault. More than a businessman, he's a philanthropist through and through. He just loves to give. It is, in fact, one of the qualities I find most attractive about him.

Some of the partners were willing, but unable, to make any investment. Others pledged to invest but, in the end, couldn't meet their full commitment. Yes, I could see that all of our partners had the highest of intentions and gave their best, but the financial burden of the company fell to us. After investing every bit of available cash into the business, personally guaranteeing everything we couldn't buy on credit, and borrowing another quarter of a million we didn't have, when there was no place left to turn and no one else to carry on, the walls of our life were crashing down on us. Somewhere in our determination to press forward despite all odds, Mark and I were destroying the most important element of our personal life.

Mark could live with the possibility of losing every penny we own, but he couldn't stand the thought of the business failing. Both of our reputations were on the line, but losing face over this was far more life threatening for Mark...and I understood that. We both wanted to find the win in this for everyone involved. But my practical, business side cried out that we couldn't keep pouring money into this all by ourselves. And, worse, this was not an equitable arrangement. Even the workload had shifted. In the beginning, ATG had agreed to oversee all aspects of product development, manufacturing, and distribution, while the Global Trust partnership was to handle setting up the office, building the field of distributors, and developing all the promotional and training materials. Through a series of defaults, responsibility for product development fell to us as well. That was okay. I wasn't complaining about it. The real problem was financing.

For Mark, it was inconsequential who actually made the investments. What mattered was that he had to make this company successful no matter what it took...his entire lifetime reputation was depending on it. His self-confident grandiosity was one of the many things most people love about my husband. Everyone and everything within his realm of experience was bigger than life.

"This company is going to become a ten-billion-dollar

company, the first in Network Marketing history to ever achieve that," he would assert. "What does it matter who makes the investments or what the disbursements are now? As the primary investor, we'll get all of our money back, and there will be plenty of profits for all of the partners as well."

He knew beyond any doubt that the company would be successful long-term. From his perspective, the only problem was short-term cash flow. Therefore, it was essential that we pour everything we had and beyond into this company to keep it going.

Initially, Mark and I had agreed to invest $150,000 into this venture as our part of the contribution. I was comfortable with that, and could live with the loss if it failed. But we had long since passed that point. Now we were investing every bit of available cash. Added to that, we had not only taken out a second mortgage against our home, but sold most of our stocks at a loss. And finally, we had the paperwork completed to borrow against our primary income, the last remaining source of funding we had. This was far more risk than I had anticipated, and I was scared. If we were going to put up the lion's share of the funding, then, at the very least, I felt that the contract of "equal partnership" should be revisited. To my way of thinking, we couldn't continue to put up most of the investment and preserve the status of everyone being equal partners.

"A deal is a deal, and we made this deal," Mark would argue.

"But they are not living up to their end of the deal. We are equal partners with equal responsibility to find or invest the money for this company. Every week, they give us hope that they will have their share next week. But next week never comes."

"But they're trying. At least ATG is trying. I think IHI knows that they can't come up with the money."

"So you're saying that it becomes our responsibility to put in all of their shares plus our own? Sweetheart, why don't we just set up a welfare system? I've never seen a business partnership work this way. This company was founded on a faulty contract. Now we're risking everything we have for one ninth of the ownership of this company."

"How do you figure that?" Mark asked disinterestedly.

"Global Trust owns one third, and we are one third of Global Trust. So we take the lion's share of the risk and receive one ninth of the profits. With both of us working full-time, that's one-eighteenth for each of us. Something is wrong with that. I just wish the partners would do what they promised. I don't want to take this big of a risk. I'm scared, Mark."

"I don't care about any of that. I know this company can succeed. I'm keeping my eye on where we're going. You are so negative. All you look at is the worst-case scenario. You pull me down, and I don't need that right now."

"I don't mean to dampen your spirits, but you're scaring me. What about you and me? What about our family? What about our putting God and our family before work? We could lose each other and every penny we have, and none of that seems to matter."

"I just can't think about that right now. Don't you understand? The success of this company rests on me, and I have to make it work. It isn't an option. I have to."

Conversations would end on that note. I would spend hours thinking about a solution, but when I tried reopening our communication, he would avoid it. He was overwhelmed by the weight of this venture. I asked if we could turn to someone who knew more about business investments than we did. That didn't work. I suggested that we get away together. No time.

Out of desperation, I decided to write a note and leave it on his pillow: "Please, can we make time for each other tonight? I'm hurting and just need to be with you."

I heard Mark rustling in the kitchen right above me. I went up to say good morning and see what frame of mind he was in. Nothing had changed.

With my note in my pocket, I hurried up to our bedroom, straightened the covers, and left it on his pillow. I showered and dressed for the day and stayed out of his way as much as I could throughout the workday. When I got home from the office, Mark was reading the note, and looked up at me.

"Jesus Christ, what have I done now? What else can possibly be wrong? I'm too wiped to be dragged into one of those long, drawn-out ordeals. Can't this wait until morning?"

There were so many things I wanted to say. *No, it can't wait. We've waited a lifetime for each other. Let's not destroy what we have over a little fatigue or distancing ourselves from each other.* But I said none of these things. "Okay, the morning will be fine, but you won't forget?"

"No, you know I'm better in the mornings anyway." He was lost in his world of television, and I lay beside him wondering how our relationship had degenerated to this point. I dozed off and on. At one o'clock in the morning I felt him climbing out of bed.

"Are you getting up?" I asked hopefully. Maybe now we could talk. No phones. No people. No interruptions.

"Yeah, I want to write for a while." My heart sank. *Please can't we talk or just lie here together?* I'm crying out but he doesn't hear.

"Are you coming back to bed later?"

"Yeah, I have to get some sleep or I'll never make it through the day."

I lay awake for a long time, feeling completely alone, thinking about our prospects for the future. *Would we pull this business together in time? There is no question that, given enough time and money, it won't be a problem. But what if we—Mark and Rene— run out of funds before the sales kick in? What if we go bankrupt over this? How well will we handle that? What will that do to our relationship? What will that do to all the people counting on us? To John Radford and Valerie Perkio, our two Global Trust partners, and to our presidential team and distributors? What will that do to Mark? Can he face it? Oh, please God, guide us through this. Only You can see what lies ahead and can know what is best for all of us.*

I lay there thinking back to our wedding vows. Mark was so committed to our marriage that he had written out every word. I kept our vows in our Memory Box and, from time to time, would get them out and read them. I had looked at them so often recently that I had parts memorized:

On this, our wedding day, I must admit that I am prepared to give up all that I hold dear in this world for your presence in my life. You are the "pearl of great price" whom I have sought for 41 years—the very completion of my destiny and nothing short of death can drag me ever from your side. Of necessity, as our responsibilities dictate, I will be separated from you for a few hours at a time but we will never again sleep alone. I am in total control of my own destiny and as such refuse to ever reach across a bed and not find the warmth of your presence. No event of any magnitude will every put "spaces in our togetherness."

I needed to be sensitive to the stress Mark was under right now. Men and women handle it differently. I knew that Mark's behavior of late was not the man I had known and lived with these past six-and-a-half years. This was far worse than anything we had ever been through together. But I too was feeling the pressure. I needed him. I needed him to live out that particular commitment now more than ever. *"No event of any magnitude will ever put 'spaces in our togetherness.'"*

Before I knew it, it was three o'clock and Mark was coming back to bed. "Are you awake?" I asked hopefully.

"Yeah, wide awake, unfortunately."

Maybe now was the time. I'd ease into it gently as I curled up next to him in a fetal position. "You know, I really love you. When I look at what we've accomplished together, I realize that we've lived a lifetime by some people's standards. But we have so much more that we still need to do. I'm worried about the business, especially with you and me out of sync. I want so much to get things back to where they belong with us...for our sake and for the company. I'm willing to try much harder, but I need to know that you want me in your life. Lately, you act like I don't matter to you at all." A long silence followed. I waited. Still nothing. Finally I broke it with, "So what do you think?"

"About what?"

"About what I just said?"

More silence followed. "Are you sure you're awake?"

"Yes, I'm wide awake. I wish I weren't." He spoke with hostility.

Should I let it go or do I keep trying, trying to find ways to communicate? I've been asking to have this conversation for nearly a month. The lack of communication was slowly destroying us. The image of the Phantom of the Opera came to mind. I sensed I was speaking to that mask. I didn't care. I reasoned that the time would never get any better. Besides, at least I could hold him while we talked. That felt better. I hoped he could feel my love and how much I wanted to understand his point of view. But I also needed him to understand mine. This wasn't a dress rehearsal. This was real life, and everything in it was at risk. I decided to approach the subject from another angle.

"You know, it tears me up when I hear Donny say that the reason he is in this company all goes back to when he came to visit and how he could see our love, the way we are with each other. He said he and Diane went home and wanted to become a part of Global Network because of the love that comes from us. They'd like to emulate us. You see, sweetheart, I want to have back what they think we are. I want to really be that again."

More silence followed. I waited. Still nothing. Finally I said, "Doesn't that bother you a little, what Donny said?"

"Donny who?"

"How many Donnys are central to our life right now? Donny Walker!"

"What did he say?"

"Mark, this conversation, if you want to call it that, is driving me nuts. Forget it, just go to sleep. We'll talk in the morning." I was angry, and I didn't want to feel that way for this talk. I felt hopeless.

Just when I thought he was really asleep, he spoke again. "What did Donny say?"

"I just told you. Are you listening? Have you heard anything I've said?"

"About what?"

My blood pressure was rising. There was never a right time to talk...never. With a slight edge to my voice, I replied, "Donny and so many people in our company, and for that matter, in our industry, look up to us. They think we have it all together. They think we love each other. I want to have what they think we have. Once upon a time, we had the fairytale. I want it back. I want our marriage to be first." Usually he held me in our favorite spoon position. But this time, it was I holding him. I could feel his body tense up. But he didn't say anything. So I continued: "And, Mark, I really believe that this company is being hurt by the way we are with each other. We can't go on like this."

"Are you saying you think you can hurt this company? I won't let you! The company doesn't need you. If you would just trust me the way you used to, and let me be the man and the decision-maker, it would be fine. It is when you stick your nose where you don't belong that you cause problems. I have twice the brains you do, and I wish you'd recognize that. You are nothing to this company except trouble. Everybody thinks so."

This isn't Mark. Who is this talking to me? What's happening to us? "Who's everybody?" I asked warily.

"Val, John, Amy, certainly Larry." Amy, our daughter, Mark's daughter by a former marriage. I wondered if that was true. Larry, the head of ATG, I could accept. He and I had reached an impasse over the money situation. I'm sure I handled this badly. But I was upset that Larry seemed willing to let Mark go as far out on a limb as he was willing to go. He acted like a close friend to Mark, but I found myself mistrusting Larry's motives. I was afraid Larry saw my husband as a way out of his own dilemmas with his company. Before I could say anything, Mark went on. "You have really overstepped your bounds there...with Larry. I've finally had enough of the way you deal with A-type men. You need to go get some pills or something to get you through menopause." Not only was my external world changing, but my body as well. And all of it combined was making me extremely emotional.

"Sweetheart, you and I handle the stress differently. The strain of this company is bringing out the worst in both of us. I just don't know how…"

"I'm just fine. I'm the way I always was. You are the one who is different. And if you want things the way they were, you are going to have to change yourself. I don't intend to do anything different."

I rolled away from him and lay there with nothing left to say. All hope was stripped for our having any meaningful communication. His words were resounding in my head. The pain went through me like shock waves—approaching a seven on the emotional Richter scale. I hurt so much I wanted to die. *The man talking this way isn't the man I knew and loved. Where did he go? I want him back. I want our old life back. To hell with partners, and the company, and the financial risks. It isn't worth it. Nothing is worth the risk of losing each other. And maybe I am being overly controlling. Maybe the way I'm supposed to love him is to trust him enough to let him do whatever he chooses with our money. Maybe we've had the good life long enough. Just maybe the divine plan is that we are supposed to hit bottom and then work together to climb back up again. Mark held our life together during our first year of marriage when I was immersed in politics. Now perhaps it is my turn while he is so completely caught up with our business venture. Yes, this time it is up to me to hold us together.*

When I was sure he was asleep, I slipped out of bed, put on a robe, and wandered downstairs to my office. This morning I dispensed with my usual morning regime. I finished all the work relevant to the immediate tasks at hand and left notes guiding Valerie and Amy about follow-up to some of my responsibilities. Then I went to the computer and let the words pour out of me as I attempted once more to explain to Mark what was going on inside of me.

Saturday Morning

Dear Mark,

This morning's conversation took the last bit of hope out of me for both our marriage and our business relationship. I always want to give you the benefit of the doubt that I have just picked the wrong moment to try to have a serious conversation. But after so many times of trying, I don't know what else I can say or how many more times I can try.

My perspective is that we are strong together and that our company needs us to reflect our love, a united message and a single spirit, back out to our partners and our distributors. For me, this is not being airy-fairy—this is real.

I miss what we had and stand ready and willing to work toward bringing it back. This is what I wanted to say, but, given how the conversation went, I don't know how to bring this back. I just know I can't do it all by myself.

Like it or not, our personal life and our business life *are* intertwined. The distance between us at home is reflected in the distance between us in building this company.

I have been talking for the past couple of weeks about needing to get away and make a retreat. I need time to sort out my life, my value as a person, my purpose, and how all that fits with you and Global Network.

I love you, and I do respect you. Your words and actions toward me are hurtful. Apparently I have hurt you too, and for that I'm truly sorry. You are a very special man. I am willing to give every ounce of energy I have to saving our relationship. My purpose in leaving is to work on my part of what has gone wrong.

The solution, if there is to be one, must come from our mutual respect for each other's talents, intelligence, and spirituality. Right now, I can only do what is in my power to do alone. I need to go work on my own relationship with God, and reflect on how I can grow and become a more loving person to everyone in my life. I have made mistakes, and I need to figure out how to correct them before it is too late. Somehow I know you will understand and give me the space to do this. I've already cleared my taking time away with John and Valerie, and feel that I have their support. I will be in touch, Rene

Making my way upstairs to his office, feeling the weight of every step I took, I laid the letter down on his desk on top of the ashtray where I was sure he wouldn't miss it. Smoking is always his first coherent act of the morning. Up another flight of stairs to our bedroom, I grabbed a suitcase and began to pack in the dark. Before 5:00 in the morning, I pulled out of the garage, glancing back through my rearview mirror at our home, which sat high on a hill overlooking the city of Reno. As I drove down the long winding driveway, every muscle in my body ached with sadness. I stopped by our office downtown to get my training manual and disks, reset my message on my voice mail, and left my desk in order. By 5:45 I was on the highway to California.

Driving through the early morning light, my mind wandered back to how beautifully Mark expressed his love for me during our early days together. Ever so gently, my heart pulsated to the enchanting flow of our favorite love song, "Somewhere in Time." Yes, how I recalled those times: his unwavering support through our first year of marriage when I was under immense strain from my days in politics, and his promise that nothing, absolutely nothing, would ever come between us. If we survived *that* year, I knew we could come through anything together. Mark was my soul mate. He was there for me when I needed him. Now it was my turn to give him my steadfast allegiance. This is nothing more than a challenge meant to measure the real depth of our love for each other.

We'll get past it. I know we will. I'm not willing to give up. I am not willing to give up.

As I headed west on the Interstate, with the warmth of the sun at my back, I watched the landscape transform from the sage-scattered brown of the Nevada desert to the forest-green of the California coastline. My soul felt like that desert at this moment, so dry and barren. I prayed that a little time spent away would bring life to my spirit.

Driving on cruise control, I let my thoughts wander back to the start of our relationship when Mark and I lay side by side in his hammock baring our souls to each other.

"Of course, I would never leave you. I could never even distance myself from you," I could remember him saying. "And if you ever leave me, I promise you...I will follow you wherever you go." *Dear God, let him mean this. Please Mark, come follow me. I know we can pull our lives back together and make it even better than before.*

PART I

Flashback

September 1988 – June 1998

CHAPTER 2

ELECTION TO PUBLIC OFFICE
1988-1989

In the far distance, I could hear ringing...ringing...ringing. I woke out of a deep sleep. It wasn't a dream. It was the phone. I glanced at the clock: 4:12. Who could be calling at this hour of the morning? Groping for the phone, I managed to gain consciousness quickly.

"Hello."

"Rene, it's Larry Beck. I just wondered if you'd read this morning's paper."

I let a few seconds go by taking in what he'd said. My eyes gazed back at the clock. Nothing was making any sense yet. "Huh? What are you talking about?"

I could hear his laughter. Whatever it was, Larry was thoroughly enjoying keeping me in suspense. Finally, he broke his chuckle long enough to spurt out, "If your delivery hasn't arrived yet, I'd suggest that you get up and drive to the nearest newspaper stand. Trust me. This little trip will be worth it.... Oh, and by the way...welcome aboard, Commissioner!" The phone went dead.

The primary election to the Board of County Commissioners was in its final days. I had only four days left in a very close race between the incumbent, Belie Williams, and myself. Larry was also on the board and had been supportive during my campaign.

"Welcome aboard." What could he mean? Wide-awake, I threw on some jeans and drove down to the nearest strip mall. I pulled up in front of the Blue Bounty storefront knowing the papers would already be in the bin for the day. I fumbled for the right change, and opened the box. Yes, it was today's paper, Friday, September 2, 1988. It wasn't hard to find what Larry wanted me to see. There it was—front-page headline news: "Commissioners Steamed by Williams' TV Spot." The by-line read: "Washoe official led water search, ad says," by Jim Mitchell/*Gazette-Journal*. With the motor still running to stay warm, I sat in the car absorbing every word of the article. I could hardly believe what I was reading:

A majority of Washoe County Commissioners are blasting fellow Commissioner Belie Williams for a television ad campaign they say inaccurately depicts him as a pioneer in the search for new water sources.

Several commissioners took issue with the television ad's claim that Williams was personally responsible for discovering additional water resources for the county. In fact, they said, he was at first opposed to importing water.

But Williams said the commercial was essentially correct in depicting him in an effort to obtain additional water sources in northern Washoe County.

"I will acknowledge to the people that the water ad is a little hokey," said Williams, who is running for re-election against Reno marketing consultant Rene Reid. *[Hmm, a free plug, how nice.]* "My advisers said we needed something to get the public's attention."

The 30-second commercial depicts Williams, shovel in hand and accompanied by his dog, finding water on a northern Washoe County ranch.

"We may never again have to live with rationed water, thanks to Belie Williams," a narrator says.

"That's absolutely not true," board Chairman Gene McDowell said. "None of us took shovel in hand and ventured forth to save our drought-stricken land. The county staff brought these projects to us."

Commissioner Jim Lillard

said he felt the commercial was inaccurate, and expressed his feelings to Williams: "I told him, 'who in the hell do you think you are?'"

"Maybe the commercial did go a shade beyond what I wanted," Williams said, "but I did push for (water importation) and I did take a leadership position on this project."

But Larry Beck, who represents the north valleys, discounted Williams' claim as an early supporter of water importation, citing Williams' initial opposition to spending $1.9 million to acquire water rights on the Winnemucca Ranch, 25 miles north of Reno.

The vote on that project, taken in August 1987, was viewed as a landmark board decision: It committed the county to the purchase of nearly 3,500 acre-feet of water and set the stage for the county's emerging role as a major player in the critical area of water resources.

Tossing the paper onto the passenger side, I threw my head back in disbelief...taking in what this article meant for me. So this is politics. This is how the game is played. One thing I clearly understood: it wasn't that they wanted me *in* so much as they wanted him *out*. Purchasing Contractors Supply Warehouse while approving development projects as a commissioner put him into a blatant conflict of interest. Developers detested the obligation they felt to buy their supplies from him if their project was approved. With this article on top of the already existing hostility toward him, I was almost sure to win the Republican primary.

Only four months earlier, at the prompting of a handful of political savvy Renoites, I had agreed to take my first run at public office. As I headed for home thinking back over the campaign, I realized it had been a good time in my life to do this. I enjoyed the process, going door-to-door talking to the people who lived in this community. I loved speaking before various groups, addressing the issues. I hated fundraising...and the personal attacks. One day I hoped someone would do something about campaign reform. I didn't mind being the newcomer, the underdog in a campaign against an eight-year incumbent. I've always loved coming from behind in any game, and have definitely had some experience coming from behind in my life.

Back home again, I couldn't sleep. I called Larry—Commissioner Beck—and chatted with him until I could see the dawn of a new morning breaking through my family room patio doors. I couldn't contain my excitement. It was after 5:00, and I called Bob and Eileen Schoeweiler and woke them. Bob, a district judge, and his wife, a Republican activist, were new friends who had played a strong role in strategizing my campaign.

"Bob, are you awake?"

"I am now. What's up?"

"It's too good to waste with a phone call. Put on the coffee. I'm on my way over."

Five minutes later, I was pulling into their driveway. Bob was in his robe bending down to get the paper from his front porch.

"Don't open it yet," I yelled. "I want to savor this moment.... Where's Eileen?"

"She's in the kitchen, making the coffee. Come on in, you crazy lady. You're one of the few people I'd let in at this hour."

Sitting around the breakfast table, I let them remove the rubber band from the rolled up newsprint...and watched their faces as they read.

"Omigod!" exclaimed Eileen as she took in the headline.

"This is unbelievable." Bob was shaking his head. "Four days before the election. Who orchestrated this?"

"I don't know. I don't know anything more than what I'm reading. I think one of the commissioners called the *Gazette*."

"But which one?"

"It could've been anyone of three of them. They were all furious."

"Omigod." Eileen was still reading.

"Do you realize what this means?"

"I think it means I just took a giant step in the polls."

"For a political novice, you're catching on real fast," the judge said in jest.

"I'm not taking anything for granted. Let's get the walkers out in masses over the Labor Day weekend. The fire department has volunteered to help with the walking. With them and the rest of our volunteers, we should be able to cover the most crucial precincts in my district."

"Now we're into my bailiwick," nodded Eileen with assurance. Her short, curly blond hair was tousled, but she looked pleased as she sipped her coffee in her fuzzy pink robe. "I knew we could do it. I just knew it. But you're right. We don't quit now. I'll organize the wards that are most decisive for us. Leave that to me."

Both in their fifties, Bob and Eileen had been married forever. His six-foot lean stature with blond-grayish hair generally depicted a stately demeanor. But at this moment, he was the picture of anything but an arrogant judge.

"I love you both. You know I couldn't have organized this without you."

"We had our moments, didn't we?" reflected Eileen. I thought having your brochures lost by the post office was the worst, but we got around that. With the help of volunteers, we managed to get thousands reprinted and hand-addressed."

"No, I think the harassing phone calls were the worst," mused Bob.

The garbage dumped on my front porch with the maggots crawling around the dead turkey carcass almost took me out of the race, I thought. My teenage son, Chris, who had been lethargic about my entering the political scene, was with me when we came home to the stench and the garbage pile blocking us from getting inside the front door. *"Whatever you do, don't quit now, Mom,"* I remember him saying as I hugged him. His support meant more to me than all the rest combined. And now even he was behind me.

"Actually, those calls helped me win the race," I said aloud, referring to the harassing phone calls threatening me to get out of the race. "That was what got the TV stations to start paying closer attention to our campaign."

"Yeah, but you were just a little frightened, weren't you?" Bob asked. I had grown to appreciate his support, sensitivity, and friendship.

"Maybe at first…but when I understood that it was all part of the game, I just felt harassed. Then when I found out what prime-time advertising cost, I came to appreciate those moments of freebies on the nightly news."

It was time for Bob to head to the courthouse, and Eileen was off to Republican headquarters to organize our final precinct walks. I had knocked on every door in District 1, but we were coming into the final stretch. With only four days left, I could see the light at the end of the tunnel. This was definitely one of the more challenging tasks I had taken on in my life...and it looked like I was about to conquer it.

The election-night celebration started at the Rap, the locals' nickname for one of Reno's finest restaurant's, The Rapscallion. At the entryway just on your left, the sign read: "193 days 'til St. Patrick's Day." *Nary a one of me countrymen would have felt out of place in this wee Irish setting*, I thought to myself. Volunteers, walkers, off-duty firemen and deputies, donors, sign people, camera crews, and friends, good friends, along with my family—all crowded into the little room behind the bar. This was the democratic system. And for everyone there, it was a moment of real celebration. John G, the owner, laid out a spread of food, and drinks poured freely.

I gazed around the room, realizing I couldn't have reached this point without the help of every person gathered here tonight and many others as well. It had been a concerted effort that began with a handful of friends and new acquaintances that broadened into the crowd here this evening. Our race had drawn quite a bit of attention over the last few weeks and had moved into a forefront position in the news. It had been a controversial battle, with a quiet, soft-spoken marketing consultant taking on the obstreperous, arrogant, and outspoken eight-year incumbent. These people gathered here this evening all contributed to the campaign. For me, it was a celebration of their part in having made it happen.

From the very first returns, with only a small percentage of the votes counted, we were in the lead and never lost it. "Reid 3,743, Williams 1,688" flashed across the screen. I felt I was back in high school, and our team had just won the homecoming game. Hugs…toasts…the crowd cheering to the TV reporters' updates. The excitement in the room was contagious and running like a current from body to body. As the newspaper photographer pointed his camera my direction, two of the campaign workers, Clark Santini and Dean Phillips, grabbed my hands and raised them up in a tribute of victory.

A microphone was shoved in front of my face by an aggressive reporter asking me for a comment. "I think it was the team effort we had. I couldn't believe the people who came out to help with this campaign. And when we hit a snag, there was always someone there to find a way around it."

"Who were your strongest supporters?"

"This particular race seemed to attract people more than conglomerates. I was fortunate to have some strong community leaders behind me: Moya Lear, Bob List, John and Nancy Flanigan, Bob Cashell, TJ Day, Rollan Melton, Bob Weiss, Bill and Nancy Bilyeu, Bob and Eileen Schouweiler. They were all backing me and introducing me around and teaching me the ropes. This is my first run at public office. And, probably because of that, mine was definitely more of a grass-roots campaign. My P.R. firm— with Bob Carroll and Bill Hull—did a great job of raising the money and spending it wisely on TV and radio spots."

The people I named were some of our strongest and most respected community leaders. "I don't know if you call people of that caliber 'grass roots,' but I get what you're saying…. So what about your opponent? How do you assess what happened? I mean, this was quite an upset," probed the reporter.

"Belie Williams has been around eight years, and that's long enough for him to have made some enemies and cast some votes that people didn't like. I think he was his own worst enemy in this race."

From there, I was whisked away to Republican headquarters where there were more supporters…more cameras…and more celebration for all the Republican victories. As I walked into the room, I received applause and cheers. I felt like a movie star. It was my first appearance at a political gathering, and I was unprepared for the accolades that accompanied winning a public election. But, then, as I gradually learned, this wasn't just any race. There were people who really wanted to see my opponent out of office. It was much more about his defeat than my victory.

Shortly after 11:00 p.m., Belie Williams conceded the race. "I think she's got a landslide. I wish her luck and I wish the commission luck in the future."

I woke up early the next morning, feeling an overwhelming sense of accomplishment. Actually, it wasn't over yet. I had only won the primary. I was still to face off against Democrat Tom Keegan in the general. But as another political newcomer, Tom wasn't as formidable as the incumbent. From this point forward, I was treated as if I had already won the general election.

I bounced out of bed, put on a robe, and grabbed my newspaper off the front porch. I couldn't wait to read about the election returns. I had made new friends through this process, and was deeply interested in several of the outcomes. Jim Gibbons readily won his seat in the Assembly, but it was our race that captured headline news: "Reid buries Williams in landslide." The article went on to say that voters gave political newcomer, Rene Reid, nearly 70 percent of their ballots.

A former nun who moved to Reno in 1980, Reid became well known to Reno residents as a talk show host on radio station KOH.

While she had some behind-the-scenes experience in earlier political campaigns, the 44-year-old Reid became involved actively when she served as co-chairwoman of Safety '88 committee—a group that successfully worked for passage of a police tax override measure last May in Reno.

Her efforts on the part of the tax override measure cemented friendships with several city politicians, and she cornered the support of several prominent Republicans.

As I sat at the breakfast bar reading the rest of the election news, I realized that the voters would have supported just about anyone who had a clean record, was honest, and without conflicting baggage.

An ex-nun met these criteria. Never mind that I had been out of religious life for half my life (I left when I was 22). Politics is so much about perception. The voters had had their fill of experienced politicians. This time the citizens of this community wanted someone they could trust. I hoped I wouldn't let them down.

I tried to go on with my life as usual, but the next couple of months took me way out of the realm of the familiar. Every few days another article appeared about the ramifications of my upset over my opponent.

I pulled up to my favorite breakfast hangout, Deux Gros Nez, a funky little upstairs hangout on California Street loved by students with spiked purple hair as well as the after-the-opera crowd. While I was waiting for my cappuccino and scone, a friend handed me his copy of this morning's paper folded to expose the headline: "Primary winner Reid amiable, but tough."

A couple of days after the election hullabaloo, my new friend and well-known local columnist, Rollan Melton, had come out with a supportive write-up. In the weeks preceding the election, he had escorted me to the Senior Citizens' Center, where we walked around visiting with the seniors who were there to enjoy a low-priced meal and the camaraderie. Rollan was beloved by this group, so he was the perfect person to make the introductions and let them know he was soliciting their support for me in the coming election. His support had far-reaching effect.

Now settled into my favorite table and sipping my coffee from the steaming mug, I began to read his column:

Political newcomer Rene Reid has sent two-term Washoe County Commissioner Belie Williams shuffling into the Sierra sunset, retiring him and his television shovel from public life.

She drubbed him in Tuesday's primary, winning seven of every ten Republican votes. Not bad for a person who six months ago had no political name recognition and claimed a meager campaign pot. The 44-year-old single mother of a teen-age son mobilized a heads-up campaign team and matched Williams dollar for dollar on fundraising.

Rene Reid is an amiable former radio talk-show host, much in command of her semantics. But some friends have told her she is "too sweet" to be in politics.

But Reid also has steel tucked under her good-natured hide.

She turned into a winner when she took on the fight with Belie Williams. On television, she pointed confidently at Williams' nameplate on the commissioner's chair, and said to voters, "I can help you if you let me sit here."

In the November 8th General Election, the voters did decide to let me occupy that seat. In the interim, I had much to learn. With an ominous drought looming over our county, I spent much of my time during these next months studying about water resources. I met with the Water Master who taught me how, through the Floriston measure, he could determine that the court-mandated rate of 500 cubic feet per second (cfs) flow from the Truckee River was being maintained at the State border. Franklyn Jeans arranged a meeting to introduce himself and explain his Honey Lake Project to me—the one that got my opponent in so much "hot water." He presented this as a viable alternative for importing water from a less populated area of our county into those areas that were being targeted for development. The county had entered into a partnership with Jeans' company, and, to date, had invested about $2 million dollars into the Project. It was stepping out in front of his fellow commissioners on this issue that was the ultimate undoing of my opponent.

I wanted to be knowledgeable but cautious about this project. It was extremely controversial among my constituents. In meeting with Franklyn, I didn't hold back in expressing their concerns.

"What if we decide we don't want to go forward with it," I inquired.

"Well, I hope you will," Franklyn responded. "It's the best hope the county has for addressing the drought problem and intelligently planning for the future."

"But are we locked in? I mean, at this point, I'm completely open to it. But what if we found reason to change our minds? Do we have an out clause in our contract?"

"Oh, yes. If you decide you want out, you will have to forfeit your original $450,000, but you can get all of the rest of the county's investment back."

"That's reassuring. But won't that leave you holding the bag?"

"Not at all. This is a really good deal for the county. You would be foolish to relinquish your part in it. But if you did, I could easily have other governmental entities in line waiting to take your place."

With that, I was satisfied. I knew what I needed to know. I then met with the folks at Sierra Pacific who were coming from a different perspective to solve our drought problems. They were outspoken in their opposition to the Honey Lake Project; rather, they supported the Truckee River Negotiated Settlement. For years the Truckee River had been tied up in lawsuits and its supporters felt the settlement would create a win for everyone.

Harry Reid—our U.S. Senator from Nevada, whom I called "Uncle Harry" in spite of the fact that we were not related—had spent years working on the Truckee River Negotiated Settlement with the Indians. If this agreement went through, it also offered solutions for granting more water usage for our community, releasing more water during our drought-ridden times but preserving it in normal times to protect the endangered cui-ui fish for the Indians.

This water controversy would dominate much of my four-year term in office, and my eventual stand would ultimately build walls between my fellow commissioners and me, much as it had with my predecessor. Just for different reasons.

Having done my homework and having met with most of the movers and shakers in the political and business world of Washoe County, I was as ready as I could be to be sworn in to my office on January 3, 1989. The local media were kind to me…at least, in the beginning. The front page headlines read: "Reid strives to balance realism, idealism" and the by-line added: "Ex-nun joins Washoe Commission Tuesday." I sat down warming myself near the wood stove with the sun streaming through the patio doors to read the article. Dated Monday, January 2nd, the *Reno Gazette-Journal* article, written by Jim Mitchell, went on to say:

In a state where voters seem to take pride in stumping the political experts, it was one of the most stunning political upsets of 1988: Marketing consultant Rene Reid, 44, emerged from nowhere to whip County Commissioner Belie Williams, a veteran campaigner who had prospered for eight years in Washoe County's wild political atmosphere. On Tuesday, Reid, a former nun with a master's degree in theology and a belief that Nevada's politics can be viewed spiritually, *[How naïve I was!]* will be sworn in as the representative of the staunchly conservative west side of Reno.

Shades of Mary Poppins?

"I've been told that," Reid said, punctuating her sentences with girlish laughs. "I think it's true. I think I have a Mary Poppins - Julie Andrews kind of image."

But anyone who thinks Reid will spend the next four years sprinkling pixie dust around the commission hearing room may be in for a surprise.

With bewildering ease, Reid can shift from a starry-eyed idealist to a cool, pragmatic politician, offering a detached appraisal of her campaign success.

A slim victory would have been spectacular enough, but Reid captured an unthinkable 70 percent of the vote over Williams in the Republican primary election, then rolled to an easy win over token Democratic and Libertarian Party opposition in November.

I read on, my gaze stopping on the following:

Reid's Idealism

Reid's idealism stems from years of service to the Roman Catholic Church, both as a nun and as a lay theologian; the realism has its roots in her later life as a businesswoman and her unsuccessful struggle to hold her marriage together.

As a teenager in Dallas, Reid had already decided on her mission in life—or so she thought. "I wanted to be an instrument of service to people," she said, "and I thought I had to be a nun to do that.

I couldn't become a priest, or I would have."

In June 1962, fresh out of high school, Reid joined the Daughters of Charity, the religious order made famous by Sally Field in the television serious, "The Flying Nun."

She began religious studies at Marillac College in St. Louis, but discovered doors were being quietly closed to her interest in theology. "In those days, nobody got a degree in theology," she said. "Priests did, but nuns didn't. Nuns lit votive candles, did the domestic work of the church, took care of the sick and taught children. They were nervous about me getting a degree in theology."

Searching for a way to pursue her calling, she resigned from the order in May 1966 at the close of the school year. After obtaining degrees in theology from the University of Dallas and the University of San Francisco, she became a lay theologian in Bay-area parishes.

It was a time of extraordinary change and tumult within the Catholic Church. "I was there during all the controversy. The liberals and conservatives were screaming at each other, priests and nuns were starting to leave. I guess I was a forerunner of those making their exodus."

She found herself more and more at odds with the church hierarchy, and job insecurity became a way of life.... As the only female on the staff at a Menlo park, Calif. seminary, she joined a faculty rebellion against an edict handed down by a bishop, and began scouting for another way to promote her views.

Marriage didn't work out

She met—and later married—James Kavanaugh, who had stirred up controversy in the 60s with his book *A Modern Priest Looks at His Outdated Church*. Much like herself, she perceived him speaking out for new personalism and humanism and less legalism in the Church.

But the tranquility she sought in marriage never materialized. "It was a revolving door," she said. "I never had

a marital situation where I could be secure financially and emotionally."

While her personal life was in turmoil, she found a way to pursue her professional goals on television. "About that time, KGO-TV in San Francisco was looking for somebody to host a religiously-oriented talk show, and guess who got the job?"

After a successful stint in San Francisco and later in Denver, Reid was hired in 1981 to host a similar talk show at KOH radio in Reno.

"I was hired to do the same kind of show about human values," she said. "But the show bombed."

She began a desperate search for a topic that would make the phones ring, and that's when she discovered Nevada politics. "That's what folks here are interested in," she said, "and all the things I care about—family, the homeless, health issues, social ethics—people in this community talk about in terms of politics.... I think this is why I've been elected to serve in this role."

...Throughout all of this, her marriage to Kavanaugh continued to be a roller-coaster ride..."I learned to enjoy the high points in our life together before he would leave again. It wasn't lack of love that destroyed our marriage. I have Jim to thank for making me more practical," she said with no trace of bitterness. "I had a pretty clear thrust in my professional life, but not so in my marital life. It was very shaky and insecure. In midstream, I found myself having to make it on my own with a son to raise." After several separations and attempts at reconciliation, the couple divorced in 1986.

No immediate plans as county commissioner

Reid said she hasn't decided upon a specific agenda as a commissioner, and plans to spend several months learning the ropes.... Historically, Nevada politics has not been kind to idealists, and Reid said she's prepared to have some holes punched in her balloon. "I don't think it's any secret that I don't have a lot of rough-and-tumble political savvy," she said. "I think I'm in for moments of disillusionment." [*Little did I know then what lay in store for me in my four-year political term.*]

But she doesn't think her backers will be disappointed. "I'm a strange bird," she said, "and I don't think that's any surprise to the voters. I think they said, 'Let's put her in there and see what she can do. It might be a welcome change.'"

There was my life poured into a fishbowl. I didn't have anything to hide so I didn't really mind. I was a "strange bird" for politics. I didn't realize it when I decided to run, but I knew it now. I didn't fit the mold. But I wasn't going to let this stop me. I was determined to become knowledgeable about the issues and cast my vote based on what I felt was in the best interest of the majority.

As a county commissioner, I served on a board of five members whose job, among others, included the disbursement of a $120 million annual budget among all of the county departments. Beyond that once-a-year decision, most of our energy was devoted to overseeing regional planning for the county and approving development projects that met the needs of both the builders and the neighbors. But, of course, without adequate water, the maintenance (much less growth) of Washoe County was in serious jeopardy.

During my first weeks in office, I was still a novice but felt reasonably educated on the challenges facing our community. Gradually I fell into my routine. Every Monday afternoon, the commissioners held a caucus meeting, giving anyone scheduled to "appear" before us the opportunity to explain their intent and answer questions in a less formidable setting. Then on Tuesday mornings, in a formal meeting, sitting at a long table on a raised platform designed, no doubt, to reinforce our power, the Board of County Commissioners of Washoe County met to hear matters coming before us and rule on issues of concern to individuals within the community.

I took my job seriously, believing that a heavy responsibility had been placed on me to oversee the development and direction of the future of our community. Joining the commission, I thought my role was to read the backup that accompanied each item on our agenda, listen openly to the public testimony, and vote my conscience. How little I knew going into office what politics was really about.

One of my first reality checks came all too soon. It was March of '89, and I'd been serving on the board just two months. Nothing about the agenda item raised any red flags for me. And no one called me ahead of time to meet and discuss the matter. It looked like any other item on this week's agenda, listed very simply as "Washoe County's bid for the 1998 Winter Olympics." As I read the backup, of course I would support this bid. Who wouldn't? What an opportunity for our little community. This hadn't happened around here since Squaw Valley was selected for this privileged event in 1960.

What surprised me was to see practically every leader in the community show up for this week's hearing. The room was packed, including reporters and camera crews. I knew most everyone from their support of me during the campaign. There was Bob Cashell, founder of Boomtown Casino, who would later serve as our state's lt. governor; Joe Crowley, president of the University; Sue Clark, wife of Dave Clark, who owned Clark and Sullivan's construction company; the columnist, Rollan Melton; Bob Rusk, a business owner, who formerly served as a county commissioner and state assemblyman. Throughout the meeting, I kept wondering what item they were all here for. Finally it became apparent.

"Madame Chairman," county manager John McIntyre spoke up following protocol as he addressed my colleague, Dianne Cornwall, "The next item is the matter of Washoe County's bid for the 1998 Winter Olympics. I suggest we defer board discussion until we hear from the chairman of the committee, Mr. Bob Cashell."

Bob, a self-confident, six-foot, burly man stepped up to the podium. Bob had been vitally involved in my campaign. Over the years, having turned Bill and Effie's truck stop, located just on our side of the Nevada-California border, into the renowned Boomtown Casino, he had become a respected pillar of our community.

In his commanding good ol' boy Texas twang, after explaining the details needed to meet the requirements of the National Olympic Committee, he wound up his presentation. "This is an opportunity for everyone in northern Nevada. Having the Winter Olympics here is not only a cause for pride for every Nevadan, but a source of tremendous revenue for our business community. The world will be watching us. With this as a catalyst," he chuckled, "we might even get our sorely ailing downtown up to snuff."

Commissioner Beck had a question about the finances. "Where is the money coming from to back this? Will the businesses who stand to profit put up the necessary funds?"

"Well, Commissioner, that is our only stumbling block. Ya see, the Olympic Committee unexpectedly tightened up their timetable on us last week. Instead of the couple of months we anticipated having to pull the fiscal plans together, they have now insisted that we have that in place on March 15th when we complete our submission forms."

"You mean next week?" Larry asked incredulously.

"Yeah," he drawled. "So that's where y'all come in. We believe we can pull the finances together with no problem, but in order to meet their deadline, we have to move quickly. There isn't time to come up with a solid plan. So we are here to ask the commission to support this effort through a tax that would reassure the Olympic Committee that we have the funds in place to carry out this event."

My antenna went up at the word *tax*. "How about a public hearing?" I asked. "I'm not comfortable putting a tax on the people without their having some say in this."

"That's the problem, Commissioner. There isn't even time for that. The Committee pulled a real fast one on us here. All of these fine people (he gestured to the crowds in attendance) are here to let you know that they support your issuance of a tax measure."

I looked out at the crowd. These were my supporters and new friends. They were counting on me. I wanted their approval, especially this early in office. But they represented the elite, the leaders and business side of our community. What about the little people, the masses of residents who were worried about running out of water? They don't own businesses. They would see the crowds descending upon our fair city as an intrusion, just using up our precious water supply. How could I impose a tax on them...without even so much as a public hearing?

One by one, each key leader approached the podium making a plea for the commission to approve the bid, and backing it up with the recommendation to increase our sales tax as needed to cover our costs. I saw many faces appear in front of me who had personally and financially backed me during my campaign. This was payback time. My gut was beginning to wrench.

Each of the commissioners was given a chance to comment before the vote. When it came my turn, I spoke slowly and could feel my heart sinking with each word. "I can feel the passion filling the room today. And I share your enthusiasm for such an important event to dignify our community. I wish we could sit around a table together and brainstorm the financial options. As much as I am with you in spirit in wanting this event here, I cannot in conscience support a tax measure without some involvement from the public at large. There must be another solution, but, for the life of me, with such short notice, I can't think of one at this moment. Short of having an alternative, given the facts before me at this moment, I am forced to cast a *no* vote on this matter."

The vote was three in favor and two opposed, with Larry Beck joining me on the issue. The motion carried, but I had lost favor with nearly everyone there.

I called my friend and political mentor, Bill Raggio, who was majority leader in our State Senate. His knowledge about handling sensitive political situations was a quality I deeply admired. I told him what had happened. He assured me I had done the right thing and, in fact, when the matter comes before him in the Senate, he would be taking a similar action. His words comforted me somewhat, but the next few days were agonizing as I heard from, or worse, didn't hear from, some of these people who were so important in my life.

Bob Rusk kept in touch with me about the matter. As a former county commissioner, I think he could identify with my dilemma. He was also still searching for solutions that would bring unanimous support from the elected officials.

"With three days notice, maybe we could still fit in at least one hearing in the time allowed. We could ask the Committee to give us an extra week for this," Bob proposed.

"Three days doesn't even give us time to post notice. But, Bob, in all honesty, what stand do you think the majority of constituents would take on this? The ramifications of this drought have been planted firmly in their minds. All they can see is that their water will be used up, and for the 'privilege' of paying higher taxes, the profits will go into the pockets of the business community. From their perspective, this will not come back to benefit them."

"You have a point. But everyone who was there wants to see the Olympics come to Reno so badly. It really is the chance of a lifetime," he speculated.

"I know. So what do they propose as a solution?"

"Well, after we left you, we all went over to Cashell's conference room and sat around the table to explore our options. Bob said it never occurred to him that we wouldn't get unanimous support on this. In fact, his exact words were, 'I told that little lady that sometime I'd be before her with some issue that was important to me, and I didn't want her feeling beholdin' just because I'd given her money for her campaign.... But, goddamn, I didn't think that moment would come so soon.'"

CHAPTER 3

BALANCING POLITICAL AND PROFESSIONAL CAREERS
1989-1991

Nevada politics is generally considered a part-time vocation. Because of the low pay, most elected officials had other professions in order to support themselves and their families. Given the history of my political seat, I was extremely sensitive to the choice I made as an additional income source.

Just prior to running for office, I had become involved in a business that was on the cusp of transition from a widely misunderstood industry wherein homemakers could create a little extra pocket change into a more sophisticated and accepted profession generating a serious income stream. While some still thought of it as a kind of pyramid scheme, more and more corporate managers and skilled workers were considering this a genuine alternative after the downsizing of corporate America.

Despite the controversy, the reality was that network marketing was a form of distribution of products and services that, through word-of-mouth promotion, used the power of duplicating the efforts of other people—or what we call *leveraging*. Unlike conventional marketing, which generally has a few representatives responsible for large volumes of sales, this form of marketing has large numbers of representatives responsible for a small number of sales. It is a form of direct selling in which the distributors are compensated on a multi-level basis as opposed to the traditional single-level pay plan. Network marketers are paid not only on the volume of sales produced by the people they bring into the business, but by those whom their people bring in (second level), and their people bring in (third level), and so on.

Carefully weighing my political situation, I concluded that representing personal care and nutritional products as a distributor for Nu Skin International would not conflict in any way that I could anticipate with my role as a public official. I joined the company in May of 1988, the same month I chose to run for office.

By the time I had won the primary, I had achieved the first significant level of success in network marketing. By the time I won the general, as a Nu Skin executive working part-time, I was already earning more than I did as a commissioner, which took nearly full-time effort. The larger my organization grew, the more it needed me. Though I was making good money, the challenge was in balancing the see-saw effect of my two careers.

As one of five on the commission, if I ever wanted to gain support to accomplish anything, it was critical to be part of a threesome. My camaraderie was with Larry Beck and Jim Lillard. I had no rapport with Dianne Cornwall, the only other woman on the board. There seemed to be many reasons for it, not the least of which was our entirely different temperaments and philosophies.

Belie and Dianne were good friends and had that all-important bond. So his departure from the board (and my replacement of him) was a serious loss to her. He also served on the board of Washoe Medical Center, a former county hospital that had, under extremely controversial arrangements, been converted to a "private hospital owned by the community"—whatever that means. Also serving on the Washoe Med Board with Belie were Gene McDowell and Jim Lillard. With three members of our commission also serving on this controversial board, that meant that three commission votes were, for all practical purposes, locked in. With Belie no longer there, Washoe Med now had only two votes, and without the third, had no power.

Coincidentally, about this same time, Dianne Cornwall was offered a job at Washoe Med in the community development department. Her starting part-time salary was somewhere in the $60,000-range annually (which over the next couple of years grew to something just short of $100,000). Not bad for a part-time job for someone with only a high school degree and no experience in fundraising. By all appearances, this would once again lock in their third vote.

One Tuesday morning all of the commissioners gathered in the caucus room before going into chambers. Ed Dannan, our legal counsel from the DA's office, was there as always. I walked in as a lively discussion was underway about the Washoe Med item on the agenda today. Several million dollars were being recommended for transfer to the hospital for taking care of the indigent in our county. Dianne was asking Ed's opinion about her ability to vote on the item, given her new job there.

Sitting at the long conference table, working a crossword puzzle, Ed leaned back in his chair, flipping the pencil against the newspaper. "No, I see no problem," Ed concluded, "as long as you declare before the vote that you are employed there and indicate that it represents no conflict of interest to you."

I couldn't believe what I was hearing. *That can't be right. Of course, it represents a conflict of interest. Just try casting a few "nay" votes and see how long that job lasts.* "You can't be serious," I said looking at Ed. "In all due respect, this is as blatant a case of conflict as anything I've ever seen. There is no way that Dianne can vote on this. I think Gene and Jim are questionable in light of their capacity as Washoe Med board members, but Dianne…there isn't even a doubt."

"This ain't right. You can't do this," Larry shouted. He looked at me with total disbelief. "Even Belie wouldn't have tried something like this. I guess doing what's right just don't matter no more." From that moment, I would always hold deep respect for Larry's integrity.

But the decision had already been made. Dianne and Gene and Jim would cast votes today. The three in favor, two opposed vote was no surprise, and millions of taxpayer dollars were transferred to Washoe Med as a result. Setting aside the issue of whether the transference was the right or wrong thing to do, the process bothered me. This issue would haunt me throughout my term in office.

I usually set Thursdays and Fridays aside to meet with anyone who had agenda items coming up the following Tuesday. Over the weekend, I would plow through the tedious backup material which gave detailed background and staff recommendations on each item.

Oh dear! There's that Honey Lake project again. I'd stayed open to this as a genuine option for water supply despite how many people were opposed to it—outside my board, of course. Continuing to look for answers, I met with the folks from Harry Reid's office and was sensitive to the years of work he had put into the Truckee River Negotiated Settlement. The City Council strongly supported this effort. The two strategies were in direct conflict. Those who supported one were constantly attacking those who supported the other.

Without forming an opinion yet as to which project I supported, something kept eating away at me about the process around Honey Lake. The first red flag was how readily we, as commissioners, kept throwing money at the project. By now, two years into my term, more than four million taxpayer dollars had been invested into the Honey Lake water importation plan.

Every other manager of a project remotely connected to the public trust had to get permission *before* the fact to spend money over a certain amount. But not Honey Lake. I kept pondering the situation. *Why? And why were there no test results coming in showing massive amounts of underground water there? My board and the county manager had determined they where going forward. If I opposed the project, it would serve as nothing more than a protest vote. Even if I concluded with absolute certainty that it was not worth pouring any more money into it, I would never convince two other commissioners of this.*

My opposition to allowing "reimbursement funding" for this

project *after* the money had already been spent was increasing the burgeoning gulch between the board and myself. If I were to oppose it outright, it would be the end of any hope of a cooperative spirit between us. I wanted to get along. Life would be so much easier. But if I thought the project was wrong for this community, there was too much money at stake for me to ignore it. Some matters just weren't worth making a fuss over. This one was.

My life was full—full of excitement and full of controversy. It was becoming increasingly difficult to keep up with everything I had to do. I hired someone to handle secretarial duties for me at home. Teresa helped me bridge my two worlds of politics and business. With staff to assist at the county, Teresa primarily took care of my phone calls, scheduling, and day-to-day activities involved in my Nu Skin business. I was committed to my role in both capacities. I also had a teenage son who was still dependent on me. There were times when Chris just needed a mom who was there to listen.

I was on a giant learning curve in all areas of my life. I was teaching, growing, and discovering so many new aspects of business and politics. I even managed to squeeze in an occasional game of tennis with my longtime group of women friends. To varying degrees, each compartment of the balance wheel of my life was filled. In all areas, that is, except, a personal relationship. It wasn't something I was actively seeking. Even if it happened, I couldn't imagine fitting it into my life at this time.

Finding a partner in life rarely happens when one obsesses on the search. More often, it comes from doing those things we love to do—recreationally, spiritually, or professionally. It was at a gathering of over 4,000 network marketers in Kansas City in 1990 that I was first introduced to Mark Yarnell. Jerry Campizi, a short, fiery, silver-haired field leader in our company with incredible energy, organized the event. He opened it to everyone who was serious about building their networking business, and that meant anyone who had reached the level of executive or higher. Jerry had asked me, now a Diamond in the company, to be one of the speakers.

Dave Johnson, two levels above me in the hierarchical structure, was a man I'd also come to know well during my time with Nu Skin. He whispered in my ear that he had someone he wanted me to meet, implying that I should stay in that general vicinity while he went to find him. As I was just finishing a conversation with someone, I turned around and there was Dave standing with a man whose face I'd seen...but only from a distance.

"Rene, I'd like to introduce you to Mark Yarnell," Dave intoned in his theatrical voice. "Mark, this is Rene. When you move to Reno, she'll be your county commissioner. But, more importantly, she is *the* Nu Skin leader there."

I had seen Mark from the stage. In fact, it was his video that first got me interested in this company. In real life, Mark was about 5'10", medium-framed, with hyperactive energy and equally vivacious facial expressions. He wasn't the Marlboro rugged type. He struck me more like an adorable little boy in a man's body who, with such vivacious enthusiasm for life, couldn't sit still or be held down.

"I had no idea you were planning to move to Reno," I said as I smiled at Mark. "What brings you to our fair city?"

"The favorable tax situation was my first attraction, but now I have even more reason. You know, I have been using your credibility for the past couple of years, telling everyone that this business must first pass the smell test. We even have a politician involved." His accent added to his charm. It sounded like a cross between Texas and the Arkansas hill country.

"Well, I'm not sure that lending a politician's name to something necessarily implies integrity," I laughed. "But if my name does that, I'm glad." I had seen Mark on several occasions at various Nu Skin events. It was nice to finally meet him in person.

"When I get to Reno, may I give you a call? I like to become a part of the community wherever I live." Although he said it casually, I could sense he was sincere.

"If it's community involvement you want, I am definitely the person to introduce you around. I'd be happy to do that." I thanked Dave and said goodbye to both of them as I headed back toward the speakers' section. Mark would later claim that he knew from that very moment that the interchange between us was a dramatic turning point in both of our lives. He realized, but I didn't.

By August of that year, Mark had moved to Reno and bought the Neeser house, known around town as the castle on the hill. Named Windara, it was an elegant Tudor home with a turret that sat high on an eight- and-a-half-acre gated parcel overlooking Caughlin Ranch, one of the most prestigious communities in the county. I had no way of knowing the first time I visited with Mark to discuss homelessness that I would one day be living with him in that castle.

During that first year, our involvement was limited to phone conversations from time to time, mostly about the inner politics of Nu Skin, or the external attacks our company was experiencing, or, on a more positive note, about our children. Once we held a Nu Skin meeting together in Reno. I introduced him to the local United Way and some of my favorite charitable projects in town. But other than that, I had little time to spare, and he traveled frequently.

On those occasions once every few weeks when we did talk, the conversations were always meaningful. Mark was a man who did not comprehend the meaning of limitations. If you didn't know anything else about him, you knew this: he lived by the principle that if anyone could do anything in life, he could too. And he had a wonderful way of making you feel that you could achieve anything you set out to do if you just believed in yourself. The more I got to know him, the more I opened up about the personal things in my life.

My son was in high school and struggling over a breakup with a close girlfriend. Chris was depressed and not motivated to do much of anything. Mark gave me some helpful guidance for handling the situation. I found myself comfortable talking about most anything with him...even politics. I knew he had deep insights; and when he called while I was in the middle of budget hearings, I talked to him about one of the challenges I was facing.

"Do you have time to talk?" Mark asked politely.

"Mmhmm, in fact, my brain needs to take a break after sitting through hours of budget hearings today."

"What does that entail? I never hung out with a 'commish' before," he teased.

I responded to his jesting but continued on quite intensely. "All the department heads want more money, and there is only so much to go around. There are many of them I want to support, but there just isn't enough in our budget without raising taxes. So I've spent a lot of time looking at making better use of our finances. You know, where can we cut? Where can we privatize and do better with taxpayer dollars?"

"That makes a lot of sense. I wish our federal politicians would think that way," Mark offered reassuringly.

"You know the Director of the United Way, Brian Bowden?" Mark had donated $150,000 to the Reno branch earlier this year and, consequently, was being offered a seat on their board.

"Yeah, I like him a lot."

"Well, I've been meeting with Brian recently. He's open-minded and helping me explore ways that we can get the homeless population out of the county's revolving door. I'd like to direct them to a more appropriate place where they can be better served and the taxpayer doesn't have to expend outlandish dollars to recycle them through a never-ending and hopelessly futile pipeline. Brian introduced me to a woman who is so caring and involved with the homeless. You'd love her. In fact, I want you to meet her. Her name is Nancy Paolini. The three of us have been meeting over this issue. We have tentatively given this project a name: Project ReStart."

"How absolutely perfect. The name says it all. You'll be teaching people how to 'restart' their lives."

"Yeah, exactly. And if we can get them off the track they're on now, we can actually move some of them into self-sufficiency. And those who aren't ready for that will usually accept our bus ticket program."

"What's that?"

"You know... 'Do you have a relative whom you would like to get back with? We will be happy to provide you a one-way ticket to get there.'"

"I love it. But what about the hard core homeless—you know, the ones who are happy being on the street and want to stay there?"

"I'm working with Sheriff Swinney on that. You'll like him too. I'll make sure you two meet. The idea is that when the homeless are arrested for breaking the vagrancy laws here, they will be tried and, if convicted, put in jail. But instead of getting free room and board and sitting around for sixty days, they will be given the *opportunity* to join the sherriff's work program. And there they will *get* to give back to the community they live in...you know, by sweeping the city streets, cleaning up the parks, things like that."

"That ought to satisfy all those who want 'the bums' off the street."

"It does. Usually, after the homeless have been through that routine once, they aren't too anxious to repeat it. So when they are released from jail, they are offered the chance to come to Project ReStart, where they will be assigned a case worker who will help them develop a resumé and get their act together. We give them an address and a phone number that doesn't broadcast they are homeless."

"Most homeless people have alcohol and addiction problems," Mark responded. "I helped put a rehab program together for the homeless just outside of Austin. I would love to get involved in what you're doing here."

"Hey, you're on. We have our next meeting scheduled on Wednesday at the county complex. There will be several people there you need to meet—Vince and Nancy and Katherine Wishart, a city councilwoman, and several others. I'd love to have you come." I knew from these conversations that Mark, who had served ten years as a Protestant minister before becoming involved with Nu Skin, was exceptionally altruistic.

Each year, by a vote of the board, the commission rotated the chairmanship. In 1991, Jim Lillard stepped into this position, and I was chosen to serve as vice-chair. Jim Lillard and I disagreed about Washoe Med and even Honey Lake. But it didn't come between us personally. We talked more frequently and became even closer during this time. Jim shared a scrapbook of his life with me including his time as Mayor of Sparks. As I flipped through the book, I loved asking him questions about various times in his political career. He had forgotten more than I'd ever know about how the game is played.

On a Friday afternoon in April, each of the commissioners was asked to sit in on a meeting explaining how a major project would come together. The open meeting law required that no more than two public officials be present in a private meeting at one time. Standing in the outer room, I was waiting for Jim to come out so I could go in. As we met in the doorway, he gave me a hug and said, "Why don't you take over my seat. I'm tired and have heard all I need to hear."

How prophetic! Over that weekend, Jim was driving back with his wife from Graeagle, his favorite get-away spot, when he had a heart attack. After only four months of serving as chairman, Jim died a few days later in Washoe Med. I wrote a poem for him which I read while lectoring at his memorial service held in a local Catholic church. I missed him terribly, as a friend and as my often-needed third vote. Just as he'd suggested, I "took over his seat" as chairman for the remainder of the year. His daughter, Tina, was appointed to replace him for the rest of his term. She immediately teamed up with Dianne and, without Jim, the remainder of my term became a living hell.

My responsibilities were mounting. As chairman, I felt a need to spend even more time at the county. Our state legislature met every other year, and this was the year it was in session. There was a reenactment of the Civil War going on between the North and the South this year. It was given the name "Fair Share," and essentially was a war waged by Southern Nevadans against the North for having, over the years, inadvertently received a greater proportion from state sales tax than we should have. They wanted their share from then on and also their fair proportion that was in arrears from past inequities. This would amount to millions of dollars taken out of our revenues for years to come. It was the central issue of the session.

Although we have 17 counties in Nevada, the war was between Clark County (Las Vegas) and Washoe County (Reno). As chairman of the board of Washoe County, I spent more than usual time down at the legislature during the session. I was the enemy, or so I felt, to every Las Vegan representative. It was a grueling experience, but I felt it was where energy needed to be directed. At best, we hoped to keep our losses down to $10 million annually. Worst case, we expected we might drop as much as $13 million. After innumerable meetings, appearances before sub-committees, bartering, and meetings with Sam McMullen, our lobbyist, in the end we forfeited nearly $17 million of ongoing, annual revenue we relied on to run our county. I sought out Bill Raggio, who championed the North's position in this battle.

"We shouldn't have lost that much. How did we miss our mark that badly?"

"Politics is rarely what it seems. There were a lot of other issues at stake. You can't let yourself feel bad. You couldn't have done anything more."

"I do feel bad. This will be one of the most impactful issues that will come up in my time on the commission. I wished we'd 'faired' better. The South is clearly the victor in this civil war."

"You're doing a fine job as a commissioner. You can't let yourself take it so personally. I remember one time talking to my wife coming back from a district attorneys' convention. I thought I was doing a pretty good job as DA back then, and I said to her, 'Dottie, how many really good DAs do you think there've been across the country?' She thought about it for a minute and responded, 'One less than you think.'"

I laughed. He was right. I couldn't take myself too seriously in this role. It was my job for that moment in time. Then I would move on and someone else would fill my seat. I just had to give my best to each cause and then let it go. It always seems far more important to us while in office than it would to anyone else when reading our memoirs.

When I wasn't involved in a public hearing or out in my

district meeting with one of the Citizens' Advisory Boards, I was back at home holding business meetings for twenty or so of the distributors in my Nu Skin organization. I was always on the run, but I loved my life. While the political battles were erupting in one part of my life, the media warfare was being discharged in my business world.

Just at the peak of our growth, in 1991, Nu Skin faced one of the most disastrous moments of its young life. Led by Attorney General Frank Kelley of Michigan, several attorneys general began an investigation of Nu Skin. Many of us were suspicious that, since Amway (one of the first network marketing companies) had its headquarters in Michigan, Frank Kelley's campaign was well financed by our competitor's contributions. And that explained, to us at least, why he made Nu Skin the target of his political campaign. We were the fastest growing company in our industry at this time and may have been perceived as posing a threat to a well-known, long-established company. The media had a heyday with all of this. They love to report controversy. Success and good news is, of course, no news. Connie Chung, Barbara Walters, Nightline, *USA Today*—every major national TV show and newspaper—went after our company.

On July 9, 1991, the Frank Kelley vs. Nu Skin drama was *USA Today's* cover story. Written by John Waggoner, the headlines read: "Marketing tactics draw scrutiny" and subtitled "Highflying firm's strategy smacks of 'pyramid scheme,' some charge." Sitting on my back deck overlooking the quiet of my park-like backyard, I bravely began to read the article:

Todd Whitthorne quit his job as a sports anchor for Washington's WRC-TV six months ago to sell skin lotion, shampoos and cosmetics. He thought being his own boss would give him more flexible hours to be with his children and still earn the "strong six-figure income" he earned as a sportscaster.

So far, it has.

Whitthorne is one of 100,000 people across the USA who has

signed on to sell a line of 60 high-quality, high-priced personal-care products made by Nu Skin International, of Provo, Utah. And sales are exploding.

The 7-year-old, privately owned company has seen its wholesale revenue leap from $40 million in 1989 to $230 million last year. It says revenue will hit $500 million this year, as it moves into Canada and other countries.

But blemishes are beginning to appear on Nu Skin. Three states—Florida, Illinois, and Utah—are investigating the company. Michigan Attorney General Frank Kelley has issued a notice of intended action against Nu Skin, charging the company is "operating an illegal pyramid marketing scheme." Nu Skin says it's close to a resolution with the state, although Chris DeWitt, spokesman for the Michigan attorney general, disagrees. "It's still a real possibility that the attorney general will file a suit," DeWitt says.

What makes some state authorities balk is that Nu Skin rewards recruiting with a higher commission rate. This type of structure is perfectly legal if it conforms to certain state guidelines. A number of companies, such as Amway, Mary Kay Cosmetics, A.L. Williams and Shaklee, successfully use multilevel marketing.

You can boost your income sharply by recruiting others to sell Nu Skin. If you recruit another person as a Nu Skin distributor, you get a commission on the products that person orders from Nu Skin for his customers. That extra commission doesn't come out of your recruit's markup; it comes from Nu Skin. The commission: 5% to 10%.

If your recruit enlists someone else, you get a commission on that person's sales volume as well. That continues down to the sixth level, "allowing you to earn commissions on hundreds or even thousands of downline distributors," as Nu Skin's literature says.

Although you can make money by selling products, clearly the road to riches is to have a network of people selling under you. State authorities—and those who have filed complaints with them—say the emphasis is on recruiting, not selling Nu Skin products. "We're trying to determine the way it actually operates, which appears to be grossly deviant from the official marketing plan," says Jim Lyons, an investigator with the Florida attorney general's office.

I scanned the rest of the article. Considering the devastating consequences, it could have been worse. Unfortunately the attacks didn't stop there. We were next hit with a *Nightline* broadcast on July 19, 1991, with Barbara Walters sitting in for Ted Koppel.

Frank Kelley was interviewed along with Mike Smith, one of the lawyers representing Nu Skin and a man whom I would later come to work with and respect.

My beloved company came under a barrage of attacks from the Michigan Attorney General. He held up a graph of our comp plan and pointed to it, saying, *"See, it even looks like a pyramid!"*

As a loyal Nu Skin distributor, I, like everyone in the company, found the show agonizing to watch. This was to cause so much needless devastation in the lives of countless innocent Nu Skin distributors who were blindsided by the repercussions that followed. I spent hours on the phone, consoling distributors in my organization. I talked to Mark Yarnell, who helped me keep my perspective.

I knew that our company was on solid legal ground. I had done my own due diligence before ever becoming involved. But we were all genuinely afraid that the goose, which had been laying the golden egg for so many of us, was about to be slaughtered. In response to the frenzy and apprehension among field distributors all over the country caused by the broadcast, Nu Skin immediately issued a letter to all of us. I knew it was coming and met the postman as he delivered my mail this day. It was right on top. Still standing by the curb, I scanned it quickly:

> ...In an effort not to jeopardize the countless hours we have spent working on the Michigan situation, it was important for Nu Skin to take a somewhat passive approach to the program. Our goal was to defend our position while insuring that the tone of the broadcast did not become hostile....
>
> Mr. Kelley referred to a test that is used to determine legitimate multi-level marketing versus a pyramid. In order to be considered legitimate, a company must be product driven rather than distributorship driven. Nu Skin agrees with Attorney General Kelley on this issue. However, in an effort to indicate that Nu Skin failed to meet the criteria, Attorney General Kelley cites an example that has no basis. He states that because Nu Skin has between

10,000 and 15,000 distributors in Michigan, the company is distributorship driven. He also states that Amway, Mary Kay and Avon pass this test because they're product driven. It is clear that these companies have many more distributors in Michigan than Nu Skin. Therefore, according to his 'test', these companies, too, would fail.

Mr. Kelley claims further evidence that Nu Skin is involved in pyramiding is the fact that we do no product advertising. The whole business philosophy of network marketing is to allow product to be promoted by word of mouth rather than spending millions of dollars in media advertising. Many network marketing companies, including some that Mr. Kelley mentioned on the broadcast, choose not to advertise their products through the media.

As I walked back into the house, I couldn't help but appreciate how our president, Blake Roney, and vice-president, Steve Lund, and the corporate team at Nu Skin were keeping their wits about them. They were being cautiously wise in the way they were handling things. I was proud to be part of their team.

It was just a couple of days later that I received a call from Sue Voyles, one of the reporters for our local paper. She began by asking me a series of questions about Nu Skin. It didn't occur to me at first that she was asking as a reporter. I naively assumed she was exploring this for personal reasons. All of a sudden it dawned on me that was not the case.

"So, Sue, give me the bottom line. Where are you going with this?"

"Better yet, I'll give you the headline," she quipped. "County Commission chairman involved in pyramid scheme."

I pleaded with her, before she ruined me politically and business-wise in one fell swoop, to get more facts. So far, she was basing her entire story from AP and UPI wire stories. At my prompting, she spoke with Frankie Sue Del Papa, our state attorney general. I would forever be indebted to our honest AG, who gave her the facts about the legality of network marketing. She provided details of three complaints that had been filed against Nu Skin in Las Vegas, and how her office had checked them out and found no wrongdoing. Frankie Sue explained that each state had different regulations about details, such as product returns, product and income claims, and the like, but that network marketing was a legitimate form of moving product and perfectly legal in our state.

Sue dropped the story, but I experienced anxiety for days on end. I called Mark Yarnell during that time to seek his help. As one of the respected pioneers in our company, he was able to put things in perspective for Sue. I'm sure his comments helped in her decision to let the story go.

In the end, Nu Skin was found to be a reputable company, and shortly after Frank Kelley won his reelection, he too dropped any and all charges against the company. Some minor adjustments were implemented but there were no changes in our compensation plan, no changes in our marketing approach, and no changes in the essential make-up of network marketing. On the contrary, from this point forward, the Direct Sales Association and the Federal Trade Commission held our company up as the benchmark by which other network marketing companies would be measured.

While it had a happy ending of sorts, over half of the distributor force dropped out or were driven out of business during this unfortunate episode. People who began their businesses in good faith, investing countless hours building a home-based business and trying to create a certain lifestyle for themselves and their families, lost everything. For those who were forced out, it left a scar of immeasurable proportions. For those who survived, most went on to become financially set. The breach between the two was as wide as the feeling of loss was deep.

However, the outcome proved one point that cannot be refuted: Network marketing has an inner strength of its own. It is here to stay and continues to flourish as an industry with burgeoning success. It will unquestionably have significant impact on the coming millennium. Over the next decade my career would lead me to play a significant role in helping raise this industry to a new level of professionalism.

CHAPTER 4

COURTSHIP
October - November 1991

J ust about the time the regulatory battle for Nu Skin was reaching its height, I found myself facing an equally challenging internal struggle. It began in October 1991, when I received a call from Mark.

"Are you sitting someplace where you can talk—I mean really talk?"

I changed phones, situated myself in a comfortable place on the couch, and sighed, "Okay, now I can talk."

He started off hesitantly, which was not like Mark. He was never without words flowing easily off his tongue. "I need to tell you something, and I can't hold it inside any longer." He paused and then went on. "I think we belong together. I think we're soul mates, and I think I want to spend the rest of my life with you." A Daniel Steele character couldn't have said it more dramatically.

There was a prolonged silence. I was caught so completely by surprise. I had never been out with Mark. Never had a romantic interchange. Never discussed anything even remotely resembling a personal relationship. We were friends who talked on the phone once every few weeks. We were business associates in Nu Skin, and I admired him and looked up to him. I considered him a kind of mentor. My mind was racing as I looked for words. He didn't make it any easier by breaking the silence. Finally I mumbled, "Mark, just one thing..."

"Anything. What?" he stammered.

"Could we go out once?"

He laughed nervously. "Well, I'm not much into the dating game, but why don't you stop by the house Sunday afternoon. We can sit out in the hammock and talk about our dreams and hopes and goals." His words drifted off.

That was my cue that it was my turn to talk. My heart was pounding. I didn't know exactly how I felt. I was so unprepared for this conversation. I was asked out very little during my time in public office. I didn't feel that I was intimidating. I still felt like the same me. But obviously there was a perception that went with the office because the occasional person who did ask me out would couch it in terms of "escorting me" to some public event. I had dated a little during this time, but never seriously. This bold breach of all social rules of order definitely got my attention. "Sunday afternoon..."

"Yeah, I really want to log some quality time with you."

Log—that seemed a funny word to use. "Okay, I'll be there."

I changed clothes three times getting ready to go. I was nervous, excited, scared, and uncertain. Something told me this was a significant moment in my life. When I arrived, he must not have heard the doorbell. I had been to his home once with Nancy for a meeting to discuss transitional housing problems for the homeless and again for a United Way fundraiser. So I had no misgiving letting myself in and sitting down in the living room while I waited for him. I tried to appear casual, but I was feeling anything but that. Soon he joined me, apologizing for not realizing I had arrived. He served me something to drink and we headed outside to the back yard. There was the hammock he had mentioned, and he headed straight for it. My mind vacillated for a moment, but my body followed without hesitation.

We spent the entire afternoon talking about our lives—where we had come from and where we were going. We were both vulnerable from failed marriages. Mark had just left another relationship in which he was living with someone who was also a distributor in Nu Skin. I wondered about it. By outward appearances, it seemed that his life was still intertwined with hers. *Had there been enough time in between? What was she feeling? I didn't want to take him away if he belonged to someone else.* He assured me that his association with her had been over for some time.

We shared our secret fears about relationships. We talked of things we wanted to do to make a difference in the world, and whether I planned to make a career out of politics. With one foot occasionally touching the ground to keep us swinging in the hammock, he directed us into some fairly weighty topics. "What is it about me that frightens you the most?"

"What a funny question!" It seemed to come out of nowhere. "But it's easy to answer. It's that you are a former minister, a writer, and a wanderer. I was married to someone who fit that same description. I loved him with all my heart...but I'm not sure I'm up for doing it again. Having it end was too agonizing, and I don't want to endure that kind of pain again. It was worse than anything I can describe." I was slightly choked and stopped speaking before it showed.

He studied me for a few moments and then said thoughtfully, "You have to have really loved someone for it to hurt that much."

"I did. I've never loved anyone the way I loved him. I'm not sure I'm ready to try again. But, it's been seven years since we...since he left. I'm over it as much as I will ever be." *There are scars left as there would be from any major trauma, but I believe they make me stronger and more sensitive at the same time.* I didn't say what I was thinking. We were both lost in our reverie for a few moments, and then I realized he was speaking softly.

"You must have been terribly hurt. Whatever happens with us, I don't want to hurt you."

After more than a year of talking now and then, it was hard

to believe that we were here: face to face, or more like side by side, swaying gently in the hammock. It was unbelievably easy to talk to him about consequential issues and deep feelings. He didn't waste words on trivial conversation, but got right to the heart of the things that really mattered.

"Mark, every man says that, at least every decent man. Believe me, I've been told that before. But my experience is that as soon as we let ourselves care about someone, really care, we are vulnerable to being hurt. The deeper the feelings, the more intense the heartache. And I have never loved someone without feeling that kind of pain. I don't think it's possible."

"So would you let that hold you back from being with someone again?"

"No, I wouldn't. But I am more cautious and reserved with my feelings. I am very careful and very selective about sharing my emotions. I have a lot of friends, especially women friends, but I guess I'm a little afraid to let a man back inside."

"So if I mean it—I really don't want to hurt you, what would it take?"

"I'm not sure I know what you mean."

"What I'm saying, if we were to come together, you and I, what would I need to do...or not do?" His brow was furrowed as he was asking. I didn't find myself doubting his sincerity for a second.

"If we were to begin seeing each other,"—*how could I be thinking this way so quickly?*—"I need continuity, a nice steady flow of being together, or talking, or keeping in communication. The pain for me is most intense with people who turn on and off, who come on strong and then back away, and then keep repeating the pattern over and over. That behavior tears my heart out. I've been there before, and I don't want to be there again."

He hugged me closer to him. "I think I understand. That doesn't sound like a lot to ask."

"You wouldn't think so. But there are people who just can't give even that much. But beyond that basic need, the only way you could hurt me deeply is if we did finally come together and then you would leave me. I can't handle abandonment. It is my deepest wound, my lifelong struggle. I need someone to love me who doesn't need a lot of 'spaces in our togetherness', as Kahlil Gibran would say, and who will never leave me—neither physically nor emotionally. I need someone who will never even threaten to leave me in the heat of an argument. I can accept differences of opinion. I can compromise. I can give in so many ways. But I can't handle starting a life together and then going through the devastation of feeling you pull away, or worse yet, walk out the door…for any reason."

My eyes were watery. Just sharing that part of me made the feelings well up all over again. I felt the pain at that moment of my loss with my former husband, James Kavanaugh. Jim, a life-long searcher, drifted in and out of my life like a seaman exploring the open seas, but always coming home to port. Like Mark, he was a former minister (a Catholic priest), a poet, a writer…and a wanderer. I thought he and I would be together until the end. I loved him so much that I wasn't sure if I would ever consider marriage again. I was lost in my thoughts and the deep sense of loss. Time had healed much of the pain but talking this openly now brought back all the feelings.

Yes, I had good reason to be afraid of Mark, the ex-minister, the writer, the wanderer who had lived in multiple states over the past several years. But as cautious as I should have been, I was also equally drawn to this side of him.

Mark's words brought me back to the present. "I can't even imagine ever pulling back from you. All I can think about right now is how I can be with you every moment. It's inconceivable that I would ever need 'space' as you call it, much less that I would ever leave you. What happened? Can you talk about it?"

"Maybe sometime. It would take a long time. It was all so convoluted; it completely consumed me at the time. I had actually been thinking recently that I may never find someone again. It's not that I'm so afraid. It just seems so unlikely that I could fall in love again, and that the kind of compatibility I would want and need could ever happen to me."

"I've been telling my daughter, Amy, about you for some time now. I even drove her by your house once just to try to introduce you. But you weren't home. I was first struck by your sweetness and your smile, but as I got to know you through our conversations, I really began to feel that you had the qualities I need in a partner."

"Really, like what?"

"Well, for starters, I've always been with women who held me back or stayed in the background and were never very interested in getting involved in business with me. What I feel about you is that you have all the supportive qualities, but also the assertive ones. This time, I want a partner, you know, a real partner, who will travel with me, and speak with me, and be so good at what we do that we are interchangeable."

"Gee, that sounds too good to be true. Most men would be intimidated by that kind of woman. I can't believe you're real."

"Actually, beyond the sweetness, it's your strength that attracts me to you. But I can understand that somewhere along the way you have been emotionally wounded. And time will heal a wound as long as it isn't reopened. I promise you I will be sensitive to that part of you. I will caress it and stroke it. But, now that I know, I will never gouge that wound."

He reached out and put his hand in mine, and we just lay there swinging in the hammock.

"What about you? What is your greatest fear about getting involved again?" Mark was a man who oozed confidence. It almost seemed incongruent that he would have any fears at all. But I asked because I was sure they were there hidden away inside him.

"Monogamy means everything to me in marriage. I have to have a wife whom I know, beyond the slightest doubt, will be totally faithful to me. I had it otherwise once. It almost killed me." There was a long pause, and then he asked, "Could you promise that and mean it?"

I realized he was serious. "It's funny, Mark. If this is the worst fear you have in the whole world and the biggest thing that could cause problems between us, then we're over the first hurdle. I have always been a one-man woman. The emotions involved in *one* loving relationship consume so much of me that I couldn't imagine dealing with more than one. It's as if you have put the easy challenge out there first. Now give me the tough ones." I squeezed his hand just a little more, and he leaned his head on my shoulder.

"That's how I feel about your request. Of course, I would never leave you. I could never even distance myself from you. And, you know what? If you ever leave me, I promise you...I would follow you wherever you go."

I had to smile. If we were to pursue this relationship, I couldn't imagine me ever being the one to leave. But if I did, the thought of him traipsing after me gave me a sense of warmth and security like I'd never felt in my life. "Do you really mean that?"

"You can't' believe how much I mean it," he said emphatically, as his arms swept outward. "No, Rene, I will never leave you. That you can absolutely take to the bank. Ask me for something difficult. Ask me to lay down my life for you. Ask me to give up all my earthly possessions. Ask me to walk away from you. That would be difficult." Mark lifted up on one elbow and kissed me lightly on the lips.

"I've had a few important relationships in my life," I responded, "but always only one at a time. Even in high school where Catholicism encouraged us to 'play the field,' I couldn't. I tried, but I couldn't get into it. I was in love with Jimmy Yeargan. And we dated all four years throughout school."

"My life has been one of serial monogamy," Mark explained. "I can only handle one woman at a time, but I have been through my share. Now I'm ready to find *the* one. I want to settle into a loving life and grow old with that person."

One thing I felt absolutely certain about at that moment was that I would never have to worry about "spaces" in our relationship. One of my worst fears had been eradicated. When I thought about what I most wanted and needed in a partnership, it was togetherness—in travel, in business, and in our personal time. It was becoming more and more clear that this was his need too.

I don't remember driving home that night. I floated home on white fluffy clouds. I couldn't stop thinking about our conversation. I realized that Mark had set his focus on me. He wanted to get married and had no hesitancy talking about it. He wasn't afraid. I was. Even though we had known each other for quite a while, our relationship had jumped overnight to a new level. My life had been moving in the fast lane, but it was down a highway where I could see what lay ahead. This interaction with Mark caught me by surprise. It had been so long since I felt romantically caught up in another person. I wanted to feel that way again, but....

Along with several other elected officials and businessmen in town, I was invited by Perry DiLoretto, a major developer in the community, to go on an Air Force tour. With all the difficulties Nu Skin was facing, the mounting demands at the county, and some challenges my son was facing, I felt overwhelmed with responsibilities but instinctively felt that this was an opportunity that would not come again. That wasn't the only reason I chose to go. I needed time and space from Mark to clear my head and be sure about the direction we seemed to be taking.

We boarded the Air Force carrier heading for the base in Dyas, Texas, where we were entertained royally after a fascinating walk-through of the B-1 Bomber. The next day, we flew to Palm Desert and were taken through the plant that was building the B-2 Bomber. We each took turns in the simulator flying the Bomber. As I set my site on the enemy fort and pressed the button, I inadvertantly hit the children's hospital. It was as close as I ever want to come to flying a bomber.

When I returned, Mark was eager to get together. So was I. We met in the afternoon on Windy Hill—a beautiful spot overlooking all of Reno. As I sat with him on the park bench, I could hardly catch my breath. He made me feel so loved, so valued as a person. He had written me a poem that reflected his feelings as he had time to think while I was away. As we sat side by side, he read it to me.

Courtship

Could I slow down my ego
And follow as you lead,
Instead of always running things
For fear we won't succeed?

Could I give up my bank account
And everything I've got,
If I knew that meant keeping you
And losing you if not?

Could I endure the anguish
Of walking from your life
If one day I could not fulfill
Your true needs as my wife?

Would I defend you to the death,
Put living on the line
In times of danger, then treasure
Your life over mine?

Perhaps those seem like questions
No couples need think through,
And yet somehow I feel compelled
To answer them for you.

Your love outweighs my ego
And money's but a game,
Before you considered becoming my wife
My only goal was fame.

Yet, now I'd give up all I own
And never shed a tear,
I'd start with nothing save your love
And launch a new career.

The tough one would be leaving you
And yet I know my heart,
If I could not fulfill your needs
I'd silently depart.

And though I'll never have to face
A warrior's demise,
Were your life truly on the line,
My own, I'd compromise.

Perhaps not all, but some of these
We'll face before we're through,
I trust my actions will translate
My depth of love for you.

As he finished reading it, I sat looking out and thinking to myself. *How am I to respond? I don't know if I'm ready to be loved like this. I've been on my own for so long now, I've become pretty self-sufficient. Do I want to give it up? Am I ready to be dependent in any way, even emotionally, on someone else again?* Finally a few disjointed thoughts came out.

"That's a beautiful poem. You make me feel so...special. I'm really overwhelmed by all of this. Is chivalry still in vogue?" It's funny how the thoughts we think sound so different than the words we speak. *I don't really want that to happen. I want such honesty in loving someone that my thoughts and my spoken words are absolutely the same. Is that naïve?*

"I've had longer to think about this than you. Do you realize it has been over a year and a half since I fell in love with you?" Mark looked at me quizzically. "Once I knew I wanted you, I began spending time getting to know you better, asking about you, talking on the phone occasionally, imagining us together. From there it was easy. Pretty soon I began to envision us together for all time, picturing what it would be like, where we would live, how we would interact... If you could see what I see, you wouldn't hesitate for a minute."

"Do you always do things in this order—I mean, imagine them first and then act on it? Most people test the waters a bit first and then start thinking about how it would feel to get in deeper." I was fascinated by the way this man's mind worked.

"Oh, yeah! I do everything this way," Mark explained. "When I first started in Nu Skin, I set my goals in writing. Then I would autogenically program myself about having a huge successful organization. I'd see myself with time to ski and teach blind skiers, and with plenty of money, enough to give away wherever I wanted. It's really fun to goal-set this way. Once I believe I am capable of achieving my goals, I can envision whatever I want. And, finally, the last step is the easy one: it is just a matter of doing whatever it takes to make it happen. But there is no question in my mind that it is going to happen. It is already a done deal. I just have to put it all in place."

"That helps me understand some things," I laughed. "Now at least that phone call you made to me—the day you told me you thought we were soul mates—makes sense now. You set goals in your mind. What I didn't know was that I was one of them." He laughed out loud. With that, I leaned over and kissed him. I was still unsure of my deeper feelings, but I was falling in love with this man's bizarre way of approaching life.

Mark was raised in Springfield, Missouri. Patsi, his mom, says Mark was always the way he is now—charged with excess energy and brain power, a natural leader serving as class president for several years, a voracious reader and great debater, mischievous, with a wild sense of humor, and completely uncontrollable.

Like most kids growing up in the 60s—he is six years younger than I—Mark tried out drugs and alcohol. His sensitivity and spiritual side seem to come from his mom and his entrepreneurial and writing propensities clearly stem from his dad.

The first thing anyone notices about Mark is his Texas-Missouri twang. Lots of network marketers have practiced imitating his speaking style and accent: "Hi, I'm Mark YARnell." He has a tendency to do whatever he does with panache. He loves to play with people's minds, asking off-the-wall questions, and then he watches playfully for their reaction. He was doing this with me; I just didn't know it.

It was a Thursday morning and my secretary had arrived to start her workday. I had just finished breakfast, brushing my teeth, and grabbing my day-planner to see what my day looked like. I was due at a meeting with the consultant whom the county had hired to help the commissioners work better together. Since I was chairman, I was supposed to be leading the charge to make that happen. Teresa was reading off my messages from my answering machine: "You've got a meeting with Jim Kent at 8:30...Your Mom called to see how your world looks today...Eleanor Waldren wanted to know if you could play tennis on the weekend...Nancy Paolini called. She needs your help in making a presentation to the City Council about Project ReStart...Mark Yarnell called to ask if you could join him in Atlanta this weekend. There's a plane leaving Reno at 11:15 the morning of November 2nd...And Russ Karlen called to ask if you are sending any of your people to the Nu Skin meeting in Orange County on Friday. He said it is filling up fast."

"Wait a minute. Go back. Mark Yarnell said what?" I couldn't believe what I thought I'd heard.

She repeated it again.

"November 2nd! That's today. Is he out of his mind? I have a job to do. I have meetings scheduled. I have my network marketing group to support. I have a son to raise. My life is governed by what's in my day-timer. His...his...serendipitous whims just don't fit in!" I went tearing out of the house slightly shaken and pushing it to be on time for my 8:30 meeting at my "other office," Deux Gros Nez.

Jim Kent was already seated when I arrived. I ordered my "cap" and scone, and joined him at the table. We got into a lively discussion about how to get the redistricting issue handled. Every ten years once the census is taken, political representatives go through a kind of reshuffling of their districts to allow for growth or whatever changes have occurred during the last decade. This is a political nightmare, and with a board of county commissioners like ours who already had serious internal problems, it was an even bigger fiasco.

We could reshape the districts any way we wanted as long as we adhered to a couple of rules: the county residents must be divided equally among the five of us and we had to live within our own district. Once we had the boundaries set, we had to vote on this by the end of December so that it could go into effect by the first of the year. We were at an impasse. Jim was giving me some pointers on how to conduct Monday's caucus so that I could enable discussion to continue.

As important as the subject was, I kept finding my thoughts drifting. Why couldn't I get Mark Yarnell out of my mind? He was crazy if he thought I was irresponsible enough to just hop on a plane because he left a message.

Finally Jim said, "Why do I have the feeling that my words are going right over your head?"

"Jim, I'm sorry. I really am concerned about how to handle this situation. The meeting is going to go nowhere Monday if we don't come up with a game plan, but I'm having a hard time keeping my mind on anything right now. I'm so distracted," I confessed.

"What's his name?" he probed with a funny smirk on his face.

I proceeded to tell him about this Man of LaMancha who not only is willing to slay windmills for me, but turns these would-be dragons into knights in shining armor. I am having a whirlwind romance with my own Don Quixote, who is also wooing me with gallant words and noble promises.

When I told him about this morning's message, he suggested that I ask myself some poignant questions. "No need to answer them out loud, but think about a few things from the perspective of what is good for you. Does this man meet your criteria for what you want in a life partner? Do you share the really important values? Do you have enough day-to-day stuff in common? Will your son be positively affected by him? Are you at a point in your life when you are ready to be with someone again? Is this an opportunity that you will regret if you don't reach out and take hold of it?"

I sipped my cappuccino thoughtfully. After a prolonged silence, slowly I nodded.

He looked at his watch, then back at me, contemplating my mood. After a moment, he said "You've got exactly fifty minutes to catch that plane."

Somehow, I made it back home, packed, called Mom, arranged for Chris to be looked after, gave instructions to Teresa, and made it to the gate with at least three minutes to spare. I couldn't believe I was really going to Atlanta. The only person more surprised than me was Mark. Still waiting at the boarding gate, he embraced me and we boarded the plane together.

It seemed to me that it took no time at all to get to Dallas although it was almost a three-hour flight. A quick layover and now taxiing onto the DFW runway, we were absorbed again in conversation. For what seemed more than an hour, we were so engaged in each other that we were greatly astonished when we stopped to regain our breath—only to discover that we were still on the ground. We both thought we were half way to Atlanta. In reality, I guess we were. Only the plane was still on the ground.

After giving a Nu Skin talk for Tom and Terry Hill, close friends and front line to Mark, we had dinner in the hotel. It was a sushi meal—some kind of raw fish that came from the stomach lining of tuna—that we will remember for the rest of our lives. I ordered a glass of wine, and I noticed he didn't join me. That gave him the opportunity to bring up a subject that he had not yet broached.

"I have had enough alcohol to last me for a lifetime. I don't know how to tell you this, except to tell you. I am a recovering alcoholic. Living a life of sobriety is one of the greatest accomplishments of my life. In fact, one of my goals is to work closely with groups of alcoholics and addicts, helping make them aware of their own dependency. I don't know how much you know about this problem, but awareness is the first step toward taking responsibility for one's actions. I want to use my experience and speaking skills to impact the lives of others who are also suffering from this disease."

When he was finished, he looked at me as if to measure my response. I wasn't surprised, but neither did I know for certain that Mark had a drinking problem. I had heard some innuendo about it from various Nu Skin people, but I've never been inclined to pay much attention to rumors. After a moment of thought, I shared my own feelings with him.

"You know, Mark, we each bring some of our own baggage into a relationship—and even more at our age. I have wounds that are healed but still scarred. If you have the problem under control, that is what matters. I'm not so interested in who you were, but who you are now is what really counts."

I had no way of knowing at this moment what additional baggage Mark was still carrying. Nor could he know all the emotional "stuff" I was bringing with me. Years of dialogue and exchange were ahead of us, years of coming to understand each other's paraphernalia. At this moment, none of that seemed to matter.

That night, ministering our own ceremony, we exchanged vows with each other. We were wedded to each other spiritually and emotionally. A more formal ceremony would come later. With so much complete honesty shared, and a prayer verbalized asking God to bless our bond, we made love. We were so out of our minds in love that nothing made a great deal of sense during this time, except to us. I fell asleep in his arms completely enveloped by his love and a sense of protectiveness. I felt certain that nothing bad could ever happen as long as I had Mark by my side.

The same feeling lingered the next morning. Not satisfied with morning lovemaking, through mind control, we tried to inhabit each other's bodies. I mean, we actually believed it was physically possible for my being to dwell within his medium-framed 5'10" body and his within my small-framed 5'3" body. We weren't satisfied with being one physically. Somehow, we wanted to be one spiritually and emotionally as well.

The next day, after spending some quality time with Tom and Terry, who recalled their own first love experiences to us, we wandered off from their house for an afternoon picnic. The grass was like carpet and so lusciously green. We spread our blanket and sipped a cool drink. While we sat under a tree, overlooking a small pond, Mark pulled out a letter he had written and said he had saved it for just the right time so when I read it, I would have time to really meditate on it. This was that moment, one that I will always hold in my heart.

Dear Rene:

When for a few brief eye-meeting moments, the world stands still, it is for love. When a park bench inspires the awe and wonder of a cathedral pew, it is for love. When merely holding another brings more joy than full intimacy with others, it is for love. When, through a series of events so totally unrelated, God brings two of His children together at one time and one place for the purpose of serving others, it is for love.

It is for love...what magical words. When Nancy asked me at lunch Tuesday why I am *really* in Reno, I didn't tell her but I knew...it is for love. Not merely a one-on-one selfish love that culminates periodically in every bed on this planet when men and women scale the heights of physical intimacy. But rather a love which comes from a unity of purpose, a love which God grants those few souls who alone can make the world better, but together can move mountains.

The question for me has most recently been about selfish isolation versus impact living. By that I mean I've felt the need to back off from the outer trappings and focus exclusively on my own personal needs and longings. For too long, it seems, I have spent wasted countless hours pursuing the power, prestige, and affluence which all seemed to be life's report card. Some would say I've earned an 'A' on that card, but to the degree that it's brought no lasting fulfillment, it matters little. So naturally I've lately been absorbed in the notion that any impact I've had thus far on the lives of others has been rendered insignificant by my own inner longings. If God could but grant me one wish, I reasoned, He would bring me a simple, uncomplicated lady with whom I could exit this outer world and raise a sweet family. I wanted nothing more than to grow old with one person, make her the very object of my total affections and bid the rest of the world a warm goodbye.

Instead, like some cosmic joke, He placed you squarely in the middle of my life and now, once again, I'm off and running on some new track of serving others. I don't know exactly how this happened, but here I am beginning a new life with someone who matters to me more than anyone, and my focus is on helping hundreds of unfortunates become sober. While most people are self-centered especially in the early stages of a new love, we seem to be other-centered opting to allow our relationship to blossom in the midst of chaos…placing the feelings and needs of others ahead of our own.

I don't question God's plan for me, nor can I look into a crystal ball and predict the outcome of our relationship even six months down the road. What I do now realize is that we can have both lives and together, synergistically, have a dramatic impact on others. I have enough capacity to love, as do you, to fulfill God's plan whatever it is.

So the purpose of my writing is to let you know that I support you in whatever direction of service you choose to pursue. I would not bind you to me alone but rather grant you the freedom to continue to make an impact in whatever manner you choose. However I do ask of you two important questions. Would you please never place outer activities ahead of our love? I won't. And would you promise to work as diligently at perpetuating our love and romance as you do in other endeavors? I will.

Because irrespective of which directions we choose, I believe we are together by design for one overwhelming reason which only God may grant a few lucky souls... it is for love.

With Mark's head in my lap, we talked for a long time about our purpose in life. What was it that each of us was being called to do? We explored how we felt we could carry it out better together than alone. We talked about challenges we might face but, like Alexander the Great, we knew with certainty there was no world we couldn't conquer. He leaned up and kissed me. We held the kiss, his tongue probing mine. My body was so alive. My emotions were overflowing with joy. It had been a long time since I had felt this symbiotic with another person. I was falling more in love with this man, more than I thought I ever could again. He was spiritual, funny, philosophical, down-to-earth, and sensitive. He was everything I could hope to find but never believed I would again. It was in this setting that I knew with certainty that I wanted to spend my life with Mark Yarnell.

Suddenly our ecstasy was interrupted by a shouting woman and a barking dog. Apparently, in our mystical explorations of each other's minds and hearts, we didn't realize that we were having our picnic on private property.

CHAPTER 5

WEDDING AND HONEYMOON
December 1991 – January 1992

B ack in Reno, we each tried to go forward with our lives as usual. But nothing was "usual" anymore. Our heads told us we should slow things down a bit, but our hearts said otherwise.

After some discussion, we made the adult decision to leave things up to our children. Mark's daughter, Amy, one year younger than my Chris, was finishing up her last year in high school and he was in his first year of college. We brought the four of us together in the Florida Keys for Thanksgiving. That would be the first time we would meet each other's children and the first time *they* would meet each other. I flew out with Mark two days earlier so we could have some private time together, and the kids could finish up their classes before the holiday break.

Mark was coming from Puerto Rico, where he was conducting business and training meetings for his Nu Skin organization there. He would connect through Miami and then on down to the Keys. I would change planes in Dallas and again in Miami. Hmm. I wondered if I could arrange to arrive in Miami at the same time as Mark.

Yes! As I landed in Miami and searched for the shuttle he'd be on, I spotted Mark. He didn't see me and didn't know my exact travel plans anyway. Walking up from behind, in my softest and sexiest voice I said: "Excuse me, sir, do you have the time?"

"Yes, it's...." At that moment, he looked around. The expression on his face was worth it all. He slipped his hand in mine and never let go...all the way to the Florida Keys.

We had two incredibly wonderful days, just the two of us. For this precious moment in time, there were no political pressures, no media upsets, no phone calls—only the serenity that comes with being in love.

When it was time for the kids to arrive, Mark was pacing. Amy was coming in from Tulsa, where she lived with her mom. Chris was attending Truckee Meadows Community College in Reno.

Mark finally broke the silence. "Jeez, I hope the kids like each other."

"Me too," I mused. Then after thinking about it more, I added, "Gosh, I hope the kids don't like each other too much."

Our eyes met and we laughed. Everything seemed perfect.

Chris got held up in Miami, so Amy arrived first. She was slightly shorter than me, with dancing brown eyes, long blond hair, and dimples. We instantly took to each other. I didn't know how Mark and I got so lucky. Most kids object to their parents remarrying. I guess ours were old enough and secure enough within themselves. They both seemed to understand that they had their own lives ahead of them. This was primarily about *our* life together.

We rented a home and two motor scooters, and for the next four days we were a family. Amy rode on the back of my scooter and Chris traveled with Mark. They were both lightweight. With Chris's 5'8" medium frame and Mark's 5'10" slim body, they balanced each other. I looked out at the two men in my life, both Capricorns, with birthdays just four days apart, and it seemed right. After a lifetime of being in search of family, this was a holiday weekend I would never forget.

We had a traditional Thanksgiving dinner at home, played at

the beach, went scuba diving, walked into town, and danced to some obnoxious music; but mostly we spent time talking and getting to know each other. At seventeen, Amy was mature beyond her years. She was well read and had good insights on a variety of topics. I loved her mind. She said she has the best of both worlds— her father's I-can-do-anything attitude and her mother's stability and calmness. She gained roots from her mom and wings from her dad. She would gradually become the daughter I never had.

On our last night together, after dinner, the four of us sat in the living room of our shared house and talked about our future. We told both of them—as if they didn't know—that we were in love and wanted to get married. We were there to ask our children for their blessing. For the rest of the evening, they talked to us about the pitfalls of marriage. Both of them were well experienced at being the children of divorce. They had survived it all, but had come away with some definite opinions about what it takes to make a marriage work.

Amy began: "You'd better have something else to hold onto after the fu-fu wears off. No matter how much you think this feeling will last forever, it won't. Then will you have enough to go on living a regular day-to-day life together?"

"Yeah," Chris added. "This is all happening pretty fast. I mean you guys are older, so maybe it's okay. But have you thought at all about those parts of each other that aren't cool? Just kidding!" He laughed nervously and then went on. "You know, Mark, Mom is awesome. She comes across really sweet, but she can also be pretty stubborn. And I've seen her get really mad. You have to worry when she's smiling while she's mad at you. That's the worst. This happens especially if you don't keep your word," he said, catching my eye with a knowing glance.

It felt as if we were the children and they were the parents. After an entire evening of exchanging ideas about what makes marriages succeed and fail, and what it would take for us to be happy as a family, Amy and Chris each gave us their blessings. They seemed appropriately cautious, but genuinely happy for us.

The first week of December, Nu Skin had scheduled a meeting with all the top field leaders, known as Blue Diamond Executives. Mark was a Blue Diamond, and I was in qualification, almost there. Mark called to see if I was planning to attend.

"I don't know. I have so much I have neglected these past few weeks. Maybe I should stay home and take care of business."

"I wish you'd come. I just want you there with me."

All he had to do was ask. I had no resistance. I wanted to be wherever he was. "How would we handle the situation? Are you ready to let everyone at Nu Skin know about us?"

"No, it's too soon. They'll think we haven't given it enough time. Let's be discreet for now. We'll tell them all after we're married."

I instinctively felt part of his reason for holding back, regardless of how long the relationship had been over, was out of concern for the feelings of his former significant other. Once we told anyone, the word would be out. I respected him for that.

"Do you think they won't see it in our eyes? I mean, we're not exactly unobtrusive when we're together."

"Well, we can register in separate rooms and at least appear to be coming independently. It's no one's business but ours right now."

"Are you sure we can pull this off?"

"Absolutely!"

We flew out together but sat apart during the meetings. It was so apparent how much everyone respected Mark. When he spoke, people listened. In the evening, a party was scheduled at Craig and Kathy Bryson's house. They were upline in the organizational structure to both Mark and me. We went out to the event together and were a little late arriving.

"Now just be yourself. Act cool and no one will think anything of our walking in together. After all, we both live in Reno, don't we?"

I nodded and agreed. Nearly everyone was already there. We could hear talking, laughter, and, as we walked through the door, we noticed a few of the distributors engaged in serious problem-solving conversations.

Wedding and Honeymoon

One of the first couples we came upon was Dave Johnson and his wife, Coni. Since Dave had been the one who introduced us a year and a half earlier, I wondered if Mark would slip away so as not to draw attention to ourselves. But what he did next shouldn't have surprised me.

"Well, Mark, Rene, how nice to see you...together," Dave remarked in his deepest baritone voice. Hearing our names, Coni turned around to say hello.

"We have something to tell you," Mark announced. "We're getting married!"

"Oh boy, oh boy, oh boy," Coni squealed as she clapped her hands together like a little girl. She hugged me. Dave hugged me. And Mark and I caught eyes. So much for keeping our cool.

He couldn't hold it inside. If he hadn't blurted it out, I probably would have. We were in love. Who were we kidding to think we could hide it from everyone? Within five minutes, the word had spread throughout the room.

We made our way over to our president, Blake Roney, and stood on the stairs talking to him for a few minutes. We wanted him to hear it from us. He gave us his blessing.

Lisa Fairbanks came rushing over. "You've given me something worthwhile to take home to everyone. This is the best news to come out of these meetings. I'm so happy for you both," she said as she put her arms around us simultaneously.

By the time we got back home, nearly everyone in Nu Skin knew of our plans. Word spreads quickly when you're in the business of networking. Congratulatory messages via our voice mail came from all over the country. Everyone seemed so happy about our news.

Everyone, that is, except for my fellow county commissioners. Every significant conflict between us came to a head at this time. Our differences about the Honey Lake Project were news items. And after three years of being unable to curtail the Washoe Med conspiracy, the Ethics Commission was about to rule on Dianne and Gene's ability to serve as paid employee/board member respectively and vote on issues pertaining to the hospital.

Facing a new year, staff recommendations were about to be made to our Board regarding the best health plan to adopt for county employees. Some staff members found inconspicuous moments to slip into my office or call me at home to let me know that they felt they were being railroaded into presenting the Washoe Med HMO as the preferred plan. They were hoping that this vote would come *after* the Ethics Commission ruling, relying on Larry Beck and me to vote against the recommendation.

On top of all of this, after months of disagreements, the vote was about to come down on redistricting. Mark and I each owned a home. His was a castle with eight bedrooms, seven baths, and six fireplaces. It was too pretentious for my comfort level. Mine I had shared with my former husband, which didn't make my house particularly inviting to Mark. So we decided to lease mine and put his up for sale, freeing us to look for our dream home together. In the meantime, we planned to lease a furnished home from a friend who resided just outside of my district. Given all the other issues, and the fact that I was creating a gray area by announcing that I would be moving just prior to our redistricting taking effect, the commissioners were not about to adjust the boundary lines a few blocks to allow me to live with my new husband *and* remain within my district.

On December 16, as the commissioners gathered for a morning study session, I noticed Gene and Dianne reading a long unfamiliar document. At first I thought I'd overlooked something in my packet. Then I realized it was the Ethics Commission decision. I had heard they had been formally reprimanded for wasting the time of the commission on such an obvious determination. They were given official notice that they may no longer vote on Washoe Med issues. The tension in the room was palpable.

Up until then, I had always tried to keep my composure in the meetings. But this particular day, neither Dianne nor I held our feelings back. The next topic on the agenda was redistricting. Knowing that the commissioners, by law, *had* to allow me to live in my district, I told them that I would be getting married on Christmas day and moving in with my new husband a few blocks further south of the currently proposed border for my district. The adjustment I was requesting was minor. But, with the Ethics Commission documentation still lying in front of her, Dianne took the position that, after all the hassling over this issue, there was no way she would make any further adjustments. I was outraged.

"I'm tired of taking your crap. I've sat here for three years and turned the other cheek…and have been accused by you, and threatened by you, and ridiculed by you for being sweet. Well, I'm tired of being sweet, and tired of taking it from you, Dianne."

"I think you've got a problem, Rene. I don't want to discuss this anymore."

Following the meeting, I went straight to my office and called Mark.

"I shouldn't be surprised by any of this. It's been this way the entire time I've served on this board. I've never met anyone like Dianne Cornwall. I thought even she would lighten up at a time that should be one of the happiest moments in my life. Instead, she is doing everything in her power to make it miserable for me."

"Well, it's the Ethics Commission decision coming down that's getting to her. She knows she can't win it. You finally beat her on an issue and she can't stand the loss."

"It's not worth it, Mark. This whole situation is tearing me apart inside."

"You've got *me*, now. You don't have to fight these battles alone."

"But do you realize they are going to exclude me from my own district?"

"They can't."

"But they are. Who's going to question them? The staff? I guess I could take this matter to the Ethics Commission too; but they are going to get tired of settling squabbles in a catfight between two women politicians who can't work out their own differences. This is just.…"

At that moment, my office door flew open and Dianne barged in ranting and raving about our confrontation in the study session.

"Sweetheart, hold on," I said to Mark. "I've got to deal with a matter that just came through my door. Don't go away." I laid the receiver down on my desk.

Dianne was going berserk, yelling and screaming at the top of her voice. Her eyes were wild, and her face seemed contorted.

Something told me this was not the time to try to have a conversation. Without saying a word, I put my hands on her back and arm, escorted her out of my office, and closed the door. She stood on the other side, trying to push it open. I held it closed from the inside until she finally went away.

Sitting back down at my desk, I picked up the phone. "Are you still there?"

"I wouldn't have believed it if I hadn't heard it with my own ears. All of this over a stupid ruling?"

"No, all of this over the loss of power from the Ethics Commission ruling and three years of buildup between us," I said, still shaking from the episode. She may not be able to hold her job now that she can't cast a vote for them. "But she is in the power position. I'm no match for Dianne."

"Get out of there and come home to me. I'll take you out for a nice dinner."

The next week sped by. Winter arrived like an unexpected and unwelcome guest. I've always been a morning person but find it harder to get out of bed when the weather turns cold. Forcing myself out of the warmth of my sheets and feathery comforter, I went to the front porch to get the morning paper. These days, I opened the paper with some fear and trepidation. As I shook the snow from the cellophane wrapper, I spotted a letter in my front door dated Thursday, 5:00 a.m. It was from Mark. I made myself a cup of coffee and nestled into my favorite morning spot. Seated on the couch in the family room, feeling the warmth of the wood-burning stove, with the sun streaming through the easterly windows, I began to read:

Wedding and Honeymoon

Dear Rene:

When I first awakened this morning, it was snowing as hard as I've ever seen it snow. I was compelled to throw on a ski jacket and go outside for a short walk. The shock of changing from a warm bed to a pelting snow was offset by the beauty all around me. The trees were already somewhat covered and bent over and the black wrought-iron fence was beautifully accented with a half inch of that magical white stuff. With all the lighting around this house, the hilltop literally looked like a movie set for some Christmas special about to be filmed. As that very thought dawned on me, I decided to make the moment into my own mental movie. I walked back inside and found my little Sony Walkman, quickly grabbed a cassette of Bing Crosby's White Christmas, popped on the earphones and began my walk again. I'm not sure I can explain exactly what happened next but here goes.

I've never, ever felt so vitally alive and fully human. I was acutely transported into a state of mind in which Santa Claus was real and Jimmy Stewart handed out money to his broke friends. I was in some ecstatic, Christmas state of mind beyond any I've ever experienced and yet I was merely shuffling through the snow alone on a hilltop I would soon be leaving. When I arrived on the back porch, the snow had let up considerably and I could see the casino lights of the valley sparkling in dramatic contrast to the white on my yard. For one brief moment the lights became a Christmas tree lying on its side lighting up all of Reno and somehow conveying a special message to me. What if this little city could become the light of giving, sharing, and Christmas spirit for this whole nation? Far-fetched? Not really.

Then Crosby clicked off and I reached into my pocket and pulled out an old Beetles tape that unbeknown to me was poised and ready to play their shortest love song. My mind shifted gears as I listened to Paul McCartney sing words which brought me back to reality: "Who knows how long I've loved you, You know I love you still, Will I wait a lonely lifetime? If you want me to I will."

McCartney's finest love song ended as the snow did. "For the things you do endear me to you, All my life they will, they will." Christmas and altruism were replaced with an overwhelming feeling of love and oneness with you. I clicked off my machine and came back inside to try to capture for you the emotions of this stroll through my early morning Christmas Love Story so that in some small way, having not been with me, you might nevertheless experience it.

What dawned on me as I searched for my pen is how very much like our lives this little experience was. We seem to be balanced between a spirit of loving service and the joy of romantic love. No sooner does one end than the other begins. My God, what a life! And then it became crystal clear to me that God had granted me a brief glimpse through this sequence of events into a much deeper awareness of His priorities. Christmas spirit, sharing and giving come first and that very activity enhances and perpetuates the very love we both want so desperately. I've had it backwards. The depth of our love will quite literally be commensurate with the extent to which we unselfishly reach out to others. God will take care of our hearts and push our love into realms we've probably never even imagined so long as we stay centered in His will, "loving our neighbors as we love ourselves."

I'm not altogether certain that any of this makes sense to you because you aren't here and much is lost in my attempt to write down my feelings. So let me just close with seven words I know you will understand: I love you with all my heart.

Missing you, Mark

I laid the letter down on the coffee table. This all seemed too good to be true. How could I be so lucky! To meet someone who understood the balance between idealism and realism, between our love for each other and our love for those outside of us. All I could think about now was how much I wanted to intertwine my life with his. I loved him; he loved me. But the personal and spiritual dimensions added so much more to our love affair.

I had always thought marrying a Catholic was important to me, but Mark had so many qualities that mattered more. Somehow, the fact that we didn't share the same heritage of religious backgrounds gradually "shrank to insignificance," as he is so fond of saying. What stood out for me was the fact that he was aware he had a purpose in life. He seemed to understand unequivocally God's plan for him, and he was vigorously engaged in pursuing it. He was encompassing me in his quest and the fulfillment of his purpose as I was him. He was generous to a fault, and really cared about people. Mark and I were coming to share all of this as the central theme of our spiritual path.

Less than two months after that phone call where he first proclaimed his love, Mark and I would be married. He chose Christmas Day so that our families could be present.

Three days before our wedding, I was coerced into sitting through one more browbeating session with my colleagues on the commission. Another special meeting was called with the five of us, the county manager, and the two consultants, Jim Kent and Bob Schultz. The morning session was heavily controlled by the consultants, forcing us to stay focused on the planning items on our agenda. The atmosphere was strained, but everything moved forward and kept to the agenda.

We took a long lunch break during which I attended my favorite Christmas celebration, Nancy Flanigan's luncheon. It was an annual event that all of her women friends eagerly anticipated. This one was an especially happy time for me. The wine flowed and, with so much to celebrate, I thoroughly enjoyed what was poured for me. Eager to share my news about my forthcoming marriage, during the luncheon I read a poem Mark had written to me, describing the fullness of his life before me, and his ten-fold joy at having me come into his life.

When I think back upon my life
Recalling all I've done,
I must admit, though challenging,
It's all been mostly fun.

I've broken stallions three years old,
Raced bikes in motorcross,
Jumped off of bridges into lakes,
Won golden gloves and lost;

Skied knee-deep powder more than once,
Hopped freight trains just for fun;
I've run off mountains with a kite,
Hit more than one home run.

I've traveled throughout these great states,
And lived in other lands,
Defeated Harvard in debate,
Played lead guitar in bands.

I've written books and articles,
Appeared on TV shows,
Owned airplanes and fancy cars,
And worn expensive clothes.

In fact, there's nothing I've not done,
As I recall the past.
It's just that now at forty-one,
With all that I've amassed,

There's nothing that compares with you,
I've done it all, my love;
You light my world with ecstasy,
And fit me like a glove.

No longer must I walk alone,
Along this path of life,
For we were two and now just one,
As soon you'll be my wife.

Take all the joy we've felt alone,
Adventures though they were,
And multiply them all by ten,
That's how much happier...

We'll be for our next phase of life.
I thank God literally,
In making you my loving wife,
He set my spirit free.

Many of these women had lived with me through the pain of my last divorce. We had grown close since my arrival in Reno more than eleven years ago.

This gathering was a conspicuous contrast to the meeting I had to resume immediately after lunch. The consultants held off the redistricting issue until the afternoon, hoping that we would have become more amicable as the meeting progressed.

Legally, I knew I had the law on my side. But this was not a matter of jurisprudence. I had not played as a team member, and I was being punished for it. Once again, led by Dianne, the commissioners made it clear that they were not going to shift their position just because I was getting married and changing my residence, even if it was only a few blocks. The vote took place; and my new residence with Mark was not in my district. With two glasses of wine at lunch, my tongue was considerably looser than I would have wanted it to be in this hostile environment. Fully realizing the consequences of this vote and using every four letter word I knew, I let my anger out on all of them.

I was inexperienced enough to let this spew out in the meeting—with the recorder going. Time out was called, and the meeting broke up. Dianne had the savvy to reserve her remarks for out in the hallway. It was me against them and she was savoring the power she had over me. As I drove home from the meeting, I made up my mind definitively that I would not seek a second term. I knew the residency issue would become a problem. I just didn't know how big of one!

Putting this behind me, I packed up things I would need in my home office over the holidays. With a new marriage and honeymoon intervening, I would have nearly a month before I would have to face county politics again.

We spent the night before Christmas, the eve of our wedding day, with my family. After everyone left, Mark and I were sitting on the couch in front of the fireplace.

"Before we take this final step tomorrow, I just want to ask you something. Do you think you will ever have a problem with fidelity in our marriage?"

For one brief moment, I felt offended. Then I looked at his face and realized how major an issue this was to him. "No, not in the least. I am a one-man woman all the way. But, sweetheart, is there something I can do to reassure you?"

"Well, vulnerability is the key. Just don't ever put yourself in a position where something could happen—I mean, something spontaneous because of the seduction of the moment. You may not premeditate getting involved with someone. I think those things happen because two people allow themselves to be put in a compromising position."

"So how do you suggest avoiding those possibilities."

"Oh, it's easy. Never allow yourself those opportunities. Just don't be alone with a man. For example, even having lunch with a guy by yourself. I know you are used to meeting with men as part of your job. I don't mind if you're in a group, but I would appreciate it if you just wouldn't meet alone. I need to know that you are mine, only mine." He reached out and put his arms around me.

I didn't think about it very long. My response was spontaneous. "If that's what it takes to provide you reassurance, I'll promise you that. I want you to know that this marriage is a forever deal with me."

"My friend Terry says it is not just ''til death do us part' but, in her belief, for a couple truly in love, their matrimonial bond is sealed for all eternity."

Getting up to leave, Mark held me close, his eyes looking down into mine. "Thank you for understanding how important this is to me."

"I do understand, and I'll never even put myself in a vulnerable situation. When a man speaks to me, he will know beyond any doubt that I am yours."

"I love you. Will you marry me in the morning?" These are words that I would hear Mark repeat frequently throughout our life together. They would come to mean more and more to me over the years.

With both of us having been married before, we chose to keep this a simple ceremony. Gathered together in my home with my parents, our children, and my close friend, Moya Lear, widow of the acclaimed inventor of the Lear Jet, who served as my matron of honor, we had a simple exchange of vows on Christmas morning with another friend, Judge Deborah Agosti, performing the ceremony.

Mark was dressed in a black tuxedo, and I wore a veil with a simple off-white, knee-length dress and a three-quarter jacket. Mark shared his thoughts from written notes, which I have preserved in our memory box forever. For Mark, the master speaker, there was a rare nervousness in his voice. It wasn't rehearsed nor did he express himself with the ease with which I had come to see him deliver a speech. It was a singular moment in time, a complete unveiling of himself with nothing held back. Facing me, with his paper held in his left hand, he began:

> Rene, so today is our special time. And I thought you might like to know my heart, my true thoughts. Today we launch a life in front of three generations who have a strong, vested interest in our future. Parents who can but hope that my assertions will prove accurate; that unlike my predecessor, I will indeed love and treasure you without imposing Kahlil Gibran's often quoted 'spaces in our togetherness.'
>
> The parents who will smile sincerely yet somewhat nervously as we exchange vows and then return home praying that we meant them.
>
> The second generation, you and I, so blinded by the intensity of romantic excitement, yet fully aware of the truth that eternity is a long time. We, my love,

will be hungry to exchange rings all the while most conscious of our former failures in the marital arena and secretly praying that this is for keeps.

And generation three, two children who have been innocently dragged through the mire of instability for nearly two decades. These loving souls will also wish us the very best, all the while hoping and praying that fifteen years from today they will, with their own families, be seated by a tree opening presents from each other and smiling as we hold hands and lovingly kiss on our 15th anniversary.

Three generations of decent people all of whom have been somewhat scarred by our former marital antics, including ourselves, will once again gather together to witness the launch of a new adventure in oneness. Today we celebrate a most special occasion and will undoubtedly be the recipients of many kind remarks, hugs, and congratulatory kisses. Let us at this time, however, not forget that, underlying the pleasantries, will be an unspoken plea for finality. All three generations will be secretly harboring the deep-seated hope that we never again subject ourselves, or indeed subject them, to the pain born of commitment gone awry. There will be love today by your fireplace, but there will also be genuine concern from three generations of displacement, instability, and heartbreak. To deny that fact would be to ignore reality.

So on this special day permit me to make some honest observations which I believe with all my heart will make the difference we all need and want between former ceremonies and today's.

First, to treasure someone as I do you, is not merely to love them, but rather to consider them priceless, and of estimable value. On this, our wedding day, I must admit that I am prepared to give up all that I hold dear in this world for your presence in my life. You are the "pearl of great price" whom I have sought for 41 years—the very completion of my destiny and nothing short of death can drag me ever from your side. Of necessity, as our responsibilities dictate, I will be separated from you for a few hours at a time but we will never again sleep alone. I am in total control of my own destiny and as such refuse to ever reach across a bed and not find the warmth of your presence. No event of any magnitude will ever put 'spaces in our togetherness.'

Second, I tacitly refuse to ever take advantage of your vulnerability or abuse the trust we are now forging. Henceforth there will be no woman in my life but you and this depth of commitment will never be altered. I am giving you myself fully without reservation and that long term oneness will never be violated by any action on my part. I am yours totally and unreservedly 'until death do us part' and beyond, for all eternity, and you may rest securely in the knowledge that no one can ever drive a wedge between us.

Third, I grant you the absolute freedom to grow immeasurably and rise to your full potential, indeed I welcome and support you in that endeavor. You were not granted existence for the purpose of elevating my stature but rather we were both put here to nurture one another as we jointly rise to levels of personal and synergistic accomplishment. Whatever we achieve together from this day forward will never be at the expense of our partner, but rather as the direct result of each other's sincere desire to see another soul mate blossom and grow. As you are here to unselfishly serve me in my efforts, I too am here to unselfishly serve you in all your strivings. And that is a role with which I find myself most comfortable.

Finally, and perhaps most important, I willingly accept God's role in our marriage and bow to his guidance. I regard our march through life as highly serendipitous and fully realize that we began our relationship with prayer and must perpetuate it with the same. Ours is not some lip-service quest of spiritual unity, but rather an impressive display of what can occur once individuals actually place their Heavenly Father at the apex of their relationship. With God, all things are possible and thus on our wedding day, I promise to always seek first this love and guidance in our lives.

Rene, what we are about to consummate is vastly different from any other bond and yet not everyone present will realize it. Only by example can we truly prove to ourselves, our parents, and our children that this new union is indeed God's will. What I want you to know going in, is that so long as I am drawing breaths of life, you will remain my number one priority. The promises I've made you leading up to this wedding day are certainly romance-motivated but are nevertheless well thought-out and calculated. You bring to me through your every action a deepening belief in the orderliness of God's universe. I have an abiding and unwavering belief in the fact that we were drawn together by some unseen force of love and that together we shall remain throughout eternity.

From this day forward you will be the very force which motivates my every action. From this day forward I will place your wishes first above my own. From this day forward I cease to be me and become us.

You are my life, my love, my best friend, and my very essence. In a brief time, you will be my wife. Rest assured that this will be your finest hour as we exchange vows before three generations of God's wonderful family. I will be unreservedly giving you the only real gift any man can ever give a woman— my heart, my attention, my respect, my love, and my life...and I know you'll be doing the same.

So today is our special time and I just wanted you to know that everything else I've ever accomplished in my life shrinks to insignificance in comparison with the joy I'm now feeling, knowing that I'll be Rene Reid's husband. In my estimation, no greater honor has ever been bestowed upon another man, and I thank you for making me whole. I love you. I love you.

For a moment, I couldn't find words. I'd never felt anything penetrate me as deeply as his betrothal. It was spoken from the very depths of his being. He may have been married before, but I was certain no former wife had ever been given promises with so much wisdom, spirituality, and sincerity. Every word he spoke was from his heart.

Deborah then indicated it was my turn to address Mark.

I hesitated, waiting for the lump in my throat to clear. I blinked away the moisture in my eyes and looked up at Mark. I spoke from my heart with no notes:

> Mark, I promise to give everything I have to making this marriage last until the end of our lives together. I have loved before but I have never succeeded at creating a lasting relationship. I promise to put our love before everything else in my life, to look for little ways every day that I can bring you some added happiness.
>
> I promise to join with you in the pursuit of our life's purpose, to be ever aware that God has a plan for us, and that it will be better carried out together than by each of us alone. I promise to join you in your giving spirit: to use much of the wealth we accumulate to give back to those who need it more.
>
> To my parents, I promise to do everything in my power to spare you the anguish of another broken marriage. I love you and thank you for being there for me, especially the times when my life wasn't so easy.
>
> To Amy, I promise to be a friend and loving stepparent. I will never take the place of your own mom, but I will be there for you when you need me as a confidante and support.
>
> To Chris, I promise that you are not losing a mom, but gaining a man in your life who cares about you and will provide a role model. You are my only son, and I will always love you and be there for you unconditionally.
>
> This is my commitment to all of you.

I made my last statement as I turned and looked out at my family. Then turning back to my betrothed, I spoke looking directly into his eyes:

To you, Mark, there are conditions. My love for you as my spouse bears some accountability in return. I ask that, after God, you put your love for me before everything else in life. If there are choices to be made, that you will choose me. In return, I promise the same to you. When those times come that challenge us, and they will come, it will be you and me standing strong together against the world. Whatever difficulties lie ahead for us, I will be there for you, and ask the same from you in return.

I promise to give myself only to you, Mark, to respect you, to stand by you, and to recognize that nothing is more important than our love for each other and for God. Through him, we will reach out to so many others and love them as we share our life's work. This is my prayer for what our life will be together. With all of this as the foundation, my dearest Mark, I promise to love you all the days of my life.

Mark looked as if he had absorbed every syllable. I knew he could feel the warmth and sincerity of my words. We held our gaze while I continued to speak to him with my thoughts. *More than anything I've ever hoped for, I want this sacrament between us to bring us closer to God and guide us to fulfilling our life's purpose. I know we will have more to give together than individually—I just know it. We truly have been brought together for a reason. Through our love for each other, I want to be able to embrace everyone who comes into our lives and give them the best of Mark and Rene's love. I feel certain that is what is being asked of us through our oneness in marriage. I love you, Mark. I give myself to you as wholly as any woman can give of herself. Because of the life we share, I believe I will become a better person. It is my intention to support you in becoming your best self as well. I believe that we each have a mission to fulfill and we will both be strengthened by our union today.*

Mark was holding my hands and squeezed them gently. He had heard my thoughts. Deborah gave a beautiful soliloquy of her own, and then smiled at me as she pronounced us husband and wife.

"Rene, you may now kiss your groom."

Mark looked momentarily startled at her twist, and then kissed me and held his lips to mine for a long, lingering moment.

Celebrating Christmas with our newly joined family, we began our life together: the birth of Christ and the birth of our pre-ordained marriage. It was so symbolically reflective of how we felt. But it wasn't just that. In part, Mark selected this day because he is not good at remembering important dates. With our anniversary on Christmas Day, he knew he could not possibly forget.

Selecting a place in the world that neither of us had ever been before, we honeymooned in New Zealand, where it was summertime in January. We spent most of our time in the south island with our first stop in Christchurch. Having lost a day in travel as we crossed the international dateline, we arrived on December 31. Jet lag got the best of us, and we arrived at our hotel and fell fast asleep. Somewhere around 10:00 p.m. I awoke. Mark was still sleeping.

"Hey, wake up. It's New Year's Eve. We don't want to sleep through it," I whispered in his ear.

No response.

"Mark," I began to shake him lightly, "don't you want to get out and see the town?"

Still nothing.

With Mark several years younger, I chose my next words carefully. "Have I married an old man who is just going to sleep through the turn of a new year?"

In fifteen minutes Mark was up, dressed, and ready for a night on the town. Asking around, we learned that the main event was going on at the biggest hotel in the city. As we walked through the main entrance, we heard music, laughter, and chatter in a wonderful new accent. Farm people had come from miles around to enjoy the festivities on this special evening. Before long, with our American accent standing out from the rest, we were a novelty. The New Zealanders took us into their community and into their hearts. We danced in group for the faster songs and snuggled in each other's arms for the slower music. We enjoyed the taste of new foods, while Mark sipped on a coke and I on a glass of white wine.

"Ten, nine, eight," the crowd began in unison. "Seven, six, five, four...." Mark grabbed my hand tighter and pulled me close to him. "Three, two, one...Happy New Year!"

We held a prolonged New Year's kiss, and dancing to Auld Lang Syne, we promised each other that this year would be like none other. We would always remember to put our love for each other first. As we spun on the dance floor, I felt so young and carefree. We had no worries, and everything beautiful to anticipate. How fortunate that we are unable to see in those precious moments all that lies ahead for us in marriage.

Renting a car, Mark maneuvered quite well driving on the opposite side of the road. We drove to the far side of the island and spent a couple of days at a fishing resort. We saw monstrous fish in the water...but never on the end of anyone's fishing pole.

We searched for the best beaches. When we inquired at a gas station, one kind countryman not only gave us directions, he led us to an incredible beach, and invited us to join his wife and himself for dinner at their home. The next day, we found our way to an expansive deserted beach, where we made love in the heat of the afternoon sun. Only later would I learn that this was completely out of character for Mark. He's a very private person, especially when it comes to nudity. Though I didn't fully understand it at the moment, this was his way of throwing caution to the wind.

I discovered Mark's love of adrenaline sports...or anything that gives him a rush. Our natural adrenaline was racing so much through this period that, when we arrived in Queenstown, there was little we didn't try.

We signed up for a boat ride down the Shotover River. In a speedboat carefully designed with curvatures underneath the water, we raced at breakneck speed, barely missing rocks jutting out at us.

In the afternoons we made love in our room with the sun beating down on us through our window.

We helicopter-skied down the Hans Josef Glacier...a moving

glacier…in summer. That meant that the 100-foot-deep and four-foot-wide cracks and crevices that would normally be covered over with inches of snow were exposed. I slipped once, and my ski pole fell into one of those deep openings. It seemed like an eternity before we heard the pole hit bottom. At another point in the adventure, our two guides asked us to spread out about a 100-yards apart so as not to create an avalanche. It was decidedly one of the riskiest and most unintelligent moves of our newly formed life together. But we lived to tell the story and brought back pictures to hang on our adventure wall.

Nothing deterred us. Arriving back at our room after skiing, we fell onto the bed, making love hungrily again as if for the first time.

It was flying over Milford Sound in a little bi-plane that was one of the most memorable parts of our trip. There were just four of us, an elderly couple riding in front, and Mark and I in the back. The old man turned to me and inquired, "So…have you been bungee jumping yet?"

Incredulously, I looked at him wide-eyed and responded, "No, have you?"

"Sure," he retorted without hesitation. "It's free if you're over sixty-five!"

Mark and I had already talked about this extensively. He was dying to go bungee jumping in Queenstown over a tributary of the Shotover River. I didn't want to. I just couldn't get up my nerve. So I turned to the old man and began querying him on things racing through my mind. "So there's one thing I'd really like to know. Were you afraid?"

"Omigod, as I looked down 143 feet over that raging river with only a cord tide around my ankles, my heart was in my throat." He described it exactly like I would only imagine it.

About that time, his 75-year-old wife spoke up. She had been quiet through this whole interchange between us. "Oh, honey, it was a cake walk."

I'll confess. I went bungee jumping, more like bungee diving, because an older woman shamed me into it. "Five, four, three, two, one," I heard the countdown. With all the confidence I could muster, I made the best swan dive of my life. With 143 feet to get it right, how could I not be magnificent? What I wasn't prepared for was that I was attached to a rope that was elasticized. It was all so scientifically measured to my body weight that, when I finally reached bottom, my head came within inches of hitting the water. Then the pendulum force brought me all the way back up again—well over 100 feet above the river—so that I could feel the rush of the Gs all over again as I headed downward. The swing gradually kept lessening until I came to a full stop with my feet dangling in the air still tied to the rope and my head down just above the rushing river. A boat came to my rescue and pulled me in to take me to shore. All of this happened without a drop of water getting on me. Mark was waiting for me in the dinghy, and we were taken safely to shore.

Would I do it again? No! The entire experience was captured on video so that I could bring it home and have Chris and Amy think I was the most awesome mom in the world. I guess "awesome" can mean anything from "far out" to courageous to having lost my mind. I knew Amy would expect this kind of action from her dad, but I wanted her to know that I, too, could demonstrate this kind of courage. But, thank God, now that I had done it once, I would never have to do it again.

I had jumped off a bridge in more ways than one. My life was on a new course filled with dangerous chances and challenging opportunities and joys beyond measure. Bungee jumping would turn out to be the least of the risks that lay ahead.

CHAPTER 6

MARRIAGE AND MERGER
January – April 1992

The temptation to prolong the time in New Zealand was only overridden by the demands of responsibilities at home. Our stay in this far-away island, with clocks turned back to another day and time, was as perfect as life gets. Political pressures and business challenges were left behind; but once we were home again, they created a formidable environment in which to begin a new life together. We were convinced that nothing could deter our resolve to put our love for each other above all else.

Settling into our life together, I realized that Mark and I came from very different lifestyle environments. His was a more placid existence. His daughter, Amy, lived with her mom. After five years, his 30,000-person organization seemed to run itself and required only as much attention as we chose to give it. With little pressure on him, Mark's priority was clearly our marriage. Even business was only of interest to him if it was in light of the consolidation of our two organizations into one. His goal was to travel together, speak together, work together, and play together. It was, in the very best sense, both a marriage and a merger.

It was my life and commitments that brought challenges to our first year of marriage. Mine was a more hectic life: raising my teenage son, who lived with me; overseeing $120-million-dollar budget for the county; and supporting my 4,000-person downline in Nu Skin. My schedule was full. Besides the special engagements I was called upon to attend, I had regularly set meetings every week: Monday, caucus at the county; Tuesday, the formal meeting of the Board of County Commissioners; Wednesday, Health Board or Water Board; Thursday through Saturday, travel with Mark to conduct a meeting for one or more of our Nu Skin groups; Sunday, read a couple hundred pages of agenda backup to prepare for the coming week's meetings.

Despite the pressures, I was happy. I couldn't wait to get home to Mark. He, on the other hand, seemed restless during the first part of every week while I was so busy with my work. More than anything, he wanted the honeymoon to last. But every week, I had new problems I was dragging home from the county.

Lying across the bed Sunday afternoon, anticipating another week ahead of us, he began to question me:

"So what are you facing with your beloved commissioners this week?" he asked sarcastically.

"I don't know. You'd think now that I've announced I'm not running again, they'd all be happy and get off my back. But they're not content with my leaving. They seem to want me to go down in humiliation."

"Even Larry Beck?" Mark asked. He had already admitted a slight jealousy of our friendship.

"No, Larry is different. I think he is being used. They've put him out in front on the Honey Lake Project, probably promising him the moon. He is their puppet, and others are pulling the strings. At a heart level, he is a good person. Right now he is just caught up in the politics.

"Does he understand what's going on?"

"Oh, yeah. He knows exactly what's going on. He's really knowledgeable about the issues before the commission. He has helped me gain a lot of insight."

"So why do you think they want to bring you down? What's the point?"

"I'm not sure I understand. Partly, it's pride—certainly the Ethics Commission decision. I haven't gone along with the program. It's Honey Lake...and Washoe Med.... and power. After three years of buildup, I think they just want to find some way to get back at me. Ever since they refused to allow our residence within my district— which, of course, was a legal violation—I am waiting for the moment when they will use this against me somehow."

"How? What can they do?"

"I'm not sure. My office and my belongings are still there, but technically, because of them I don't live in my district when I'm with you. And even if it is a matter of a few blocks, you watch. Sooner or later, this will become an issue. I just know it."

"Why don't you just walk away from it all? You don't need that pressure."

"I just can't quit. I was elected to serve in this role. I committed to four years. I'm not going to pull out just because it's getting a little rough.

"They treat you like crap. I can give you so much more. Let me take you away from all of this. We can travel, and work with our people, and gradually expand into new countries as we open there."

"Sweetheart, it is only for one more year. Then we'll be free to do all of that and more. But I have to see this through."

This would end the conversation for the time, but it would recur. He wanted to see me carefree and happy. We had the freedom to do anything we wanted. Why would I endure the idiocy of one more year serving on a board with people who openly disdained me? Especially when I could be with him and our Nu Skin family, who welcomed and loved us. It made no sense to him.

Learning to share responsibilities was a new experience for us. We were each accustomed to running our own lives; and now that we lived and worked together, we needed to create some semblance of a cooperative arrangement. For the first few months we struggled with this until we came up with a solution that was acceptable to both of us. Going down the list of responsibilities, we assigned each task to the one who was better at it. We also agreed that, while the other person could make suggestions, the one in charge of that task had the final say. It took a while to make this work, but overall, we were both satisfied with the results.

Our first business challenge came so unobtrusively that it caught us both by surprise. In February, Mark's Colorado contingency called to invite us to come out the following month to do Nu Skin opportunity meetings in Denver and Colorado Springs. This meant that the distributors who lived in the area would invite their family, friends, and prospective business partners to attend our meetings. The top distributor would make arrangements at a hotel and, via voice mail and networking, spread the word about our speaking schedule. This was the first time that I would be traveling and speaking with my husband. We were both looking forward to it. County business came between us, but Nu Skin business brought us together.

Before marrying Mark, whenever I traveled I had always notified the distributors throughout my organization of my touring schedule in the event that they had contacts nearby whom they might want to send to the meetings. They would often run ads in those cities to draw additional prospects.

As always, some of my people began to organize for the Colorado tour. But when ads began showing up in the local papers, Mark's distributors called, quite concerned. They knew from experience that Mark never competed with them but always came to support them. So what's with the ads, they wanted to know. It was our first conflict over *his* organization versus *mine*.

"Rene, this is critical. You've got to get your people to back off."

"Sweetheart, I need your help on this. I've assured them that my marriage to you meant they weren't losing *me* but were gaining *you*. Now, suddenly, for the first time, because there is an 'us' they're feeling restricted in how they can go about getting people to our meetings in order to build their own organizations."

"Can't you see how awkward this is for me? My people need

me to do this meeting for them. You're my wife. You need to be there helping me support them. This meeting isn't for your people. It's for mine...ours now."

I understood the problem. I just didn't know what to do about it. "If my people can't generate prospects for my meetings, what should I tell them?"

"Tell them next time we'll do a meeting for them."

I felt torn, much like a mother in a second marriage is asked to choose between her husband and her children. The ads gradually tapered off, but I chided myself for not acting more decisively to respect the dilemma Mark faced with his people. *Why did I let myself get caught in the middle? I could have handled the situation more responsibly. Mark was right. He made a simple request, and I let him down.* I learned from the experience. From then on, when Mark's people called the meeting, I would show my respect by encouraging my people to invite their family and friends to the meeting by word of mouth and not by advertising. With this change, the blending of our two groups went relatively smoothly.

Our first joint speaking tour went well. Mark was an outstanding public speaker. As a child I had had a speech impediment and couldn't pronounce my Rs. With the name Rene Reid, that was a problem. I went through most of grade school introducing myself as "Weenie Weed." I'd come a ways since then, but I was still just a good classroom teacher. Mark assessed my talk and gave me some excellent coaching afterwards to help me transition from classroom teaching to stage presentation.

On the flight home, Mark seemed unusually quiet.

"Sweetheart, is something wrong? You don't seem like yourself," I said with concern.

"I guess I'm just not looking forward to going home. I like it better when we're on the road."

"I know. We're away from the stress of my political life. It's really getting to you, isn't it?"

"Damned right. You think I like seeing my wife get death threats in the mail? Or having the sheriff show us how to tape the hood of our car to be sure no one has been fooling with anything under the hood? I just don't know why you want to put up with all of that. And no one appreciates what you're going through. Who are you doing it for? I mean, what are you trying to prove?"

"I don't know if I'm trying to prove anything. But I'm sure not going to back off because someone doesn't like my stand on Honey Lake or Washoe Med. If I quit, I'd just be giving into them. Whoever it is doing these obnoxious things, that's exactly what they want me to do."

"It's more than obnoxious. It's frightening. I'm really worried. You're precious to me. I've spent my life looking for you. I don't want to lose you."

A lump suddenly bulged in my throat and got in the way of my words. I couldn't speak for a minute. I was touched by his concern. It had been a long time since I had a man care about my well-being like this. I loved it. I loved him for loving me this way. "I don't think this is a real death threat. This is a scare tactic. They want me to quit. That's all."

"But why? Do you really think this whole thing is tied to this crazy water deal?"

"It has to be more than that. They've got the votes tied up. Four out of five members of the board plus the county manager are solidly behind it. Why would they care about my one little vote? Other than my meeting with Uncle Harry, I'm virtually powerless to stop the project."

"Who?"

"Senator Harry Reid," I smiled. "I met with him and one of his staff to get his perspective. Of course, with all the years he has put into the Truckee River Negotiated Settlement, he is obviously not an advocate of the Honey Lake solution. By the end of our meeting, I sensed he had a plan in mind that would thwart Honey Lake, but he didn't lay it out for me." It would be another year after I left office before the Senator fromNevada was able to get Bruce Babbitt, the Secretary of the Interior, to prevent the Honey Lake Project from going forward. The Bureau of Land

Management ultimately denied the needed permits to pipe water across the agency's land, which lies between Honey Lake Valley and the Truckee Meadows. That political maneuver would put an end once and for all to the Honey Lake Project.

"Don't you think their upset has a lot more to do with Washoe Med?"

"I suppose. But ever since the Ethics Commission finally ruled that Dianne and Gene couldn't vote on issues related to the hospital, that matter has quieted down. I'm just sorry it took three out of my four years on this board to get that resolved. Now commissioners who have jobs or serve on boards related to issues that come before our board won't be able to vote. I don't know why that took an act of Congress to figure out. It definitely deepened the rift between us, but it's a done deal. Getting rid of me isn't going to change anything."

"But that's the point. Now that they can't vote, you have more power over this matter. You can control the money that goes to the hospital. Maybe somebody doesn't like that."

"Hmm. The Washoe Med situation does continue to haunt me. The way it was transferred from a county hospital to a 'community-owned private one,' the way it was given away for almost nothing, the promises that were made to the Legislature and not kept about keeping healthcare costs down—it just all seems so fraudulent. They stole something of tremendous value from the people in this community. It has bothered me throughout my whole term. But what can I do about it?"

"There's plenty you can do. You can take the matter before the Grand Jury. You can call a press conference. You're a public official, and when you speak out, it carries some weight." Mark seemed to get excited for a moment about my job and helping me do what is right about this situation. Then, as if it suddenly dawned on him what he was saying, he backed off. "But frankly, I'd like to see you drop the whole thing...for your sake and ours. I love you and don't want anything to happen to you."

For the rest of the flight, I sat staring out the window, thinking about our conversation and what I faced when I returned home.

Mark is a take-charge person. That's part of his attraction. Seeing me so restricted in what I can accomplish frustrates him. He would fight to the death for anything that was worthwhile. Whatever he does, he does passionately and with all of his energy behind it. I did too, normally. But after three years on this board, and especially since Jim Lillard's death, I have felt beaten down. Mark is right. Few people know what is really going on. Because of Honey Lake, I've even lost my bond with Larry Beck. I have no one to talk to. I am completely cut off when I'm at the meetings now. It's a living hell for me to go to the county anymore. Maybe Mark is right. Maybe I've done all that I can do and should quit. But something in me just won't let me do it.

I pulled out this week's thicker-than-usual agenda from my briefcase. With a yellow highlighter in my hand, I began to go through it, giving my full concentration to the somewhat dry reading.

About 5:30, I walked through the door from our Monday caucus and plopped down on the couch. Mark sat beside me, and I put my head on his shoulder.

"God, it is good to have you to come home to. I love you so much," I said lifting my head up just enough to kiss his neck.

"Are you hungry?"

"Mmhmm. But do you mind going out? It just takes too much energy to fix anything tonight."

"It's all ready. I fixed one of my Missouri favorites—chicken and my special dumplings. I think you'll love them."

Mark always cooked up the most wonderful meals, and this one was no exception. His mother was often sick when he was growing up, and he learned to fix dinner for the family. Melissa, his sister, was too young so the responsibility fell to him. He didn't talk readily about his family life, but he seemed to recall time spent in the kitchen with much happiness.

Over dinner he caught me up on the Nu Skin situation. Things were settling down. More and more positive news articles were coming out in our favor, indicating that the investigations were winding down, and nothing substantive had been found wrong with our company.

"It's a shame that we have lost so many good people. It wrenches my gut every time I'm on the phone with someone who is telling me how they lost their home, their life savings, or had to take their kids out of private school. That damned Kelley. He ought to be hung at high noon for what he's caused."

"It sounds like you spent your day counseling."

"That's how I spend most of my time these days. There are just so many innocent people who got blindsided by this media campaign. I stay optimistic with them; but deep down, I wonder if Nu Skin will ever recover from this."

As I kissed Mark goodbye the next morning, I could tell he was still carrying the burden of so many of our people being wiped out by all that happened to our company. I was off to the county for my Tuesday hearings, preoccupied with trying to work things out between neighbors and developers or making last-minute calls to devise a solution to disputes between homeowners and trail users along the Steamboat Ditch.

When I arrived home mid-afternoon, Mark wasn't there. Probably out running errands. As I sat down at my desk, I found a letter propped up so I wouldn't miss it. I sat back in my chair, put my feet up on the desk, and began to read:

Dear Rene,

First and foremost, you're a great wife and I love you very much. That, I hope, will never change.

Now to the point. I don't like what I'm becoming....
When we got into this thing, I took your insecurities and needs at face value. Everything shrank to insignificance in your life in comparison to our love and you made it abundantly clear that you didn't want a man who created "space." So I've continued in my endeavor to create and sustain a relationship as the number one priority in my life while you've gone back to business as usual...which has now resulted in death threats, more work for you, insane telephone records, and life-preserving checkpoints for me.

When you have been with me, it has been an

incessant discussion of "all the work you have to do," and "how much you're falling behind." In Atlanta I never heard those things, nor did I in Florida or New Zealand. Therein lies the problem. Together, we created a dream world of oneness, one which I truly believed would outlast the honeymoon.... In my idealism, I thought that because we have the money and freedom to make any choices, you would continue to choose me over "business as usual." You did in the early days and I just naturally assumed it would continue. So I created this fairytale relationship in my mind and then cringed every time you stepped out of it....

My intent is not to punish you because of your choices. I love you. No, my intent is to plug the holes left in my life when you went back to your business as usual. If I don't plug those holes then I'm going to continue to live in a perfect world designed for two but predominately occupied by one. That's when I get upset and frustrated. So, I'm off to your reality. I'm heading back into the practical world of appointments and meetings and all that important stuff. When we are together, I'm sure we can always create a little segment of idealism because we truly love each other deeply. I'm not bitter and I'm not upset. I don't think you are a bad person nor do I consider you any less than my soul mate. I intend to make this marriage work no matter what.

Who knows, maybe someday we'll slip back into the fairytale and never emerge. But even if we don't, we did glimpse it and that's something most other couples never achieve. And we even have photo albums and a charcoal portrait to remind us of that alternate life should we ever stray too far from our original course....

I want the ultimate life shared with you, and if you ever really want to get back into it, I have the time and the money...and more important, I have the desire. I do love you and always will... and I still want you to marry me in the morning. And if love is a crime, I'm guilty. Mark

Marriage and Merger

I pondered each word as I reread the letter. Its tone sent a warning: *Will I ever be able to measure up to his ideal of a loving wife as totally available to him. But Mark was right. He was giving his all to our marriage, and I was giving everything I had left after my work at the county. I had my own downline to support, and now, as his wife, I had his to support as well. I had a son who needed me, and now, a daughter who visited us at holidays. My plate was full. Dear God, show me what to do. How do I balance all of this?*

I knew I wasn't going to run again. It wasn't how unpleasant it was to serve with this particular board that stopped me. They would be moving on soon, and I would have new people with whom I could work. Or I could run for a different office. It was my marriage and Mark that made me want to leave office. I wanted a life with him. I wanted the fairytale. And I felt so much more on track with my life purpose working with him, speaking and training around the world, than I did holding office in one small county.

There were loose ends I wanted to tie up if this was to be my last year in office. Mark and I were strong. We would work through this. That was all there was to it. I couldn't quit, and I didn't want to lose what we had with each other. I would find a way to balance my two worlds for the few remaining months left in my term.

Having a family and a life outside of politics was my preservation. Amy was graduating from high school, and Mark, Chris, and I flew to Tulsa to celebrate with her. It was my first time to meet Mark's Mom, Patsi Yarnell, who radiated a zeal for life.

The event was a special celebration in so many ways, but especially because Amy was class president and her father was asked to be the keynote speaker for the ceremony. Mark was upbeat and made everyone believe in whatever it was he was promoting. By the time he finished, the audience would have laughed with him and cried with him, and often given him a standing ovation.

For this graduation keynote, Mark gave one of his all-time favorite talks about pursuing the career that you love, not what you are being programmed to do by your parents and teachers. He told the story of two of his high school friends, one, who loved to fish and eventually built a multi-million dollar business selling boats and fishing equipment, who today has a wonderful family and a great deal of wealth, and seems genuinely happy; and the other, who felt compelled to follow the plan laid out for him by his family and all those watching out for his well-being. He committed suicide last year. As his words cast silence over the audience, Mark ended the talk as he closed all of his Nu Skin presentations: "And, folks, I want you to know that there are just two kinds of people in this world: people who think they can and people who think they can't. And they're both right. I just hope and pray to God that you think you can."

The talk was well received by the kids. A few parents stormed out, truly shaken by Mark's comments. As I sat next to Patsi and observed her response to Mark's talk, it was easy to see where Mark gained his positive attitude. The only thing I concluded with certainty was that she was proud of her son, and it wouldn't have mattered what he had said. And for that matter, I felt the same way.

Following her father's talk, Amy read the benediction, and the ceremony was complete. When we got back to the hotel, mom called to tell me about the front-page article in the *Gazette-Journal*. The headline read: "Bitter feud hampers Washoe Commission." The article, which continued to the inside and included a full page of related articles about the infighting, was written by Jim Mitchell, the same reporter who had interviewed me at the beginning of my term. He had been fair with me then, and I had come to trust him. I had agreed to be interviewed for this piece but felt an intuitive anxiety about the article coming out. With so much bitterness and ego at stake, it couldn't be an item that would reflect well on the county—or its commissioners.

Once I was back home again, I found a hideaway spot upstairs in the loft with a cup of hot tea and slowly began to read:

It was supposed to be a routine meeting of Washoe County Commissioners and key staffers for a study session last December.

Marriage and Merger

But it would turn out to be anything but routine.

County Commissioner Rene Reid was still angry about being snubbed the week before when she asked her fellow commissioners to shift the boundary of her district a short distance to include the home of her fiancé, Mark Yarnell. *[I wished he'd stressed that the law said the adjusted boundaries must include the residence of the commissioner in that district.]* They planned to be married on Christmas Day, and the change would allow them to reside in his home. *[O god, here it comes. My outburst just after leaving Nancy's Christmas luncheon. If only I hadn't had wine…]*

"Sh—, I can't stand it!" she shouted. "You know, the rest of the world is celebrating something very exciting for me, and supporting me, and the only persons I'm having trouble communicating with and talking about this is the g—damn four of you. The one place where I ought to have the most support I can't even f—ing talk about it!"

It was one of the first significant signs of a growing rift in commission chambers—a feud that last Tuesday resulted in her four commission colleagues issuing an unprecedented open letter condemning Reid.

On the surface, the scathing rebuke came after Reid accused County Manager John MacIntyre of pressuring staffers to produce a financial report that supported continued use of a controversial employee health insurance program with Washoe Medical Center. *[There was that Washoe Med favoritism coming through again.]*

A landslide election

Reid, a former nun, succeeded in her first try for political office when she buried longtime Commissioner Belie Williams in a landslide. *[Oh great! It can't just be "outraged commissioner" loses her temper and swears at her colleagues over disagreements. They have to say "former nun" uses the F word. I am mortified. I just had to wonder what Jim Mitchell hoped to accomplish.]*

She saw her 70-percent vote from residents of west Reno as a mandate for change from the "clubby" county government atmosphere.

At the same time, she admitted that her background as a nun, businesswoman and radio talk show host did little to prepare her for rigors of political life….

Reid said she first clashed with commissioners when she discovered that three members of the board with ties to Washoe Medical Center were voting on health-related contracts affecting the hospital….

"I was aghast," Reid said, "and we fought over that."

Reid said she also challenged decisions on some of the commissioners' pet projects, including water importation, and questioned strategic plans that would position county government's emerging role as the area's principal provider of municipal services….

In an effort to defuse the growing turmoil, MacIntyre ordered Bob Schultz, a management consultant brought in to assist in strategic planning, to conduct a series of workshops with commission members. What emerged last October was a list of "ground rules for policy makers." The rules included elementary suggestions, such as that all five board members should be informed of major issues, and when "personalization" of an issue occurs, someone should declare "time out."

"It didn't work," said Commission Chairman Gene McDowell. "Two or three days later, she was off doing things by herself again." *[Translation: that meant I wasn't voting with the rest of them on certain key issues.]*

By December, no one was declaring "time out," and commission meetings were turning into contests of will, punctuated by sniping and invective.

By then, the State Ethics Commission had ruled that McDowell and Cornwall could not vote on matters affecting Washoe Medical Center, and Reid appeared victorious in her two-year battle over the issue.

I scanned farther down the page:

Hate mail and phone calls

Shortly after the ruling came out, Reid said, she began getting harassing phone calls, including death threats. A pieced-together note arrived in the mail, reading, "brutal death to sluts."

Reid said she reported the threats to the county sheriff's office, and a call-tracing device was placed on her phone. But detectives were never able to determine the source of the calls.

By late December, after more altercations with commissioners, including a name-calling and shoving match with Cornwall, Reid announced she would not seek reelection.

"It was just too much for me," she said. "I had to think about my family."

But the threats, she said, continued, and political enemies began leaking damaging documents to the media.

One packet, received by the Gazette-Journal, included a Sept. 23, 1988, letter from real estate developer Robert L. Weise indicating that he was forwarding her more than $3,000 in campaign contributions.

All of the checks, collected from nine different sources, were written for $500 or less, and did not have to be reported by name as campaign contributions under Nevada's campaign contribution laws. *[Of course! They were developers who feared retaliation from my opponent.]*

Will any work get done?

Of her four colleagues, only Beck held out any hope that Reid could continue to function effectively. *[I knew Larry had to be hurting over this.]*

"I'm hoping she will understand what everybody is trying to say," he said. "I hope she's willing to be a part of the team, so we can get a lot of things done." Reid said her decision to go public with her grievances was prompted by a desire to promote discussion of the issues.

"If this leads to the commission sitting down and talking...then all of this will have been worthwhile."

The following week, the journalist, Jim Mitchell, quit the paper and went to work for Franklyn Jeans on the Honey Lake Project. *So much for objective reporting.*

My reaction was to bury my head in the sand. I was humiliated beyond words, but friends rallied their support.

"I always said your sweetness would be your undoing. Thank God Betty Bitch is finally emerging. I knew you had it in you," chided Linda Cook. "I tried to draw it out of you, but it finally took Dianne to do it."

"I'm so proud of you for fighting back," added Kathryn Wishart over the phone. "Sue Smith, Karen Bryan, we're all rooting for you. (These were all members of the City Council.) Even Pete (Mayor Pete Sferrazza) said he didn't know you had it in you." Reno Councilman Judd Allen had originally tried to get me to run for a seat on the council. Maybe I made the wrong choice. I had such a good rapport with all of them.

"Now we know how you come back from love forty so often in our games," remarked Eleanor Waldren, as we walked out onto the court together. "Yeah, you play tennis like you play politics," added Lynn Carasali.

"Where did you get that mouth?" teased Gail Brunetti. "And all these years you've tried to make us all think you were just a sweet little ex-nun."

Feeling empathy, Kathy List called to be sure I was okay. She had been through similar embarrassments as the former first lady of Nevada when she was married to Governor Bob List.

That week, I appeared before the Board of Catholic Community Services requesting their participation in the move to centralize homeless services away from downtown where our tourism prevailed. Our proposal, known to everyone as Project ReStart, was to move all homeless-related programs to a site a couple of miles east of town where the clients would be better served and at a greatly reduced cost to the taxpayers.

"You're my kind of woman," Al Pulitz spouted out in his less than usual gravelly voice. Al was the owner of Pulitz Moving and

Storage, an active Catholic, and a CCS board member. "I never paid much attention to this Project ReStart deal of yours, but any woman who can stand up to the likes of them the way you did has my support."

I told Nancy Paolini, who had become ReStart's director, how the meeting went. "Nance, I never expected to get their backing. It was so encouraging."

"When you stand up for what is right, the rest begins to fall into place. I mean, which is more important? A little public humiliation or getting our project supported and underway?"

"Well, I guess that does help put things in perspective. I still feel terrible about the whole situation...and even worse now that it is publicized. It just looks like a catfight between two women. I'm not sure that the issues are being heard at all."

"Just hold your ground, lady. You're doing just fine. They may have beaten up on you a little, but they haven't gotten rid of you," she said to encourage me.

"...Yet! I don't know how much longer I can hold out. Mark wants me to quit."

"Sure. He loves you. No one wants to see you put through this kind of anguish. But it was a choice you made. I know you. You're not going to quit. Besides, we still have work to do to get Project ReStart centralized and the agencies pulling together. Until that's done, you can't leave office. We need you there."

She was right. I still had a purpose to fulfill, and only a few months left to accomplish it. I knew I would stay to see it through.

CHAPTER 7

BALANCING TWO CAREERS AND MARRIAGE
May – December 1992

Over the next month, anticipating that time when I would be leaving office, we began looking for our home. We both envisioned land and room to walk, with trees and wild animals meandering on our property. There aren't many places that fit that description in the high desert area surrounding Reno, Nevada.

"Let's take a serendipitous drive and see where it leads us," Mark suggested.

"That sounds fun. So what direction should we head in?"

"You know this area better than I do, Commish," Mark teased.

"I know. Let's go out toward Washoe Valley where my friends, Ursula and Richard Tracy, live."

As we exited onto Old Highway 395 and passed Bowers Mansion, I suggested we turn onto Franktown Road. That is where we would find houses set in the trees. As we came up to Old Ranch Road, I recognized this as the street that led to the Tracy's house. "Turn here, and I can show you the area where Richard and Ursula live."

As the county road ran out and we were about to start up the hill into a private homeowners community, Mark said excitedly, "Look, over there!"

There it was. Our home. We both knew it instantly. With a "for sale" sign out in front, it sat there calling out to us. A wood-and-glass contemporary design nestled in the trees, it was a hideaway with decks off of every room for outdoor living.

"Dickson Realty has the listing. Kathy List is with them. Let's go find a phone and call her."

We settled on this five-acre retreat surrounded by national forest the same way we were making most of our decisions together—easily, quickly, and in complete accord. We loved this home.

The downside was that this house was far outside of my district. Even though I was not going to seek reelection and had only six months left in my term, I knew that this would become an issue with Dianne. I was just giving her ammunition to attack me.

I called the Attorney General's office asking for an official opinion, and Attorney General Frankie Sue Del Papa called me back personally. I explained my situation and asked how I meet my legal obligations for living within my district and have this as a second home. She had one of her deputies respond to me formally about dual residency. Upon advice from the AG's office, I rented out my home and set up residency at my mom's house. Hers was within my district, and I could easily stay there more than half the week to meet my obligations for living within my district for the short time I had left in office. Fortunately, our travel time away from home counted as days spent in residence. Knowing that this was only for a few months, Mark and I felt we could tolerate the separation.

It was the start of a new week and time to face the commission. While I was accustomed to taking care of myself, still I loved the way Mark worried about my safety during my late night meetings. He seemed afraid some discontented constituent would attack me in the parking lot. While I didn't share that concern, I appreciated his protectiveness. After all the years of living alone, it was a new and welcomed experience.

Balancing Two Careers and Marriage

Our commission meeting this week was scheduled in the evening to accommodate those who work and might want to attend. I wasn't looking forward to the evening. No matter how I voted, I would displease someone important to me.

For years the Washoe Valley area plan had minimum five-acre parcels. Bob Weise, who had been very supportive during my campaign, was requesting that the commission depart from this plan and allow smaller acreage with open spaces surrounding the Lightning W, his proposed golf course and clubhouse.

Perry DiLoretto, the man who had organized the Air Force tour and a well-known developer who lived in the area, was experienced with housing developments surrounding golf courses. In discussing the feasibility of Lightning W, Perry told me privately that he had written a letter to Bob strongly discouraging him from going forward with the project. The weather wasn't conducive, Perry wrote; but more importantly, there weren't enough residents to support the golf course financially. Sooner or later, it would go under.

Emotions were at an all-time high as each person came to the podium to speak. The public comments went on for hours as homeowners poured their hearts out. I gave each of them my full attention. I wanted to weigh all possibilities before casting my vote. I had no conflict of interest because the vote would not affect our new property either way, since it was and would remain a five-acre parcel.

As I looked out over the crowded room, I spotted Mark sitting in the audience. How comforting to know that he was there. He smiled when our eyes met.

At last, as this year's chairman, Gene called for the vote. Tina and Larry voted for the project. Dianne and I voted against the project. What a novelty to have us in agreement. It was the chairman's role to break the tie. I already knew his decision—or so I thought. But, contrary to how he told me he was going to vote the day before in caucus, Gene voted *for* the project! The vote carried in favor, three to two. Lightning W Golf Course was given life, and five-acre minimums were history. Tears of sadness and hugs of joy prevailed simultaneously across the room. As I walked out with Gene, I was more than curious. "So what happened? What changed your mind?"

"Perry DiLoretto's letter. Bob Weise waved it in front of me yesterday, and knowing that he had Perry's support—that did it for me," he replied.

"Did you read it? The letter from Perry. Did you read it?"

"No, what difference...."

"Gene, I read the letter and I spoke with Perry. It wasn't a letter of support. He was doing everything in his power to convince Bob *not* to go forward with the golf course. He said he has looked at dozens of these, and, in his opinion, there weren't enough residents to support it. Bottom line, he said don't do it. It won't work!"

Gene turned for half a minute and looked at me. Then he shrugged his shoulders and walked on. *How many political votes across our nation are decided on just such a set of circumstances?* I wondered. I could imagine innumerable decisions changing the fate of our country, of our cities and counties across America, based on appearances.

The Lightning W was built and opened. It is a beautiful course and clubhouse with walking paths and open space. It would be another seven years before it became public knowledge that the development was facing serious financial difficulties and struggling to stay open.

After a frenetic month with numerous phone calls from those on both sides of the issue, but mostly from those who wanted to see the area plan preserved, Mark and I moved into our new residence. We took the month of July to settle into it and make some desired renovations. But beginning in August, I split my time between my home in the district and my home with Mark. It was our first time to spend nights apart. As I made my way down Old 395 heading home on that first Friday evening, I was mentally fatigued from a busy week, and couldn't wait to get back to our little paradise.

Mark was waiting for me with his hands outstretched. I walked straight into his arms and stayed there for minutes before either of us let go. It was good to be home.

Getting ready for bed, I found, propped up on my pillow, a

poem—one he'd written based on that infamous night in the commission chambers. Just seeing it there made me teary. The contrast was unmistakable—how I was shunned by my colleagues at the county and revered at home. Throwing myself across the bed and turning up my bedside light, I absorbed every word of this new poem. Having sat through this hearing watching me in my official capacity, he reminded me how shallow our lives would be if all we had were politics and our network marketing business. So he concluded:

No arguments, no wasted nights
concerned with thoughts of stress,
Just warmth and passion in our home,
a place of tenderness.
I'm proud of my commissioner,
your strength is clear to see,
But it's your heart and gentle soul
that really captured me.

On the long weekends I spent with Mark, we took extended walks through the Forest Service and BLM land out behind our house. Our favorite hike was to a beautiful waterfall about a mile behind our property. It was a nature-lover's paradise.

During the summer we traveled less, spending more of our free time together at the house. Sitting down by the waterfall, we watched the last glow of a sunset slip behind the mountain range, casting a golden hue across the land.

Mark was gazing off into the sky, watching for any remaining paragliders who hadn't had the sense to come down yet. Most paragliders, I learned from Mark, preferred the early morning thermals, but a few daredevils loved the wind that came up late afternoons until dusk. Out of the blue, he turned to me and said almost inaudibly, "Do you remember that goober on the video?"

"What video?" I had no idea what he was talking about.

"The video that got you into Nu Skin years ago. You know,

the one with me and my three-day growth of beard and my jeans and suspenders."

"Yeah, and the hick accent from the Boston mountains of northern Arkansas," I mimicked. "Of course, I remember." For years I had teased him about it.

"Well, you know what's really funny?" He paused to be sure we had eye contact.

"What?"

"You married him!"

We laughed uncontrollably. Mark had an incredible sense of humor. I never knew what he was going to say next.

One of the many things that kept our focus on our priority was a book of poetry Mark compiled for me over our years together. We were sitting out on the southeasterly deck off our upstairs bedroom, overlooking the trees and watching a deer nibble the salt lick Mark had set out. The sky was just lighting up with the early morning sunrise, as I began to read the letter in the front of the book he had just handed me.

> My Dearest Rene,
>
> As a youth I was frequently ridiculed for my love of poetry until, at the tender age of nine, I took up boxing and thereafter silenced a number of my critics. I hated boxing but loved poetry more and even today find myself arising early several times a week in order to satisfy my desire to be creative.
>
> This little book is a compilation of only those poems that you have inspired. Never before has anyone come into my life and brought about such intense creativity nor have I ever even sought to publish any love poems. These poems are strictly for you and as such will always remain in your control to do with as you wish. If one day you feel they should be shared with others, so be it. The important thing is for you to know that I love you and in some small way I hope these poems provide you with a glimpse into both the scope and depth of my love for you.

What did I ever do to deserve this? I thought. *I never ever want to take the love we have for granted. Help me to love him with all that I have to give and nothing held back. I want to show more love for him by paying closer attention to little things throughout the day.*

Mark's fun-loving, but sensitive nature often demonstrated itself in some of his poetry. One of the first lyrics he had included in the book was one written on our last trip just as we were taking off on a Nu Skin tour. Recognizing that several months had passed and the poetry had diminished somewhat, but in spite of our having to spend some days apart, he was convinced our love would last. It then continued:

> *I still see you as no man has,*
> *The woman of my dreams,*
> *And though these poems have slowed down,*
> *Or so that's how it seems...*
>
> *The romance rhymes are always there,*
> *I've never loved you more;*
> *I love you more than any man*
> *Has ever loved before.*
>
> *I'll never take for granted*
> *That girl who took my name,*
> *The only one on planet earth*
> *Whom God made my twin flame.*
>
> *And as the days and weeks roll by*
> *While you remain my wife,*
> *Ohio or Atlanta-bound,*
> *You're my entire life.*
>
> *So as we lift off on this trip,*
> *I'd like to plant one seed:*
> *I thank God daily for the fact*
> *That I got Rene Reid.*

The poem made me laugh and cry. *Dear God, please let these feelings remain ten, twenty years from now. I want stability in a relationship more than anything else in life. I want to grow old with Mark, although I cannot even imagine either of us "elderly" in mind or body or spirit.*

How strange that I had drawn two poets into my life. My previous husband, Jim Kavanaugh, was a poet—"America's poet laureate," as Wayne Dyer stated in one of the cover quotes. Dear Abby proclaimed him "the poet of the American people." All I knew is that he was my poet. Many of his poems were inspired by our relationship. Some deeply romantic. Some dry wit. But, all too often, his verses emphasized the incompatibility of men and women and the sadness of relationships ending, especially ours. Ours would end...and begin again...and end...and begin again—with him drifting in and out of my life.

Though Mark Yarnell was not a published poet and his style was more dilettante than was Kavanaugh's, he expressed a theme that offered me reassurance. His writings were consistently about the joy of loving, about staying together forever, about the wholeness of a shared life.

Whenever time allowed and I needed a break from reading my commission agenda packet, I liked to slip out onto the lower deck off the dining room with my book from Mark. Reading it replenished my soul and served as a constant reminder of my good fortune in having such a loving partner with whom to share my life.

Mark loved being married. I did too. After so many years of being alone, I loved having him to come home to. I craved stability and longevity. In my political life, I felt pressure every moment of every day. Despite the outside support, I continued to feel alone at the county. More and more, I was carrying my problems home with me. It was getting harder to switch gears and be a gentle, loving wife at home.

The strain of it all was getting to Mark too. Feeling the stress, one afternoon when I was able to be working at home, Mark launched into a tirade about how much he objected to the secretary that he inherited by our marriage. Teresa, who had been my assistant, now worked for both of us.

"She can't spell. She can't keep books. I feel like we're keeping her on as a charity case."

My savior instincts sprang into action. "But I care about her. I just can't let her go."

"Dammit, Rene, you can't save the whole world. I like her too, but she is absolutely hopeless as a secretary. It would be an embarrassment to let any letter go out unless I have personally scrutinized it. You couldn't imagine some of the errors I've caught. Unbelievable! We don't seem to have any accounting of where our money is going. The whole thing stinks." When he felt strongly about something, his arms would meet in the middle and then be flung apart as wide as he could stretch them.

"Then *you* fire her. I can't!" I yelled at him. It was the first time that I had ever raised my voice to Mark. I didn't even know where it was coming from. I was brushing my hair while we were talking and, before I knew what I was doing, I threw the brush in his direction in a state of rage. I knew she wasn't the secretarial type; but she was my protégé, and I couldn't stand the thought of losing her. Almost immediately I could see that I was in the wrong. He had every right to want a professional office person to work with us. It was only later that I understood this fight was all about control. In the midst of living in the vortex of the tornado, I couldn't gain perspective on the day-to-day reality of our newly merged life. We were facing some pressing challenges regarding the power struggle that went hand in hand with sharing a business partnership and a personal relationship. For both to work, we were going to have to come to grips with some of these issues.

I drove out to see my friend, Moya Lear, whom I found to be full of good counsel on the subject of marriage. We sat and talked out on the patio just off her bedroom overlooking the Truckee River; we read poetry and old letters she had written to her husband, Bill. She had helped me through the rise and fall of my last marriage, and I knew she could help me now. When it came right down to it, she almost always offered the same advice, and in a moment of levity, would break into song: "You've got to give a little, take a little, let your poor heart break a little. That's the story of...that's the glory of...love."

With some wise guidance and a few days away just for us, Mark and I moved past this hurdle. A few months later, we hired a new administrative assistant, Cathy Hatch, who was extremely capable of handling many of our business affairs.

My husband was in love with being in love. The state of feeling so loving toward another person was itself a high for him. Sitting out on our deck, I began reflecting. *I know I can't sustain this early stage of love. What happens when the newness wears off? Can I continue to satisfy him? His temperament requires massive adrenaline flow. More than anything, let me never take our love for granted. He has been sent into my life for a reason.*

I didn't realize how long I had been sitting out there. The sun was going down. Ursula passed by walking her dogs and told me how good it was to have me as a neighbor. I went inside to join Mark for the evening.

After all the years of searching for my soul mate, the one person whom I could love and who would love me, I had found my own reflection in Mark. Despite our little challenges, I so appreciated the way he expressed himself throughout the day—a phone call, a note, a poem, a look, a hug, a touch. He worried about me like I have never been worried about, except by my mother.

Mark's greatest pleasure has always been flying. It doesn't matter what he's in as long as he is in the air. Even a hang-gliding crash in 1979 that fractured his pelvis and left him hospitalized for weeks did not squelch his passion. He simply took pain pills and, as they say, got back on that horse and rode her again.

His toy of the moment was an ultralite, a small one-passenger (Thank God!) motorized carrier with a wide wing-span and propelled from the top much like a helicopter. He kept it in a barn just down from our house, where there was a dirt runway out in the fields. Some of his happiest moments were taking off in this contraption and flying over the house, waving his wings at me while I stood on the balcony.

By now it was fall and the leaves were turning beautiful shades of reds and yellows. Saturday afternoon Chris was home, and we were looking up at the sky watching Mark fly over the trees. My heart stopped at the same time as his engine. He continued to glide, but something didn't seem right. I didn't know if he had turned off the engine or if it locked up on its own. I watched until I couldn't see him anymore.

Suddenly Ursula's car came speeding down the road in what seemed like hot pursuit. She and Richard are experienced aircraft people whom I felt would recognize a stalled engine from one manually shut down. By the time I got out of the house, into the car, and down to the field, there was Mark brushing himself off and walking away from a pile of metal left in the cow pasture. He had crashed and walked away from it.

"Why didn't you pull the emergency chute?" I shouted out.

"Because I thought I could pull out of the stall and make it back to the runway. If I could, I wouldn't have to jack with folding the chute back up." Somewhere in that explanation was some logic. There must have been. But it didn't matter. Even a crash didn't hinder him from finding yet another medium for getting up in the air.

Later that evening, while Mark was still out cleaning up the wreckage, I took a phone call for him from the Federal Aviation Agency. When I asked what this was concerning, I was told "a noise complaint that had been filed." Concerned, when he came home, I asked Mark to return the call first thing Monday morning. As Mark was dialing the last number, he suddenly put down the receiver and looked at me, smiling. "Since when did the FAA start sharing the same phone line with the Tracy's?" he asked. Ursula had pulled a fast one on me.

He would soon take up paragliding, convincing me that this was, by far, the safest of all airborne sports. "You just can't believe how safe this sport is. You'd have to be brain-dead to get hurt paragliding—I mean a total idiot. Anyone can paraglide. Maybe you'll want to take it up with me. There is absolutely nothing to worry about." I could always tell when he was forcing his own belief in what he was saying by the hand motions. There they were again: his hands crossing in front of him and then spreading as wide as he could reach, demonstrating dramatically the unfathomable ridiculousness of any accident conceivable in running off mountains into the sky with only the wind for support.

We appreciated our quiet moments because wherever we turned, Mark and I were embroiled in politics. While the pressures of the county were escalating, Nu Skin politics were heightening at an equally fast pace.

There was an understood code of honor among the distributors in our company that included open meetings, respect for relationships between distributors and their personal contacts, no "downline switching," that is, transferring distributors from one organization to another, and no preferential treatment. Network marketing was known for its level playing field. Regardless of one's background, financial standing, sex, religion, or education, there was equal opportunity for all. The field leaders supported not only the letter of the law but also the spirit of the Nu Skin policies and procedures. Because of this, Nu Skin continued to grow and to flourish, and emerged as the fastest growing network marketing company at this time. This spirit was a large part of what attracted many of us to the company.

What Mark and I were able to accomplish each as individuals, we augmented substantially by working together as a couple. As independent distributors for Nu Skin, our organization was expanding voluminously since our marriage and merger of our two organizations. Mark was the motivator and closer, while I loved the follow-up and training. We complemented each other's strengths.

The next major period of explosive growth for Nu Skin distributors was anticipated to be in Japan. All the requirements for success in network marketing are in place in the Asian world—they are hard workers, well-connected within their own community, and loyal to each other. For all these reasons, there was a great deal of excitement as we prepared for the opening of Japan. Making connections with serious players was energy well spent as we all geared up for the launch, still nearly a year away.

"I don't believe this. I fucking don't believe this," Mark was shouting as he walked into my downstairs office. He usually reserved the F word for occasions that warranted it. I knew something major had happened.

"It's Nathan Ricks again. This is unbelievable. He's over in Japan before anyone else can be, spreading a lot of hype with illicit flyers about his being the family line, the only line to join. When is the company going to stop this guy?"

Every company has its own form of politics. In Nu Skin, there were three founding family distributors—Clara McDermott, Craig Bryson, and Craig Tillotson. Clara is Craig Tillotson's mother. Craig Bryson and Craig Tillotson are brothers in law; their wives are sisters. Craig Tillotson's wife, Sandy, is one of the company founders and stockholders, and therefore, an owner. Nathan married Clara's daughter, thus making him a part of the family too. It is a close-knit situation. The family is purported to have loaned Blake Roney, the president and founder of Nu Skin, his first $5,000 to begin this company.

"I'd heard something. I just didn't want to believe it. What do you think we should do?"

"We're going to speak out until we're heard. I'll do whatever I have to do to get it fixed! After all we've withstood from the outside, it would be a crying shame to have us destruct from within." Mark was referring to the regulatory investigations and negative press that we overcame the previous year.

"You're right. We have to do something before this gets out of hand. Too many people will get hurt if it isn't handled fairly." I stopped and looked directly at him. Mark carried so much weight in the company that we both knew much of the responsibility rested on him. "Are you going to call the company?"

"You bet I am. And I'll go right up the line until I get someone to listen."

"Is Richard with you on this one?" I was referring to Richard Kall, immediate upline to us. Mark and Richard were close friends, and they spoke several times a week early in the mornings.

"Absolutely. I just got off the phone with him. He's hearing it too, and we're both mad as hell. We never used to have to put up with this sort of thing. If we have to, the two of us are ready to get on a plane and fly out to Provo."

Mark's passion for fighting causes worth fighting—my lovable
Man of La Mancha—carried over into my world of politics as
well. Holding down two careers was a constant balancing act for
me. As I knew it would, the residency issue heated up. Mark couldn't
stand to see me beaten up so badly. It was time to match power for
power. My husband went to my longtime friend and the former
governor, Bob List, and hired him to represent me on this matter.

When I chose to run for office, I had such high ideals. I never
thought I would end up in this situation. I made certain choices early
on. *How many of us fully comprehend the consequences of the choices we
make? I could have decided to keep the waters of my political life smooth.
It would have been so much easier. All I had to do was go along with the
programs set in motion. Then I would have gotten along with my board
members and, more than likely, my constituents wouldn't have known
the difference. But I would have known.* I did some soul-searching
examining my own motives now. Was my intention merely to win? If
so, the cause wasn't worth fighting. But if I am acting on principle
exposing some real issues having harmful impact on our community,
then perhaps I can still achieve the goals of my original idealism.

Thursday morning, September 10, as I came downstairs ready to
start my day, Mom was waiting for me with the morning paper. "You're
not going to like today's news." There was real concern in her voice.

On the front page, the headline read, "Nevada Politics. Spies?"
and led readers to the more detailed article on page 1B. Still standing
and flipping to the next section, I scanned the headline quickly: "County
conflict—Reid says officials spying on her home." Mom poured me a
cup of coffee while I sat at the breakfast bar and carefully read the
entire article by one of the local reporters, Faith Bremner.

County Commissioner Rene
Reid on Wednesday accused
Washoe County Manager John
MacIntyre of using sheriff's
deputies to spy on her to determine
whether she lives in her district.

Undersheriff Dan Coppa said he
was unaware of any spying.
Speaking through the county's
public information officer,
MacIntyre denied any knowledge of
investigating Reid's residency.

Reid said she rented out her home at 95 Rancho Manor Drive July 4 and moved into her parents' condominium within her district. Since then, however, patrol cars have constantly paraded past her new husband's new home in Washoe Valley, Reid said.

Commission concerns

During their caucus, commissioners asked for a legal opinion on whether Reid was violating state residency laws by splitting her time between the condo in her district and the Washoe Valley home.

"Our concern was whether a vacancy had been created and, if it had been, how it would affect votes taken by the board," Commissioner Dianne Cornwall said. *[How noble of you to have such concern!]*

An attorney general's opinion dated July 25 said Reid has met the legal requirements as a resident of her district.

Reid's views on the Honey Lake Valley water importation project and Washoe Medical Center have put her at odds with the rest of the commission.

This saga played itself out in the newspaper all week. With Mark's support, I was able to let myself feel angry—finally angry enough to fight back. I spent hours at Bob's law firm, counting on him to help me get the truth out. For the first time since Jim Lillard's death more than a year ago, I felt some inner political strength returning.

As I walked into the caucus room on Monday afternoon, September 14, the atmosphere was exceptionally strained. My colleagues seemed surprised to see me, somehow expecting me to fold under the pressure of such a public display with all of them against me.

There was only one person in the room who was my friend. She was Dorothy Nash Holmes, the DA who had her own attackers and personal struggles as the first woman district attorney in our county. She was most empathetic to my situation. As the legal advisor to the county, she was helpful in keeping me on track so I could perform the job I was elected to do.

"Have you seen this?" Dorothy discreetly handed me the *Daily Sparks Tribune* with the front-page headline: "Residency flap latest in commission war." While the commissioners and staff were seating themselves, and since no one was speaking to me, I quietly sat and read the article.

Our weekly caucus was tense but we got through it. Larry Beck glanced at me across the table a couple of times. I wasn't certain, but I sensed him reaching out to me. Gene never liked conflict, and he didn't appear to feel particularly good about the way this was all playing out before the public.

As I came downstairs the next morning dressed to go to the commission chambers for the regular Tuesday meeting, Mom was standing in the kitchen with a grin on her face and the morning newspaper in her hand. It was opened to the Nevada section. Stretching across the top in the biggest, boldest letters possible, the headline read: "Sheriff admits checking on Reid." *Yes! Hooray! Good ol' Vince. Somehow, if anyone was going to come forward, I should have known that it would be the sheriff.* Mom read me the parts that were pertinent while I sat on the bar stool munching on a bowl of cereal.

Washoe County Sheriff Vince Swinney admitted Monday that one of his detectives investigated Commissioner Rene Reid earlier this year to see if she lives in her district....

Copies of the detective's report were leaked to the news media and Reid late last week.... The detective concluded Reid lives full-time in Washoe Valley, which is not in her district.

"We verified an address at the request of a commissioner, end of story," Swinney said.

Reid said Swinney told her that Reid's political nemesis and fellow county commissioner, Dianne Cornwall, requested the surveillance. Reid said the investigation amounts to political dirty tricks and a waste of tax dollars.

"I don't think one commissioner should have that kind of power," Reid said. "This is a personal vendetta Dianne Cornwall has against me."

Cornwall and Reid have sparred for years *"blah, blah, blah," Mom inserted, skipping over the repetitive parts.*

Cornwall would not say whether she requested the investigation. She said the four commissioners collectively wanted verification of Reid's address because of concerns their votes could be nullified if Reid's residency was not valid....

Commissioner Tina Leighton remembers asking for the investigation. *[Of course.]* Commissioners Larry Beck and Gene McDowell do not. *[Hmmm.]* Beck said the first he heard about it was at an August 26 caucus meeting when Cornwall handed out copies of the detective's report.

District Attorney Dorothy Nash Holmes said the report is worthless.

"I don't think from an occasional review, a half an hour here and a half an hour there, you can tell what someone's residence is," Nash Holmes said.

"Nobody tells me they've taken pictures of the clothes in her closet."

I called Mark and read him the story. He was elated. I knew I wouldn't be winning this battle if it weren't for his support and strategy. As I drove to the county, my spirits were lifted. The truth eventually comes out. I felt vindicated. Gene was warmer to me now. I'd always felt comfortable with him and sensed we *could* have been on the same team if it weren't for one small hospital connected by a "bridge over troubled Honey Lake waters." Larry was downright nice. I think they both felt Dianne had gone too far. I'm sure they believed that I could have handled my differences with them better. And they're right. There were so many things I could have done better. But they could no longer stand behind Dianne in her approach to the situation.

That evening the *Sparks Tribune* covered the story as well. A supportive constituent called and read me the highlights of the article by Alisa Hicks over the phone:

A residency challenge is just the most recent battle in a four-year war between Washoe County Commissioners Rene Reid and Dianne Cornwall, according to Reid....

When an elected official is found to be residing outside of her district, the seat is declared vacant and all of the decisions made during the illegal holding of the seat can be nullified and repeated with a commissioner who resides in the district.

Reid said the sheriff's report is not a true indication of her residency. Of the four spot checks at her Washoe Valley home (outside her district), she was out of town for two. She said she was in Texas August 7 and 8 for a class reunion and will happily produce her airplane stub and names of some of her classmates who attended the reunion.

All four checks were made on the weekends. Reid readily admits to living in Washoe Valley on the weekends.

During the week Reid lives with her parents in a condominium within her district, she said.

Reid said the main conflict with Cornwall is her past insistence that Cornwall's connection to Wahsoe Medical Center has made all of her commission decisions regarding the hospital a conflict of interest.

She said that issue is what put her in the dual residency role in the first place since, after the Nevada Ethics commission confirmed the conflict of interest. Reid's district lines were not extended four tenths of a mile as required by law during the redistricting period to have her new home with her husband included in District 1,

Reid is not seeking re-election this year.

As I hung up the phone, Mark came bouncing into my office. "I'm really happy for the way this is turning out for you."

"Thanks." Hugging him, I added. "I wouldn't have been this assertive if you hadn't pushed me."

"Hey, speaking of being assertive, I've gotten Nu Skin to agree to a meeting of all the Blue Diamonds in Provo. I don't care what's going on in this damn county. I need you to be there with me."

"When's the meeting?"

"Next Friday."

"No problem. I can get away."

Mark spoke with Russ Karlen, who is parallel to Richard in the organizational structure. And with the other key leaders under Richard—Jerry Campisi and his partner, Gary Lemerise, and John Sexsmith and his wife, Giselle—everyone worked well together even though they were in different lines and did not stand to benefit financially from each other. They all agreed to be there and make sure their main field leaders were there as well.

Because of the respect for Mark held by so many field leaders, our phone rang constantly over the next few days. Almost every executive in the company felt contempt for Nathan and concern about stopping him from playing by a different set of rules. By policy, no one was allowed to actively pre-market, introduce products, collect money, or otherwise pre-sign people in a country that was not yet open for business to our distributors. Prior to the launch, we were limited to phone contacts and correspondence. What Nathan was doing was equivalent to insider trading, using his ties to the family to entice newcomers to his group.

The potential revenue for what could be earned (or lost) in Japan alone was staggering. Nu Skin was projected to double the first-year earnings of IBM. That meant the company could sell the equivalent in yen of $130 million in annualized sales in just the first year. With approximately half of that going back to the distributor force, we were talking about more than Monopoly money. When all goes well in network marketing, sales continue month after month and year after year for decades to come. The stakes were high. With Nathan's defiant attitude, even if he were fined for disregarding the policies, he would consider that nothing more than the cost of doing business.

One of the many tactics that frustrated everyone was the way Nathan and his partner, Scott Tillotson (brother to Craig Tillotson), separated their group from the rest by giving it a name, the NS Group. They would have us believe that the initials stood for Nathan and Scott. But the coincidence of it sounding like an acronym for Nu Skin was just too great.

I walked into Mark's office while he was on a conference call. He was expounding his views to some of the leaders in our downline: "It would be like three guys who worked for IBM—Iggy, Bob, and Melvin—all joining forces and deciding to call themselves the IBM Group. Nobody would put up that kind of crap!"

Mark pushed the speaker button so I could hear the conversation.

"Yeah," Mark Barrett added, "so when they go into Japan early flaunting the NS name, prospective distributors naively take it as being an official logo of the company."

"Corporate politics is corporate politics," Jay Primm was quick to point out. He had come out of the corporate world and understood it better than most of the leaders. "It exists everywhere, and we're no different."

"But we want to be different," Dennis Clifton responded. "The fairness is a big part of what drew my brother and me into this industry. We can't let that slip away because Nathan's off playing by his own rules. He's not Nu Skin. We are."

"I agree," Mark added. "One day those corporate guys are going to want to leave their world and come over into ours. If we don't stand up for this issue now, we will never be able to control it later. We have to do whatever we have to do to ensure that network marketing has the highest standards."

Thirty Blue Diamond Executives gathered for the meeting in Provo to recommend changes to the international policies, and *demanded* strict compliance and enforcement of the rules.

"All we want is to know what the rules are and that they apply to everyone. And that goes for you too, Nathan," said one of the leaders, who was totally exasperated with the discussion so far.

Nathan and Scott stood in the back of the room. Scott spoke first. "Lay out what you want to do, and we'll take a look at it and let you know if we can live with it." His arrogance angered every Blue Diamond present.

Verbal warfare broke out. Everyone was talking at one time. Steve Lund stood up and tried to regain order in the room. "We just want you all to get along. This is your chance to help us define the policies. We're here to listen."

"Steve, it won't do any good to set more policies unless you guys are willing to enforce them. And we're getting sick and tired of this wimpy excuse that you *are* enforcing them. But you're not telling us *who* you fined or *how much*! Who do you think you're kidding?" David Clifton spoke for everyone in the room.

"We have to be concerned about slander and libel and those kinds of things. That's why...." Steve's voice trailed off. He looked defeated as the din and chatter in the room overpowered his legal semantics.

"Yeah, let 's be sure we protect the guilty and the family. Never mind about the good guys who play by the rules."

Scott Schwerdt stood up at the front of the room to come to Steve's rescue. "We treat everyone the same. Nate is not given any special treatment. (The word 'Nate' grated on everyone.) If anything, he takes more riding than most anyone else."

"Yeah? Well how come his latest 'Jumpstart' training has the Nu Skin logo on it? The rest of us can't use it on our materials."

"Actually, you can. We changed that policy recently. You are all allowed to use it once your material has been approved by the review committee."

There was grumbling around the room, everyone asking each other if they knew that. Dennis Clifton spoke up: "Scott, how come there are more than thirty Blue Diamonds in this room and *Nate* is the only one who knew about that change in policy?"

"I thought I had put that out to everyone. I don't know why you all didn't get the word," Scott said sheepishly.

Heads were nodding and eyes were rolling. "It's just so typical. When your brother-in-law and mother-in-law sit in on board meetings, I guess you just hear things sooner," one Blue Diamond snarled.

The room was in a state of frenzy; except for Nathan and Scott, everyone was in favor of tightening the policies forbidding premature advancement into a country prior to launch. The majority won the battle, but Nathan won the war. The policies were rewritten as suggested by the team of leaders. But details about the enforcement of these policies continued to be ambiguous. Even this gathering of the strongest field leaders did not result in a satisfactory conclusion.

Back home again, I had been weighing whether or not to call for a Grand Jury investigation into Washoe Med. I had accumulated four years of evidence about the transfer of this facility from a county hospital to a private one, the conflicts of interest surrounding it, the profits to special interest groups, the millions of tax dollars lost to the community, the sky-rocketing healthcare costs that resulted, and the secrets preserved in the non-disclosed files that had been given to me. I finally decided to bring closure to this issue by turning the matter over to the Grand Jury for thorough examination.

In Saturday's Opinion section of our newspaper, the final saga of my woeful commission battle was played out by editors of the *Reno Gazette-Journal*. For the first time in months, I felt understood as I read their headline: "*County's spying operation against Reid disgusting.*" I was too hyper to sit down and read the article. I held the folded paper in my hand and paced up and down as I tried to assimilate what this support meant to me. My eyes went to the summary at the top of the article:

Commissioner Watched
- Board member's enemies tried to prove she didn't live in her district.
- But they didn't prove anything except their vindictiveness.
- Washoe residents should be repulsed by this Big Brotherism.

As I began reading, I thought of all the people to whom I owed a debt of gratitude: to Sheriff Swinney for telling the truth, to Bob List for getting to the bottom of all of this, and to my husband for hiring him. Yes, especially to Mark, who stood by me through one of the most oppressive periods of my public life. How many new marriages could have withstood living apart and having our lives played out in the daily paper? Dear God, thank you for giving me the stamina to get through this. No one will know how close I came to giving up.

Calming myself down, I read on:

Anyone who doubts whether there are vicious and petty politicians in our midst need look no further than the Washoe County Commission for evidence. If you look into this nasty nest, you are also likely to find some board members with questionable motives and selective memories.

This is the obvious conclusion after looking at the surveillance operation against Commissioner Rene Reid to see if she truly lives within her district....Why it was arranged is really not much of a mystery. Reid has sparred with her fellow commissioners on a number of issues—especially the Honey Lake Valley water importation project and Washoe Medical Center policy. To say she has made enemies during her tenure is to put it mildly.

Commissioner Dianne Cornwall is no doubt near the top of the list of those who dislike Reid and would like to embarrass her—even though Reid only has a few months left on her term and is not running for reelection. Reid might have suspected there would be retaliation from the board, but that does not make it less reprehensible.

Somebody on the commission—naturally, no one is saying who—asked the Sheriff's Department for an investigation of Reid's residency.

Swinney has admitted that one of his detectives was assigned to the case, but will only say that it was requested by "a commissioner." That's real helpful, sheriff. But then Swinney probably didn't expect copies of the detective's report to be leaked to Reid and the news media.

Cornwall says there was a concern that if Reid was asked about her residence in a public hearing, she would somehow weasel out of telling the truth. The only sure-fire way was to spy on her.

The irony is that the detective's report notes that the surveillance consisted of four drives past Reid's new husband's home in Washoe Valley—hardly the basis for solid evidence.

Reid has explained that, after she rented out her residence, she moved into her parent's home, which is also in her district. Her position that this is her primary residence was upheld in an attorney general's opinion, but it's almost irrelevant at this point.

What is relevant is that county officials are constantly bickering with each other—to the point that it interferes with legitimate public business. Residents now almost expect such things as clandestine operations, officials attacking political enemies through the use of rumor and innuendo and a general nastiness. It is getting to be awfully disgusting.

And it also raises the question: Who else is being watched?

"I think I'll save this article," I said, smiling at Mark.

"Maybe now you can live out the rest of your term in peace."

As I walked through the county doors on Monday morning, I was greeted by beaming faces from county employees. They didn't say a word. They didn't have to. Their smiles said it all.

Larry followed me into my office, shut the door, and sat down. "Uh, I don't know what to say exactly. Just that I'm proud of you. There aren't many people who could have withstood what you just went through. I don't know how you did it."

"Thanks, Larry. I had a husband who stood right by my side through it all."

"Yeah, and apparently had the savvy to hire the biggest gun in town."

"That didn't hurt any. Bob was good. He has a way of getting people to tell the truth."

"I'm really sorry about everything. Sometimes it just seems that all our hard work don't amount to nothing. Nobody really appreciates what we do. I was already feeling down. And then you made me so mad when…."

"It's okay. You don't have to go back over it. I'm sorry too. I believe in the principles I've tried to uphold. But I made a lot of mistakes in how I went about carrying them out. I was so green."

"You're not anymore. You may be the only person who could actually go up against Dianne and win. She's a tough lady. But you broke her down."

"No way! No one could break her down."

"Oh, yeah. We all sat in John's office this morning doing a post locker room session. She broke down and cried."

"Who cried? Dianne?"

"Yep."

"I can't even imagine it. Why?"

"She was whipped. The two of you had a trial by press, and the jury came back with their verdict in your favor. It's over, and you won't have to deal with any of it no more."

"I'm sorry. I'm just so sorry about the whole damn thing. It was so…"

"Unnecessary." Larry supplied the word.

How I would like to have the chance to relive some of my term. I wish I knew as much at the beginning as I know on my way out. Oh, the wisdom of hindsight. "Neither of us came off looking good. I mean, every time I glance up at that seal and see the words, 'to protect and to serve,' I keep wondering what happened to that idealism? After giving several years of our life to public service, all either of us will be remembered for is this petty catfight."

"No, you will be remembered as a woman who stood for what you believed in. You never had nothing but good intentions. Like Project ReStart. You will leave that as a legacy. That's what matters. All the rest of it—well, it just don't matter."

"I hope so. ReStart still has a lot of challenges ahead. I'm not sure if it will survive without more financial support, but I plan to work more closely with it after I leave office." It would take us another three years to agree upon the location for the centralized homeless site. It was the Sage Street site that passed the NIMBY test—Not In

My Back Yard—from the public. But in August of 1995, we would lose approval from the Reno City Council by one vote because several newly elected members didn't understand the issue. Until that vote, the Reno City Council had supported this site. Still another five years after that loss I would attend a Rotary Club luncheon at which the formal announcement was made by the mayor and council members that the centralized homeless center was at long last about to come to pass. It would be located. . .at Sage Street. Politics moves at its own pace.

"Well, if you put the same energy into that project that you have put into fighting your causes here, Project ReStart will be around for a long time to come."

"Any advice for me, Larry? How could I have accomplished my goals better?"

"Who am I to tell you?"

"But I really want to know."

"Maybe just be a little more patient. Work behind the scenes more. Make sure you have your support in place before you go charging out to change things."

"Good advice. I'll try to remember that in the future."

We hugged, and Larry was out the door. He is a good person. He'd worked hard as a commissioner. I worried about him being used, and I hoped the political puppeteers wouldn't pull his strings too tightly.

My remaining two months on the commission went more smoothly. I had learned some lessons. I had gained some respect. And I was less inclined to go charging out on my own. I worked on resolving the Steamboat trail issue between land owners and hikers. I found a temporary home for Project ReStart in an empty county office next to the Social Services office. I met with the Grand Jury regarding the Washoe Med report I'd filed. Months after I left office, they found 14 improprieties on this matter but the case was dropped. I talked further with Senator Harry Reid about the Honey Lake project and what I knew from personal observation and from staff. We were beginning to gain new levels of water from the snow and rain. The drought issue was beginning to dissipate slightly. . .almost as much as the tension had let up at the county.

By December the entire Nu Skin field leadership banded together. It appeared that the company still wasn't taking measurable action. Corporate leaders continued to beg all distributors to withhold pre-market activities or lose our right to do business in Japan. Unfortunately, as long as one group ignored these pleas, the problem remained unsolved.

Mark and I were in complete agreement that we had to take a strong stand on this issue. About 5:00 a.m. every morning, he and Richard were on the phone strategizing how to "beat the bastards at their own game." At last, the two of them had a plan. In an effort to face the matter head on, nearly every leader in the company, from the Karlen line to the Kall line, was invited to Kay Smith's home in Florida for an entire weekend of strategizing. There was dogged determination on the part of the Nu Skin field leaders to put Nu Skin back in sync with the integrity upon which it was founded.

The meeting was opened by Richard Kall, who invited everyone to state their reason for being there. One after another, astonishing stories were told of long-time distributors who had believed in this company and in its founding family of distributors. There was tremendous support for Blake Roney and Steve Lund, but they had lost trust in the founding family.

The group of powerful Nu Skin leaders representing a wide cross-section of the company concluded that there was unity in strength. If we were to win, we were going to have to form an organization. We named it the International Training Network. Its mission was to create an organization of members committed to the very principles intrinsic to network marketing: shared training, mutual support, fair recruiting practices, and a policy of non-solicitation of distributors from other downlines. ITN would unify its members across lines, protect them from unethical practices, and encourage that high-integrity behavior be voluntarily practiced by the members. It was our hope that everyone (well...nearly everyone) in the company would join ITN, committing to one code of ethics within the company and thereby eliminating any other splinter groups.

We saw membership to ITN as an opportunity to belong to the largest and most powerful international support group in Nu Skin history. This was to be an organization with the power and respect necessary to motivate the home office staff to *enforce and uphold* legal and ethical principles as well as policies and procedures that were in the best interest of Nu Skin and its distributor force as a whole.

The meeting closed with an agreement to send a letter to Blake Roney explaining our position and why we felt the need to form our own group. Because of Mark's writing skills, he was asked to draft it.

Once he'd finished the letter, he read it aloud to get the approval of everyone present. It was addressed to Blake and concluded with, "We love this company and respect its founders. If we didn't believe that you and Steve share our mutual desire for integrity, we wouldn't be spending so much valuable time seeking change. We eagerly anticipate sitting down with you both in order to achieve these ends....Respectfully submitted, Founding Members of International Training Network." Cheers went around the room and the letter was signed by everyone present.

Despite the approaching Christmas holidays, a meeting was set for the following week with the leaders who had been in the company the longest representing our group. It was obvious that Blake wanted what we wanted but didn't believe our starting a competing group was the answer. For him, we were all one Nu Skin family. It had always been that way and he wanted to keep it that way. Out of respect for Blake, who was esteemed by everyone in Nu Skin, our group backed off, leaving him with the charge to resolve the matter. Unfortunately, facing confrontation was not his strong suit. As a result, the Nu Skin saga was yet to be played out.

A few days before Christmas, Mark and I celebrated our first wedding anniversary with several hundred friends whom we knew socially, politically, and as our Nu Skin associates. It was a gala formal affair, complete with live band and dancing, held in the ballroom at the Nugget in Sparks. I felt proud to dance with Mark, he in his tux and me in my black sequined gown. It was not only a celebration of our marriage surviving this first year; it was a "bon voyage" to public life and a "bien venue" to my new life of unrestrained freedom with Mark. At this event, I was awarded a plaque "welcoming me home" to my shared abode with Mark after all my turmoil over the residency issue.

This Christmas was truly family time, with presents and turkey, a warm fire in the fireplace, and Christmas music.

It snowed relentlessly over the next two weeks. Cabin fever got the best of Mark and Chris as they used their pent-up energy to exercise their lungs at each other. With Mark in one of his bearish moods, I took the kids and their friends skiing to give us all a break. As we saw Amy off at the airport to finish out her freshman year at the University of Missouri at Columbia, she and I hugged, agreeing that women cope better than men under stress.

The house seemed quiet. Alone, Mark and I snuggled up by the fireplace. I lay in his arms as he leaned his back against the couch.

"I love you so much. I'm sorry I've been so short-fused these past couple of weeks."

"Don't worry. It's a lot of adjustment. You probably don't know what to do with me home all the time. No more county. No more worries about what spin the newspaper will put on our life. No more politics. Just you and me, babe."

I pulled out his book of poetry, and together, we read some of the poems he'd written for me this past year. Even he laughed at himself as we read another one of his Kavanaugh take-offs, countering thought by thought what Jim had expressed. I think Mark admired Jim's poetic style. The satire was never to put him down, but rather to let me know that, while Jim may have left me, he wouldn't. The verse ended assuring me that, no matter what, he would never, never leave me.

> *I need not be mad to see our lives through,*
> *to stand at your side facing each day anew,*
> *I need only love you and care for you...*
> *forever and ever, and Rene, I do.*

CHAPTER 8

ADDICTION:
THE INTRUSIVE MISTRESS
January – August 1993

F ree! Free at Last! With my life in public service over, Mark and I were at liberty to do whatever we wanted. We chose to celebrate our new freedom by spending a month over January and February in Australia and New Zealand, where Nu Skin was just opening. There we would have the balance of a working trip combined with personal time. Now there was only our shared life and work—the moment we had anticipated since we first dreamed together.

We flew from Reno to LA to Sydney to Perth, which is situated on the southwesternmost coast of Australia, proported to be the most remote city in the world. It was a grueling trip—some twelve-thousand miles and twenty-four hours of travel. Once we acclimated ourselves to the change in time and season, we were happy to be enjoying summer on the Australian coast. We were scheduled to deliver Nu Skin presentations across Australia, gradually making our way back east to Melbourne and then up to Sydney. From there we were going on to speak in various cities throughout New Zealand, where we had such fond memories from just the year before. Living much of this time on various beaches, we had our freedom, our health, no demands, and each other. What more could we ask?

But almost immediately after arriving, our life changed in a startling way. Mark began complaining about his old pelvic injury from the '79 hang-gliding accident, in which he had fallen 54 feet to the ground, fracturing part of his pelvis. The doctor had prescribed fairly strong doses of Vicodin to help alleviate the pain.

Lying across the bed in our hotel room, Mark began nervously: "Yeah, the old injury is flaring up. I didn't want to concern you, but I've started taking fairly strong doses of this painkiller again."

How could I not know this? For the first time, I felt myself holding back with Mark, carefully choosing my words...afraid of setting him off. "I knew something was wrong. You've been...short with everyone."

"Yeah, well, I'm sorry. But you wouldn't believe how terrible the pain is." His brow was furrowed as his hands swept outward to demonstrate his point. "It's really bad, honey. I've got to do something."

"So why didn't you bring the medication with you?"

He paused before he spoke. He didn't usually do that. He always had his answers ready before I could get the question out. Slowly he spoke. "I guess I was concerned about bringing so much medication across international borders."

"How much are we talking about?"

"Well, I've been under a doctor's care on pain medication most of the time since the accident. Gradually you have to build up to pretty big doses. Otherwise it doesn't have any effect."

"How big?"

"Twenty-thirty a day."

"A *day?*"

"That's what it takes for me to get rid of the pain and feel normal."

I was stunned. I was so distressed that I had to search for the right words. "Has this been going on all year?" I asked with serious misgivings.

"No. I was getting by okay during most of last year. I didn't have to start on it again until a couple of months ago." *Could that explain the cabin-fever episode during the holidays?*

I agreed to help him search for a doctor who could or would

give him a similar appropriate Aussie prescription to relieve the pain. With the help of some of our Nu Skin connections, we found someone relatively easily.

The problem was solved—or so I thought. But within days, Mark was out of medicine and needed more.

"I know what you're thinking, but it's not like that," he explained. "My body has built up such a tolerance for the medication that the paltry amount that the doctor gave me doesn't do anything unless I take it in larger doses."

"So let's go back and see him again, and explain what's going on."

"No, you don't understand. I can't go back to him. He made it clear that this is all he can give me. He doesn't get it either. After all these years, I need massive doses to do me any good at all."

"So what do we do?"

"I have to find another doctor."

"But how will that help? You'll have the same problem all over again."

"I just keep hoping that I can find a doctor who will x-ray me, see the problem, and give me the dosage I need. Otherwise, I'll always be in pain."

At first I was torn between concern for his discomfort and worry that he was addicted to the prescription. By the end of our month in Australia and New Zealand, going from city to city and doctor to doctor, I was no longer reeling with doubt and confusion. I knew with certainty: my husband was seriously addicted to a prescription drug. I was fully cognizant of his alcoholism because he had told me about it, but he was in recovery for that and doing extraordinarily well. The chemical dependency on Vicodin was a new revelation. Other than what Betty Ford had shared with the world about her own similar situation, I knew nothing about this disease.

By the time we returned home, we had agreed on a plan of action. We were going to see a doctor friend of his who would help transition Mark off this drug. He gave Mark a complete physical, including an EKG and MRI. After two days of testing and consultation, we arrived at a plan. Mark would immediately be taken down from 30 Vicodin a day to 18. Over the next four months, he would continue to reduce the amount until he was completely free of the habit. By the start of summer, I was told, we'd have the problem under control. But Mark didn't completely buy into the program.

I had no experience with drug addition either personally or with anyone else. Consequently, the four months of implementing this plan only heightened the tension between us.

Mark spent hours at the medical library at the University of Nevada researching cases to back up his point of view. "Rene, I want you to read this," he said handing me an article. "This explains me. I know you don't know a lot about pain medication, but this will help you understand that certain body types simply require more mood-altering substances in order to be 'normal.'"

"Sweetheart, I love you, but I'm not buying this. You agreed to go through the program and you're not doing it. Your doctor has asked you to go into therapy. He has lined up Rolfing sessions and a pain clinic. Why won't you go along with him? He seems like he really cares about you and wants to help."

"Yeah, well, he doesn't understand this either. Maybe I made a mistake going to a friend."

When Mark couldn't convince me, he had lunch with our friend Kathy List, trying to win her over so that she would in turn persuade me. By the time she called me, she was wavering.

"Rene, I don't know. He's pretty convincing. Maybe there is something to what he's saying."

"Kathy, Mark could sell ice to Eskimos. That's his strength. That's what has made him so successful in Nu Skin. He is a professional persuader."

"I know. I don't know what to tell you. He's pretty upset that you won't buy into his theory."

"Kathy, how did I get myself in this situation? How come I didn't know this before we got married?"

"What does he say?"

"He says it was hard enough for him to tell me that he was an alcoholic—a recovering alcoholic. And he's been really good about that. He has had only one slip. Remember when you and I went up to Ashland to see Jack and Linda Cook?

"Yeah, Thelma and Louise," Kathy recalled what we said to Mark as we headed out the door.

"Well, when I left him home alone, he fell off the wagon."

"So why is this harder?"

"I'm not sure. I think he's more ashamed of being an addict. He often talks about his alcoholism from the stage. Being open about it is part of his AA mission. But he doesn't seem to see the addiction in the same light."

"I don't know what to tell you."

"I guess nobody can tell me. I'm just going to have to work this one out by myself. Something tells me this will be the ultimate test of how strong we are together. Death threats, commission battles, and my life being played out in the media didn't destroy us. After all we've already been through in our first year, it would be a shame to have an addiction problem tear us apart in our second."

The weeks went by with Mark bringing home more and more articles for me to read from the Med School library. Through it all, we continued to travel and do meetings for our distributors. In early April, while we were speaking in Austin, Mark went with me to see my father who was hospitalized in Burnet, Texas. He was dying of cancer. Except for a year in my infancy, my dad and I had not lived together, and, consequently, weren't very close. He was serving in World War II when I was born in 1944, and he and Mom were divorced when I was a baby. Dad and his wife, Dixie, had been married 46 years.

"Rene, I'm so glad to see you." He could barely speak, so I did more of the talking.

"Dad, I want you to meet my husband. This is Mark."

As a minister, Mark had spent a great deal of time at sick beds. He was at ease with the circumstances. Mark reached out to my dad and spoke quietly as he leaned over him. "I'm going to take good care of your daughter, Mr. Reid. There is nothing I wouldn't do for her."

"Call me Bill. I can't tell you how much it means to me to know that she is with someone who loves her and will care for her, someone who won't leave her." He was referring to my previous marriage. Dixie, Mark, and I all knew it. "I may not have been able to be a part of her growing-up years, but I've worried about her nonetheless, especially these last few years." I felt as if I were in the rite of marriage, being given away by my father. Never before had this happened.

"Well, there is no reason to worry now. She is with me. And I won't ever leave her." As Mark spoke those words, our eyes caught. At that moment, the strain that had been ever present lately seemed to dissipate. Mark hadn't been as expressive of his love for me these past couple of months. He had been too frustrated with me and too preoccupied with his own internal struggle. But now, as my father lay dying, I could feel love pervading the room—my father's commingled with my husband's, a feeling so warm and protective, like nothing I have ever felt before or since. My entire life had been entrusted completely to women—to my grandmother, my mother, the nuns, my guardians. Always to women. For the first time in my life, I felt safeguarded and cherished by not one but two men. I would remember this moment as long as I lived. On April 13, my father passed away.

For the next two months, we worked with our Nu Skin organization and traveled extensively for business purposes. But, unlike the previous year, we seemed to be making less personal time for ourselves. I struggled within myself not knowing when to talk about "the program" and when to let it go and say nothing. By mid-June, we were no further along than we had been in February. I was distraught, and the trust level was severely damaged between us.

Four years in politics should have given me more insight into dealing with conflict. But even that didn't seem to help. I was constantly battling with myself. If I ignored the problem, I was an enabler. If I addressed the problem, I was a controller. And to a man with the ego and pride of a Mark Yarnell, the latter was by far the greater of the two evils.

Mark was becoming more and more upset that I was still

expecting him to be clean by summer. He just wasn't the same person anymore. His temper flared up easily. I was coming to understand that the addictive personality must take the spotlight off of his own shortcomings by redirecting it at his partner.

"You just want to control me. No woman has ever done that, and I won't let you. I've got to do this my way. I'll get off these things when I'm damned ready. Just back off, goddamn it. Just back way off."

There was a time I would have. Maybe if you had known me as a younger woman, you would have appreciated me more. I would have rolled over, looked the other way, done whatever I had to do to keep you happy. My objective would have been to preserve our togetherness and avoid your abandoning me. But you didn't get me at that phase of my life, sweetheart. I've been through a few trials before you. I'm stronger now. Maybe, just maybe, you were drawn to me because you knew I would stand up to you on this matter...even if it means losing you. "Mark, I can't take this," I shouted. "We've got to get help...and *this* doctor isn't the answer. We need someone who can really help us. Both of us." I broke down in tears. I may have been strong at that moment, but not without a barrage of deeply-felt emotions.

Mark couldn't stand it when I cried. It made him want to distance himself from me, and he had the perfect excuse to leave early. He was due to be in Dallas, where he was going to meet with our friend, Charles King. The three of us had been exploring the possibility of beginning a certification course on network marketing at the university where Charles was a professor in the school of business.

Mark walked out the door in a huff and wouldn't let me drive him to the airport. I could tell by the amount of clothes he packed that this was more than a two-day trip. I was devastated, and still not sure what had gone wrong with the program. There were so few people to whom I could really talk. Days passed and I didn't hear from him. Out of fear for his well-being, I called his mom.

"Don't you worry, honey. He's here."

Does she know about the pills? How much do I say? "I'm so worried about him, Patsi. What should I do?"

"There's not a lot you can do when he's like this. Just let him be for now. I'll let you know if anything changes. And Rene...try not to worry." Right. Well, at least I knew where he was and that he was safe. I was deeply hurt by our separation. Mark *promised* that this would never happen. But I was even more distraught over the disease that I now undersood had afflicted my husband since he was in high school. The windmills of his life had caught my Man of La Mancha in their centrifugal whirl.

In the meantime, our Nu Skin business went on. I had to keep up a front with everyone who called. In our business, it is essential to keep a positive attitude. If anyone knew that Mark had walked out of our marriage, it would have taken its toll on the distributors in our organization. Most of our people look up to him and, I feared, might even be demoralized by his struggle with this disease. So I made up excuses and covered up in every way possible. I couldn't let anyone know that our life was falling apart.

I took long walks, sometimes alone and sometimes with my friend and now neighbor, Ursula. We'd walk into the backwoods behind our houses while I poured everything out to her. She really liked Mark and encouraged me to stand by him. I knew she wanted him to get the help he needed and come home to me.

I spoke with two doctors, one a personal friend and one my physician, trying to learn more about drug addiction. They left little room for doubt in my mind. Mark was a full-fledged addict, and his doctor was not helping the situation. In fact, in their opinion, he was seriously jeopardizing his medical practice by the way he was handling Mark.

After a week or so of thought, and prayer, and more investigation into the whole situation, I decided to write to Mark's closest family—his mother and daughter—and appeal to them to try to help him. I couldn't bring myself to say anything to Patsi on the phone. It was too hard. A letter would be easier. As I wrote the date, July 3, 1993, at the top of the letter, it was the first time I realized a holiday was coming.

Addiction: the Intrusive Mistress

Dear Patsi and Amy,

It is with some fear coupled with deep concern and love for Mark that I write this letter. Mark would be displeased if he knew that I am contacting you. At this time, I ask your confidence while I or we explore the best options of what we can do for our son and father and husband. If, after reading this, you decide that it is beyond your ability to do anything, no one will understand that better than I. I have felt helpless about the situation ever since learning of it in January of this year.

Mark believes, and would have you believe, that the problems we are experiencing are solely marital. I wanted to believe that because problems regarding shared responsibility of mutual business tasks, some challenges with Nu Skin, and the parenting of my son living with us are all items that can be faced and fixed. What can't be as easily fixed is Mark's drug addiction.

After recounting our time abroad and the purported program Mark was on, I went on to share my concern and ask for their help.

Since Mark left home about a week ago, I have discovered a letter from a Dr. Ann Mass in Aspen, Colorado, dated 1987 and another dated 1988. Even back then, she was concerned about Mark's possible addiction to this habit-forming drug. She diagnosed him as having "somatiform disorder," which means using a condition in the body as a secondary issue in order to justify another primary intent; in other words, using the pelvic pain as a justification for accessing a drug to which he is addicted. Yes, there was real pain from the hang-gliding accident. But it is possible that he has unwittingly—and I stress, without full realization of what he is doing—nurtured and exaggerated that pain in order to satisfy his addiction.

With somatization, I understand that the body can even create pain in order to keep the medication coming. This past year, he had given up alcohol but revived using his drug of choice—Vicodin.

I called Mark's doctor and shared the letter with him. He dismissed it as not having any significance, and suggested I just throw the letter away. I still had doubts, so I turned to two local and trusted doctor friends while they patiently listened to every detail. The first one told me that my husband has a serious drug addiction and it is critical that I face that fact. The second doctor reaffirmed that even more strongly and added that what Mark's doctor is doing is criminal and he could lose his medical license over it. He said there isn't a legitimate doctor anywhere who would risk his license prescribing this quantity of a habit-forming drug to anyone, much less to a self-proclaimed addict and alcoholic. Further, I was told that if, as Mark has said, the chronic pain is arthritic in nature as Mark grows older, still the proper medical application for arthritis is not a painkiller like hydracodone. No matter how I try to look at it, the facts just don't add up.

I am turning to the two of you because I don't know what else to do. If you think I am over-reacting, please tell me so. I suggest you not take my research as gospel, and go to someone you trust in the medical field, preferably a doctor who understands addiction, and describe these circumstances. Check it out for yourselves if you wish. I am at a loss as to what to do. The one thing I can't do is discuss it intelligently with Mark. When I try, it only leads to an argument and accusations of my being controlling. His position is that his doctor should be prescribing more pills than he is and, by not doing so, is causing Mark unnecessary pain.

I accept and am fully facing the fact that Mark is a practicing addict. I am equally convinced that the program he is now on is not working. As I weigh my options, I narrow them down to these two: (1) With your help (or without, if I must), do everything within my power to get Mark to a rehabilitation clinic and get help. (2) Conclude that Mark knows his own body better than any doctor, and support him in getting back on 30 Vicodin a day. The first option is by far, in my opinion, the best for Mark but one that could lead to his anger at me (or us) beyond our wildest dreams. The second seems pretty bizarre to me but still an option. It requires that I accept that my husband is an addict, but having an addiction that is "controlled" by his definition, so that he can manage his pain and we can return to the kind of shared life we had the first year of marriage. I don't mean to dismiss other marital challenges between us. But I honestly believe they would fall into perspective if Mark were more himself and less preoccupied with acquiring more drugs or coping with less.

None of this offers any guarantees. No matter what I do, Mark and I may end up in divorce. But I do not consider it an option just to walk away because I can't stand the heat. I love Mark and want him to be whole, healthy and happy. Even more, I hope this can happen with us together to the end. But I believe I cannot ignore the symptoms, and that I have some responsibility to try to do what I believe is the right thing. He would consider any action I took toward getting him help as controlling. And now that he has his doctor doing more or less what he wants, he doesn't want me to interfere.

I chose writing to you so that you could have time to absorb what I am saying before responding to me. Maybe I am telling you both something you already know. I am more concerned than I can tell you. I don't know what else to do but to turn to the people who love Mark as much as I do. There are very few people I can talk to about this problem.

Please call me when and if you feel you want to. I love you both. For some reason, we have been brought together as a family. Hopefully, as a family, we will stand strong and work this out together.

Love, Rene

It wasn't long before Mark's mom called to thank me for the letter. "You know, honey, Mark has been his own person and done his own thing for most of his life. I have very little ability to change him now. We just have to pray and put this in the Lord's hands."

"How does he seem to be doing? I'm mean, is he okay? Does he miss me?" I asked.

"Well, he's drinking fairly heavily at the moment, but he seems able to function reasonably well. In fact, he gave a sermon at church on the 4th of July, and he was just fabulous. He got everyone fired up like only he can. Actually, I was proud of him and a lot of my friends said really nice things afterwards."

Omigod. This sounds horrible to me. Excessive alcohol mixed with massive doses of Vicodin. He's going to kill himself. My mind was racing. There must be something I could do. But all I said was, "Patsi, I'm here if you need me. I wish I knew what to do."

"Honey, this has been going on for years before you. You're not going to be able to do any kind of quick fix."

"But why, Patsi? Why did this happen to him? He's a good person. He doesn't deserve this."

"It goes way back. When he was growing up, we had some challenges as a family. Someday, I'll tell you about it. Mark's dad was not always the easiest person to live with. I guess you know Duane was an alcoholic. Melissa was five years younger than Mark and he took more of the brunt of his father's wrath. He must have learned to cope with our situation by taking drugs."

I was choked up as I listened. It was hard to find words, but finally I said, "That helps me understand him. I just wish I knew what I'm supposed to do."

"Just keep praying for him. These things always work out. They just happen in His time, not in ours."

As I hung up the phone, I admired her faith. She truly could leave it in His hands. Patsi's words clarified the dilemma we faced. Understanding the background helped put the situation into perspective. Mark didn't sit down one day and say, "I think I'll become an alcoholic and an addict." His life circumstances led him to it. It was in his genes. It could have been me as easily as him. I didn't find myself blaming him, only wanting to do something before he killed himself with the combination of booze and pain pills. My love for him would not permit me to sit back and do nothing.

I picked up the phone again and called the infamous doctor. "Hi, this is Rene. I need to talk to you. Are you in touch with Mark?"

"Yes, we spoke a couple of days ago. He still seems resistant to doing anything for himself. I'm trying to get him to go to a pain clinic, but he won't do it."

"Look, I've gone along with this pain stuff from the very beginning. I've waited out the four months. I've been the supportive wife in every way I know how. But I am finally facing the bottom-line truth, and it's very hard to face."

"What's that?"

"That my husband is a drug addict, and you, doctor, are nothing more than his supplier!"

There was a prolonged silence before he spoke again. "Yeah, well, I can't argue with that. But I believe this is the only effective way to deal with someone like Mark."

"How would you be dealing with anyone else...anyone, that is, who is not your friend and mentor?"

"Much tougher, that's for sure."

"Then that is what we should be doing. The course of action you prescribed isn't working. That's pretty evident." I was really angry at this man for allowing this situation to get this far out of hand.

"Look, I'm doing the best I can here under the circumstances. There's no reason to get testy with me. Just back off and I'll handle this."

"No, I think it is time that you back off. Listen to me. Don't give him any more drugs! I've talked to St. Mary's Rehab Program here in town. You are not helping the situation. This has to stop."

"You can't stop this. I don't know who you think you are," he yelled.

"You're right. I can't stop *him*, but I sure as hell can stop *you*." My whole body was tense as I unleashed on him.

"Oh, yeah, and how are you going to do that?"

"By turning you into the Medical Board. What you are doing is wrong. You are hurting Mark. You think you're a friend, but you're not a good one. A real friend would say *no* to him."

"You have no right, goddamn you. All I've tried to do is help. You're crazy, do you know that? You've really lost it. I'm going to hang up now. This conversation is going nowhere. I'm calling Mark. Goodbye!"

I could just hear friends saying "Rene, you are such a strong woman." Oh yeah, then why I am sitting here waiting by the phone and trembling all over? I knew it was only a matter of time before it would ring. It took about thirty minutes.

"Rene, this is Mark. Have you lost your mind? What do you think you're doing? This is my life, and I will live it as I see fit. You are a control freak. First me and now my friend. When will you ever be satisfied? Just stay out of this. You have no business getting involved. This is between my doctor and me. Just stay out! Do you hear me? Stay the hell out!"

"Sweetheart, this does involve me. You and I have a life together, and your behavior affects me. Right now, I'm more concerned than I can tell you."

"Well, you can stop worrying. I'm a big boy, and I can take care of myself. I don't need you to be watching out for me. Now look what you've gone and done. You've got the doc so upset, he's cutting me off. I really hate you for this. You have no idea what you've caused. I can't stand the thought of you right now."

"Mark, listen to yourself. This is not you. We have to do something to get you past this state. Will you consider calling the clinic that your doctor keeps bringing up to you? It's right there in Springfield."

"Hell, no. I'm just fine the way I am. I don't need you butting into my life. And I'm going to go do something about that right now." He hung up.

I collapsed into tears realizing that addiction was more intrusive than a mistress to a marriage. *Dear God, where are you? Don't abandon me now. How did this happen to us? I know that you brought me into Mark's life to help him overcome this. But what am I supposed to do now? What is the right thing to do? Show me. Please, show me.*

I must have been lying on the bed sobbing for hours. Ursula brought me some supper. I hadn't thought about food all day. It felt good to have someone there.

"There is a clinic in Springfield that his doctor told me about. He had hoped to get Mark into it. Ursula, do you think there is any chance at all that he might check himself in?"

"There is always a chance. Mark is a pretty smart fellow," she stated rather solemnly in her Swiss accent. "He's cornered right now. He's like a wild animal that is going to do whatever he has to in order to escape. But in the end, there's something in him that desperately wants to find a way out of drugs. He wants a life with you, Rene. I've seen it when he's with you. He just has to work it through in his own way."

"What do I do?"

"You've already done it. You've set the stage. Now he has to decide how the acts will unfold." Wise advice.

With Mom and Ursula as my confidantes, I got through the week. I didn't hear a word from my husband all during that time.

Mark and I generally filed an extension on our taxes. With August 15 not too far away, I had to get on with day-to-day business. As I was sitting with our accountant, Dick Coonradt, going over our IRS forms for our delayed filing, the phone rang. I excused myself and went into the kitchen to take the call.

"Hello, is this Rene?" It was a male voice I didn't recognize.

"Yes."

"Rene, you don't know me. I'm an attorney from Reno. My name is Joel Barber. We've not met before, but I know who you are. I admired your stance on the commission. I am calling on behalf of Mark. He has asked me to help the two of you work through a quick divorce. I have drawn up some papers and just wanted to do this as amicably as possible."

So many thoughts were racing through my mind. *Mark doesn't really mean this...he isn't thinking clearly...I don't want a divorce...I don't want to lose him ...I can't handle another failed marriage...what about all the promises to our kids and parents?...what impact will this have on our entire Nu Skin organization?* But I simply said, "I need some time to think about this. I'll get back to you."

I cried for a few minutes, apologizing to Dick, who just happened to be there at the wrong time. He was kind and showed a great deal of compassion. We didn't try to do any more tax work after that. As he drove off, I sat there staring into space. The phone rang again, and I forced myself to answer it. The call was someone in our Nu Skin group wanting to speak to Mark.

"I'm sorry, he isn't here right now."

"Well, I really need to talk to him. Where is he?"

Believe me, I know how you feel. I really need to talk to him too. "He's spending some much-needed time with his mom. But if there is anything I can do..."

Our distributor began telling me about his challenges in building an organization. Someone in something called the NS group had stolen the most lucrative leg of his organization and he was devastated. I agreed it was deplorable, that the company should step in, and promised to call the home office and follow up on this.

I hung up the phone and with my hand still on the receiver, picked it back up and called Ron Logar, another Reno attorney. I had met him through Kathy List when he handled her divorce from Bob. I gave him a quick synopsis of what was happening, assuring him that I had no interest in moving forward on this but wanted him to send a letter to Mark's attorney on my behalf. We composed the letter briefly together on the phone:

Dear Mr. Barber:

I have been asked to respond to your recent communication on behalf of Mrs. Yarnell. She was both surprised and disheartened by your proposal. I'm sure it was not an easy call for you to make. Mrs. Yarnell has instructed me to let her husband know through you that she doesn't care to have a divorce at this time. Perhaps we can take another look at it sometime in the future if the situation doesn't remedy itself.

Cordially, Ron Logar

I told Ursula about my letter to Mark's attorney.

"I don't care for any," she mimicked. "Only you would respond to a divorce request like you'd been offered a tray of hors d'oeuvres. "I don't care for any, but thank you for offering."

For the first time since Mark's attorney called, I laughed. It felt better than crying.

Amy called the next morning. She was only nineteen and, I felt sure, was feeling caught in the middle. We were beginning to build a bond, but I didn't know if it could withstand the strain between her dad and me.

"I got your letter, and I don't know what to say. The whole thing makes me feel yucky."

"You don't have to say anything, Amy. I just needed to tell you what was really going on."

"Well, Dad thinks you're trying to control him. And, with him, that's about the worst thing you could do."

"So what do you think I—or we—should do?"

"Well, I've heard his side of this and I've read your letter. I mean, maybe Dad really does need that much medication to handle his pain. I don't know."

"Do you really believe that? I mean, really?"

"I don't know what I believe, but I don't like being in the middle."

"I wasn't trying to put you there. I just thought maybe he'd listen if we both suggested that he go for help. I thought maybe if we did a kind of intervention...."

"No way. I can't. He's my dad. Besides...I'm not sure if you're right or if he's right. I've been thinking about talking to Doug Duey about this." Doug was a long-time friend of Mark's who was himself a recovering alcoholic and had guided Mark to a rehab center in the past.

"That sounds like a great idea. Why don't you? He's got experience with this. Maybe he will know what we should do," I said hopefully. Somewhere in all of this, I just wanted to find someone who would confirm that I'm doing the right thing, or if I'm not, tell me what to do.

Amy did talk to Doug, who then promised to talk to Mark. But first Doug called me. He seemed somewhat critical of how I was handling the situation. His attitude was that eventually Mark would get sick and tired of this and do something for himself. In the meantime, I should back off.

From my perspective, except for Ursula and Mom, it felt like everyone was on Mark's side. I felt alone and powerless over the situation, trapped in freezing waters batting my head against the icy ceiling. I didn't want there to be any sides at all. I just wanted my husband back, the one I married. I knew Doug was right. I had to back off now. I had done everything I could. Now it was time to take care of my own needs. I began reading everything I could on co-dependency. I started attending AA meetings for spouses of alcoholics and addicts, and kept my focus on what I *was* able to change. I couldn't fix the situation. I could learn how to cope with it and emerge as a whole person.

I needed an outlet. I could face any battle *with* Mark. Confronting one *alone*, and especially one that questioned the inherent bond of our relationship, was tearing me apart. Hidden away in the back of mind, I remembered that I had kept a diary as a kid. I wasn't satisfied to lock it and hide the key. I also hid it in the Mexican sombrero that hung on the wall of the room I shared with someone who was like a sister. I always loved writing in it. It was private and truly contained the deepest secrets in my life—as deep as they come in pre-puberty. I could express anything I felt without holding back. Keeping a diary was becoming popular again. The new adult name for it was "journaling." It was as a safety valve for these pressures occurring in my life that I began keeping my journal. Only this time, on my computer, of course, locked away in a secret file that only I would know.

Addiction: the Intrusive Mistress

Facing a drug and/or alcohol problem in a relationship requires a spine of steel. All the literature I've been reading stresses the likelihood that the spouse will serve as the enabler. Although I am a "co-dependent" with Mark, I am most definitely not an enabler. I would have been ten years ago. But somewhere along the way, I gained some confidence in myself and became stronger in this area.

The reality of this situation hit me hard, but once it sunk in, I believe I've done all that is within my power to place Mark's well-being ahead of everything, even taking the risk of jeopardizing our marriage. The hardest part for someone like me is recognizing when I've done all that I can do and can do no more. I can't change the situation. I can only change me. Lately, I've begun to focus on those steps that would help me through the crisis—programs, books, classes, counseling, whatever gave me some comfort and understanding of what was happening. Beyond my prayers, what Mark will do is completely up to him now. I understand that. By letting go and focusing on my own healing, I can feel that I am becoming healthier.

For the first time in my life, I believe I am able to love someone enough to let him walk away...if I have to. I have never been strong enough in the past, and most especially in my previous marriage, to handle a major challenge without putting my own fears first. Formerly, I would have clung to the relationship no matter what, couching such dependency as love.

I don't mean to sound indifferent about whether Mark and I make it together. I know, after only a year and a half of marriage, my life will go on if that is what is to be. But I so want him to work through this. Maybe part of it is that I want to know that I am loved and that, in the final analysis, he will choose me over drugs. But I also hope, that as I'm faced with choices now, I will choose the path that will produce the greatest good for Mark.

It is hard to say exactly how it happened—probably a combination of prayers, pressure from the supply being withdrawn, conversations with his mom and others, and an intrinsic readiness on my husband's part—but within two weeks, Mark went off the booze and pills cold turkey and checked himself into the rehab facility in Springfield. I thanked God he was under medical care for that dangerous transition. He also had an excellent counselor who was herself a recovering alcoholic and addict. She understood everything Mark was going through. The counselor and I talked every day, and some days I spoke with the counselor *and* Mark. We didn't talk about our getting back together, only of getting him well.

Getting off prescription drugs would prove to be, over time, the biggest challenge of Mark's life. He was able to do it because he wanted it so badly...because he had a reason not to be on drugs...because he felt support from me...and because he knew he would soon die if he didn't quit. Toward the end of his stay, he gave me a call just to talk—no counselor, just the two of us.

"I was afraid to tell you the truth. It was hard enough to admit I was an alcoholic. But, once I got on the road to recovery with that, I thought I would lose you if I told you that I was still a practicing addict. I knew you would make me choose between you and this habit, and I didn't think I could do it."

I felt Mark was never more honest with me than he was at this moment. "I'm sure you're right. I couldn't have lived with you knowing that. But I have come to know how strong you really are. You have incredible strength, you really do. You have slain so many dragons in your life. I know you can conquer this one. And I give you my word that as long as you are working toward some resolution, I'll stand by you."

"Thank you. I really love you."

"I love you too, sweetheart...so much."

"It's been so hard to be here without you. But I had to do this on my own."

"I know. But if you hadn't called me soon, I may have followed you there. Kind of like you told me you would do if ever I left you."

Addiction: the Intrusive Mistress

I sensed him smiling through the receiver. As I hung up the phone, I felt my whole body trembling. I didn't know exactly what lay ahead for us, but I was grateful that Mark was on the road to recovery. I admired his courage. I couldn't empathize because I'd never been where he is, but I'd read enough to know that it was a sheer act of bravery that led him to go for help. Not that this was his first time in treatment. It wasn't. But I felt that Mark was driven like never before to get his act together now. I knew he had to do it for himself, but I hoped that he was motivated, in part, by his desire to share his life with me. More than any mistress, drugs can come between two people and destroy the harmony of their relationship.

I thought back over the past month and my own handling of the situation. When I discovered the challenge in our marriage, at first I pressed hard to face what was happening head on. Then, once I had done all that I could do, I backed off, concentrating on my own coping mechanisms and personal growth. Both steps were necessary, but I believe that the more critical step was my withdrawing. That is what gave Mark the space to come to his own conclusions about what *he* wanted for himself. The Serenity Prayer that is so much a part of Alcoholics Anonymous fits the role of the co-dependent perfectly: "God, grant me the serenity to accept the things I cannot change, the courage to change the things I can, and the wisdom to know the difference." I said this prayer daily through this period.

It was only two days before Mark called again and said simply, "I want to come home."

"Do you want me to come get you?" I asked softly.

"No, I want to walk through the door into your arms."

Chris and I hung a banner over the fireplace that said "Welcome Home." When Mark walked in, he looked as if he had been to hell and back. This was not going to be easy for him, or for us. But with the two of us in unison now, I knew there was no challenge over which we wouldn't triumph...together.

CHAPTER 9

RELAPSE

August 1993 – August 1994

While we were living in Washoe Valley, Mark had a pending sale on his former home on Neeser Lane and had allowed the buyer to move into it. Actually, it was the same man who had sold him the house originally. While Mark was back in Missouri in rehab, the former owner called to let me know that his financing was not coming together and that meant the house sale was going to fall through. *Oh, great! Mark really needs to be dealing with this on top of everything else.*

In lieu of charging him rent for the house, we mutually agreed that we would forego paying the second mortgage to him. Knowing that Mark was out of town, the pseudo-buyer chose this moment to drop his bomb on me.

"So, sweetheart, it looks like the situation leaves me no choice. Since Mark hasn't paid the second mortgage for the past three months, I'm going to have to foreclose on him."

I sat holding the phone in utter disbelief. *God, I hate it when a man calls me "sweetheart" in the middle of a business deal...but especially when he is in the process of defrauding me.* I wasn't sure what I *would* do, but I was very sure what I *wouldn't* do: I wasn't going to roll over for him.

Before I found words to speak, he continued: "Oh, and I see you have taken some of the furniture out of the house. You see, honey, a lot of the furniture was part of the house sale, and I want certain key pieces returned."

Honey! Dammit, now he has really gone too far! His choice of words added fuel to the fire of my indignation. "Wait, let me get this straight. You can't work out the financing to buy our house, so you are going to steal it under the pretext of our failing to pay your second mortgage payments while you lived in the house rent-free."

"Business is business, sweetheart. I've checked with my lawyer and I'm in the right. Now I want you to return the roll-top desk that belongs in my office and also the bronze statue of the four cowboys on horseback. You know the one?"

Not agreeing to anything, I felt uncontrollable rage. Had he been in the same room with me, I could have easily wrapped the telephone cord around his neck and squeezed. Without Mark at home to work out a strategy together, I called my real estate friend, TJ Day, and asked for his guidance. He put me in touch with Mike Malarkey, a real estate attorney, and I began fighting back. I didn't say anything to Mark while he was gone because I felt he had all he could handle at the moment. But after he got home, I filled him in on what was happening. Mark was pleased with what I'd done so far and met with Mike to pick up where I left off.

While the lawsuit was pending, we were required to pay three months' back mortgage payments while he paid us nothing for living in the house. By August, this conniving encroacher moved out and, because of the house's size and upkeep requirements, we felt compelled to move in. Given its value, it was going to be difficult to sell and impossible to lease. Instead, we leased out our Washoe Valley home, knowing that we would be on Neeser Lane for a while. At first, I was uncomfortable in this mansion. It was too big, too ostentatious for my less affluent upbringing. It seemed more haunted than inviting, but gradually we made it into a home—*our* home named Windara. I actually loved the process of warming it up, creating our adventure wall in the library with all the photos of our trips and escapades in, under, and over water, as well as on and off the ground.

Mark had just hung up from giving Dennis Clifton our new phone numbers. "God, I love that guy. He said something today that is really true. 'If money will solve it, it isn't a problem.'"

Mark and I were facing two challenges simultaneously — neither of which money would solve. While we continued to work alongside the other leaders trying to preserve a level playing field for everyone in Nu Skin, we were still embroiled in finding solutions for Mark's addiction. Going through rehab didn't end the problem. Mark had good days and bad days as he searched for solutions that would work for him. We talked openly about the options open to us, but we were far from out of the woods on conquering his chemical dependency.

"I've never known anyone who has struggled with this before. I had no idea how tough it is," I told him.

"You wouldn't believe how hard it is. It's on your mind every minute of every day."

"You're through the worst of it, you know." I was overwhelmed with respect for his strength. Standing behind him, I put my arms around his neck, and whispered, "Sweetheart, I love you so much."

"Why?"

"I can't explain it. But I've never loved you more."

"Just trust me to solve this, okay? And no matter what, don't give up on me. I know we have some adjustments to make." We had been backing away from some of our social interaction during this time. Mark didn't need the added pressure of covering this up in front of friends. "And thanks for not judging me."

"What's to judge? It's a disease. I don't know if it happened genetically or circumstantially, but it happened. All we have to figure out is how to get it behind you."

"You know, I would understand if you want out. You hadn't bargained for this."

"You have no idea how much I thought about it while you were gone. But now...now I couldn't leave you."

"I don't want your pity."

"Ogod, it is nothing like that. It's...it's you. You're one of the strongest people I've ever known. I don't know if I could handle it. But you're so determined to find some resolution."

"You are part of what drives me. I don't want to lose you."

"Don't worry, sweetheart. I'm not going anywhere. And if *you* ever do again, I'll follow you."

He smiled. It was our inside joke.

I knew he was getting better when the poetry started flowing again. We went out to dinner, just the two of us; and while we were waiting to be served, he read his latest prose poem to me.

They all began as mere thoughts one afternoon, simple, lazy thoughts that would drift through my mind and awaken me to a new life fraught with infinite possibilities. And I, lost in those thoughts, became awakened to a part of my own heart and soul that had lay dormant for so many years as to nearly perish.

It began with a thought of her smile, the perfect white teeth, the all-consuming facial posture that so transcends a superficial grin. Yes, I first thought of that smile and something began to stir in the very depth of my being.

Then I thought of her power and gently, mentally walked through so many recent events in which her powerful spirit dominated the room...a non-threatening power that brought others present to the unmistakable realization that her strength permeated through each conversation. Yes, I then felt her power.

Then I thought of her movements, a frisky colt prancing wildly through dew-covered, misty Kentucky pastures, kicking, pent-up, frolicking energy dying to be released one untamed step at a time. I next saw her movements and breathed deeply with awe.

Then I experienced her kiss, and the world became for me a furnace of passion burning non-destructively in the darkest corner of my soul... but burning to be sure. And when she left my bed and walked from the room, she took all the oxygen with her. I next felt her kiss, and for the first time lost myself in her.

Last I experienced her body, a man and a woman scaling the heights together, tentative for fear of a plunge to emotional death. Yet filled with the reckless abandon of two starving animals who, having stumbled upon a lesser species, devour it until satisfied. Such was the all-consuming intimacy of that first penetration. She breathed me and I her.

I now realize it was God, the omniscient Creator, manifest in a touch between two hungry souls. Two spirits of light who but days prior refused eternal union, yet now, so immersed in one another could dwell upon little else. We love... we love as none before us and in this realm of dreams-become-reality, I thank you for the smile, the power, the movements, the kiss, the body, which together have fed my starved soul.

This then is love, this then is the God I've sought for a lifetime and found buried within the depths of my own heart, dormant until you.

"Sweetheart, where does that come from? I wish I could express myself like that."

"Frankly, I like the way you express yourself. Speaking of that, how about a foot, butt, and back rub tonight? I'm feeling pretty achy."

We had made a significant turnaround in our relationship. Yet I knew we weren't over all the hurdles. We were taking one day at a time. I would stand by him as long as his goal was recovery. I didn't know how, but I knew we'd find answers for him. They had to be out there. How did other recovering addicts cope with their habit? I could picture Mark saying to crowds of Nu Skin distributors as he attempted to send them out motivated and confident in their own abilities, "If anyone can, you can too." Well, he was right. And we could too.

"Are you awake?" Mark asked softly early the next morning.

"Yeah...are you?" The absurdity of the question made me start to giggle.

"Don't go away."

"No fair brushing your teeth."

"You know me. I have to go to the bathroom."

"But if you brush your teeth, I want to brush mine."

He didn't say anything. I watched him walk back into the room and walk over to the stereo. On came our favorite theme song, "Somewhere in Time." It had been a while since we had made love in the morning.

As we wandered downstairs together hand in hand, it was still early, almost 5:30. We each put on our coffee. We made separate pots because his could walk on its own power, and he was the only person who could drink it.

"Hey, come back after you pour your coffee. I have something I want to read to you."

Sitting in one of the two red leather chairs in front of his desk, clasping my creamed and sweetened coffee with both hands, I was ready.

"This is something I wrote for you. Actually, I have been working on it for a while. But I think I have it to the point that I'm ready to share it with you.

> *Within this world of countless souls*
> *We've come and gone through many lives,*
> *As men who fought in valiant wars,*
> *And women who have been their wives.*
>
> *We've been together many times*
> *Like fishing boats returned to shore,*
> *It is again a Powerful Force*
> *Uniting our two lives once more.*

As Teilhard noted in his works,
It is through love that we are born
By loving others we love Him
Whether they're family or forlorn.

Drawn ever closer to the Omega
By the example of our shared life
Raising the consciousness of love,
Through harmony as well as strife.

Would that Love becomes the focal point
As we watch our species evolve
Transforming hurts and personal discord
Into harmonious resolve.

Let's never take for granted
One single precious waking hour,
We'll show our love throughout each day
And sharing it we'll sense His Power.

To have finally found our soul mate
Is to discover the priceless pearl
The depth of this far-reaching love
Impacts every aspect of our world.

The lives we touch together
Will draw us closer to our goal,
Creating new ways to serve and love
radiating from our inmost soul.

I grasped the meaning behind the words and appreciated how
Mark had captured my love for Teilhard de Chardin. My discovery
of Teilhard back in the 60s was a life-changing event. I wrote the
thesis for my theology degree on this man's worldview.

Mark seemed determined to recapture the time we'd lost while
apart. While it may have only been a month physically, it felt like
at least half a year emotionally. After reading the poem aloud, he
handed it to me, and I sat reading and rereading it. The phone
rang. It was 6:00 a.m., and our day was begun.

As I left the room, I heard his usual opener. "If I were any
better, I'd be twins." I searched through our library and pulled

out an old copy of Teilhard's *The Divine Milieu*. The book fell open to a passage I had read many times: "It is easy to love those who love us, to love those with whom we share an affinity. It is relatively easy to love the poor and the sick and the lame—out of sympathy if nothing else. But to be drawn to someone with whom we share no common values, who is completely out of sync with our world—through the magnetism of the world movement to become one with itself and toward that end to become one with God—that is Love."

As I walked back into Mark's office, I heard him signing off. "I love you, too, brother."

"Dennis Clifton?"

"Yeah, he wanted to talk about the Nathan situation. He is so frustrated over it."

"What did you say to him?"

"I don't know. The guy makes me as mad as anyone else. It's okay if I rant and rave about him to you. But when other people do, I find myself defending him. Underneath all the b.s. is a guy I could like."

With the Teilhard book still in my hand, I read Mark the passage. "Do you think this might apply to Nathan? I mean, what if we reached out to him, could it change anything?"

"I've always liked Nathan...apart from the difference in our business ethics, I mean. He's a bright guy. I like the way he sees the bigger picture."

"Your poem got me thinking about the Teilhardian philosophy. Somehow I think it fits what we're battling with Nathan."

Mark had a short attention span. I often found that I had to avoid superfluous words and get right to the point to hold his attention. But this morning, he was as eager to sit and philosophize as I was. "What's that?" he asked with apparent genuine interest.

"Teilhard often compares the process of drawing closer to God and to other people to an upside-down cone with the round base representing the Alpha (the beginning) and the tip of the point symbolizing the Omega (the ultimate final point of convergence). The Force attracting all things to itself runs from the Alpha to the

Omega like an axial rod. As this Charismatic Power pulls all things inward towards Itself, we become closer both to each other and to this Central Shaft. As time itself moves us from Alpha toward Omega, we come to understand that we are simultaneously becoming closer to everything around us. Whether we are aspiring to become one with the Axis or one with the periphery of the cone, it doesn't matter. It is one and the same. In striving for unity, we ultimately become one with each other and one with the Omega."

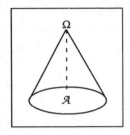

"Hey, I like that. I may borrow it for my next talk. That's absolutely perfect to describe what we're all about in our business. Maybe instead of whining to Blake, I should try to work it out with Nathan."

After more discussion, Mark phoned Nathan and left a message on his answering machine. Later, when Nathan got back to him, they talked at length. I walked in the room as Mark was winding down the conversation.

"Hey, stud, you wouldn't believe what we could do with you and me on the same team. I mean, it would be phenomenal!" Mark came away from the conversation feeling hopeful. At least the groundwork was set.

With fall coming, Mark and I began having some friends over for Monday night football. This was a tradition with our friends, John and Nancy Flanigan. As they chose to ease up on hosting weekly gatherings, we offered to have them at our home once a month or so. The real football fans gathered in the library and watched on the big screen, and those of us who loved the social part gathered in the over-sized kitchen. Mark loved to cook up a big batch of his famous chili, and I made the corn bread and salad. Dinner was served at halftime with the help of our housekeeper, Cyndi.

We still had our challenges, but all in all, life felt balanced again with a solid marriage, close friends, and our family nearby.

The house was a perfect gathering place for Christmas

celebrations. What started out with the aura of a haunted house soon was transformed into a warm, loving home. With a large gathering of family and friends, we celebrated our second anniversary and, with Amy home, welcomed in the holidays. Mark described it as "just a wee little bit of heaven" as I found another poem inside a card on Christmas morning. It began:

> *These two have been the finest years*
> *Of any in my life,*
> *Since you abandoned politics*
> *And chose to be my wife.*

I scanned down the poem and felt his honesty in these lines:

> *Sometimes I fear that couples*
> *Enduring countless years,*
> *So fraught with daily challenges,*
> *With trials, toil and tears...*
>
> *Begin to take for granted,*
> *The joys they early knew,*
> *As if what once attracted both,*
> *They, through the years, outgrew.*
>
> *But that is not the way I feel,*
> *And on this Christmas morn,*
> *I recommit my heart to you,*
> *My Christmas love reborn.*

During those special times, it always seemed that nothing could disturb our peace. But life is a series of ups and downs. It just is. No matter how much we may want to cling to a joyous, peace-filled moment, it slips away from us; and nothing that we do can hold it forever.

The New Year brought a recurrence of the old problem. I

was in the office going over bills when my eye caught one from a pharmacy in Idaho. It was for a few hundred dollars for two prescriptions of Lorcet, a trade name for Vicodin, which apparently had been sent here in December. As I scanned the invoice, I noted in the annual summary that there had been more than $2,200 in prescriptions from this pharmacy for 1993. I kept staring at it in disbelief.

This has to be a mistake. Maybe it's a summary of the past year. I broke out in a cold sweat, and my teeth started chattering. I sat there for a long time before I finally picked up the phone and made the long-distance call to the pharmacy, asking to speak with the owner. It wasn't a mistake. He told me both prescriptions had been filled last month and issued by the same doctor as before. The chills were dissipating as I felt my whole body trembling with anger. I challenged the owner of the pharmacy for having sent prescriptions across state lines. He didn't argue. He acted mortified to be caught in the act of what I was describing as an interstate crime. We ended the conversation with him assuring me that this wouldn't happen again. I guaranteed him I had no intention of participating in this sham by paying the bill. That should definitely discourage any future shipments. And it did.

My next phone call was to the doctor. No call back. I tried to talk to Mark, but he was in absolute denial—the first response of an addict. By Mark's own definition, one I'd heard him give innumerable times from the stage, denial is a self-imposed coping mechanism designed to protect the ego from information it just can't handle.

The next couple of weeks were abysmal. Every fax we received about the pre-activity of Nu Skin running amok in Japan depressed us further. Countless phone calls came in with varying stories of how enthusiasm turned to despair as good people lost their best leads to operators who had been taught how to advance into a country prior to its official opening. Mark was avoiding me. The doctor was avoiding me. I felt completely isolated and powerless over everything happening in my life.

Finally, on February 4, I did the only thing that was within my power to do: I sent the doctor a strong letter confronting him with the situation. I told him how sickened I was to discover that just five months since our last confrontation, he was willing to risk everything and prescribe this medication again. I reminded him how the drugs nearly destroyed my marriage to Mark and, in fact, according to the treatment center staff, nearly destroyed Mark. I assured him that I would not drop the matter—not until I was convinced beyond any doubt that this would *never* happen again.

I waited a few days and still received no response. It was then that I decided to call his State Medical Board. It was a difficult call to make; but once I was on the phone, there was no turning back. I reported the details of the entire situation to a man who identified himself as an examiner, explaining how I had held off exposing the doctor the first time it had happened.

Much to my surprise, the Medical Board made a call to the doctor right away. I wasn't accustomed to having government bureaucracy move on anything swiftly. The doctor called Mark and pleaded with him to get me to back off. With everything on the line, Mark finally admitted to me that he was back up to full dosage on the same drug again.

"Goddamn it, Rene. Why can't you stay out of this? It isn't his fault. I'm the one to blame."

"I agree. But it took both of you to make this happen. He is a doctor, and he should have stood up to you. I backed off the first time it happened. I'm not backing off this time. He needs to be stopped from ever doing this again."

"You're just being vindictive. You don't care about me. If you did, you'd back off."

"Actually, under the circumstances, my stand on this is the deepest sign of love I can give you. It may not look or feel like it, but I believe anything short of this would be enabling. And I don't care how far back your friendship goes. What he is doing is harmful to you, and this needs to be stopped. That's all there is to it."

"This is about control. You are a controller—do you know that? Okay, so you've made your point. Now let it go. It's over."

"Mark, how will I ever know that? When is an addiction ever really over?" I enunciated every single word precisely, emphasizing that this was the ultimate question.

I felt he heard me because of the pause before he spoke. "Look, we're talking about someone's life here. I don't want to see my friend hurt because of me. Can't we just let him off the hook, and you and I will work things out between us?"

"First, I have to make certain that the supply is cut off."

"Oh, you don't have to worry about that. You've cut me off with the doc and the pharmacy. Neither of them will ever be involved with me again after you put the fear of God into them. No, you don't have to worry about that at all. It's over with them. Period. End of the story."

The tension between Mark and me was at an all-time high. He moved downstairs to one of the other bedrooms. We didn't talk. We didn't sleep or eat in the same room. We didn't have any kind of interchange for days. Chris and Amy, both living in dorms at college, were acutely aware of what was happening and seemed affected by the cold war. Though we generally avoided that subject, I communicated more frequently with each of them. The unspoken message I felt from them was their seeking my reassurance that we would all come through this with our family intact.

Paradoxically, on Valentines' Day, Mark left town to do a meeting for a new distributor and, out of character, went without me. I felt the pain of his not-so-subtle message and used the opportunity to pour my heart out to him in a letter. When I finished, I reread the core parts of my message to be sure I was saying what I really meant.

> There is no other way to say this but to reinforce bluntly what I have already said. I don't like drugs. I don't like your being on drugs. I don't like drugs controlling our lives.... But I realize that I can't change this. As long as you choose to be on them, you will be. I also realize that it is *your* choice.

So what are my options? Stick with my philosophy that I have pledged all along—you must choose between drugs and me. Or stay with this marriage and find a way to cope. Either choice is because I love you, so love has no bearing on my decision. I told you a few days ago that I want to work out a way that I can stand by you through this. Before I could ever choose to leave, I want to first try to stay. I realize that what I decide for me may be preempted by you at any time. You may decide that you want to leave, thereby freeing yourself to take your pills with no one to look over your shoulder—no one to love you, but no one to deter you either.

One thing I am going to do, regardless of what happens, is seek help. Beginning tomorrow morning, I am getting counseling for myself. But I realize that there are limits to what anyone can do for me. That is only one step. Secondly, I am going to reinforce inside myself, almost like a mantra, that I can't change the situation—I can only change me. Thirdly, I want to work on areas of personal growth within myself beyond the effect of your drugs on my life, things that I want to improve about myself. And, lastly, I want to work on the growth of our relationship.

Even this didn't break the silence. *Sweetheart, tell me you don't like what I did. Tell me you're angry. But talk to me. I need to know what is going on inside of you.* Silence is the most deadly weapon of all for me. The cold war continued both with Nu Skin and my marriage. Nothing was being resolved in any facet of my life. I felt utterly depressed. Mark couldn't forgive me for going after the doctor and cutting off his supply. He was still sleeping downstairs, and the distance between us was crushing my spirit. I desperately needed communication. Finally, unable to hold it inside anymore, I knocked on his door late one night. He was lying in bed reading. I asked if I could come in and sat down on the bed. I didn't say anything. I couldn't. I felt the veins in my neck quivering and my bottom lip trembling.

"What's the matter?" Mark asked curtly.

"I can't go on like this. Please, talk to me. Say something. Say anything."

Neither of us spoke for a long painful moment. Then the floodgate opened, and I couldn't hold it back. I started crying and couldn't stop. I lay down in his arms and sobbed uncontrollably. I couldn't catch my breath. My nose was running. My eyes were stinging and swollen. I just wanted him to acknowledge me. That's all. It was a long time before I finally quieted down. We lay motionless, and I could hear coyotes crying in the distance. I wondered if their cry was ever like a human cry—of loss or fear or loneliness.

As I lay in his arms, I was emotionally spent. I welcomed the silence. But it was Mark who finally broke it. "I'm sorry for causing you so much pain."

Actually, I had already forgiven him weeks ago. I was gradually coming to understand the plight an addict faces. No one who hasn't experienced it or lived with it can comprehend the intensity of the struggle. Relapse is an inevitable part of the recovery process. I gradually came to expect it and not be surprised by the slips. I still didn't know how we were going to get past this, but I believed that, "if anyone could, we could too."

"I'm sorry if I didn't handle things well. I did the only thing I knew to do. I had to take some action, even if it meant losing you." I was sorry it had taken so much out of both of us to get to this point. "So now what? Can we pick up the pieces and go on with our life...together?"

"Yeah, how 'bout starting by moving back upstairs into our room?" he said quietly.

It was finally over. We held each other most of the night in silence, but it was a tranquil silence unlike that of the previous weeks. We passed through the moment and survived the aftermath of one of the worst conflicts of our married life.

I spoke only to a therapist friend about the situation. While I demonstrated strength on one level, she pointed out to me, I was operating from fear on another—fear that Mark would abandon me. Even more devastating than physical leaving was to have someone I love withdraw emotionally. While I recognized that the addiction issue was the central focus of our life at this time, what I was unable to see, even with the help of counseling, was the lifetime pattern we were both exemplifying. Neither of us could fully know the emotional baggage we each brought with us into our relationship. Few couples ever do. Nor could we possibly comprehend the pain that we would continue to cause each other...because of our baggage.

When Mark Yarnell puts his mind to achieving something, nothing, but nothing, can stand in his way. Mark was motivated like never before to overcome his addiction to Vicodin. Now it became our *mutual* objective to conquer this demon. We considered moving to another state for a few months while he went into a treatment program. But it was conversations with two of my closest friends that led to the decision we ultimately made.

Along with her MSW degree, my friend Nancy had extensive experience in drug counseling because of her longtime work with the homeless population. She recommended that we explore methadone as an option. She had seen many heroin addicts straighten up their lives by going onto this government-sponsored program.

I found Mark in the kitchen rustling up one of his famous home-cooked meals and decided to broach the subject.

"What do you think, sweetheart? Is it worth looking into?" I asked.

"I don't think I could handle it. Methadone clinics have such a...a negative image. I mean, you are really the scum of the earth to have to lower yourself to go on methadone. No, forget it. I wouldn't even consider it."

"I don't know enough about it to have any aversion to trying it. Actually, I don't know anything about it. I'd never heard of it before Nancy brought it up. How many people do?"

"I don't know. Why don't you ask Dorothy Nash Holmes. As DA, I guarantee you she will have an opinion about it."

I immediately picked up the phone and called her. After explaining our situation, I asked what she thought about methadone as an answer for Mark.

"You know, it works. I mean, I've seen lifetime users go on methadone and lead very normal lives."

"But what about people's perception about taking it?" I asked.

"Well, it's legal. It is government-approved. I guess it beats the hell out of illicit use of prescription or street drugs."

"Mark has never used street drugs. His only addiction is to Vicodin, which for years now has been prescribed to him."

"If Mark continues taking those massive doses of Vicodin, he will kill himself. That kind of quantity is deadly, and I would prosecute anyone who was dosing it out to him like that."

"Yeah, I know. That's already happening to the doctor who did. His State Board is investigating the matter right now."

"Well, good for them! I'm glad to hear they take that sort of thing seriously. It really is inexcusable."

"But would Mark's image be hurt if people knew he was on methadone?"

"Well, why does anyone have to know? Can't you just keep it quiet?"

"I suppose, but it bothers him. I guess if there is a negative conotation, it would bother me if I were thinking of taking it."

"In the end, you guys have to be the ones to decide. But when you weigh everything, I think it is a viable solution. It won't give him a high, but it will take away his craving. The downside is that he will have to go into the clinic every morning. They dispense it one day at a time until you prove yourself. And even then, the dispensing of the drug is very controlled. You have to account for every single bottle when they finally approve you for take-home use."

"Why is that?"

"It's a serious drug. If you begin taking it and don't use it properly, or worse, stop taking it too suddenly, it can be fatal. We've had problems at the jail with prisoners who didn't tell us they were on methadone and went into serious withdrawal. It can be scary. If Mark wants to, I would be happy to share with him everything I know about it."

After my conversations with Nancy and Dorothy, Mark talked with them and, though still skeptical, decided to go talk to the director of the local clinic. The director admitted that a person of Mark's stature was not your normal methadone user. But he felt, after hearing Mark's history, that it was a good solution for him. After exploring every other option, we both concluded that this was the answer.

As part of his own recovery, Mark chose to begin working directly with people who suffered from substance abuse. He founded a program called School of Sobriety dedicated to helping alcoholics and addicts become aware that they have a problem and then begin to do something about it. The local district and municipal court judges, whom I introduced to Mark, provided him with "students" who were offered this alternative to serving time in jail. They didn't start out as eager participants. Rarely did they think they had a problem—only bad luck at getting caught. But by the time the class was over, Mark usually had them laughing at themselves and admitting to the wildest things. He loved to come home and share the day's episodes with me.

"I hide my booze in the toilet tank," one woman admitted.

"So what's so strange about that?" Mark probed. "Most alcoholics hide their booze from their family and peers."

"Yeah," she responded, "but I live alone."

Mark was also instrumental in starting a Toastmasters program for prisoners. While they were still incarcerated, the guys would learn to stand in front of an audience and talk about those things—most frequently drugs and alcohol—that put them in prison in the first place. It was designed to give ex-convicts a tool to help them reenter society as a contributing member. They would gain a comfort level talking to schools, clubs, and organizations about avoiding those things that can bring people down and showing, by their example, how it is possible to transform one's life into a force for good.

Mark took on a protégé, David Avery, a prisoner in the Nevada State Penitentiary, who worked closely with him to implement the program. If David typifies what this course can do for prisoners, every warden would want this as part of the prison curriculum. After his release, David later began working with us in our business. He is one of the most positive people to be around and radiates his enthusiasm for life.

Mark began writing for *Success* magazine as well. Through sheer persistence, he convinced the publisher to let him write articles about network marketing for the magazine. It was a major breakthrough for a mainstream periodical to honor our industry by giving Mark a regular column. I busied myself doing a major rewrite, preparing a new edition of Mark's former book, *Power Multi-Level Marketing*. This was the beginning of a writing career that would eventually shape both of our professional lives.

With Mark on the methadone program, our lives settled down. After six months, Mark had been granted "privileges" at the clinic, which allowed him to leave the country with a month's supply of methadone. We were traveling again in our usual style and living a life of carefree abandon, working where we wanted to work, playing where we wanted to play, serving others wherever we could.

Most men who speak for a living use a laser to call the audience's attention to illustrative examples, but few use it as Mark did. Late one afternoon, just before leaving for a speaking engagement, I found him out on our hotel balcony making what sounded like loud bird calls. There he was, holding his laser and shooting the notorious little red ball all over the place as he played with people's minds down on the street. Whether it was on an airplane, a hotel balcony, or with the dog Amy would soon bring home to us, flashing that little red ball around to create wonder was one of his favorite pastimes. At that moment, I knew for certain that everything was back to normal.

From that engagement, we headed to Chicago to teach our first University Certificate Seminar in Network Marketing. After a year of negotiations with the University of Illinois, Chicago, Charles King, Mark and I were ready to launch this historical event—one that would have far-reaching effects on our industry. As I came back to our room after delivering my opening talk, there lying on my pillow was a hurriedly scrawled note on a yellow pad. Oh, not a note, but a poem in true Yarnell style.

> *Oh how I truly love thee*
> *My widdle Weenie Weed,*
> *But now I've got to hurry,*
> *Five minutes to succeed.*
> *I've got to get my tie on,*
> *And change into clean clothes,*
> *Brush my hair, shine my shoes,*
> *Make sure no bald spot shows.*
> *It's twenty after four o'clock*
> *No wait, it's twenty five!*
> *Oh, God, and now the telephone,*
> *And Scott will soon arrive.*
> *That's all for now, as you can see*
> *I've got so much to do,*
> *But never there's too little time*
> *for poetry for you!"*
> *P.S. I love you.*
> *Will you marry me in the morning?*

After all the hoop-la, Nu Skin finally opened in Japan. We enjoyed our time staying in the Ginza district of Tokyo and visiting the less populated parts of Sapporo and Osaka while we worked with our Japanese downline. On the flight home, I took time to do some much-needed journaling. Hurrying through my meal, I cleared my tray table so I could set my laptop on it. With my last entry on the screen, I began to write:

> As we speak at various meetings, I've noticed that Mark is using these opportunities much more frequently to talk about his struggle with substance abuse. I'm so proud of him when he does this. I think it must take tremendous courage. One of the best things addicts or alcoholics can do while in recovery is willingly share their struggle with others. Each time the addiction is shared openly, it reaffirms the recovery of those individuals and radiates outward to help in the recovery

of every person touched by hearing the story. And if they in turn duplicate the process, like network marketing, recovery will begin to reach out exponentially to everyone fighting the disease. Lately I've begun to realize that I've been behaving as if all of this has little to do with me. It has everything to do with me. I live with an alcoholic/addict. My life is enmeshed in his and, as such, I am a co-dependent. If he has the courage to share his experience, why shouldn't I? There are hundreds of thousands of spouses and partners like me who have had little or no experience with substance abuse and are as naïve as I was in understanding it and knowing how to cope with it. Maybe once I gain more perspective, I will one day write about it.

From the co-dependent perspective, addiction is more damaging to a marriage than any adulterous situation. How often I had heard Mark say from stage, "Never trust a man whose wife can't." I often thought I could handle his having an affair more readily. But that is easy for me to say because I knew Mark never would.

Substance abuse can lead to all the "D" words— dishonesty, dissension, divisiveness, denial, if not divorce, and certainly distrust...even in the best of relationships. When it came to drugs, I knew I couldn't trust Mark. His obsession with chemical dependency had built a huge wall between us and exaggerated the smallest of problems into larger ones. But if the Great Wall of China and the Berlin Wall in Germany could come down, so could ours.

The monotonous announcement came on telling us to turn our electronic equipment off and return our seats to their upright position. I leaned over and kissed Mark. Writing about the situation welled up in me incredible appreciation for him and his inner strength in dealing with his disease.

Coming home after a long trip away was always a good feeling. We had so much joy in our lives again. Not the least of which,

Amy had moved home to be with us and finish out her last two years of college. Chris was thrilled. Mark was ecstatic. It was the first time father and daughter had lived together since she was four—sixteen years since the time of his divorce from her mother. Over Christmas break, Amy set out to get us a family dog and cat. She and Chris made a day trip to Sacramento in search of the perfect puppy. They settled on a golden retriever named Codiac. We called him Cody. Mark named the kitten Scuddy Dives, and he quickly became Chris's cat.

All my life I had wanted family, and have always had to go to great lengths to create it. Now for the first time in my life I had an intact family—a husband, a wife, a son, a daughter, a dog, and a cat—all living under one roof and I loved it. Amy worked with us in our office at home, helping support our Nu Skin organization, doing all the computer, e-mail, and web page entries. She assisted her dad in editing his books. She was an aspiring actress and continued to teach me a great deal about step-mother/daughter relationships. My son was also on track to graduate from UNR while working nearly full-time at Project ReStart, serving as an intake worker for homeless people. As a project that I had nurtured, developed, and supported since 1989, it was particularly meaningful to have our daughter helping bring in our revenue and our son working in a field where we could give it away.

Returning from our long road trip, it was comforting to get to my morning routine: affirmations, journaling, catching up with my mail after two weeks on the road. I was just beginning to gain some awareness about my co-dependency, and I wanted to capture it while it was fresh.

> I realize as I look back over this past year, I am still learning how to handle a relapse and to understand that it is an inevitable part of living with an addict. I must constantly remind myself that I can't change the situation and I can't transform my husband. I can only change myself and how I react to the situation. Knowing this takes some of the

pressure off of me. Deciding what to do actually becomes easier because the only transformation that I have control over is my own attitude.

I know now how important it is to be true to myself in these situations, holding on to those things that really matter: the relationship, my family, my values, belief in myself, and belief in us that Mark and I will have the strength to pull through these setbacks. I must say to myself: "It is just a relapse. Nothing more. He slipped and he will recover."

Sometimes I find that it helps me to concentrate on two things. First, using this time to pay closer attention to those aspects within myself I want to change. The greatest spurts of personal growth happen in times of stress and adversity. Second, using this time to focus on Mark's strengths. Substance abusers are already well enough aware of their weaknesses and certainly don't need their partners to remind them. People with addictive personalities often experience major victories in other parts of their lives. They are obsessive about everything, and that very quality can often result in business success or athletic prowess or simply having tremendous perseverance to reach their goals. Concentrating on his successes is an approach I will work harder at mastering.

I was pulled out of my reverie when the phone rang. It came in on my line but was for Mark. I didn't recognize his voice at first, but when I heard Mark take the call, I realized it was the would-be buyer who attempted foreclosure on our home.

"Mark, how are you doing, buddy?"

"Fine, what's up?" Mark responded curtly.

"I don't know if you know, but I had a heart attack."

"I'm sorry to hear that," he responded, removing some of the ice from his voice.

"Well, it wasn't just any ol' heart attack. I actually died on the table. It was an experience I can't even begin to expect anyone to understand. But I felt a white light surrounding me. It was the greatest peace I've ever known. I don't know how long it lasted. The doctor said my heart stopped for about four minutes. Anyway, you know this is not like me to be talking this way, but I am very grateful to be alive. It made me rethink a lot of things. And I just wanted to get back to you, and especially Rene, and say how sorry I am for what I did. It was wrong of me. And I want to make it up to you."

"I'm really proud of you. What you are doing right now takes a very big man. And you are that." Mark was completely sincere.

"Well, I didn't call to get any kudos. I don't deserve them. I want to put a check in the mail to you and let my attorney and Judge Breen know that this stupid lawsuit is over. I'd like to have you and Rene over to the house for dinner sometime...if you'll agree to that. It would make the wife and me very happy. She never did agree with what I had done."

CHAPTER 10

Drug-free at last!
December 1994 – September 1997

B y December Mark was refocused on building our Nu Skin business. "Let's put the past behind us and give Europe our all," Mark said to me one evening. "Craig Bryson thinks we should get over to the UK as soon after the first of the year as possible. Sometime in 1995 Nu Skin will open there."

Nu Skin had made a genuine effort to deal with the international challenges. The company changed its policy and now encouraged distributors with contacts in the new country to go there prior to the opening and have small meetings—no more than five—introducing people from that country to the coming Nu Skin opportunity. I felt this was Craig's way of reaching out to Mark to tilt the scale back to neutral after all that had gone wrong in Japan. Although Craig was part of the founding family and indirectly tied to Nathan, we had always liked him and were glad to have him back in our lives.

"You've never been to Europe," I said to Mark. "I passed through Gatwick in the early eighties on my way to Ireland several times, but I haven't spent any real time in London since I graduated from college in the sixties. This could be a fun adventure." I loved the thought of spending time there with Mark.

With that thought planted, it was just a couple of weeks later that Mark received a call from John Kavanagh, a Brit well experienced in network marketing in his country.

"Mark, my partner, Trisha Derham, and I are looking for a stable network marketing company. We read the book you and your wife wrote, *Power Multi-Level Marketing*, and we thought we'd ring you up and see if you know if there is a good company coming to the UK."

"How fortuitous!" Mark exclaimed. "Your timing is phenomenal."

"Timing is everything, as they say. Trisha and I are keen to get started and really build a dynamic group. But we want to check everything out thoroughly before we begin the process of bringing everyone we know into a company. Can we come out and visit you and Rene?"

John and Trisha spent some time in December with us, and the following month, per Craig's encouragement, we went to visit them. They helped us lease a flat in the Kensington district near Harrods where we both loved to shop. There, the couple began introducing us to many of their friends and people formerly associated with the networking industry from all around London.

It was good to see Mark fired up again. We knew we had spent way too much time fighting the system in Japan. This time we were just going to lead our people by example and build an organization in the UK. We didn't want any more battles in our life. Mark absolutely loved the recruiting phase of our business. When he was building our organization, he was the happiest man alive.

But there was Nathan, right in the thick of things again, teaching people, "to sign up with the family line where you will get information sooner and better than everyone else," as he was recorded saying. Gary Wattenburg, a competitor of Nathan's, emerged on the scene with similar but innovative ways to violate the policies and claim his share of the market out in front of everyone else. When the Brits got wind of their tactics, their reaction was, "At the end of the day, why hasn't the company just kicked the bloody blokes out?" Of course we wondered the same, but the Brits do have a way with words.

"What should we do if someone wants to switch lines because they're not being supported where they are?" distributors would ask Mark.

Mark had a reputation for guiding distributors to take the high road. "Tell them they are welcome to use our system, but they need to stay where they are. Otherwise it will destroy the integral structure which makes our industry so extraordinary."

"There is this prospect whom I meant to call, and now I ran into him at one of the meetings. Is he fair game before he signs?"

"Absolutely not. Whoever thought enough of him to be the first to invite him to look at the business deserves to sign him. Even if the prospect hints that he is looking for a sponsor, tell him to respect the integrity of the system and stay with the person who brought him to the meeting. What goes around will come back around to you in the long run."

Mark was torn up inside about the changing culture that permitted unfair competition within the company. He was the champion of the little guy, the distributor who had only one contact in a new country and was banking everything on that person building a dynasty.

Back home in Reno again, standing in the kitchen fixing a snack, Mark looked defeated. "I'm running out of steam. This whole thing is a giant whirlwind that can't be contained."

"They could have contained it a couple of years ago. Had the problem been nipped in the bud...." My words trailed off. Mark knew where I was going with that thought.

"Yeah, but they didn't. And I don't feel right about much of anything anymore."

"The hard part is knowing how to guide people. Before, it was always so clear."

"I just don't think I can speak with the same conviction anymore. I mean, you and I are so driven by the ethics of the situation. But where did it get some of our people in Japan? They followed my advice, and now they're out of the company and lost out on a great opportunity. Their people bought into the pitch for the family line.

Every time I think about it, I get mad all over again. What happened wasn't right. It just wasn't right. Period. End of the story."

We gradually backed away from giving distributors moral advice about building a network in a foreign market. For us, it was a Catch-22. If we guided them to operate on our set of principles, we could easily curtail their ability to build a business that would allow them to support their families. But neither was it an option for us to guide them to follow the standard business procedures that seemed to be infiltrating our company. So we said very little, leaving distributors the freedom to run their businesses by their own set of values as they saw fit.

During the pre-launch, as fate would have it, one of our second-level British prospects sent out direct mailings announcing the new opportunity coming to the UK and touted the Yarnell Organization as part of the attraction for joining his team. This activity led to our receiving a letter from the legal department. The letter dated May 31, 1995, was destined to change our lives forever. Addressed to both of us, it read like a legal document.

Since the Company has found evidence that the aforementioned activity has taken place in relation to your distributorship, the Distributor Violations Review Committee (DVRC) has decided that the following disciplinary action will be imposed: (1) 10% of total worldwide commissions to be withheld for 1 month; (2) 10% of total European commissions for 3 months; (3) Sponsorship hold in Europe for 3 months (during this period of time, you may not introduce any individual into the business, nor may Distributor Agreements be submitted under your account or on behalf of anyone in your organization.); (4) Correspondence to downline which acknowledges prior mistakes, offers restitution to anyone who feels they may have been misled, and asks all affected individuals to discontinue any and all European activity until specific countries are officially opened.

"After years of putting pressure on Nu Skin to take action on violators, this is the monster we created?" Mark said in disbelief.

"It looks like for the crime of having our name extolled by our prospective downline, we have been penalized big time!"

"Wait a minute. Let me get this straight. Are they saying we can't bring anybody into the business ourselves *and* neither can anyone in our entire organization for the first three months?"

"It's ambiguous, but that's how it reads to me," I responded.

"Are they out of their minds? John Kavanagh isn't going to sit around and wait for three months until our penalty time lapses. Wait 'til I tell Clifton. 'Oh, by the way, brother, no one in your organization can sign anyone up for three months in Europe.' Jeez! They've lost it. They've really lost it. Because of one goddamn brochure, our entire organization is being held hostage. This is outrageous!"

After nearly two months of letters and phone calls back and forth, we received another letter from the Nu Skin Appeals Committee. I took it up to Mark, and he read it to himself.

"Hey, get this," Mark exclaimed, while he read from the document.

> The Committee is cognizant of the fact that Mark and Rene Yarnell may not have been the direct catalyst behind the creation and distribution of each of the violative documents. *[Thanks a lot.]* However, in conjunction with enjoying the upside of the business from distributors in their organization, they are also responsible as leaders for the downside of their organization's actions. Therefore, the following disciplinary action will be imposed against the Yarnell Organization....

"It goes on to issue the same penalties as before, omitting the one preventing us and our entire downline from being able to sponsor distributors from Europe in the first three months. Wow! We're making headway with an appeal board that we didn't know existed."

"I think I would have liked to meet my accusers and judges face to face," I said. "But even without us present, someone had the presence of mind to realize that you can't penalize a hundred thousand people for the actions of one."

Once again, instead of focusing our energy exclusively on building this new market, we were sidetracked into wasting energy arguing with the Nu Skin legal department. Unconsciously, Mark and I divided our responsibilities so as to diffuse our energies as little as possible. He was the master recruiter. I would take on the battle with Nu Skin so that he could stay focused on building our group.

I phoned Mike Smith, the legal head honcho. After weeks of delay, he finally returned my calls. Mark and I both liked Mike. This couldn't be a pleasant experience for him either. I tried to keep that thought in mind as I spoke to him. He wasn't the enemy, just the liaison. We didn't think Blake or Steve were adversaries either. Maybe it was all a simple matter of a bunch of guys who were just too nice to lower the boom on the real culprits. And in lieu of that, they didn't know what to do. So the pendulum was swinging from far left to far right. And with the creation of the Distributor Violations Review Committee, we happened to get caught in the oscillation.

"Mike, Mark and I appreciate your acknowledging our innocence in your letter and the fact that we are being punished because of our 'upside' earnings potential rather than our illegal activities."

"Well, Rene, you know I think the world of you and Mark. In fact, you are the ones who pressed us so hard to take definitive action."

"Mike, you're the lawyer, but it would really help if you'd explain this legalese to me. Even though you don't believe we were, as your letter states, the 'direct catalyst behind the creation and distribution of the violative documents,'—by the way, 'violative', who dreams up words like that?—we are being penalized because of our 'enjoying the upside of the business from distributors in our organization.' What does that mean exactly?"

"What part of it don't you understand?" he asked cautiously.

"Well, based on what I think I understand, and following this kind of logic, would it not make sense that Richard Kall, Craig

Bryson (who encouraged us to get over to the UK), Craig Tillotson, and Clara McDermott—everyone upline to us—be penalized as well since they all stand to benefit just as much as we will?"

"But you were the ones specifically named in the brochure. It was highlighting the Yarnell Organization."

"Exactly like the 'family's name' was flaunted outrageously by Nathan in Japan and now again in Europe. We still have reams of evidence of this, as I'm sure you do. So, are Clara, Craig, and Craig penalized for Nathan's using their name? They certainly stand to benefit from the 'upside' of that activity."

"I can't say, Rene. You know that."

"The company's policy that refuses to acknowledge who has been nailed and for what amount makes me and everyone else crazy. But it doesn't matter. You know and I know that 'the family' isn't being penalized for this. But, Mike, what's the difference between their situation and ours? The only circumstance that would make sense holding upline responsible for downline activity is if the upline directly coached the downline (and we certainly have instances of that happening in Japan and now in the UK). Short of that, I think this is something you may want to rethink before you set it as a precedent."

"But this is also the very point that you were making in regard to Nathan. All of you wanted him held accountable."

"Of course, because he taught everyone how to 'push the envelope.' And we have him on cassette and video as evidence. Don't you see the difference? Mike, tell me the truth. Is this all a ruse to get Mark and me to back off of our campaign to try to stop Nathan?"

"You can be sure Nathan and I have had some conversations similar to this one."

"And no matter what you ask him to do or not do, he does whatever suits him. And you let him get away with it. It is clear to everyone in the know that 'the family' does not play by the same rules as the rest of us."

"I know you feel that way, but there is a lot more to it."

"I know, and you just can't say...."

"But I can't. I really can't."

"So, Mike, how can you justify the times when Nathan, the beloved son-in-law, has been caught red-handed, repeatedly going into countries early when it was against policy? And teaching others how to sign up early in Hong Kong, how to advance illegal products across borders, how to set up warehouses of products, how to steal distributors on opening day, how to offer bribes to switch lines, and, of course, always flaunting the advantages of belonging to 'the family line'. And, Mike, excuse me, but the sad part is…he is right. There are advantages."

"We are as upset about some of these problems as you are, and we are addressing them. It's just that we can't tell you our specific actions, and I know that is hard for you to accept."

I hung up the phone shaking with emotion. But I felt better because, in my heart, I knew Mike and I wanted the same things. At least, I'd gotten it off my chest and felt I'd been heard. I ran up to Mark's office and gave him a blow by blow of my conversation with Mike.

"I'm glad you're handling that end, honey. I'd be wringing someone's neck by now if I had to deal with it. I'm trying to focus all of my energy on building a positive spirit among our UK group."

"I know there is some frustration with them; but for the most part, they are keeping their eye on the bigger picture, thanks to you."

We stood and held each other. We needed one another more than ever as we fought our way through these battles. Other than some incidental income from books and training materials, Nu Skin was our sole source of income. But more than that, it had become our family and our way of life. Understandably, these issues consumed us. Mark and I were not going to become silent on this matter of ethics until we solved the problem.

Mark and I weren't alone. Richard, after one of his many 5:00 a.m. calls to my husband, without fanfare or concern for how the company felt, called together a group of his leaders in Stamford, Connecticut, and officially formed the Kall Global Network

(KGN). It was a meeting charged with emotion. Richard relied heavily on Mark's perceptions as to whether he was moving the group in the right direction. Neither Mark nor Richard had any doubt that this was the right action to take. It was less about blame toward anyone at the company and more of a realization that Nu Skin had grown too large for us to be able to monitor every new or prospective distributor. Much like the last attempt at forming our own group, the work session resulted in a petition, which expressed the anguish that many of us were experiencing and our sincere desire to work with the company to get things back on track. Specific requests were made as to what was needed. In order to keep attracting others to this opportunity, we insisted that there must be a level playing field for all people in both the national and international realms. The company took the formation of the KGN seriously. This time, no attempt was made to stop it.

With our ability to go into Europe as a united group and the strength of the entire KGN behind our organization, Mark and I redirected our entire focus on building our group through teleconference calls with our UK connections. They were "keen" on this form of support, and it was an effective and *approved* method for introducing their prospective business associates to our business.

Just at the perfect time for our European launch, a new magazine published by *Success* called *Working at Home* was introduced to the industry. Mark and I were one of twenty or so business owners to be featured in the magazine—all entrepreneurs who had achieved their success by working home-based businesses. Our six-page article, with full-page pictures of our home, entitled "King and Queen of the Castle" was used by our downline worldwide to build their organizations. Although it was more helpful to the English-speaking countries—America, Britain, Australia, and New Zealand—we were told the Japanese found it just as useful for the pictures.

On October 9, Nu Skin dismissed all restrictions on us and

issued us a refund lowering our entire fine to $5,000. I knew we had Mike to thank for this. At the same time, it was announced that Nu Skin Europe would open the following month.

"We have some phenomenal people joining us in Europe." Mark's arms spread wide as he said *phenomenal.* "And I'm looking forward to logging some quality time in Europe. I'm going to have to find some solution about the methadone. We may want to spend a couple of months at a time over there, and I can't take that large a supply with me."

"We'll figure it out. You've really made a beautiful adjustment. When we're out traveling and working with our people, I'm so proud to be your wife."

"I'm proud that you *are* my wife. You did a helluva job handling the Nu Skin ordeal. You're so much more...diplomatic than I could be. And patient. God, how could you keep writing all those letters?"

"I'm not sure the Nu Skin management would describe me that way. But how could I not keep persisting? And while I did that, you stayed focused. And look what you've built, sweetie, with John and Trisha there to organize it all. We are really fortunate to have had them come into our lives. They've worked hard with me to get our training materials in place too. We're ready to open."

"Over 1,500 people have signed in. This is unbelievable." Mark let out that squeal that sounded like a cross between a chimpanzee and a wild birdcall. He was elated, to say the least.

"With so much chaos on opening day at the home office, I'm glad we chose to hold our own private celebration at this elegant hotel in London."

"Yeah, I agree. And besides, Peter Powderham will be out later this evening to speak to our people." Peter was the newly appointed General Manager of Nu Skin in the UK. He was a friend of John Kavanagh's, and we had been instrumental in recommending that he be considered for the position.

I loved to see Mark this happy. He was smiling that boyish

grin that spoke volumes. The launch of Nu Skin UK was one of the most exciting events in which either of us had ever participated. Organized by one of John's top distributors, Scott Lucy, and with the coordinated effort of so many of our British leaders, our grand opening of the Yarnell Organization was beyond our wildest expectations. All of those who signed up were part of John and Trisha's organization, the only UK distributorship we chose to have on our frontline.

With Amy and Chris holding down the fort at home, Cyndi housekeeping, and Mom and Amy running our office, Mark and I were free to begin searching for the ideal spot for a second home in Europe. Finally, after a fun-filled exploration, we settled on a small village on the westerly side of Switzerland at about 1,000 meters elevation. Gstaad was a perfect place for paragliders, which met Mark's adrenaline craving. It was where the Swiss Open was held every year, which met my tennis needs. There we felt we could enjoy the excitement of experiencing a new culture while also living close to the European distributors joining our organization. We welcomed the opportunity to expand our horizons culturally while introducing our industry and our company to a whole new part of the world.

We gradually developed a routine. We'd fly on TWA from Reno to St. Louis and from there to London, where we'd conduct meetings for our distributors. We loved walking through the Kensington district, shopping at Harrods, taking in an occasional play, and finding quaint little spots for cappuccino in the Chiswick district, where John and Trisha lived.

With our largest group in the United Kingdom, we had ample opportunity to travel by train all over Great Britain, Scotland, and Ireland—b'gosh and b'gora, lands of both of our ancestors. We made new friends, stayed in their homes, dined with them, and shared some of the intimacies of their lives and hopes and disappointments. On our way to and from the UK, we would occasionally stop in Amsterdam, where our Nu Skin European corporate office was located. Then onto Paris.

We would romp through the back streets of the Left Bank, hand in hand, listening to barkers on the street enticing us into their Greek restaurants. Mark loved to stop and talk with them. Language was never a barrier to a man as demonstrative as Mark Yarnell.

"Hey, brother, you are good at convincing me to try food in this window that I've never heard of before. With your enthusiasm, you'd be unbelievable in my business."

"Hey, man, it is difficult, yes?" the barker said in broken English.

"Are you kidding? I could get a dog with a note in its mouth to fifty thousand francs a month."

They laughed. Who knows if they understood what he was saying? It didn't matter. Mark was passionate about recruiting. He didn't speak a word of French, and even that didn't stop him. He loved people and enjoyed the process of arousing their interest.

Sometimes I wandered through the city on my own, stopping in Nôtre Däme for morning Mass or visiting the motherhouse of my former religious community on Rue de Bac. There the body of St. Catherine Labouré is fully preserved and laid out wearing the habit that I wore while I belonged to the order of the Daughters of Charity of St. Vincent de Paul. Just being there put me in touch with my roots and reminded me of a saying from Simone Weil: "We possess no other life...then the treasures stored up from the past and digested, assimilated, and created afresh by us."

From Paris, we would catch the train to Geneva. We loved our layover in Montreaux, where we discovered some of the best calamari anywhere in the world—in the train station of all places. But the ride through the Swiss Alps from Montreaux to Gstaad took our breath away. Summer or winter, it was one of the most spectacular scenic areas either of us had ever seen.

"I didn't know places like this even existed," I whispered to Mark as I leaned my head on his shoulder, looking up through the glass roof to catch another glimpse of the Alps.

"No wonder Prince Charles brings his sons skiing here...and Julie Andrews has made this her second home. I can't believe the number of famous people who have made this discovery."

"Gstaad next," called out the conductor. We got to know many of the conductors after so many months of living there. In Europe we went everywhere by train.

"We'll send for you if we find work," Mark teased them as he stepped off the platform, reaching for his backpack. As I grabbed my own and waved goodbye, I knew they didn't understand the joke, but they played along with him.

It was only a few blocks to our chalet, so we loved to walk home from the station. Saying hello to the shopkeepers along the way and stopping for a "croque madame" (a Swiss version of a grilled ham and cheese sandwich with an egg on top), we knew we were home. "Gstaad, how I love you," was the slogan of the village. Our sentiments exactly! We had made the right decision in selecting Switzerland as our European base. The Swiss people were so caring, the country so clean, and their manner so welcoming.

Mark and I led a simple life in Gstaad. Early in the mornings, he could hardly wait to go into town to buy bread just out of the oven along with farm-fresh eggs and yogurt. He discovered arugula, which he loved to have with Swiss mozzarella cheese and garden-grown tomatoes. We found joy in little things—a slower pace of life, the sweetness of the people, and the acts of kindness they showed us.

There was only one dry cleaner in the village, run by a heavyset Swiss-German frau. The first time Mark and I went there, we were getting ready to do a series of Nu Skin meetings and needed our clothes back within a couple of days.

"Thursday would be good," Mark said graciously.

"Nein!" she blurted out with her hands on her ample hips. "You get on Saturday," she announced in a voice that I would not have questioned.

I looked at Mark and could see moonbeams dancing in his head. Here it comes. I just didn't know what it would be. Suddenly Mark was down on his knees, reaching out to grasp the hand of this mannish, overbearing woman. "Oh, please, could we have them back in two days? I have to go on a tour and speak to lots of people. It would be humiliating if I had to do it in my underwear.

You could save me from this embarrassment. Such a beautiful woman like yourself wouldn't want to see a grown man put to such shame."

I could tell this woman hadn't a clue what Mark was saying. It was the voice, the mannerisms, the posturing that was her undoing. Her hands left her hips and began to clutch at her heart, while she looked heavenward, fluttering her eyes. Mark had penetrated what I thought was one of the thickest human walls imaginable. "You are crazy man. But for you, I do. Thursday, ya!"

From that moment on, we never had trouble getting our dry cleaning when we needed it. Sometimes Mark would come in with clothes in his "special" laundry bag, and take her in his arms and dance her around the store. She would stop whatever she was doing for her "crazy man." On those rare occasions when I came in alone, she would show obvious disappointment. "Where is my crazy man?" she would inquire. "Tell my crazy man come see me." I'm not sure she'd ever had such excitement as during the two years that her crazy man lived in Gstaad.

This little village was a wonderful place to share with friends. John Kavanagh and Trisha Derham spent time with us there, and Ursula and Richard Tracy came to visit. Since Ursula is Swiss, she introduced us to places like Gruyere and enjoyed showing us her country. Our children joined us during the 1996-97 New Year's break. Everyone who came to see us went away joining in the village slogan, "Gstaad, how I love you!"

The cow drives down the main street were typical of our little village. Drivers would patiently pull the cars to the side as one person would lead and at least one would follow behind, moving the herd from one grazing area to another. With gigantic bells dangling around their necks, there was no way to ignore a Swiss cow drive. No matter how many of them passed my window, each time I was compelled to throw open the shutters and watch them go by.

Spending so much time in Europe isolated us somewhat from communication with other Nu Skin leaders. We were off in our own little world.

"I'm so happy here," I commented to Mark as we crawled into bed, snuggling under the down comforter.

"Yeah, it's good for us to get away from all the battles going on back home. I'm sick of it."

"It's better that we can just concentrate on building our group in Europe and not let ourselves get caught up in all that turmoil."

"Absolutely," Mark said as he pulled me closer to him. "But I want to enjoy my life too. I can hardly wait to get up in the morning and go hit the slopes."

"Skiing?"

"Paragliding!" He knew I was egging him on. "Where else in the world do I get to ride up Wispley Mountain and then fly down it? It's a wee bit of heaven," Mark said feigning an Irish accent. "What are you going to do today?"

"I'm not sure. For the first time in my adult life, I have free time. I mean I have more time than I have work or projects. This is a turning point for me."

"Why don't you take up writing?" Mark suggested.

"I don't know. I think I am more the teacher type than the writer."

"I don't think so. I've watched you grow as a writer: first the manual you did for our UIC Certificate Seminar and then all the new stuff you added to *Power MLM*. Your writing just keeps getting more polished. And I can help edit. You're good, honey. You should use your time here and go for it."

Maybe he was right. Maybe I should go for it. I do love to write. And for the first time, I have the time. Sitting at my desk with the shutters thrown open, looking out at the Swiss Alps, I began. Not knowing exactly where I would go with it, I started with what was most familiar—my life with Mark. It was idyllic to write about the man I adored while I watched him playfully catching thermals as he paraglided outside my window. He was happiest when he was more than 1,000 feet off the ground. For an addictive personality, this was a true "high."

During one of our tours through the UK, Mark's briefcase was stolen. It happened in Nottingham, the home of Robin Hood, where we were delivering a Nu Skin presentation. We speculated that the thief was part of Robin Hood's merry men, stealing from the rich to give to the poor. The personal tragedy was that Mark had a two-week supply of methadone in his briefcase. Knowing that sudden withdrawal from the drug could be fatal, Mark panicked. Seeing my husband somewhat debilitated, I was determined to find a solution. Based on what I knew about methadone withdrawal, we had very little time—and we were in a foreign country. Finding nothing listed in the phone directory, I confided the situation to John Kavanagh, hoping that he could help us find a methadone clinic in London. John didn't know where to turn but asked my permission to bring Scott Lucy into the loop because he had contacts throughout London. Scott led us to Dr. Brewer, a small-framed man with a gigantic heart. He was published and often invited to the US to speak on the subject of detoxification. Speaking in an upper-class British accent, Dr. Brewer took Mark under his wing. Despite how proper he sounded, he was relaxed and flexible about his dispensation of methadone. He had a wonderful attitude, and Mark took to him immediately.

Although we solved the problem, Mark was annoyed that John and Trisha, *and now* Scott, were aware of his methadone dependency. He grew cold and distant. I could handle Mark's explosive anger better than I did his emotional withdrawal from me. That silence was screaming at me again; it became worse than verbal abuse. *How much did this have to do with the brief lapse off the drug, or was there a difference in the chemical consistency between countries?*

We were in the midst of the silent cold war when John and Trisha came for a visit. They immediately sensed something was wrong between us because we were usually so demonstrative and loving toward each other. After a few days (and perhaps after he made the adjustment to his new meds), he forgave me, and we moved past it. It was one of our rare arguments while in Gstaad. Most of our time there was peaceful and without stress.

Throughout the day, our phone and fax machine would put us back in touch with the real world. The attitudes of top Nu Skin leaders continued to be subdued, but Mark and I found our own way of lifting our spirits. We were living between our home in Reno and our home in Gstaad. Our life was reasonably well balanced between work and playtime, writing and reading for personal growth and pleasure, travel, tennis, and paragliding. We took train trips to Lucerne or just over to the next "willage" as the town people would say. We worked avidly with our distributors, returning their calls, boosting their morale, training them, and taking calls from their prospective associates. We took walks by the stream or just wandered into town for dinner. Coping with the ongoing battles back home was relatively easy as we stayed thousands of miles away from it all.

If we compared our challenges to any Fortune 500 company, we knew ours would probably have looked small. But when your tooth aches, it's difficult to feel good about the rest of your body. The part that is diseased, however miniscule, consumes your entire attention. For nearly four years, no matter how hard we tried and despite all that was good about our company, we were preoccupied with the inequities that pervaded our international growth.

In April of '96, exactly ten years to the month that Mark joined the company, we returned home to the States to prepare to go to the Hyatt Regency in Kauai. There we would celebrate our annual week of fun in the sun with top Nu Skin corporate staff and all of the Hawaiian Blue Diamonds. While a board meeting was planned, it was essentially meant to be a time of fun spent with our Nu Skin family. This was an event to which we always looked forward; but this year, the closer it got, the less Mark felt like going.

"I don't really want to go hang out with Nathan and Wattenburg. There's a board meeting, but all they're going to do is try to placate us. It's just going to be a lot of bullshit."

I knew he was right but I still wanted to go. "We could hang out with the Karlens, the Johnsons, Betty Sung...."

"Richard and Carol aren't going. He can't stand it any more

than I can. And our downline has gradually fallen out of qualification." Our strongest leaders no longer met the requirements that allowed them to attend the Hawaiian gathering. "The Cliftons, Barrett, Primm—none of those guys will be there," Mark continued. "And that's bullshit too. Some of the people who built this company and pioneered it through the early days aren't getting the thanks. And the guys who cheated to get to the top will be there. The whole thing is just screwed up. It's not like it used to be. You can go if you want to…and take Amy."

I really wanted to go, screwed up or not. But Mark felt strongly about it, and I wanted to stand by him on this. Our togetherness was too critical. After a lot of soul searching, we chose not to attend and instead to address our concerns to Blake in a letter. We had no sooner sent the letter to key individuals when a phone call came in that lifted my husband's spirits.

"Hey, you won't believe what just happened. It's unbelievable," Mark called down on the intercom. "Come on up so I can tell you in person."

Everything was either "phenomenal" or "unbelievable" to Mark, so I never knew whether it was major unbelievable or just average unbelievable. As I walked into his office and slipped into my usual chair, he was already breaking the news to me.

"You know how we like to have a sign that we made the right move. Well, we got it. If we were off in Hawaii right now playing dodge games with the Watenburgs and Ricks, this would never have happened!"

"What would never have happened?" I knew he was dragging this out for effect.

"Being honored as the Nevada recipient for the 1996 Philanthropist award. That's what!" he said emphatically. "The event is being held in Washington DC and aired on CNN this week. They are flying us out. There's a big dinner and all these Legislative mucky-mucks will be there dispensing the awards. I guess ours is supposed to be given by Senator Reid."

"Uncle Harry? How nice."

"Nice. I think we're seeing the clouds parting and the voice from the heavens saying, "You were right, my children, to stand your ground and put your energy to better use." Mark was standing with his hands outstretched as if playing God talking to Moses on Mount Sinai.

I still felt a little sad at not going to Hawaii. Just because there were people there I didn't respect didn't mean I couldn't have fun with everyone else. We loved Nu Skin. We knew it was a remarkable company. The challenges that bothered us were small on the scale of things, but they still bothered us. Knowing that, I convinced myself that Mark was right. Somehow, getting this call did make it seem as if we were supposed to be doing something of greater value. We flew to Washington and met with several friends and network marketing associates. We thoroughly enjoyed ourselves and were honored by the recognition.

Though our letter wasn't answered, we heard from various corporate people who attended that it was the catalyst for some in-depth conversation in Hawaii. This made us feel that our message might finally be reaching them. A better sign was that a meeting of Blue Diamonds was called about two months later—thanks to so many requests. In addition, a business builder position that gave strong incentive to Blue Diamond executives to keep building their organization was added to the compensation plan. Some good dialogue resulted and there seemed to be a lifting of spirits among the leaders...well, at least until the next opening of a foreign market.

Nu Skin's launch in Korea was like every other foreign market opening—the usual shenanigans plus a few new ones. Policy violations in this country had gone beyond anyone's ability to control.

What worried so many of us was that our industry had struggled for nearly forty years to overcome certain negative images...and was making extraordinary progress toward that goal. The negative perception of network marketing as a pyramid scheme and get-rich-quick scam was being replaced by an industry offering freedom and integrity, particularly to the growing number of professionals being downsized right out of corporate America.

It was gradually being seen as a serious entrepreneurial opportunity where teamwork was more prevalent than dog-eat-dog competition, where people at any level could rise to their full potential simply because they worked harder. Such is not usually the case in corporations and government hierarchies. Rarely, if ever, can someone in the lower ranks pass over someone above them just because of old-fashioned hard work. More and more Baby Boomers wanting to change the world were joining network marketing companies that shared their altruistic vision. These realities along with the financial and lifestyle opportunities were attracting massive numbers of people into network marketing.

We loved our industry. And for that matter, we loved our company. Of the 200,000 members in our organization world-wide, crossing into 28 countries, we were proud of the success so many of our distributors had experienced. The products were fabulous, the compensation plan was lucrative, and we had good friends throughout the company. But we could no longer, in good conscience, encourage people into our company or our organization until Nu Skin corporate managers did something to stop the illicit activity in foreign markets and level the playing field for all distributors to truly have an equal opportunity.

Mark and I were looking for a sign—anything that would provide us with answers. Would we resolve our differences with Nu Skin and live happily ever after with the company or would we ultimately divorce ourselves from the situation and become involved with something entirely new? The response came clearly, leaving little doubt as to what we were supposed to do.

"Did you see this?" I asked Mark.

"You mean our being honored at the convention for ten years of loyal service?" He put the quote marks around "ten years of loyal service" with his fingers in the air. "Why does it feel so perfunctory and with so little actual appreciation?"

"Well, maybe it is because of this." I handed Mark a letter that had just come in. He read it and looked up at me, furrowing his brow in total disbelief. It was from Scott Schwardt, Mark's nemesis, informing us that, due to a certain violation of non-approved materials that were released in the UK earlier this year (the matter I thought I had resolved with Mike), we would be prohibited from speaking at the convention. And just the week before, we had received a letter informing us that we were being fined $10,000 for a generic audio (non Nu Skin for use industry-wide) that had been turned into Nu Skin *and* our long-standing Nu Skin training manual had been pulled by the sales aids review department. We were finding all of this pettiness hard to take in such a short time span.

I was offended by the letter but Mark looked genuinely and deeply wounded. Standing beside him, I could feel his pain. "You've spoken at every convention since the company's inception. Some of the old guard still remember your giving the keynote address at the very first convention. Who do you think is behind this?"

"It's not Blake or Steve. I doubt if they even know. Scott wrote the letter, and I have to believe he would revel in being the one to tell us."

Mark made a couple of phone calls and found out we were not alone. Nathan Ricks and Gary Wattenburg had also received the same notice. "Great! We're the ones who encouraged Nu Skin not to elevate violators and now we've been cast in the same category with these two jerks. I've had it. I've finally had it with this company!" Throwing the letter down, Mark stormed out of the room.

Even before Mark and I came together, I too had been invited to do workshops at the convention. For us to attend and be "honored for ten years of faithful service" while also being precluded from speaking was utterly humiliating. In light of the fact that we had hundreds of thousands of generic training materials, books, audio and video tapes out in the marketplace, we were livid that some department at Nu Skin now felt they had the right to exercise authority over our generic materials. Obviously, if there was something of concern, all they had to do was request that we change it, and we would have. The situation didn't warrant treating us like criminals. It was extremely painful to be dealt with so insensitively. We felt like the prophet "without honor in his own land."

Waiting until late in the day for the nine-hour time difference back to the States, Mark called Steve Lund, who was extremely kind and understanding on the phone. He promised to have a resolution no later than the following Monday. No call and no resolution came. Mark and I flew back to the States and reluctantly attended the convention out of loyalty—not to the company but to our people. However, we chose not to participate in the ten-year honoring process. It seemed hypocritical. As it turned out, the ceremony was so mishandled that we were grateful not to be included.

It was the last convention that Mark ever attended. By its end, we knew that our life with Nu Skin was over. We had not prepared ourselves for that eventuality, so we had no alternate plan.

Shortly after the annual convention, in November of 1996, I wrote a final letter, which I held onto for some time before sending. It was written and signed only by me so that I had the liberty to talk about Mark's personal contributions to the company over the last decade and his devastation over the way he had been treated at the end. I lay across the bed and showed it to him looking for his feedback. Holding me with one hand and the letter to Blake in the other, he skipped over parts and read the highlights out loud.

> ...What motivates me is probably no different than what motivates most people in building any business. We all want to be a part of a company in which (1) the financial rewards are really possible; (2) there is a sense of long-term stability; (3) there exists a strong sense of fair play; and (4) everyone feels appreciated for their efforts. For Mark and me, the first two requirements are solidly in place. Our concerns are centered around the last two points.
>
> After observing firsthand the evolution of this company for a decade, it is clear that there is still a good opportunity for people with smaller dreams or for those who limit themselves to the domestic market. The seriously unleveled playing field is not felt until a distributor enters the major leagues of international

sponsoring. Blake, you have made the choice not to involve yourself in all of this at a personal level. Now you must live with the fact that others with differing values are the pacesetters for company ethics....

Until this problem is resolved, the spirit for continuing to build this company has been taken out of us. Maybe ten or twelve years are enough and we would have burned out anyway. We have come to a crossroads. It is time for us to move on and find another cause in which we can believe and to which we can once again give totally of ourselves!

I do want to sincerely thank you for the many good things that have come to us through the experience of Nu Skin—not the least of which is that Mark and I met each other. I should also thank the company for indirectly nudging us out of our comfort zone and giving us incentive to move on to the next chapter of our lives.

I know I speak for Mark as well when I tell you that we will always be grateful for the opportunity and the lifestyle given to us by Nu Skin. The strengths of the company far outweigh the weaknesses. It's just that the weaknesses that do exist deeply violate our personal integrity....

Our departure will be made respectfully and gradually over the next year. We will work with your legal department to ensure as little agitation for all of the distributors as possible. We bid you adieu wishing you every good for the future and know you want the same for us.

Sincerely, Rene Reid Yarnell

"You should send it. It is time that, at least mentally, we move on with our lives," Mark said solemnly. After all the build-up, our decision came so quietly.

Knowing that there would be a gradual winding down before we officially retired from the company, we each felt a relief from all the tension that had built up within us. Having no particular schedule, we continued to go back and forth between Reno and Gstaad whenever the mood struck us. With a more carefree attitude and far less intensity about building our organization, we spent more time traveling for pleasure. We loved staying a night or two on the Left Bank of Paris and wandering the cobblestone streets. Mark was always drawn to the Greek restaurants with the food displayed in the windows. We danced one evening at a disco on the Champs Elysees, where we were undoubtedly the oldest couple on the floor.

Driving down into the south of France, we allowed ourselves to be pampered in a wonderful old estate. Our bedroom was in the round turret overlooking the garden-like grounds. Now we truly did feel like "king and queen of the castle," as the *Working at Home* article had described us.

The train was still our preferred mode of transportation. From our home in Switzerland, we made our way to the northernmost parts of Germany on a sleeper car and occasionally conducted Nu Skin meetings in East Berlin for Mark's longtime friend, Chris Ebersberg. Then on down into Frankfort and Munich, we would meet with our German contingency as we helped them build their Nu Skin organizations. It was easier to offer support to our people with a laissez-faire attitude. But no matter what wonderful places we visited, after a few days out, we always looked forward to coming home—to Gstaad.

Then we were off again to Madrid for the wedding of a friend, and afterward spent a week on the island of Majorca, east of Spain. We took side trips all over Italy as far down as the southernmost tip of Naples. Our favorite place, beyond question, was Venice. There's nothing more romantic than being taken by gondola through the moonlit back waterways of this quixotic city, and I will never forget the evening that we were gliding along by moonlight, Mark whispering in my ear, "*There is only you.*" For the moment, we had rediscovered the fairy tale.

Whatever struggle I may have experienced with Mark's addiction, for him it was tenfold. The next Valentine's Day, Mark wrote a poem for me that perhaps meant more than all the rest because of his absolute sincerity. It was on a train leaving Italy and on our way to Austria that he gave it to me hand-written inside a card.

Drug-free at Last!

Perhaps I've been deceptive
My throughts at times unclear;
I've hidden pain and challenges
Which plagued me our first year.

I've shattered some of your beliefs
And kept my own inside;
At times I could have told the truth
Yet can't believe I lied.

I know I didn't always give
The kind of love you need;
What started out as poetry
Wound up sometimes as greed.

This all-consuming passion
So focused once on you
Was soon reduced to Shakespeare's words:
"To thine own self be true."

But now that I've discovered
My selfishness and pride,
The first step has been taken
To regain you as my bride.

And, frankly, as I now look back
At all that we've come through,
In spite of all the adjustments
I still do treasure you.

I still believe you love me
In spite of all the strife;
I still cling to the fervent prayer
That you're glad you're my wife.

So as we start all over
Begin a brand new year
Though I reflect on past mistakes
I truly have no fear...

That we can't march through anything,
Together, conquer all,
That I can't live more honestly
And we can have it all!

So Happy Valentine's, my love,
And please believe in me,
For if my lies imprisoned us,
Your trust will set us free.

We spent a few days in Austria, residing in a quaint old hotel dating back to medieval times. With the shutters thrown open, we could look over the village and then walk to the nearby castle for Wiener schnitzel. Amy's birthday was also in February, and I shopped... and shopped...and shopped for her. I loved having a daughter—and not just for the shopping. We promised each other that, no matter what happened, we would never lose our bond.

Back home again, in late spring of '97, we received a phone call from Ben Dominitz, the owner/publisher of Prima Publishing. He had previously released a book called *Wave Three,* written by Richard Poe, which quoted Mark frequently. It was a runaway best seller. Now Ben wanted a book *by* us rather than merely *about* us. Over lunch, we discussed the concept, possible titles, terms, and time parameters. Mark didn't like to drag anything out too long, so he committed us to a two-month period in which to complete the book. I thought that was a bit ambitious, but, what the heck? A chapter a week? We could do it! We tentatively titled it, Network Marketing 101, but following Ben's lead, we soon changed it to *Your First Year in Network Marketing.* We allotted ourselves the months of June and July, when we would be back in Gstaad, to write the book.

As much as we traveled, it became more and more of a nuisance for Mark to organize his meds and carry them across international borders. We had discussed the possibility of his gradually getting off of methadone, but it was in June of '97 on our way to Paris that the decision was made for us.

I was sitting in the St. Louis airport lounge for business class passengers working on my laptop when Mark came storming in the room. His face was flushed and his whole body was shaking.

"I've lost them. Someone stole them. A whole month's supply! I've retraced my steps and looked everywhere. They're gone! They're fucking gone! I don't know what I'm going to do."

I knew what he was talking about. This was the second time that he had lost his meds in less than a year. The first time they were stolen, and this time he must have set the carrying-case down. Everyone within fifty feet thought he had gone ballistic as he vented his rage. I knew he wasn't mad at me. He was panicked, and with good reason. Mark was on such a high dosage of methadone that a few days of unsupervised withdrawal could be critical, if not fatal.

As I looked up at him, I saw a frightened little boy standing in front of me. The look on his face said it all. He was beyond scared. It was such a privilege to be trusted with this large a supply that the methadone center in Reno would never replace lost pills. We couldn't return home and we couldn't go on to Paris. We had no connection there to solve the problem, and the language barrier made things even more difficult.

"Wait here, sweetheart. You watch our bags and let me see what I can do to switch our flight to London. At least we have Dr. Brewer there." Approaching the ticket counter, I was determined to find a solution.

"Sir, my husband has a medical emergency. I need to switch our flight to London where we can get the medication he needs. Can you help me?"

"The TWA clerk must have read the look on my face. He didn't question me or argue. He simply said, "Follow me."

We walked only about twenty yards to another counter, where he spoke quietly to the attendant in charge, looking back and pointing to me. They beckoned me to join them; and the second clerk, in a British accent, assured me that they would do everything they could to accommodate us. They were rewriting our tickets and booking us standby on the flight to London that was scheduled to leave only fifteen minutes later than the flight to Paris. I felt the weight of the world on my shoulders—well, at least the weight of my husband. He was far too shaken to wheel and deal diplomatically with bureaucrats. The minutes seemed like hours.

At last, I heard the name "Yarnell" called by the ticket agent. "You are on the flight, ma'am...still in business class. We're getting your bags switched now."

I didn't have to throw a fit or exaggerate the truth. I'm sure they could sense my determination. Once we were on the plane, Mark relaxed and went right to sleep. The next morning, upon arriving in London, I called Dr. Brewer. His receptionist scheduled us in to see him that same day.

Mark explained up front how much he wanted to sever his dependency on this drug.

"These bloody American doctors," Dr. Brewer muttered to no one in particular. "They don't have a clue about methadone. But it's not really their fault. It's your government that legalizes this serious drug and makes the use of less dangerous ones a felony if you're caught." Turning to Mark, "You're on a very high dosage of an extremely potent drug. They should have told you when they put you on this that you'd more than likely be on it the rest of your life."

I watched Mark bristle. "What do you mean?"

"I mean this is a powerful drug. It's meant for lifetime heroin addicts and other serious users. It's effective. It curbs the craving. But at your dosage, it will be the most difficult thing you've ever done in your life if you decide to come off it."

"I hate the dependency. This is the second time that...."

"I know. And, under normal circumstances, I would encourage a person of your caliber to get off of this drug and clean up your act all the way. But, I don't know...."

"I want off!" Whenever Mark decided he wanted something, he always went after it. But I had never heard such conviction in his voice, especially as it pertained to drugs. "I can't take this anymore. I don't want to spend the rest of my life a prisoner."

"We have a program that I could put you in. It's called rapid detox. But I have to be honest with you. It's not an easy program. I don't know if you can handle it. If you were on heroin, it would be a cakewalk to bring you down. But with methadone, and especially your high dosage, I cannot stress enough what a challenge you will face."

After further conversation, Dr. Brewer dispensed the supply needed for now, and Mark and I made our way slowly back home to Gstaad.

"Honey, this is like a hundred-pound weight that I'm carrying around my neck. It gave me the semblance of a normal life these past few years, but it is time for me to learn to live without even this crutch."

"If you're ready to take this step, I'm with you. I gather from our conversation with Dr. Brewer that we are in store for a really tough transition."

"I can handle anything knowing you're with me. But are you sure you're up for this? It's not going to be easy for you, either."

"The only part that scares me is the unknown. Dr. Brewer indicated that you'll go through some significant changes. You will likely be an entirely different person—a person that neither of us knows. You will be a drug-free Mark, and no one can predict exactly what that will be like."

As he put his arms around me, he spoke quietly, "We've gotten over lots of hurdles together. We'll get over this one." Sitting silently on the couch in his office, we held each other, drifting in our own thoughts.

We spent all of June working on our book. It was a full-time job for me. We both worked on the same chapter, taking one at a time. Since Mark was not a computer person, he wrote in longhand and I would type his part into my laptop. I loved writing on my computer and couldn't imagine doing it any other way. Blending my work with Mark's, I took the first shot at editing the merged chapter. Then I'd send it back to Mark for more extensive editing. Mark was outstanding at writing stories, catching grammatical errors, and creating stronger sentencing structure. I would type in his corrections, giving it one final edit. If anything concerned me, I would send it back to Mark one more time. Every Friday, I e-mailed that week's chapter to our editor at Prima. At the end of June, we were halfway done.

On the Fourth of July weekend, not a highly celebrated holiday in this part of the world, Mark was waiting anxiously for Dr. Brewer to call from London. The phone rang and, at the doctor's request, Mark asked me to pick up my extension.

"I'm glad to have the chance to talk to both of you. I have taken hundreds of people through the rapid detox program, and I always like to prepare the family for what to expect," Dr. Brewer explained.

"I wanted my wife to hear all that you have told me about it. She needs to understand some of the implications it may have on our lives." Mark sounded genuinely concerned.

"The first thing you need to know is that the 'rapid' part of a rapid detox program only refers to the first few days. By putting Mark under sedation and keeping him essentially unconscious for the first twenty-four hours, we are able to expedite the process. He will have the benefits of going through ten days to two weeks of detoxification in this short period. Then from that point on, the process is in real time."

"Is there any danger during that first twenty-four-hour interval?" I asked. I didn't realize from what Mark had told me that he would be unconscious through that whole time. That part worried me.

"No more than with any anesthesia. We have him in intensive-care, monitoring him through every single phase of the program. You see, the first few days of a serious withdrawal are the worst for any patient. We essentially get them through all of that in an unconscious state."

"When can I expect to come out of it?" Mark queried.

"You'll go under at the top of the morning on Friday and come out of it about the same time the next morning. As I said, 24 hours under sedation will get you through the equivalent of a couple of weeks of withdrawal. And something you need to understand, Mark. Withdrawal from methadone is a far more difficult thing than from heroin and some of the street drugs. For those on these drugs, it's a valuable support. I'm keen on dispensing methadone to those who really need it. I just don't happen to believe that you're one of them. You have too much going for you and much too full a life to have to deal with this albatross."

As I listened, I was becoming less fearful of the process and more comfortable with Dr. Brewer's expertise. I gradually shifted my concern to the side-effects and after-effects. "What will Mark's life be like by the time we get back to the States? I mean, what kind of aftermath can we expect? And what kind of followup will we need to do when we get home?"

"Good questions, and the very reason I wanted you on this call. There will be numerous after-effects. You can expect Mark's thinking to be clouded for a while. He will be lightheaded and weak. You will likely need to be here with him so you can assist him in getting back to your home in Gstaad."

"So I should come over with him this Friday?" Mark was insisting that he could do this on his own, and would call for me if and when he needed help.

"That's up to Mark, but I would highly recommend it. But there's more. Mark will be in a fog for a while but gradually his mind will become clearer and clearer, probably more so than it has ever been since he first took drugs into his system. All of this might change his perspective on a variety of things. You can expect that he will have a great difficulty sleeping. That is the most predictable side-effect. I will be prescribing some rather heavy-duty non-addictive sleeping pills for the first several months."

"What about our sex life?" Mark questioned.

"That will likely change too. It's hard to say in what way. Could be more. Could be less. Could be a loss of interest or an increase. It varies with each person. Change is the only thing I can tell you is predictable."

"Doctor, do you believe that this is the best thing we could possibly do for my husband?"

"Yes, I do. I wouldn't be this far along recommending it if I didn't feel that way."

"Is there anything else I should be prepared for?" I knew there must be more questions I should be asking. I just didn't know what they were. I thought back to my conversations with Dorothy and Nancy. My friends and I were primarily instrumental in getting Mark to consider going on methadone. We encouraged him into the program without a full grasp of its long-term effects. The director of the center never explained that it was likely a lifetime decision for Mark, given his high dosage. So now, to withdraw from it after more than three years was evidently a much bigger undertaking than I had understood.

"Only to be ready to stand by him. The next six months will not be easy. And I can't tell you what to expect after that except that there will be notable changes in your husband. I expect that most of them will be good ones, but there will be behaviors that you will need to adjust to. You see, you have only known your husband on drugs or in withdrawal from them. You can expect to experience an entirely different man when his system is completely free of all chemical dependency. It's just impossible to predict exactly what those changes will be. Everyone is different. Look, Mrs. Yarnell, Mark has been on drugs a very long time, the better part of his life. This is not like taking a heroin addict off the habit after a couple of years. It's a much more serious step." I felt a shiver run through my body as he finished speaking. I was beginning to feel frightened of going through with this, but what was the alternative? There seemed no turning back.

"As long as I'm going through all this, I might as well stop smoking too." Mark added almost as an afterthought.

"I'd be careful about that. Don't try to undertake more than you can handle. This is a life-altering process that you will be going through. You might want to hold off on that addiction until you are through this one."

We chatted a few minutes longer, and then Mark and I went out for lunch together to continue our conversation. Mark was still insistent that he go to London on his own. He felt strongly about that. I expressed concern that I would be about six hours away by train and plane. Mark assured me that there was nothing I could do while he was sedated. When he came out of it the next morning, he would decide then how he felt.

I was lying in bed waiting for the early-morning call when the phone rang. I didn't recognize Mark's voice, it was so weak. "Honey, please come. I need you." My bag was already packed. I took the train to Zurich and then flew to London. It took the better part of the day to get there, so when I arrived, supper had already been served and Mark was sleeping. As I looked down at him wrapped in his white gown lying in the hospital bed, he looked so helpless and innocent. I could tell by looking at him that he'd been through an unbelievable ordeal. I sat on the edge of the bed and stroked his arm. It was nearly an hour before he awoke. The look on his face said it all. He was grateful to have me there. The strong, independent man who could do this all on his own, for this one brief instant in time, acknowledged needing me. I would treasure this moment and treat him with the dignity he deserved.

I arranged to have a recliner chair brought into the room so that I could stay there with him through the night. Mark will never remember, and I will never forget, the anguish he suffered during those next two days. I hadn't ever witnessed such physical agony before. I held him while he vomited and dressed him in a fresh gown. The orderlies and I changed sheets several times through the night, and I rinsed my own splattered clothes out in the sink. He couldn't stand up alone, and I felt all of his weight leaning on me as I walked him back to his bed.

I used my time while he slept working on my laptop. I just kept plugging away at the next chapter of our book.

When I called home to let Amy and Chris know his progress, he couldn't talk to them. Except to Dr. Brewer and me, he didn't speak unless it was absolutely necessary. I couldn't help but reflect on the fact that all of his life he had such an incredible gift for using words. They were his friends, but in this hospital setting even they seemed powerless. It was as if he was in withdrawal even from his dependency on words. He did what the nurses told him to do; he ate and slept, and took his meds.

Gradually he was strong enough to be discharged, but only to a nearby hotel where Dr. Brewer could continue to visit him. Every time a new medication was needed, I went from pharmacy to pharmacy in search of it. Finally it was time for us to begin the trek home to Gstaad for the first month of recovery. Mark was still very weak, and we were assisted in the airport by wheelchair attendants. This humiliated Mark; but as I was helping him out of the chair onto the plane, he turned to me and whispered softly, "As long as I live, I will always remember you for standing by me like this." I kissed him gently on the forehead. I loved him more than any words could describe at that moment. Together we had slain his most ferocious dragon. I was certain he'd never relapse again. He would never put himself through this kind of misery a second time.

Gstaad had truly become our home away from home. It was a wonderful place for Mark to recover. Dr. Brewer's description of how Mark would act was accurate. His behavior during these first days reminded me of Harrison Ford's character in *Regarding Henry*—a film we both loved. His brain was foggy, but his temperament was the gentlest I had ever known. This final month in Gstaad was a peaceful time. No tours. No outside battles. We shut it all out so that Mark could recuperate, just the two of us, writing in our chalet, walking into town for meals, holding hands as we ambled down the main street of our little village. We finished the last half of our book, and met our July deadline. We would always remember Gstaad as the place where we wrote *Your First Year in Network Marketing*.

It was with some sadness that we closed out the lease on our chalet in Switzerland and returned home to the States. Mark left a card on my pillow on our return. It very simply said: "If we were together for all time...I'd want more. And I'd get it. Thanks for standing by me through the tough times. I love you, Mark."

In August, just a month after our return home, Mark and I joined Robert and Karen Holloway, experienced yachtsmen, for two beautiful weeks cruising through the British Virgin Islands. We went bareboat sailing (just the four of us with no other crew) on a 47' yacht we rented from The Moorings in Tartola. With our book in the hands of our publisher, we were under no pressure. Mark had regained much of his strength and, though sleep was still a challenge, he seemed the most relaxed I had seen him in months. With nothing but the wind carrying us across the open sea, we made our way to Norman Island, where Robert Louis Stevenson wrote *Treasure Island*. Stopping briefly at Peter Island, we headed down to Virgin Gorda, where we swam and snorkeled through the Baths, an area of huge boulders where we saw some of the largest and most colorful schools of fish in the world. Each evening we had dinner on a different island—Bittersend, Briar's Cove (a writers' paradise), Jost Van Dyke. We fell in love with a small island where, caught up in the magic of the moment, we actually toyed with buying or leasing a home. Returning around the southern tip of St. John's, we ended where we began in Tartola. Our time there was, in Mark's words, "a wee little bit of heaven."

The entire rapid detox program—a misnomer for sure—took nearly six months, the latter half of 1997, and continued to be one of the most excruciating experiences of Mark's life. Throughout this period, he struggled to get even a few hours sleep each night. With drugs out of his system, he was left with no alternative coping mechanism. No one ever discussed this. No one ever suggested that he enter a program that would teach him new life skills for coping with stress and challenges. Mark was like a baby animal abandoned in the wild with no survival skills.

Mark's decision and my support of him to withdraw from the methadone program was a colossal turning point in both of our lives. Mark had spent the better part of his life dependent on mood-altering substances. I could only see the good of having his body cleansed from all of that, but I was not at all prepared for the changes and how they would effect our lives. It wasn't just Mark who experienced change. Our marriage was destined to undergo a dramatic transformation.

Dr. Brewer had certainly warned me: "You have only known your husband on drugs or in withdrawal from them. You can expect to experience an entirely different man when his system is completely free of all chemical dependency." As I recalled those words, I realized how little I had understood their full meaning. Only as the next year unfolded would I come to grasp it.

CHAPTER 11

A NEW PARTNERSHIP
October 1997 – January 1998

Lying in bed one evening, I asked Mark, "Do you miss Gstaad?" "Yeah. We were protected over there. Here, with every phone call, it's all hitting me in the face. I don't want to take the wind out of anyone's sails by letting them know we're moving on, but when I hear all the Nu Skin complaints about all the crap on the international front, I just want to cry out, 'Frankly, Scarlet, I don't give a damn' anymore."

"It doesn't help any that you are having so much trouble sleeping. I wish there were something I could do for you."

"You've done plenty," he reassured me as he grabbed hold of my hand. We both drifted off in our thoughts for a few minutes.

"So what's next for us? Neither of us is satisfied unless we are moving toward some goal or doing something worthwhile. I just feel we are at such loose ends right now."

"It's twue. It's twue," Mark said, imitating Tweedy Bird. "Do you remember that guy, Rick Tonita, who called some time ago?"

"Remind me. I'm not sure."

"The guy from Canada, Vancouver, I think. He called early this year and keeps calling back every few weeks. He phoned again today."

"What does he want?"

"He said that he and some partners were exploring the possibility of forming a network marketing consulting group and would be interested in having us join the team."

"Hmm. Who are the others?"

"He mentioned a woman named Valerie Perkio. She is also a Canadian and some kind of a facilitator and conflict resolution consultant to corporations. And another guy, Dr. John Radford, who is living in Vancouver, having recently left his home in South Africa. He apparently had something to do with helping Nelson Mandela's office bring about a peaceful settlement to end apartheid there."

"Well, I can see why they need us."

"Why?"

"Well, if they are forming a network marketing consulting group, it would seem they need someone with some network marketing experience," I said grinning at him.

"Well, I guess Tonita has some. He and his wife have been with Shaklee for some time now and are starting to build something there. To tell you the truth, I wasn't too interested when he called the first few times, but now I'm open to possibilities. I think we should check it out."

"It can't hurt to see what they have in mind."

After several calls back and forth, we agreed to meet Rick Tonita and the other prospective partners in Seattle. One of the conditions of joining the team was that we take a personal development course from The Pacific Institute there. Lou Tice was a fascinating man who had been developing this TPI curriculum, "Investment in Excellence," for twenty years. Part of Rick's concept was that we would carry this program into the network marketing world. We agreed to take the program to familiarize ourselves with the course and have the partners all on the same wavelength.

At the conclusion of the course, Valerie Perkio and John Radford, who had already taken it, met us in Seattle. Valerie was about my height, a brunette with shoulder-length hair, a lean, small body, and sharp facial features. She appeared very professional but somewhat aloof. John, on the other hand, seemed like a loveable teddy bear, tall, a bit on the heavy side, with thinning hair and a round, gentle face.

Rick was right. It did help that we had all taken the same course. It gave us a common link and openness in our communication that might not have been there otherwise . Our meeting went well. We felt at ease with everyone. We were all married, so the partnership would, to varying degrees, involve eight people. Rick had already begun operating under the name "Global Partners," a name we all readily accepted. With our slogan, "transforming human potential into purposeful lives," we saw ourselves consulting with various network marketing companies and, through our personal development curriculum, helping raise the industry to a new professional standard.

All of the partners worked intensely over the next few weeks to create a revenue stream. Valerie worked with the facilitators who would be helping us take the TPI course into the network marketing arena. John and I began outlining our training system for the industry based on human potential principles. Mark and Rick were responsible for bringing in the companies who would appreciate our competencies and contributions, knowing that we had value to add to their already existing establishments.

The first time our venture made money, the partners and Rick had a falling out over the distribution of funds. After some discussion, we encouraged Rick to go forward with the name Global Partners, keeping the contracts he had personally brought to the table. We would take the name Global Trust and the pending contracts that had come through us. It was as if Rick Tonita had been sent as an intermediary to bring us together with John and Valerie. His job was completed, and he moved on.

During the next month, we explored our options but were, admittedly, at loose ends. With The Pacific Institute association tied to Rick, we met with Bob Mowab, president of the Edge

Program, and a former partner of Lou Tice's. We took his program and found some valuable parts to his curriculum as well. But in the end, we concluded that neither program was perfectly suited to meet our needs. The only recourse was to develop our own.

During this transition in our partnership makeup, Mark and I had hit another downturn. That deadly silence was back again. A giant abyss separated our worlds, and Mark began to spend more and more time hiding away in our bedroom or his office. How ironic that our objective was "to help people live purposeful lives." Ours at this moment were anything but.

We both felt that it was the other one who had changed. He blamed my transformation on menopause. As a woman in my mid-fifties, I was experiencing changes within my body. I was teary and feeling desperately needy. How much of this was menopause and how much was just wanting the old Mark back, I didn't know.

I felt his personality change was directly related to the treatment program. Could this be the real Mark—the drug free Mark? It was as if his body had gone through detox, but his mind and heart were not prepared to cope. In fact, without drugs he had no coping mechanism whatsoever. But then, why should he? He had been dependent on drugs of one form or another since he started sneaking whatever was available out of the medicine cabinet at home when he was in junior high. He had never known a life without them. This was hardly the juncture to be going through a major transition in our lives. Our timing was anything but well thought out.

All through Christmas and the New Year, Mark seemed depressed. I wasn't much better. The heaviness pervaded our home and our children. His anniversary card to me hurt me deeply. It was a man and woman arm wrestling with the message that read: "still holding hands." Mark continued to insist that we needed to bring things between us to some resolution. We put it off long enough to deal with the departure of Rick Tonita, but finally there were no more excuses.

Deciding to have an early dinner, we headed for Mark's favorite steak house, The Glory Hole. This was also where we had had heavy discussions in the past, and I believe he chose it as the setting for this long-overdue discussion. We were seated in our familiar back corner booth. Mark ordered his old standby meal: steak, grilled zucchini, and baked potato. I ordered something light, as I had no appetite.

Once our meals were ordered and I was nibbling on my salad—more like using my fork to move it around on my plate—I began searching for the right words. I was frightened of saying the wrong ones. "Is this the right time to talk, sweetheart? I can't stand the coldness and distance between us much longer. I'm dying inside."

"Yeah, I guess this is as good a time as any." He paused and then began as if he had rehearsed a speech. "Look, Rene, it all comes down to this. You aren't the same person I married, and you won't do anything about it. Everyone notices it. Even Amy has talked to me about it. But you just don't see it. You have to control everything, and I just won't let you control me. If you can't handle that, then leave. I don't care anymore. I won't be controlled by you. I will be in charge of my own house and my own life. If you can't or won't respect that, then it is all over between us."

"Sweetheart, talk to me more about what's really causing this. I hear your words, but we made some pretty strong promises to each other when we brought our lives together. I can hardly believe you are willing to let a little menopause, if that's what you think it is, come between us. There has to be something more that is upsetting you. I just keep wondering...."

"Look, why won't you accept it? It is you, Rene. It is your controlling, take-charge-of-everything manner that is the problem. Why can't you see that?" *How quickly his regard for my independent thinking eroded in times of stress.*

"We're both under some stress because our life isn't tracking right now. We don't have our joint purpose clearly in sight, and I believe that has a lot to do with what's wrong," I said carefully.

"I don't want to do anything joint with you. It's impossible.

You do things your way, and I do them mine. There is no 'us' when it comes to business."

"There is no 'us'...period. We have no personal life. I never see you. We never talk. We don't touch. This is the first time we've had a meal together since Christmas, and that was with a table full of people. I need to have a shared life with you. Is that too much to ask?"

"You're not going to win by laying a guilt trip on me. I'll do what I want and I'm not going to allow you to control everything I do."

"Like what? What are you talking about?" I could only assume that he still resented me for how I had handled the drug problem. But his answer was something different.

"Like finances. You and your mother handle all the money. And if I try to make an investment or buy some land, you balk. I'm tired of it. The only way to handle things is to split everything down the middle. That way, I can do whatever I want with my half, and you can sit and preserve your half."

If I could have foreseen what lay ahead, I would have accepted his offer. Instead I merely replied, "That sounds like the first step toward divorce."

"That's fine too. Frankly, I don't give a damn about that either."

"Why? What's happened to us?"

"It's you, Rene. Don't you get it? Everyone else does. You are a complete bitch. You are not the sweet, adoring person that I married. I don't like who you've become."

He sounded so intransigent. This wasn't the Mark I had married.

"Whatever it is, isn't it something we can work on or get help with? Is there any hope in your mind?" I asked.

"Whatever needs to be done has to come from you. I'm fine just the way I am. But I won't let my life be manipulated by you. I'm sick and tired of everything about you."

I was speechless. I could feel a tear running down my face. I still didn't know what had happened. His words weren't telling me the whole story.

We went home and crawled into bed...without touching. He fell asleep, and I lay there not knowing what to do.

A New Partnership

Over the next few days, Mark went into deep isolation. I found myself crying in the closet, the bathroom, the boiler room, wherever I could find space in the house where I could be alone. Even with nearly 9,000 square feet of house, I didn't have one place that I could call my own. My office was open and shared. Of course, my bedroom was shared. I needed a place where I could hide away and just be with my thoughts and emotions. Above the kitchen was a small balcony and to the left, although it appeared to be a wall, was a secret door to what we called the playroom. Children who came to visit us loved to go up there. All of Chris's books, Star Wars toys, and games from childhood were housed in that room. Once in a while, I would sneak away there.

The silence became a weapon, and I felt totally battered by it. Every time I walked into our bedroom, Mark was there. He seemed to never come out. If he spoke to me, it was only to pummel me with hateful and degrading words. I moved into my son's old room for a couple of nights. I couldn't cope with the situation anymore. Somehow, I believed this was not Mark. This was some alter ego, some demon occupying his body. Whatever I had done—and I accepted my part in this—it couldn't have elicited this kind of a response.

Then it hit me: it was either drugs or alcohol, I wasn't sure which. After the ordeal he had gone through to get off drugs, I couldn't believe he would slip back into that world. It must be alcohol, I decided. He had kept his distance from me, perhaps so I wouldn't smell it on his breath or coming through his pores. Around four in the morning, I got up and went straight to the cabinet where we kept the liquor. Since Christmas and our holiday parties, we had more than usual on hand. He wasn't even subtle. There were the bottles, almost all empty: scotch, bourbon, vodka, rum, brandy, even peach schnapps. In his old drinking days, Mark told me that his habit was to hide the bottles. He wasn't even trying to do that now. *But why, after his conquering drugs, would he revert back to alcohol?*

At first, I didn't say anything to anyone, not even Amy. Mark was on his fifth straight day of holing up in our bedroom and drinking. I had to talk to someone. I was afraid for him.

After reaching Nancy on the phone and telling her I needed her, soon we were sitting in Rapscallion over a glass of wine and some coconut prawns.

"Nancy, what is going on? I mean, what leads to this?"

Nancy had extensive experience counseling alcoholic and drug addicts. "It could be so many things, Rene. You see, alcoholics or addicts will do anything for their drink or their fix. It becomes paramount in their lives, and everything else becomes secondary. He's in clear focus on getting that next drink while the rest of life becomes foggy and blurred. Alcohol is an alcoholic's drug of choice. Socially, he may find it more acceptable to use prescription drugs. But make no mistake: Mark is first and foremost an alcoholic who also uses drugs—not the other way around."

"That makes a lot of sense. But what I really want to know is, what part did I play in bringing this on? And what do I do now? I feel so...helpless. Nance, what if he's right? What if I've been such a bitch about his drugging that I have driven him to drinking? I mean, that is possible. I can be a controller. Maybe I've handled everything wrong in this situation. It's possible that most of this is my fault."

"Addicts want you to believe that, Rene. They want to pass the blame off on anyone but themselves. You are not going to do yourself or him any good if you let the thought that you are responsible consume you. As a participant in this relationship, you can't accept responsibility for what Mark is doing. But what you can do is look at your own actions and reactions, and decide if what you are doing is promoting a healthy relationship."

"I do believe it has taken two of us to get to where we are. But there is something missing that I just don't understand. We seemed to do everything right in going through the detox program, and yet everything is turning out so wrong.

"Maybe that's because you didn't know—no one could know— what Mark would be like without drugs in his system. And with all the stress you guys are under, he had to find some way to deal with it. He went back to the only other alternative he knows. And, Rene, Mark is going to keep on drinking until *he* decides to stop, and there isn't a thing you can do about it."

"But he may kill himself."

"This is the hardest thing I will ever say to you, sweetie. If that's what he decides to do, there isn't a damn thing you can do to stop it. The more controlling you are, the more you are promoting Mark's dependency and, therefore, the more responsible you *are* making yourself for the outcome."

I sat quietly thinking about that. I knew she was right. I tried to imagine what it must be like for those afflicted with substance abuse to find a healthy alternative on their own. It would be about as difficult as my choosing to stop driving a car and replace it with walking or bicycling for the rest of my life. Few people can comprehend the ominous challenge involved in recovery. For now, it was time to let go. Mark first went into a treatment program only when he was ready. He will stop drinking only when he is ready.

Mark drank his way through his birthday, January 16. We had my parents over for dinner to celebrate it, but he never came downstairs. I made up some excuse and did my best to keep it from everyone: the partners, our family, and especially any distributors.

The morning after, I walked into the kitchen and found Amy standing in front of the liquor cabinet. She had figured it out too.

"What do you think we should do?" she asked sweetly. I thought back to the last time we had faced this situation. At that time, she was unable to face the reality. She had certainly matured. This time, she couldn't mistake it.

"Believe me, Ame, I've asked myself that question over and over. If there were anything to be doing, I'd be doing it. I talked to Nancy about it."

"What'd she say?" Amy asked eagerly.

"She said what any good counselor would say. I can't do anything for him. Certainly I can't change him or make him get off this binge. I can only change me. So I've spent more time analyzing what my part is in all this, and what is within my power to do. I can't do anything more about the situation. The only change I can make is within me." Seeing the concern in her eyes, I asked, "How's *your* relationship with him right now?"

"Mmm, distant. He's kind of in denial about...you know. He just kind of avoids me."

"Well, God knows that I don't have any special wisdom about all of this. But I would guide you the same way I am talking to myself. This is a time for us to work on being at peace within ourselves. I know I haven't been myself since we closed out our home in Gstaad. The stress of Mark's challenges, leaving Nu Skin, my change of life, our being at loose ends with what we are doing with our lives—all of this is getting to me.

"Yeah, you haven't exactly been yourself lately."

"I know. I'm short-tempered; I'm making mountains out of molehills in the office, and, most of all, I can't get hold of my emotions. They are running away with me. I seem to cry all the time."

"It's hard for me not to get caught up in it all when you and Dad are having problems. I still worry about him...well, about you both."

"I had to process this whole thing for myself. I also talked it over with Dr. Lovett." Jeff Lovett was our family physician who, by coincidence, also had taken over as the medical advisor for the methadone clinic in town. "What I've come to understand is that this is a disease, and I want to respond the best way I can to this. I keep asking myself: What would I do if he had cancer?"

"So what are you really saying?"

"I guess...that your dad has an illness. Nothing more and nothing less. It's not like he deserves to be judged or criticized. Like cancer, a lot of the healing will come from his own will to make himself whole and healthy. In the meantime, all we can do is just love him...and pray that he decides to do something about this soon. But we should be doing everything we can for ourselves right now to create our own inner peace."

Her eyes got a little watery. I reached out and held her. We prolonged our hug. I reached up and closed the liquor cabinet as if shutting the door would somehow shut out the reality.

A New Partnership

As we both headed downstairs to our office, I realized there was one more thing I needed to say. "By the way, part of my inner peace is needing to tell you how sorry I am if I've been impossible to work with lately."

"Oh, I'm pretty good at separating our work time and our personal time. I don't let them get mixed up."

She was maturing into a beautiful woman. I felt fortunate to have her in my life...and to be in hers, particularly at this time.

It happened on its own. Mark got a call from Dr. Graham Simpson, a longtime acquaintance and former client of mine, inviting him to a meeting in Pasadena on January 22 for a critical meeting representing Global Trust. It was a command performance, and Mark rose to the occasion like a superhero. Few people could pull themselves out of a stupor cold turkey like he did. He was shaky but composed. He had a job to do, and he was going to do it. I wish he knew how much I admired him for that. But instead we chose not to talk about the incident. And since we didn't acknowledge that it happened, I could hardly offer praise for how he pulled out of it.

"What do you expect to happen at this meeting?" I asked by way of making conversation as I drove him to the airport.

"I don't know for sure, but it could be important to us. Graham's company, Integral Health Inc., is comprised of over 50 medical doctors and healthcare specialists. They want to completely restructure healthcare delivery systems by placing more emphasis on balanced, preventative medicine, which of course would result in increased longevity. They are in the process of establishing a series of Longevity MetaCenters nationwide. Right now these centers are only in northern and southern California, but there will be lots more to come. It is tied in closely with American Technologies Group. Larry Brady is the CEO of ATG and his son, Marc Brady, is the CFO of IHI."

"Sounds a little incestuous."

"Don't be so quick to judge," Mark snapped at me. "Let's give it a chance. We need a break, and this could be it."

"I'm sorry. I just don't want to see us grasping at straws out of desperation. You and I are not desperate. We can afford to take all the time we need to discover what it is we should be doing next. The urgency you're feeling is more for Valerie and John. They don't have that luxury."

"You see what I mean—you and I can't agree on anything about business! We really shouldn't be in business together. It was a mistake that we even tried."

I took a deep breath. We were at least talking. That was progress. I didn't want to send him off with us fighting again. There was a brief silence as I watched a couple, hand-in-hand, cross the street in front of us. *God, I wanted to be that couple right this moment. Why have we allowed our life to become so complicated?* "So tell me, what does ATG do?"

Seeming relieved that I didn't choose that moment to pick a fight, Mark responded as if eager to talk about it. "They are a research and development company committed to finding solutions to the environmental problems in today's world. Their mission is to introduce innovative technologies." They manufacture something called I_E crystals, which are some kind of water molecules that offer all kinds of benefits that would otherwise require the use of chemicals. From what little I know, when added to other ingredients they help with cleaning and lowering calcium scaling, and will have a really positive effect on the environment. I'm hoping that we can connect them to a network marketing company that is looking for something like this."

I pulled up to the curb and Mark got out and grabbed his bag out of the backseat. I felt as awkward as being on a first date. Nothing felt natural anymore. He broke the moment of discomfort by leaning over and giving me a peck on the lips. I pecked him back, and he was off. I watched him walk through the doors until I couldn't see him anymore. There was almost the old bounce to his walk.

Having come to the conclusion that we weren't ready to plug into someone else's human potential curriculum, we sought out expertise on developing our own program. One of the leading authorities on the subject was Dr. Albert Bandura, a Professor of Social Sciences in Psychology as well as the Department of Psychology Chairman at Stanford University. He had authored countless articles and nine books on a wide range of issues in psychology. In his most recent book, *Self-Efficacy: The Exercise of Control,* Dr. Bandura laid out a premise that belief in ourselves and our own intrinsic value is the foundation for taking positive actions to better our lives. Without such "self-efficacy," we get bogged down in our own complacency.

On behalf of ourselves and our partners, Mark contracted for us all to spend a day seeking advice from this wise man about how to organize and implement our program. The meeting was scheduled for January 23, the day after Mark's meeting in Pasadena. We all gathered in Palo Alto for the encounter, anxious for Mark to arrive and catch us up on his meeting with IHI and ATG.

At dinner, Mark seemed to be his old self. "You won't believe these people," Mark began. *It was wonderful to have the old Mark back, full of exuberance and larger-than-life salesmanship.* "They are just what we've been looking for. They have a product that is so exciting I don't think we want to give it away. It's unbelievable...." That old familiar body language was back: his brow furrowed and his hands starting at his heart and stretching as wide as he could stretch.

"So what do you think we should do?" John asked.

"Start our own network marketing company! I've wanted to do this for a long time, and here is our chance. It's phenomenal what we could do with these other two companies.

"Mark, I'm overwhelmed. How does it all tie together?" Valerie inquired.

"Okay, let me explain what each of them are about, and I think you'll begin to see it." Mark went on to explain IHI's mission to reform healthcare and how ATG's I_E Crystal could take the place of chemicals and be the foundation of a whole new natural product line.

We all looked at each other, and an excitement sparked. Not one of us fully grasped exactly what the I_E Crystal actually did yet, but Mark's enthusiasm was contagious. I had held mine back up to this point. My focus was not really on our partnership. I was preoccupied about my husband, our marriage, and our future. But as I heard Mark describe what was possible, even I got caught up in the moment.

"Couldn't part of IHI's role in the joint venture be to provide scientific credibility to the products and services through their network of physicians and healthcare professionals?" John offered somewhat reflectively.

"Absolutely!" Mark responded, thrilled that we were starting to see the possibilities.

"So where do we fit in?" Valerie probed.

"Our job is to market the IHI services and the products that we create with ATG's I_E Crystals. We bring in the distributor force and build the network marketing company. ATG oversees the manufacturing of the products with the Crystals. And IHI—well, they keep on developing their MetaCenters and Resorts, and we'll market them when they get them up and running. In the meantime, they will add immense credibility to the testing and approval of the products ATG roles out."

"But where do John and I fit in?" Valerie repeated her real intention in asking the question. "We don't have any real network marketing experience. And we don't have any money to contribute. So how do we contribute equitably in this venture?" Valerie pressed.

Val's emphasis went up at the end of each sentence and, for the first time, I could notice her Canadian accent. I looked at Mark, curious how he would respond. She was right. And they were both critical points.

"Rene and I can handle the distributor side of all of this. But someone has to run the corporate side. That's where you and John fit it." *"Rene and I...." That was the first time in a long time that I had heard Mark refer to us together. It felt good to hear him speak of us as a couple or a team or whatever.*

"Are you sure, Mark," Valerie continued. "It just doesn't feel like we are carrying our weight. You and Rene are known for your network marketing experience. But we aren't. And, besides that, I don't see how we can make up in effort what we lack in financial contributions." I admired her for speaking up so forthrightly on this subject. What she was saying made so much sense.

"This is going to be a gigantic company. What difference does it make who puts up the money? We'll get it back, and we're all going to be billionaires. Don't you get it? Don't you all see how big this is?" Mark gave us that little boy look that said: Are you blind? How can you not see what I see?

"How much do you think we'll have to put up?" I asked warily. I may have been the only one not convinced.

"I don't know. Whatever it is, our company, Global Trust, will probably put up a third, ATG will put up a third, and IHI will put up a third. If we decide to do this, then we need to set up a time for all of us to go down next week, and we'll work out those details at that time."

It seemed to be a consensus that we should meet and explore the possibility further. I hadn't seen Mark this happy since before he entered the treatment program the previous July. I was scared but didn't want to rain on his parade. If it worked, it would be an extraordinary company, but there were so many hurdles.

Our meeting the next day with Dr. Bandura was jam-packed with information. "Efficacy," he explained, "refers to the value or the effectiveness of something. Self-efficacy is recognizing our own worth, our own competency and ability to master a certain task or conquer a bad habit." He spoke at length about the importance of knowing how to deal with obstacles, with failure. We were well into our talk when Mark asked: "With access to over 30-million people in the network marketing industry who want to improve their lives, can we offer them something of value?"

"You can give them knowledge, and determine what skills are needed, but the question continually comes back to how you persuade them that they have the capabilities to succeed. Identify the impediments they are going to run into and then teach them how to overcome them."

"Gosh, how interesting that Mark and I did this in the book we just wrote. *Your First Year in Network Marketing* is hitting the bookstores as we speak. All we did was list the most common impediments to building a successful network organization and then tell them how to overcome these hurdles."

"If there are enough people wanting to know how to succeed at network marketing, by taking that approach, your book is destined to be a bestseller," Dr. Bandura said. "You are providing them with exactly what they need and want to know. It would be nice if there were an efficacy scale that could measure results in all situations. But it doesn't exist. So you have to link your belief system with the domain you are coping with."

"So everything you are saying comes back to the fact that we must begin by dealing with the likely failures," Valerie said.

"Yes, whether you are talking about individual or collective efficacy, focus on the real problem in adversity, not just under ideal settings. Guide them in applying the knowledge. Give them good guides for prototypic problems. Allow your people to try it and fail, and train them to deal with the failures and setbacks. You will get good ratings from your students if you give them a program that is tough in training and easy in reality."

"I'm really interested in body building, but it is so hard to motivate myself to do what I have to do and stick with it," Amy shared as an example. "So, how do I..."

"That's a great example. Here's the efficacy scale used in the medical school for exercise: What makes it hard for you to exercise? List all the things that would prevent you from doing your exercise program. Get them to write everything down: such as when I'm tired, or after work, or when I'm depressed, or when there is something more interesting to do. Make a profile on their challenges to this particular issue. Now with guidelines in place, you can inform them how to overcome those specific obstacles. What you are doing is translating self-motivation into hard work."

"But how do we get from the knowledge of what the obstacles are to the act of facing and overcoming them?" I asked.

"In designing a curriculum, you want to translate the knowledge into guidance about how to handle the problems. Your distributors need strategies for how to get there. Break the goals down into sub-goals. They will never get there in one big leap. Now help them get focused on the first thing they have to do. However slow it may seem, they need the reassurance that they are making progress."

"Dr. Bandura," Mark began, "my wife and I bungee jumped while we were in New Zealand, and there was one young Asian girl ahead of us who had a transforming experience right in front of our eyes. At first she was too petrified too jump. But she finally did. Then, after our own dives, a more accurate description of a bungee jump, we saw her again in the office where the video was being shown. She had all of her friends gathered around her. She was not the same intimidated young woman. She was confident and extremely self-assured. There was no question that she had experienced something internal that changed her. Should we create mastery experiences to solidify their efficacy?"

"Be careful. No single powerful experience will change people permanently. Ask them what they fear. Show them that the fear won't happen. In other words, disconfirm by example that their fear is misguided. We have had considerable success by having people who are afraid of snakes observe others handling them through a one-way mirror to see that what they fear isn't happening. After a while, they come into the room and walk closer to the snake. Take people gradually step by step. You want to provide both graduated tasks over a graduated timespan. However, in this instance with the fear of snakes, in one and half hours we were able to cure every single person in the experiment. Always structure an example that won't fail."

"So how could we do the same with broad effectiveness?" John asked.

"If you help them in one area, it may not translate into other areas. You must decide over which domain in their lives you want them to gain control. Transforming experiences must deal with the prime issue. Work at understanding their reality. Guide them through baby steps that create a true sense of progress.

"Look at your project as an experiment. Keep refining it. Some may respond very quickly. Others will need more guidance. Still others will be very dependent and need a lot of help. You must decide which level you are targeting. Give people a program with specific strategies, anticipate the impediments, and give them attainable steps so that they can experience success. Then give them tougher challenges, have them track themselves, get good feedback, and adjust their strategy. Create lifetime curricula—not magic fixes. Enable them to weather the tough times."

Our brains were saturated from sitting at the feet of this master. We drove into downtown Palo Alto together and had lunch at one of Dr. Bandura's favorite local spots and the conversation didn't lighten up. As we returned from lunch, Dr. Bandura asked if there was any particular direction we wanted to take the discussion. Much to my surprise and pleasure, Mark inquired about the efficacy of overcoming alcoholism and addiction.

"People who come for help with alcoholism and drug addiction aren't necessarily ready for help. You can only help them get help when they're ready. *How I've learned that to be true.* Build up to some successes in life that convince them that they can lead a more productive life without substance abuse. We don't put enough emphasis on people's ability to overcome it. Recent studies showed that 72 percent of heroin users got off the drug without any help. We don't know how they did it because we only study what doesn't work, not what does. If you look at the history of alcoholism, we have tended to accentuate the negatives. We need to study how people recover and build models around that.

"Take an addict whose life is centered on getting drugs. When he goes into treatment, we ask him to give up all of that, but we don't provide substitute structures. We provide nothing positive in their lives. *Bingo! That's it. That is exactly what we are dealing with right at this moment. Of course Mark went back on alcohol. Where else would he turn? He made an heroic decision to give up pills but he has nothing to take their place. Mark's body is drug-free, but it has left a vacuum. Unless the drugs are replaced with healthier forms for dealing with life and coping with stress, he is trapped into a no-win situation.* I understood this intellectually at the time we went through the detox program, but I didn't think it through. *Why didn't we make it part of the program to follow up with some counseling and forming new habits once we were back home? It seems so obvious.* I could only hope that maybe now, listening to Dr Bandura, Mark would choose this on his own.

Mark had the courage to bring this subject up. I guess I shouldn't be afraid to ask the question on my mind too. "So what about the co-alcoholic and co-addict. What should the person do who is living with them?" I didn't look at Mark. I was afraid he'd be angry at my question.

"We would often make recommendations to AA. Why don't we build our own social structures where the entire family can come? When one person in a family faces alcoholism or addiction, it becomes a family problem. DeLancy's program works with hardcore addicts. They bring in the spouses, the children, run their own school system, find them jobs, etc. The failure or success of conquering an addiction has everything to do with the degree of self-efficacy in that individual. The rest of the family cannot do anything about that.

"The greater the efficacy of the alcoholic or addict after treatment, the greater the chance they'll make it." *On a scale of one to ten, Mark Yarnell is off the charts in grandiosity and belief in himself. If anyone can conquer this monster, I know my husband can and will.* "But as the person involved and living with them," the professor continued, "you need to know that the chance of relapse is very high. This is a process with which the addict will always struggle. The ideal situation is, while the addict is of a mind to withdraw, that you would have an agreed upon plan for recovery from a slip. People who have had a slip make the acknowledgement that they have no control over booze or drugs. Given the chance, they will always be inclined to abuse them. A slip will not set them back. Rather, those who have strong self-efficacy will

recognize it as only a slip and continue on with their conviction."
*So I shouldn't feel that I have to ignore a slip. Pretending that I don't
notice would be dishonest and enabling. Rather, I should acknowledge
when a slip occurs, without blame, and support him in picking up
the pieces and going on with his original conviction. A relapse is a
natural part of the flow. Slips will happen, and with enough self-
efficacy within himself and my showing my belief in his ability to
move past them, the slips will become less and less frequent.*

After several more questions and answers, Mark said, "I have
one last question. I think of myself as a motivational speaker, but
is it really possible to motivate people?"

"Yes, I believe so. There are three classes of incentives: material
costs and benefits (financial rewards), social costs and benefits
(what people think of us), and the measures we use in adopting
our own personal standards and regulating our behavior. People
are usually motivated by a mixture of how they perceive their own
efficacy, what they are going to get from their actions, their own
aspirations and goals, and how they perceive the impediments.
Once you know how high or low their efficacy, you can help them
determine what they will have to do next. If they have a low self-
efficacy, you will need to take them through more baby steps as
you lay out a plan of action."

The day was ended. We thanked Dr. Bandura and asked if we
could stay in touch to let him know our progress in putting the
curriculum together. As we left his office, I spotted a poster on his
wall: "No snowflake in an avalanche ever feels responsible." How
prophetic this would become.

After an intense and exhilarating day, John and Valerie headed
home to Canada. Amy, Mark, and I spent the night in Palo Alto and
drove home the next day. The four-hour drive gave us time to pull
ourselves back together as a family. I treasured the very idea of family.
Mark, Amy, and Chris were my real-life family, the one I had longed
for all of my life. I wasn't going to let this slip away. We had an enormous
task ahead of us. We were moving into a larger arena of life, and, to
face it, it was critical for us to be in sync with each other.

CHAPTER 12

FORMING OUR COMPANY
February - June, 1998

The following week we all gathered in Pasadena, California, to formally enter into an agreement to go forward with the formation of our network marketing company: 21st Century Global Network. The name had a sound of grandeur to it—one that we thought would last forever, or at least for a hundred years. The plan was to form an equal partnership between IHI, ATG, and Global Trust. That might have been simple enough except that Global Trust was made up of John and his wife, Valerie and her husband, and Mark and me with Amy working fulltime in the project as well. Each joint-venture partnership represented one-third of the ownership and, therefore, one-third of the profits. Mark's offer to put up the agreed-upon $150,000 on behalf of the three partners within our partnership meant that Mark and I would each own just one-eighteenth of the company in exchange for being the only individuals among us to invest our personal finances *and* our full-time energy as a couple. The very mathematics frightened me. How would we ever come out of this as winners? And somehow Amy needed to be compensated... I presumed, out of our share.

All of the partners worked intensely to get our company up and running with the fastest start in network marketing history. It was the beginning of February, and our objective was to launch the beginning of May. We had three months to accomplish a year's work. John and I spent hours developing the outline and general thrust of our training program, incorporating his expertise on the orderly flow of information linked step-by-step with my knowledge of network marketing. When we were ready to develop the step on goal setting, Valerie contributed her years of facilitation training and leadership management skills. Mark's role was to bring in the leading distributors who would form our presidential team, frontline to the company.

March rolled around before we knew it, and it was time for the Nu Skin annual convention. Mark and I were asked to speak at one of the workshop sessions. As important as this had been to us the year before, this year our hearts weren't in it. Mark couldn't even bring himself to go. He had moved on mentally, and his heart and mind were fully into building the new company. After some discussion, we decided that Amy and I would attend and make the announcement that, not so unlike other Nu Skin leaders, we were bringing our daughter into the business and would begin to pass the baton to her. Throughout the conference I had to field questions about why Mark wasn't there. Everyone noticed.

Standing in front of 1,400 people at the breakout session, it hit me really hard. This had been my family for a decade. I felt a wave of anxiety and sadness. I thought about the lifestyle we'd led and the close friends we'd made as we were building this company. My heart went out to Carol Kall, who was valiantly attending the convention in her final stages of cancer with Richard watching protectively over her. What wonderful times the four of us had had together. I remembered our Hawaiian Blue Diamond trips: we were a family, playing tug-of-war on the beach, lying by the pool talking to Blake or Steve, hanging out with the Kalls, the Karlens, the Johnsons, Betty

Sung. I thought about our ski trips to Breckenridge with Dennis Clifton and his wife, Georgia. I remembered Mark serving as the minister for the wedding of Kathy Dennison when she married her husband; the time in Atlanta with Tom and Terry Hill; standing on the stairs at Craig Bryson's house with Mark proudly telling Blake of our plans to marry. It all came flashing back to me, and I was going to miss everyone terribly.

My promise to Steve Lund was that I would not say goodbye formally, nor would we tell anyone we were leaving. We would just slip away quietly. This was one of the more difficult talks I ever delivered. The lump in my throat got in the way of my words. I knew that this would be the last time I would see many of the people present. At that moment, I wanted to turn the clock back...to stop time. The memory of Nu Skin, even with its challenges in the foreign markets, was far more comforting to me than what I felt lay ahead in our own company.

I would learn more than two years later of Nathan Rick's "retirement" from the business. The Kall Global Network, now known as Global Internetworks, has become an active online support group for professional network marketers. The issues that we'd fought for with all our hearts gradually improved over time. For so many reasons, I felt blessed to have been guided into this company and to have spent so many wonderful years with them.

As soon as I returned from the convention, we hit our first serious holdup, when the man whom ATG had selected to develop and manufacture our product line failed to meet his deadline. Further, despite our insistence that the products be all-natural, he had included a significant amount of chemicals. A unanimous decision of the partners led to his dismissal. With six weeks lost, we were beginning from scratch to find someone to create our product line.

A second attempt with our next company, Westwood, essentially produced the same results. When we asked for a predominance of aloe vera in our skincare products, they provided us with approximately two percent, telling us we had no idea of the expense that would be incurred if we added the 50-plus percent we had requisitioned. Although ATG was responsible for product development, it was we at Global Trust who discovered this incongruity along with chemicals in our "all-natural" products. "How could such a serious omission occur?" we asked them in a letter dated April 6. "And how is it possible that ATG had no awareness of this, despite the fact that they were only ten minutes from the lab and were the project manager for product development?" At the root of all of this was our concern over the failure of ATG to exercise quality control over our products.

The final straw came when we received a copy of a fully signed contract regarding the warehousing space Global Network was leasing from ATG. It was appropriately signed by Harold Rapp as the landlord and, surprisingly, by Mike, the employee assigned as liaison for this project, as if he were representing Global Network. Our concern was less over the impropriety of two ATG employees having sole legal control over a matter that clearly should involve the full partnership than the implication that Mike would think he represents Global Network and would feel he has the authority to sign contracts either now or in the future on our behalf.

In response to our letter, ATG acknowledged that they did not have the personnel to oversee the production and manufacturing of the product. If we wanted this job done, it would have to fall to us at Global Trust to do it. They also agreed that the first round of quality control was unacceptable.

This should have been our first sign that this project was in serious jeopardy, but we didn't see it coming. Instead, Valerie and I took the lead on product development, with neither of us having any background or experience in this phase of business. The bond between us deepened as we gave our all to this task so crucial to our company. We were two capable women, accustomed to making decisions with conviction, but we had never sailed these waters before. Over dinner at Kyoto's, sipping our sake, we giggled over the decisions we were facing. We knew we didn't have the expertise to be doing what we were doing, but we had more confidence in ourselves than in the alternatives.

We could not improve the situation at Westwood, so we found a third and ultimately a fourth company to handle the production and development for us. On a trip to Dallas, Mark and I met with Aloe Dynamics, the developer and manufacturer we finally trusted to produce all-natural products for us. It was now April, and we were just beginning the production.

Bottling issues became our next nightmare. We chose Arroyo, a company who agreed to meet our tight deadline and did not require any up-front deposit. A month passed, and they acknowledged they were clearly reneging on their time commitment. For the next several hours, I got on the phone and began asking for other referrals. I found Pacific Bottling Company and spoke with their top sales rep. In order to get our business, he eagerly agreed to the same terms as our former company: he could meet our deadline, and his company would require no deposit up front. With our partners all on the line, I introduced this new bottling company as our knight on a white horse. After intensely grilling the rep, we all agreed to leave Arroyo and go with this new company. Much to our dismay, especially after our recent letter, ATG once again put their only available employee, Mike, on this task.

"Mike signed what?" I raised my voice in utter disbelief.

"Mike signed an agreement committing us to put up a reserve of $250,000 that is accessible to Pacific Bottling if anything should go wrong," Val repeated not so calmly.

"He can't do that. On what authority?"

"He once again signed as a representative of 21st Century Global Network," she said with her voice lowering a decibel.

"This is outrageous. We can't come up with that kind of money."

"Rene, I've just come back from there. The deal is done and we can't get out of it. We are completely locked in."

"Omigod." My voice trailed off. Val and I just sat looking at each other. Neither of us could think of anything to say.

I phoned the rep. He, of course, said the matter was out of his hands. The owner made this decision. "Sensing we were desperate," I muttered.

"Until you put up the money, we will not be able to proceed. We have to have some kind of assurance on this."

All the partners participated in a conference call within the hour. It was time to call in the chips. No use wasting time on the absurdity of why we were in this mess. We simply were and couldn't get out it.

"Each entity is going to have to come up with about eighty some-odd thousand," John was explaining.

"We hadn't counted on this," I heard Graham say. "We need more time to gather the money."

"We don't have that kind of cash just lying around either," Larry Brady echoed. "We should never have gone with this other company. We had this resolved with the first one."

No, we should never have signed an agreement to pay this kind of money. When they wanted our business—that was the time to get these details ironed out. I could feel the blame coming my way for having introduced this second company. I let it go and chose not to over-react.

"We can't let this hold us up," Mark said. If we are locked into the deal, then we're locked in. We can't quit now. Rene and I will put up the reserve."

A thunderous unspoken relief breathed into the phone at his words, by everyone but me. *First we're putting up the money for John and Valerie. Now we are putting up the money for ATG and IHI. This will never work. We can't run a business this way.* Mark was right. We could no longer run a business together. Suddenly we were thinking so differently about every aspect of business. I tried to talk to Mark about how I felt, but it was clear that this company mattered to him more than life itself. His pride, his name, his reputation and credibility were all on the line.

Once the reserve was securely in place, of course, it became apparent that Pacific Packaging couldn't meet the deadline for silk-screening the bottles. The infamous contract that had been signed by Mike somehow failed to protect us against this fiasco.

Valerie and I made the unilateral decision to order a few thousand bottles of each of our products with printed labels. Forget the beautiful bottles—our only thought was to get on with the business. We had a deadline to meet.

Mike assured us that the manufacturing of the household products being contributed by ATG was under control. They had been ready for months prior to the formation of our partnership.

"These ugly-looking bottles for the skincare and household products are just coming off the assembly line, and we were ready to begin filling them," Valerie reported to Mike.

"Um," he stammered. "Our original formulator had been in charge of this. I relied on what he told me," Mike explained. We thought we had let this man go. How did he get back into the picture?

"So what's the problem?" Valerie asked, trying to stay calm.

"Well, the household products aren't ready. Apparently, it's going to take another three weeks at least."

Valerie was so beside herself, she didn't even respond to him. Instead, she called me from her home in Vancouver. "The problems are just continuing to compound themselves. I don't see how we're going to work our way out of this one."

"We've been able to think of something to do about every mishap, but I think we've finally hit a wall," I replied.

That was the moment when, if all that had happened up until now wasn't enough, we should have pulled out. So much wasted energy. So much wasted money going down the tubes. Mark was barely speaking to me. Our differences in attitude about the financing were tearing us apart.

Out of frustration, I picked up the phone to call Harold and Larry. I knew better: Never, never make a phone call in a state of anger. You will undoubtedly regret it. If I could have thought of a solution, I would have pursued it. If I had the unilateral power to pull out, I would have done that. But neither was an option. I made the call.

"One moment, please, and I will connect you," said the cheery receptionist at ATG.

While I was on hold, I was thinking about what I wanted to say.

"Larry here...Good morning, this is Harold."

"This is the last straw! We've finally hit a wall that even *we* can't work around."

"What are you talking about?" Larry asked, exasperated.

"It's Mike. First, he can't oversee the product and keep chemicals out. He signs a warehousing contract that he had no right to sign. He can't keep the product development on schedule. He commits us to an unnecessary quarter of a million we shouldn't have had to spend, and Mark and I have to pick up those pieces. Then after we put out the money, he can't keep that project on schedule. But now, now, after giving us every assurance that the homecare products were under control, now we learn that that isn't going to happen either. It is delayed another three weeks. You are the ones who are so desperate to get this company launched for the sake of your almighty stockholders. Well, thanks to your inability to do your job, we might as well face it! We aren't going to make it. Period. There is no way out this time. We are not going to be able to launch in May!"

The edge in my voice was unmistakable. I wanted these guys to pull Mike from the job and give us their best employee. I wanted them to care, to put up their financial share, to meet deadlines—I wanted them to save our company. I wanted them to save my marriage. Truthfully, it wasn't anger I felt at all. I was terrified. *Dammit! What will it take for you guys to get your act together?*

I was so lost in my own thoughts that it was a minute before I realized that Larry was yelling into the receiver. He was equally terrified. His entire company was riding on the success of this venture. He had stockholders to answer to. Probably his very job was on the line, so he was taking his anger out on me as I was taking mine out on him.

"I'm sick and tired of you people blaming Mike for everything. He's doing the best he can. You're the one who took us to that godawful bottling company who is ripping us off and still missing deadlines. We should have stayed where we were. That was your bright idea. Why don't you step to the plate and accept some of the blame here."

"Now, let's all calm down." Harold tried to be a peacemaker, but it was useless. Larry and I were beyond peacemaking. Mark was Larry's hope. I was nothing more than a giant nuisance. I laid down the receiver and realized I was shaking all over. During previous crises, as long as Mark and I were together and we could envision a plan and take steps to implement it, no matter how bad the situation was, I could always pull myself together. This time I could not see a way out. I saw us caught in a whirlpool, being sucked in by its powerful vortex, inexorably pulling us deeper and deeper into personal and financial ruin.

The phone rang. It was Dean Schmanski, the son of close personal friends, who had come to work for us. Dean had a good head for business, having worked with his dad in running their company. Overseeing the ordering of our computer and office equipment, he had called earlier in the week to report to Mark and me that we couldn't wait any longer if we were going to launch in May. The phone company had been unwilling to accept the credit of our new company since we had no credit history. They evaluated the financial track of our three joint-venture companies, and concluded that none had sufficient credit to satisfy our creditors. Dean told us the only way they would go forward was on a personal guarantee from the Yarnells. There seemed to be no other way. Next it was the computer company, who would not turn over the computers without our personal guarantee. We had found office space in the Bank of America building in downtown Reno, but the same problem cropped up again.

"I know, I know," Mark said to Dean, "they want our personal guarantee."

"You got it," Dean replied.

Before we were done, it felt to me that Mark had placed our personal guarantee on the entire world and everything in it to launch this business. In the end, ATG put up a fraction of what we needed to launch this company, and IHI even less. Neither company was able to deliver on its promises for financial or product contributions. Nearly all of the financial responsibilities fell to Mark and me, and nearly all of the work responsibilities fell to us at Global Trust. Mark was showing the stress, and I was feeling it. We were living a nightmare.

Typical of us during these days, we were both up before 4:00 a.m. But this particular morning, Mark acted strangely. I heard a crash coming from his office bathroom and watched him stagger out, bumping into walls. I guided him to the couch in the library and helped him lie down. He fell instantly asleep, but his breathing wasn't normal; and when I spoke to him, he didn't respond. I took him by the shoulders and lifted him up, but he still didn't come to. *God help me. Who can I call at this hour of the morning?* Mark had become friends with a doctor who was the husband of one of my friends. I rang them, apologized for the hour, and asked for help. The doctor urged me to do everything humanly possible to wake Mark...and if I succeeded, to keep him awake. If I couldn't do that, he advised I should call 911 immediately.

After several futile tries, I called for help and within minutes, the REMSA ambulance appeared at our door. A handful of men and women came rushing into our home and took over. They were also unable to awaken him, so one of them gave him an injection and within a few minutes, Mark came to. He was disoriented and then outraged to find his home filled with people who were asking him questions he didn't want to answer. What is your name? What day of the week is it? Do you know where you are?

Mark glared at me as if to say "how could you do this to me?" I didn't know if I was more afraid that he might die or that he would live and hate me forever for this. The EMTs kept assuring me I had done the right thing and, unsure what the problem was, transported him to the hospital against his will. I followed in my car, and Amy joined me at the hospital shortly thereafter. We spent the day by his bedside as they ran tests. Nothing was found in his bloodstream, and no one could explain why this happened. He was released by the end of the day. The incident added to the strain on our relationship. I think Mark was torn between being appreciative for my concern and furious at the invasion of our home.

About a week later, he and I were upstairs getting ready for bed when he said, "I think I know what happened last week."

I was surprised he was willing to talk about it. "What?" I asked with genuine curiosity. I had been unable to put the incident out of my mind.

"Lately, I've been taking doses of human growth hormone, you know, HGH, to help me with sleep. That morning it didn't seem to work, so I took a second dose and I didn't think any more about it. But I just read the label: 'Warning: do not drive a vehicle when taking this and do not exceed dosage. In the event that an overdose occurs, notify medical attendants that you have taken this remedy. They may otherwise misdiagnose the symptoms. This can have serious consequences on the human body.'"

"Omigod. Where do you get that?"

"From a health food store. It's the hottest thing on the market right now. I figured if it is all-natural, I was safe using it."

"You're the only person I know who can overdose on vitamins and herbs," I teased. We hugged and fell into bed together. It was the first time in a long time that I felt close to him. I treasured the moment because I knew it wouldn't last.

Each day passed with no resolution of the fiscal pressures from our business. I shared my feelings about this with Valerie and John. They agreed that Mark and I couldn't go on single-handedly financing the company.

"Maybe we need to talk to Larry and Harold again," John offered.

"How many more times can we do that? They don't have the money, period. And now they are getting used to Mark and me bailing all of us out." I responded resentfully.

"But, Rene, it's your money too. You have a right to speak up about this," Valerie suggested.

"Easy for you to say. You don't have to be the one to say it. I'm getting used to Larry's wrath, but I dread Mark's. He isn't himself right now. He is so determined to have this company go that his decisions seem borderline desperate to me. I feel torn apart inside. On the one hand, I want to be supportive to my husband and on the other, I am watching our life savings go down the drain. We will run out of funds long before we have this company on solid ground."

"Maybe *we* should be the ones to say it. It isn't right that all of this financial burden should be falling to you," suggested John.

Valerie jumped in. "You're scared, Rene, and you have every right to be. This is not just Mark's money."

"But I can't say that. I will alienate myself permanently from the joint-venture partners and destroy what's left of my relationship to Mark. He is looking at all of this entirely differently than I am."

"John is right. It shouldn't be you who brings it up. John and I should. Granted, it is a little awkward since we have no money in this at all, but we owe you that much."

I felt a growing bond between Valerie and me at that moment. What she and John were saying meant so much to me. "What about Mark?" I asked fearfully.

"He needn't be in on the call," John replied. This should be between the three of us and Larry and Harold," John retorted.

"What about Graham?" I asked.

"What's the point?" Valerie responded. She was right. He has no prayer of contributing to this venture and never did. He knew that going in.

"So you honestly think that if you bare my frightened soul to the ATG guys, they will see the bigger picture and suddenly find the money that they have previously been unable to dig up?"

"It's a long shot," John replied, "but it's the only shot we've got. It's clearly better that we say it than you. Leave it to us, Rene. I will call and organize this with Harold right now."

The teleconference was set for 2:00 that afternoon. Mark was upstairs in his office, and I felt funny not telling him about it.

This was the first time in our married life that I consciously kept something important from him.

"Thanks for agreeing to this meeting on such short notice," John said to Larry and Harold.

"Not a problem," Harold responded. "We're a team, aren't we?"

I hope so. We are about to find out just how much of a team we really are. I said nothing. I knew this was one time that getting through the call with as few words as possible was my best strategy.

"We are at a pivotal point in our strategic planning," John began. "We are about to pour thousands and thousands of dollars into this project, and we can't continue the way we have been going. It just won't work unless we can pin everyone down to specific dollar amounts and specific times for remitting the money."

"This is Larry. Look, we are doing the best we can. I have stockholders to answer to, and I can't just pull the money from here and yonder any time I feel like it. I have to take it slowly so as not to upset them."

"Larry...." John's voice was always soft, but it seemed unusually delicate now. "We are attempting to move at lightning speed because of your quarterly reports to your stockholders. We've reached a point where you have to make a decision. Do you want to go forward and keep on schedule, or do you want to slow down and take more time to call in your resources? We at Global Trust are comfortable either way. What is not acceptable is to charge forward without our funding in place."

There was a pause, a long one. "We'd like to continue forward and keep on schedule," Larry said a little less arrogantly.

Harold went into a long diatribe about his potential funding sources. I had heard it all before. None of it ended in anything definitive.

"Harold, that is all fine," said John. "But the fact of the matter is that if we keep on schedule, the money has to be paid up front now. Where is it going to come from?"

Again, Harold reeled off a long-winded description of how close he was to collecting the funds to meet ATG's obligation.

"So, I propose that we move forward on this the moment that you have that in place." Valerie suggested. I could have hugged her. That is exactly what I wanted to say.

"But we can't afford to lose the time," Larry said, raising his voice. We can't let the schedule slip."

"So where do you propose that the money come from?" John asked again.

After a long pause, Harold suggested meekly, "Mark said that he can keep us going."

"But it is Rene's money too," interjected Valerie. No one said a word. *She might as well have hit both men over the head with a two-by-four. I wanted to be anyplace but on this call at this moment.*

"What are you saying, exactly?" Larry asked warily.

"Just that Rene is part of that funding source, and it is getting uncomfortable for her. Besides, she shouldn't be put in this position."

"But Mark said...."

"You see, Harold, Mark doesn't keep the books," I said reluctantly. "My mom does. But I'm right here watching them everyday, and we're running out of money. The well is about to dry up. Now Mark is talking about selling off our stocks at a loss or getting a loan against our Nu Skin income, grasping at straws as if the whole burden were on our shoulders. To be honest, I'm scared. I don't want to lose our life savings over this. But Mark is so determined to keep this ship afloat that he is willing to risk everything we have. I have different priorities. I just don't want to do that."

"Give us until Friday,' Harold suggested. "We need a little more time to pull in our resources."

"Let's set a time now, gentlemen," John said more forcefully than usual.

We agreed on Friday at 3:00 p.m. and that all the partners, including IHI and Mark, would be on the call.

I was grateful to both my partners. They did what they agreed to do, and it wasn't easy for them. Maybe now the pressure on Mark and me would be spread among the partners as originally agreed. It was my only hope.

Friday, June 6, at 3:00 sharp, all the partners were present and accounted for. Valerie was calling in from her home in Vancouver, BC, as was John. Larry and Harold were in Pasadena. Mark Brady, Larry's son, was calling from San Diego. My Mark was calling from our home. Graham came into the Global Network office and sat with me in my office as we took the call on my speakerphone.

Valerie usually facilitated the meetings; but since this one was called by John and had to do with the finances, John started things off.

"We asked all the partners to participate in this call because we are facing some serious financial crises. We have run out of time and money. It is critical that we have a specific time and dollar commitment from each partnership for their share of the funding. But more to the immediate point, the first shift leaves in an hour—and we haven't the funds to meet payroll."

John stopped talking. He had made his point. It was a powerful place to stop.

No one seemed overly eager to speak next. It was Harold who braved it first. "We at ATG are very close to bringing in our part. We have had several conversations with our East Indian connection. They are most interested in the project and think they are good for $50,000."

Larry said one of his stockholders was interested in possibly upping the ante on his investment. "Could be as much as $100,000."

Graham began talking about some of the doctors and backers of IHI. He thought for sure he could eventually bring in at least a $100,000 more.

For forty-five minutes that conversation droned on...each male voice full of more bravado than the last. Payroll had to be met in 15 minutes. It was I who had to address it. Dean was literally pacing up and down the hallway, waiting for a release of funds so he could pass out the checks.

"Gentlemen, may I remind you that we have 15 minutes left to meet today's deadline. Beyond the long-range planning, we have immediate needs." I felt that I was the voice of doom-and-gloom reality. They were flexing their muscles about what they will do in the future, and I had to spoil it all with a reminder of the now.

I expected a knock at my door any minute and could picture the discussions in the hallway. "Should we knock? Should we tell everyone to wait? Should we give them the checks and hope the bank will cover us?" But no knock came. They must have decided it was not wise under the circumstances.

By 4:15 no resolution had been reached; and it was clearly not forthcoming. I looked over at Graham. He seemed so much more detached from this conversation than I. Amazing! How did he do it? It was as if these problems had nothing to do with him personally.

I waited to hear from John or Valerie. As the call progessed, they both became noticeably less vocal. Mark had hardly said a word throughout the entire conversation. I'm sure he was hoping that someone would take the burden off of his shoulders.

There was a long awkward hush. No one seemed compelled to break the silence. No, that isn't quite true. I couldn't stand it anymore. I was going to be the one to face our employees.

I was trembling inside as I spoke. It was almost as if I were having an out-of-body experience. My voice seemed to be coming from somewhere outside of me. I was past anger—way past anger. I just felt sickened by what we had permitted to happen to us. With great effort, I found my voice: "We are out of time and have to come to some conclusion now. I would like to make a proposal. Mark, we haven't had a chance to discuss this, so let me know if this meets with your approval as well. We have to have more money infused into the company this minute or we send employees out of here with no pay. So this is my suggestion: Mark and I put in the $25,000 we need to keep us going this week. Let's give this until Tuesday and all meet again by phone. At that time, each of the partners would submit a plan for meeting their commitment. Each of you agrees to a date, a reasonable one, by which you will come up with the committed dollar figure. I suggest we put this in writing. When that date arrives and the commitment is met, we go forward as planned. In the unlikely event that the date should arrive and the commitment not be met, then and only then do we renegotiate stock ownership of this company."

I knew about a primordial scream but had never actually heard one until that moment. It was Larry Brady. The sound began at the bottom of his gut and roared out of his mouth. It was loud and bloodcurdling, sending shivers through my entire body.

"Noooooooooooooooooooooooooooo!"

Just when I thought it couldn't get any worse, it did. Mark spoke next, not as loudly but equally formidable. "Never! I would never agree to that. A deal is a deal, and we made a deal to go into this venture together. I would never back away from that. Never. Do you hear me? Never!"

Mark Brady jumped in. He was his father's son. "IHI would never agree to that. That would destroy the whole reason for our coming into this. You are out of your mind if you think you can bully us like this."

I knew my proposal would not be well received, but I didn't anticipate the intensity of the reactions to it.

Graham spoke next, his voice calm. "Look, guys. Some adjustment will have to be made for any investor that would be brought in. Why not Mark and Rene if they are the ones who deliver the funds?" But no one was listening.

Mark said we would put up the $25,000 and the call ended.

Graham scooted out the door, uttering something about not letting this get me too upset.

I wrote the check and took it down to Dean. I knew he knew what I was feeling. We didn't need to say a word.

I went back to my office, closed the door, and watched the sun set over the Reno skyline. Glittering signs and lights began to outline Virginia Street. This was my town, my community. I had had my talk show here. I had worked to establish Nevada's only law school. I had served it politically. I had developed a world of friends and acquaintances over my eighteen years in Reno, but never had I felt so alone.

I didn't know where to go. I knew I could not go home. I called Nancy. "I need you." That's all I could say.

"Come on over. I'm here alone, and I'll have a bottle of good wine open and breathing."

By the time I got to her home, I was despondent. Our company was doomed, and I knew it. Even an infusion of money would not solve the problem. My marriage was collapsing and I had never felt so hopeless.

Nancy put her arms around me and just held me. She didn't pull back, and neither did I. Tears were running down my face and onto her shoulder. It was the safest, most comforting place I could be at that moment. I thanked God for her. How incredible to have a friend who is really there for you when you really need her.

Nancy poured us each a glass of Merlot. I settled into the couch looking out over our beautiful Rancho San Rafael Park. Even before serving in office, I had been involved in its preservation and development. As a commissioner, I served on its board. I could remember having a life before 21st Century Global Network. But at this moment, I was unable to see myself having one after it.

"I blew it, Nance. Every time I open my mouth, I seem to alienate myself further from the partners. But that isn't what is killing me. It's Mark. I don't even know him. If I never came home again, I don't think he'd even bother looking for me. It's worse than his having fallen out of love. It feels like he hates me. There is nothing in his life but the company. That's all that matters to him."

"Maybe your time with Mark has come to an end, Rene. You had some wonderful years together, but now it may be time for you to move apart with your lives. Can you accept that yet?"

"No. I can't even conceive of my life without Mark. Our lives are so intertwined personally and professionally—that's how Mark wanted it. "Mark and Rene Yarnell!" We have people all over the world who consider us the epitome of what they want to become. They see us as a couple deeply in love, with success, freedom, and purposeful lives. That's who we *were*. What happened to us?"

"It came, and it went. Those things are often passing in our lives. The secret is to appreciate them while we have them."

We let the silence linger while I thought about that. I could feel the tears welling up in me again. "I don't want to lose it. It's not the money. It's my life with him."

"Do you think you have a choice?"

"I must think so. I'm not ready to give up."

"When you look ahead six months from now, what do you see?"

"I see Mark and me lying on our hammock together and him saying: 'I thank God for you every day. I'm so glad we put each other first and didn't let the company consume us. You are my number one priority, Rene. I almost lost you. I won't ever let that happen again.'"

"And then he kisses you and the curtain goes down." Nancy finished my fantasy for me.

I knew she was gently trying to prod me away from building castles in the sky and push me in the direction of reality. I wasn't ready to go there. I just couldn't face another failed marriage. I was slower to fall in love with Mark than he with me, but my love for him had grown over time. Now I couldn't even imagine a life without him.

"Yeah, and he just keeps holding me and never lets go."

"You are going to get hurt really badly, girlfriend. You know that, don't you?"

"Going to?"

"Umhum. If you think you hurt now, it can only get worse. I just wish I could protect you from that. But you have to move at your own pace. I can see you're not ready to let go."

"No, I can't. I could never feel good about myself if I didn't try even harder to put things back together. I need to step back and figure out what my part is in all of this. I want to work on me and change what I can. Mark didn't do this all alone. I helped get us to this point. I can't fix him, but I can fix me."

"You're challenge is that Mark doesn't think he needs fixing but he would vehemently agree that you do."

"So isn't that a good first step? We both agree I need to work on me. So I will."

"You're going to get hurt, Rene. You're going to get hurt really badly. You are setting yourself up for a fall."

"Nance, what else can I do? I can't give up yet. I just can't."

"So what do you want to do?"

"Clear things up with the partners to the best of my ability and then put my whole effort into my relationship with Mark. No matter what happens, I have to know I gave it my all. I have no control over what is happening in our company. If I did, I would put it on hold until we have the money in place, but not a single one of the partners would agree to that. Why should they? Can you imagine their reaction had I suggested *that* on the call?"

"It sounds like everybody is hanging their hopes on this company—and this company's survival depends on Mark and Rene. Without you two, there is no company."

"And there is no 'Mark and Rene.' There is only a 'Mark' and a 'Rene.' So, in a very strange sense, if I put my effort into working on us, I may inadvertently be giving the company the only thread of hope it has." I could see Nancy didn't agree with my conclusions, but she didn't try to persuade me otherwise. "I don't think there are any really bad guys in this drama," I continued. "I think Mark is being used by ATG and IHI, but he doesn't see it that way. You're right, Nance. Everyone, including John and Valerie, are putting all their hopes on Mark. And he and I are going to lose everything financially. I guess I could try to stop it, but then even if I won that battle, I would lose him."

"What can I do to support you and be your friend? This is going to be one of the most difficult phases of your life."

At that point, the floodgate opened. I began crying, then sobbing until my gut was wrenching. Nancy moved over and held me. "What can I do?" she asked softly.

"I just want him to love me, Nance. All I want is for him to keep his promise and put our love before everything else. Please, God, just give me my old life back. Please. Please."

I stayed on that couch for hours. Nancy stroked me and rocked me until I had no tears left. We didn't say a word. There was nothing left to say. At some point, I must have drifted off to sleep. When I awoke, the house was empty. Nancy left me a note saying that her sister came by and they had gone out for dinner. I looked at the clock. It was after 11:00. I had made up my mind. My marriage came first. I was going home to devote myself to saving it.

I crawled into bed next to Mark. I'm sure he felt me arrive, but he didn't acknowledge me. He pretended to be asleep.

When I awoke the next morning, he was already up. I washed my face, but nothing would wash away the pain or the aftermath of last night's weeping. My face still looked swollen and tear-stained, and my eyes were puffy and bloodshot. I went downstairs and found Mark in his office. .

"Where were you last night?" he demanded to know.

"I went to Nancy's."

"Why didn't you come home?"

"I needed time. I didn't know what to expect here. I needed to be with someone whose support I could count on."

"You should have come home."

I wondered what that meant. Could it be that he was saying I would have found support here with him? Before I could let that possibility in, he added. "You really blew it. You will never have respect from the partners. It's all over." *It is the partners who have let us down. If there is any disrespect here, it should be cast in their direction.*

"The only respect that matters to me is yours, sweetheart. I really want to talk. I would give anything in the world if we could get away—just for a day or two—and be together, sort things out, get ourselves back on track."

"That's ridiculous. We are at an all-time crucial point in this company. I am its president. I have to stay strong. I'm needed here."

"Then let's talk here. Let's make the time."

"I can't now. I have a conference call coming in any minute. I have to try to repair the damage you caused on yesterday's call. This isn't the time."

I felt my heart fall. *When will the time ever be right? Please, Mark. Don't give up on us. We are good together.*

The phone rang. Mark was saved from any more dialogue with me.

I made my way downstairs to my office and went through my morning motions. Flip on the computer, make coffee, let Cody out. As I sat at my computer and opened the file to my affirmations, certain ones jumped out at me because they were so far from reality. I said them, repeated them, and repeated them again, as if somehow by saying them more intently I would move toward making them happen.

> ➤ I feel supported working with a team of positive people who share my values. *A little ways to go here.*
> ➤ I feel loving when I find positive solutions to problems and sensitively share these constructive approaches with my associates. *Hmm, not doing so well on this one either.*
> ➤ People listen to me when I speak because I have something of value to say. *Everyone but my partners..*
> ➤ I am thrilled to see our current book hit number one on the bestseller list, thereby putting network marketing into the mainstream. *In the midst of all of our trauma, this one is actually happening, and we are missing the joy of it. People everywhere are reading and benefiting from our book, writing to "Mark and Rene," thanking us for having helped them. How is it that we can help the whole world and can't help ourselves?*
> ➤ I have the strength to be loving toward Mark without expectations during this period when he rejects and criticizes me. I am supportive of him in becoming his best self as I am working to accomplish the same. By being empathetic and truthful with him, I will turn his heart toward being a loving and caring person—toward me and especially toward those he is supposed to be serving.
> ➤ I can feel my love being transferred into Mark as clearly as the time in Atlanta when we envisioned exchanging bodies with each other.

Forming Our Company

> I am a warm and compassionate woman, expressing this sensitivity first to my husband *regardless of the distance between us* and also to others who need my understanding. I am not holding onto any expectation of what this will bring.

> I am passionate as I show my love for Mark, making our relationship the highest priority, opening up our communication, and doing little acts of kindness that are meaningful to him.

Sipping my coffee, having dwelled on my list of thirty or so affirmations, I felt slightly uplifted. I was ready to do whatever I had to do to take my relationship with Mark to the next level. This was a milestone, a bump in the road. We would get past it. We would. We would.

I closed that file and opened a new one. With a blank screen in front of me, I began constructing a letter to our joint-venture partners. I wasn't sure if I would send it, but I knew I needed to write it.

Dear Larry, Harold, and Graham,

Let me begin by telling you how scared I am. And I suspect I'm not the only one. Larry Brady's outcry may have been a primal scream indicating his fear is as deep as mine. Each one of us, in our own way, stands to lose much if this project is not a success. So the only real question is this: Is it possible to find a solution that will address the concerns and meet each of our needs? And if so, how?

Not only is my business relationship on the line, but our differing outlook about finances is driving a wedge between Mark and me in our personal life. Mark is willing to risk everything we have in the world and go beg (literally) for a few million more from our friends, and not ask for any compensation from ATG or IHI. While this is a generous spirit, from my perspective it is not an acceptable approach for either a public company like yours or a private one like ours.

The choice for Mark and me is this: We either stand together on this matter or we divide our assets and stand apart. I can understand if some of you prefer to have only Mark involved in this company and me gone. If that is the group consensus, I would immediately accept

Mark's proposal of divided assets and move on to find another way to fulfill my purpose in life. However, it is a bit late for that. Everything we have has already been spent or promised. And for more heartfelt reasons than I can possibly tell you, I prefer to stand beside my husband on our decision about the financing of this company. Along with Valerie and John, Mark and I have more to contribute to this company as a partnership than either of us alone.

I hope that you will search your hearts and find a means for coming up with your share of your committed contribution to this venture. Or in lieu of that, you will agree to reasonably compensate any partner who is able and willing to fill in the giant hole to fund this company. This is what will make it possible for me to stand with Mark in our financial decisions.

There are other alternatives, and I suspect that, among us, we have considered them all. For now, I have chosen to concentrate on the most positive one, namely, working to renew my relationship with my husband that we may continue to work together to build the first truly giant company in the network marketing industry.

I hope that each of you accepts this memorandum in the spirit it is intended. Whatever options we explore together, it is my hope that, beyond the funding issue, we can find a way to preserve the spirit of cooperation we had in the beginning. While I admit to being frightened, I am searching to find a belief in our future together. I look forward to your response.

Sincerely, Rene Reid Yarnell

I read the letter over. It was exactly how I felt. I knew that I wasn't asking anything unreasonable. I said a quiet, reflective prayer wondering if I should share it with Mark. I knew that was pointless. Without further hesitation, I pressed the send button on the fax machine. Now I would wait for their response.

None came. No one said a word. No angry outburst. No cool response. Nothing.

In the meantime, I kept waiting for Mark to make time for us. Not a word from him either. Not a single word. If we didn't communicate soon, I knew I would have to take a much bolder step.

PART II

Present

June 1998 – July 1999

CHAPTER 13

SEARCHING FOR ANSWERS
June 1998

As I headed west on the Interstate, with the warmth of the sun at my back, I watched the landscape transform from the sage-scattered brown of the Nevada desert to the forest-green of the California coastline. My soul felt like that desert at this moment, so dry and barren. I prayed that a little time spent away would bring life to my spirit.

Driving on cruise control, I let my thoughts wander back to the start of our relationship when Mark and I lay side by side in his hammock baring our souls to each other.

"Of course, I would never leave you. I could never even distance myself from you," I could remember him saying. "And if you ever leave me, I promise you...I will follow you wherever you go." *Dear God, let him mean this. Please Mark, come follow me. I know we can pull our lives back together and make it even better than before.*

Having decided to return to my roots, I headed for San Francisco, where life began for me after graduating from college. I stopped outside of Sacramento and found a pay phone so that I could do my regularly scheduled Saturday training call. This was a time when I spoke by teleconference to all our representatives in the company who wanted to be trained to use our system for building their businesses. It was also an opportunity for them to ask questions and offer suggestions for things that we could do to make their work in the field more productive. In the words of George Burns, "All I needed was a little honesty and sincerity, and if I could *fake* that, I had it made." I could do it. I knew I could do it.

As I joined the call, I heard Amy's voice. I wondered if she knew. And if she knew, what did she think? Then I heard Mark's voice talking to Ranya Alexander, Jonathan Goldsmith, John DeHart, and Donnie Walker, all presidential team members. It was unusual for Mark to be on the call. For a fleeting moment, I prayed it was to beg me to turn around and come home. Please, let him tell me how much he loves me in front of every distributor on the call. But that didn't happen. It couldn't happen. Mark kept up a great front, and once he knew I hadn't shunned my responsibility for this teleconference, he excused himself from the call. It was a loud and clear message to me. He didn't need me. I did the training that morning apparently without anyone suspecting a problem.

As I drove over the Bay Bridge, the City was a welcomed sight. Its spirit of peace, hope, and love awakened my whole being.

I knew I needed to spend time with someone who would give me objective feedback about my situation. I wasn't at a point in my life where I needed to be told that I'm okay and he's all wrong. No, I needed to become clear about what was within my power to do. Where had I gone wrong? How could I have handled things better? What did I want from Mark, and what was I willing to give to him? And, most importantly, and what I had lost sight of, what was it that God wanted of both of us? As I drove on, I kept asking myself who I could turn to for guidance.

It had been thirty-two years since I had taken my leave from my religious order, the Daughters of Charity, but they were still my family. I had kept in touch with many of the Sisters over the years. Yes, like Julie Andrews in the Sound of Music, I would head to the motherhouse.

I drove to Los Altos Hills where the West-coast headquarters was located. I'd never been to this branch before. I had entered the Community through Marillac Seminary in St. Louis. The beauty and tranquility reminded me of my seminary days. There was no doubt that God resided here.

The Sisters greeted me warmly. I inquired about Sister Josephine, the person who might give me spiritual counsel now. We had kept up with each other over the years, ever since she taught me philosophy at Marillac College. I knew she was somewhere in California, Santa Barbara, the last I'd heard. Great news! She had been missioned to San Francisco. I dialed the number and the extension, and she answered on the second ring.

"Jody!"

"Rene!" It had been only a couple of years since we had written but at least five or six since we had spoken. It always amazed me when people recognized my voice. It also made me feel loved and remembered, which, at that moment, was the most important thing in the world to me. It was what I didn't have at home.

We met at St. Agnes Church in the Haight-Ashbury—ah, days of my youth! I had moved to the Haight in the famous summer of '67 to begin my master's study at the University of San Francisco. It was the season of flower children, love, and peace marches. The memories came flooding back as we went to Saturday afternoon Mass and then back to St. Elizabeth's, where Jody lived, to have dinner with the Sisters. After dinner, we found time to be alone and talk.

"So what's going on?"

"Jody, I don't know if I really know anymore. It's so hard to say."

"Problems with your marriage?"

"Umhmm, major ones. And I don't know what to do or where to turn. So here I am." I tried to explain about the pressures of the business, the changing relationship, the growing distance between Mark and me, the lack of any semblance of love between us. "I'm here because I feel I need to make a retreat. I was hoping I might be able to do it at the motherhouse."

Sister picked up the phone and called our mutual friend, Sister Audrey, who was now on the counsel with the Community. Audrey said this was the busiest time of the year to try to get me in. Then Jody tried one of her elderly friends who had a home on the beach. It too was occupied for the moment. But I knew with certainty that was what I had to do—get to the beach, where I could feel the draw of the ocean and experience its healing power.

Saying a temporary goodbye to Jody, I headed south on Highway 1 along the coast. It was unusually foggy for a summer day—El Nino, everyone explained. I was bound and determined to find sun. I stopped at Half Moon Bay Lodge. It was a perfect setting, but still no sun. The clerk at the front desk said I might end up in Mexico before I felt the warmth of the rays. I kept driving, knowing that when sunshine appeared, that was where I was supposed to stop.

By the time I reached Santa Cruz, the sun was shining brightly. I should have known—Santa Cruz, the place where I'd come in the past when my life was in crisis. As I drove toward the boardwalk, I could hear Bette Midler singing, *Under the Boardwalk*. This is where I lived twenty-six years ago when I was pregnant with my son and separated from his father. I should have thought of this on my own. It was a healing place for me then, and I was sure it would be now. It was the perfect *déjà vu* spot for a retreat.

I bought a newspaper and began checking the short-term and vacation rentals—on the beach. It had to be on the beach. I set up an office in my car, and began calling on ads and leaving the number of my cell phone. On my second try, I found what I was looking for. A single mom, Meera, and her daughter, Crystal, were going to Mexico for three weeks, and were looking for someone to housesit and take care of their dog, cat, and bird. The house overlooked Sunset Beach, about 20 miles south of Santa Cruz. I had found my home away from home.

I called Mom to let her know I was making a retreat, I phoned Jody to let her know I had found a place, and e-mailed Valerie and John to let them know I was gone.

>Hi! I'm sorry about slipping away so quickly. My
>repeated and last attempt at communication with
>Mark blew up on me in the wee hours. I just can't
>go on the way we are. Something has to give. So
>I've decided to make that retreat I talked about
>with you.

>I'm settled in for now. I found sun and surf and it
>brings me peace. I just came from a long walk on
>the beach, and already feel somewhat renewed.
>My plan is to go on working as usual. I'll do my
>training teleconferences, return calls, work on
>updates for our fax-on-demand and Web site,
>and keep moving forward on the September
>convention. I can do those things just as well from
>here...maybe better.

>Will look forward to hearing from you. We need to
>all pray for each other, for our relationships, and for
>our company. Try to take care of Mark. I love him
>but just can't go on living with the way things are. I
>am trying to become more open and more receptive
>to new and better ways to improve our relationship.

>For now, I feel I am doing what I must. I pray that
>God will lead me to where I am supposed to be and
>doing what I am supposed to be doing.

> Stay in close touch, please. I miss you. Love, Rene

It was early Monday morning and I couldn't wait to get down to the beach. It was foggy, but this was still my ocean, and I felt the pull of the tide drawing me to the water. Walking down the path with Doji, my new four-legged friend, I could feel the healing power as I breathed in the air. I sat down on the bench overlooking miles of beach and realized that, without the ability to see the ocean through the fog, it looked like I hadn't left Nevada. This verse came pouring out of me as I looked out over the gray mist, with only the isolated sand and driftwood peeking through.

The beach is like the desert on a foggy day
Barren, desolate, without ocean or bay
Just me, alone, with the sound of the wind and the waves
Looking for snails...or seals...or any sign of life
Amidst the strife

I was looking for any sign of life amidst the strife of my marriage. I believed it was there; it was just fogged over. The haze would pass. Life would reappear and love would flourish. As I sat looking out, I let my thoughts drift with the mist. I thought I saw a lone figure of a fisherman standing out near the water. How appropriate—a fisherman. So biblical. So Christ-like. I found myself slipping into a kind of meditation as I talked to the lone Fisherman.

What is it Mark wants of me? Not what he says, but what he really feels. What am I supposed to do with my life? Do Mark and I belong together? What is the Divine plan for us? If we're supposed to work this out, how could I make changes in myself to effect the needed change in our relationship? And if we cannot rebuild our marriage, how will I know? Will it be evident to me whether we are meant to be together or go apart? And if the latter, where would I go and what would I do? My God, show me the way through this fog.

When I got back up to the house, I called Mom to let her know what was really going on. She was concerned. I could only imagine what she was thinking. Then I called Nancy. For now, I'd covered my bases. I didn't want anyone else to know where I was, or why. With a phone and a computer, I could keep up with the rest of the world without their knowing of my problems.

From biblical times, seekers of truth fled to the desert for solitude with God. I needed to be alone with Him, to listen, to pray, to journal, and to turn within for answers. I needed this time away from the distractions of my life to sit quietly with myself and rediscover my own inner-strength, my authentic power. Over the next few days, I spent long hours on this desert-beach trying to understand how things could have gotten so far off track between

Mark and me. I knew that no matter how much a marriage disintegrates, it is always salvageable—if both parties want that. The challenge for me was that Mark had no interest at this time in renewing our relationship. If it was to happen, with only me working toward this end, it would be a slower, more circuitous route leading down more arduous paths. Though there were no guarantees, I believed I could still turn things around; but I knew it was going to be a long road home.

I spent my time in reflection, seeking to gain an awareness of Mark and me, respectively and together. The newness and passion of our love had waned. While this is the normal course of events, it seemed to have caught Mark by surprise. He didn't seem to believe that should ever happen: Somehow our love would supersede the mundane; it would rise above all other customary passages. While some might see this as myopic, I found it to be part of Mark's charm. Everything was bigger than life; no person or event was ordinary in his eyes.

I thought back to that evening in the Florida Keys when we sat talking with our children about our pending marriage. It was Amy who so wisely said, "You'd better have something else to hold onto after the fu-fu wears off. No matter how much you think this feeling will last forever, it won't. Then will you have enough to go on living a regular day-to-day life together?"

From the very beginning, there was a kind of symbiosis to our life together. We were two very dissimilar individuals who integrated our lives in order to create something of mutual benefit. We brought our respective theological backgrounds into our relationship. We had similar life purposes, mine being to stimulate others to lead purposeful lives by maximizing their potential to turn challenges into positive life changes. His was to instill self-belief in others. We had independently chosen network marketing as the medium for delivering our respective messages and touching people's lives. We had found a compatibility for teaching and writing, whereby our different styles blended well to produce balance in our message. I felt that our relationship was begun on a solid foundation. It may have happened quickly, but we thought it through carefully, and established goals and priorities that reflected the values of each of us. As I examined our early beginnings, I could not find fault with any aspect.

Mark, of late, had been quick to point out our differences: he liked paragliding and adventure sports; I favored tennis and more grounded activities. He was drawn to horror and adventure films; I preferred drama, romance, and feel-good movies. He was, by nature, more solitary; I enjoyed my alone time, but I was more sociable than he. But those differences did not make for incompatibility. As I headed home, brushing the sand off my feet, I had convinced myself that we had hit hard times, but our marriage was worth "saving." I was ready to uncover the wounds and begin the healing process.

One question kept popping into my head. It was one John Radford had raised over breakfast recently following a disrupted partners' meeting. "What do you have to offer to Mark?" I felt this was as good a place to begin as any.

> June 18, 1998
> What do I have to offer Mark? So much.
> I contribute a balance and stability to his life. Looking back over that part of his life he has shared with me, he has rarely been alone. He has always jumped out of one relationship and immediately into another. It might be good for Mark to spend some time alone to see if he tuly wants an interdependent relationship.
> I bring a softness and mellowness to his hyper-activity. Mark can't sit still. In the course of a conversation, he will be up and down innumerable times. I smooth out the rough edges of his eccentricities.
> I listen to him with an empowered listening. He's generally better at talking than hearing so I think Mark needs this in his life. He is always coming up with new ideas—very creative ones—and likes to bounce them off of me. He dominates our

conversations so we tend to talk about what ever is on his mind more than mine. I enjoy this part of our time together, but it would be nice if we could balance this more. I would love to feel *heard* more than I do. But, for now, I am content to be his sounding board.

He likes to lead a solitary life, and I give him space to do this. Often he will be on the phone or reading or writing at his desk while I am downstairs doing the same in my own office. For nearly seven years we have spent twenty-four hours a day, seven days a week in each other's company. Compared to most couples who go off to separate jobs, we have lived a lifetime together. On the other hand, when he wants a partner, I am there for him. We are great travel companions and have literally traversed the world together. A balance of togetherness and intervals of solidarity have been my gift to him.

I add the gift of perseverance to Mark's visionary side. I hadn't thought of this before: Mark usually starts the process and has the vision to see where we might go with a project. But seeing projects through and keeping them on track is a gift I offer him.

I bring a different, and I feel more grounded, perspective to his life. Although we have opposite personalities, at one time he saw me as his soul mate and someone interchangeable with him. Not with identical talents, but complementary ones. Through my contribution, I round out the gaps in his disparities.

I love his touch, to hold and be held, to feel my hand in his. I love the feeling of slipping in bed next to him, just knowing that we have the whole night together. I offer Mark the gift of my love.

We spent much more time in the early days of our married life praying together and talking about things of the heart. As I look over our life more recently, this is an area where our relationship has slipped. I want to renew this, and I know we can. But overall, I offer him the gift of spiritual nourishment.

I offer continued support for Mark to stay clean and sober. It was a long road home to sobriety, but we got there...together. While I stood by him, it was he who conquered this by his own determination, knowing that there was a better life for him without this albatross. From my perspective, our life together has been measured by Mark on drugs, off drugs, or withdrawing from drugs. The final stage, a year-long cleansing process, was the hardest. I believe that some of the challenges we are now facing, as Dr. Brewer predicted, are due to the changes that inevitably occur when one goes from strong dependency to total independence. He knows beyond a shadow of a doubt that this was my ultimate gift to him. Whatever happens, I believe Mark Yarnell is once and for all drug free, and if it means that I have to lose him so that he could gain mastery over this, I would do it all over again.

I lay my head back on the chair and closed my eyes for a moment. It was crucial that I begin my retreat being totally honest with myself about my situation.

My relationship with Mark was so closely intertwined with our business that the two were inseparable. That was how both of us had wanted it. I realized that I didn't have an inkling of what being married to him would look or feel like apart from our working together. A question I needed to answer was whether I could, for the sake of the marriage, separate our personal life from our business partnership. And, if so, what form would it take? This would be a question I would be resolving for days and perhaps weeks ahead.

Just then, the phone rang. It was Nancy calling to check up on me.

"Are you hanging in there?"

"Yeah...by my fingernails. Do you really think I'm doing the right thing?" I needed reassurance.

"Absolutely. You're taking care of yourself, and that's what you need to be doing right now. You were dying back here. I know. I was watching you and felt so helpless to do anything."

"These past couple of months haven't been real good for either one of us." I was referring to the homeless project we shared together. With Nancy as executive director and me as board chair, we spent a lot of time dealing with political issues in our community. Project ReStart came under fire when another agency wanted our funding. The sheriff had been our partner and strong supporter until, for personal reasons, he switched his allegiance and strongly urged key public officials to back the other agency.

"I'm sure you won't be surprised that we didn't get our funding for ReStart this year. With all that you have going on, I didn't want to bother you with this news. But Joanne Bond and Jeff Griffin both acquiesced to the sheriff on this." (Joanne was the chairman of the county commission this year. Jeff was the mayor of Reno. They were both my friends.) They had heard my version of the facts and the sheriff's, and chose to act on his recommendation. The county and city had been funding ReStart and working closely with us since 1990 when we first started the project while I was serving on the commission. Losing their support was a giant blow to our program. I felt betrayed on both grounds: in business and in my community project. No words could get past the lump in my throat. I heard Nancy crying too. As we hung up the phone, it was clear that we were both at turning points in our lives.

Walking anywhere is therapeutic, but walking on the beach is like none other. The next day, as I trod barefoot through the sand, I decided it was a good time to examine the other side of the question I had explored the day before. Part of the answer to my quest lay in coming to grips with what it is that Mark has to offer me. I wanted to place my focus on what he *was* capable of giving and not on what he *wasn't* contributing to our marriage at this time. If I was going to be realistic and bring about valuable change, I needed to look at this.

Wandering along the packed sand close to the water with Doji at my side, I thought about how Mark had once manifested his love for me in unmistakable ways: with lovemaking and poetry and insisting on being with me always. While he asked fidelity of me, I simply needed to be reassured that he would never leave me. That exchange of emotional stability was the basis of our marriage vows. Although, this time, I was the one who physically left the relationship, I felt he had long since abandoned me emotionally. I only wanted him to come back and simply "be" with me in the deepest sense of the word. Be—one of the most complex words in our vocabulary. In spite of what was happening, I knew from experience that Mark was capable of loving me in the way I needed to be loved. The only question was whether he would choose this again.

Once, Mark wouldn't consider taking a significant step without seeking my opinion or involving me in the discussions. He offered me a sense of inclusion in all of our affairs. He respected my mind, and I so needed this again.

Once, Mark had encouraged me to reach my full potential by encouraging me to write and having me join him on stage in making presentations. Over the years, I knew I had grown in my writing and public speaking skills because of the confidence and coaching he gave me. I appreciated this gift and I wanted to return to that life. I loved our working and traveling together, and I yearned to have that back.

Once, Mark had offered me financial stability like I had never known. Today, I feared impending bankruptcy. We'd never been at such risk before. While he thrives on living on the edge, I become insecure and frightened. I knew he was capable of generating a solid income again, but I feared things had gone too far. One question weighed on me: If we relinquished everything outward about our life that we had known up until this moment—all financial security—could Mark and I reconstruct our life by putting our priorities in order? Could we be happy with each other if we had to start over financially? Without hesitating, I felt certain we could do that.

Doji got bored walking with me and found some people to play Frisbee with him. There was a lesson to learn even from him. He made friends easily and was the happiest animal I had ever known. As I watched him frolic in the ocean, I felt comforted by his playfulness.

Sitting down on the beach and digging my toes into the warm sand, I began exploring the reverse of today's question. So I knew what we had to offer each other, but what was it we really *needed* from each other?

I wanted Mark to continue to encourage me in living up to my full potential. I craved to return to the time when it was the two of us together ready to face any conflict that might arise in our life. Why had we degenerated into taking opposite sides in front of our partners? Why was he so quick to support anyone who spoke ill of me? I hungered for a marriage that was a genuine, caring relationship between two people who respected each other and wanted to grow spiritually together—two people drawn to share their day-to-day lives and life purpose together.

Mark was now asking me to back away from the business. He no longer needed me as an equal in his life but wanted me to let him run the business and make all the descions related to it. Whew! I didn't know if I could do that. But, I would flow with the idea for the moment. Is it possible that what we both wanted could come about if I were to back away from our business? Would he still see me as an equal in the rest of our life? Could we create a new life with less entanglement? Did he still want to? Did I? I had always loved working together. I didn't know how our life would be without this.

The next morning, I woke up at my usual time, fixed coffee, did my morning journaling and visualizations, and checked my e-mail. Doji's eyes-said, "Let's go for a walk....pleeeeeease." It was early dawn, and the light of day was just breaking. We headed down the road above the ocean, with Doji leading the way. Lately I had been feeling physical discomfort from my isolation and self-examination. I found it hard to breathe this morning, but I forced myself to drink in the ocean air. It was so pure and clean. And as I walked, my thoughts picked up from where I left off the day before.

I felt it was time to examine those aspects of our relationship that were in conflict, imagining myself living out the opposing alternatives and giving each side serious—and to the best of my ability, objective—consideration. I began thinking back to all that we had agreed to when we first came together and which of those aspects had changed over time. What was he asking of me now, and what would it look like if I went along with him on this?

We were two of a kind, he and I. Back then, he'd been quite vocal about wanting an equal partner, as opposed to someone who merely walked in his shadow and admired his talents. He wanted a life partner who could interchange with him and fill the needed roles. We would be alter egos, soul mates in every sense. Now he had dramatically changed this stance, demanding that he be in charge of our business and finances, while I would passively trust in his ability to be successful. Neither of us was willing to subjugate our fundamental beliefs about finances to the other. He wanted the freedom to invest every last penny into this business if he so chose.

I tried to imagine myself as the kind of wife Mark was envisioning now. What would our life be like? Could I feel good about myself? Was I capable of playing such a passive role? I pictured the company being run by Valerie, John, and Mark, while I sat on the sidelines restricting my participation to some occasional training. I felt hurt, left out, and completely off track from what I perceived to be my life purpose.

I played with Doji while this visualization settled into my subconscious. Wait a minute. A breakthrough! What if I devoted my time to writing as my new primary professional focus? After all, *Your First Year in Network Marketing* was doing well. I knew that I enjoyed writing. And I would still be teaching the University Certificate Seminar, which I loved. If I could find another way to feel fulfilled through my work, still on track to impact people's lives, then I could be the supportive wife that Mark said he now wanted. I could encourage him in business while he supported me in my writing. I could continue to play a smaller role in our company, while putting most of my energy into becoming a full-fledged author.

I could even picture our traveling together—he doing a company tour and I doing book signings. Maybe I would be a guest speaker with him for our company because the pressure of working together would finally be off of us. If I could let go and offer him what he is asking, diverting my energy in new directions, it was conceivable that we could eventually have a blending of both worlds—the old one and the new one. What a concept! I liked it. For just this moment, I actually liked it.

I thought back to the early days of our courtship and how he had shared with me that his greatest vulnerability was a wife who was not faithful to him. I never caused him the slightest doubt about this. Even when my former husband sent his newest book or a personal letter, although I would have liked to respond to him, I chose not to—out of loyalty to Mark. This may be the only area of our life that wasn't being questioned by either of us. I had always been faithful to him and he to me. We trusted each other implicitly.

Using all of my creative visualization skills, I began to picture the coming together of both extremes of our relationship—loving Mark was still my first priority; being successful in our new business was now his. I tried to imagine the moment when our company had received new capital and was financially solvent. Our intentions in our personal life and in our business life were all about growth—our own and that of all those who joined our company. I could see us traveling together, as I spoke to groups about the subject of my new book and we spoke to distributors joining our company. Our love was strong as we were once again focused on our spiritual journey together which overlapped into our respective business involvements. In all aspects of our lives, we were working toward helping advance human potential. With some significant adjustments to our original promises, we had a down-to-earth version of the fairytale back. Through one simple visualization, everything that we both wanted had come together in my mind.

Until now, my identity and purpose in life had been tied to our work together and the projects we shared. The pressing question was whether I could, for the sake of our marriage, separate our married life from our professional work. For the first time, I felt I could.

Jody drove down from San Francisco to visit me. She'd known me since I first entered the Community and understood my life philosophy as well as my theology. She was the perfect person to break my monastic silence and isolation. Doji loved her and immediately accepted her into our home.

"Have you been in communication with him?" she asked softly.

"No. We've had nothing…written or verbal."

"That's not good, Rene. Have you tried?"

"No," I responded, feeling somewhat remiss. "I just didn't feel ready."

"You might think about putting your thoughts in writing to him. That is always a safer way to go if you think an argument might errupt during a conversation."

She was right. I used our beach time to reflect back with her to the very beginning of my relationship with Mark: our goals, our shared vision, the place that God occupied in our lives, the promises we made. Jody offered so much support to the process I was putting myself through that by the time she left, I felt ready to write to him.

It had been a long time since I had hand-written a letter. As I wrote the date, I realized it had been ten days since I left home.

Wednesday, June 23
Dear Mark,

It is officially summer. And I'm where I feel the most comfort when I can't be with you—in the sun with the wind and the waves. I walk on the beach everyday. It is healing for me like no other place in the world.

I know you are preoccupied with getting the business underway. I understand that. There is nothing more important in your life at this moment. This company will be a phenomenal success. I know it. It began with all the right motivation. It is driven by the right causes. The only concern is temporary—cash flow. But if God intended for us to do this, he will provide us with the necessary bridges to link all the pieces together in some meaningful way.

I am concerned about the company too and all the people who are counting on us. But my greater concern is for us, for you and me: the power we derive from each other and the depletion of our energy when we are out of sync. I believe that there are many people—our partners, our distributors, our friends and family—who are sustained by our energy. The best of your strength and the best of mine respectively do not equate to the melding of both of ours together.

In the years we've shared, we have always had the freedom to work or not to work. There has never been any real stress from a financial perspective. With our decision to start this company, all that has changed. And you and I are both feeling the pressure. That is how I explain to myself why our conversations have deteriorated so, why I am not the wife you want me to be, and why you are filled with anger and hate whenever you speak to me. You are willing to risk every penny we have in the world and mortgage the rest for this business. Doing that frightens me. It's not so unusual that we might have different ideas about how to cope with all of this. What is out of the ordinary is that we would not listen to each other and find a solution acceptable to both of us.

I've raised a thousand questions since I've been away. Was it all a mistake? In the beginning, did we just kid ourselves and create our own make-believe world? All the words of shared destiny and never letting outer activities take precedence over our love? The commitments to our parents and our children that we would not drag them needlessly through another failed marriage? The promise that we would never put 'spaces in our togetherness'? There are worse kinds of spaces than physical ones. The withdrawal of affection and continued emotional distancing while still sleeping in the same bed are even more devastating.

The question I keep asking myself is whether there is hope. And the answer—only if we both want there to be. But, sweetheart, I don't want to settle for just living under the same roof, come what may. I don't want to be able to say twenty years from now, "We made it. We endured each other!" Unless we can rediscover an innate passion for our shared purpose and for each other, I lose all desire to want to continue in a sham. I'm fully aware of my own faults that are difficult for you to accept. I have recounted them a hundred times since I've been away. One thing I am sure of: if there is such a thing as long-term enduring love, each day must begin and end with forgiveness.

So let me close this letter for now by asking for allowances as I struggle to become a better person, sometimes succeeding and sometimes not. In turn, I understand that you are under severe stress and I forgive you for the coldness and hostility that you have directed my way over the last few months. If we can begin with this, perhaps we can carry on a discussion about a renewal of our love and shared destiny. I want this. I can only hope that you want it too.

If you feel like responding, I would love to hear from you. And if you are too caught up in things right now, I understand. My intention is not to rush this. I'm ready to talk when you are. I'm ready to see each other when you are. Whether you respond or not, I'll write more soon.

All my love, Rene

I felt rejuvenated after writing this. Although I had experienced some personal growth already, I knew it was just a first step. I put the letter in the mail box and flipped the red flag up for the postman. I prayed that I had said what needed to be said for now.

Two days later, on Friday, as I came walking in from the beach, I noticed the red light was flashing on the answering machine. As I pushed the play button, I heard: "Rene, hi! It's Mark. Sorry I missed you. I'm very, very busy. I'm sorry we haven't visited before now. I got your letter. Want to visit with you. I'll be calling you this evening probably as soon as I finish up with several people here at the house. Jonathan Goldsmith is leaving tonight. So I'll call you this evening around 7:00. Thanks."

It was hard to concentrate on anything else all afternoon. A few minutes before 7:00, I nervously picked up the phone to be sure it had a dial tone. Without even a ring, there was Mark.

"So how's the training going?" he asked, referring to my Saturday training calls for our company.

"Fine."

"Are there very many people on the calls?"

"No, not as many people as I would like. I would have hoped it would be growing more by now."

"You see, it's just not working. I knew it wouldn't. I have people on a new training track now. They love it. But some are confused about which track to run on."

I felt my heart sink. *Of all the topics we have to discuss after two weeks apart, here we are talking about training; and, what's worse, we are in competition over it. How are we going to get this company off the ground if Mark and I aren't leading them down the same path?* "I'm sorry to hear that you and I are causing them any confusion."

"I'm in my element. I've never felt stronger. It's like when I was running the Chevrolet dealership with 16 salesmen and 59 employees." *You mean your first job twenty-six years ago?* "I'm great at working the corporate side…with John and Val's help, of course. What I've come to understand is that you're lousy at it. There isn't room for the four of us. You're going to have to make a decision between the marriage and the business."

"You may be right, and I'm willing to talk about that. But I think we need to make *us* work first and then we can talk about the business. I do think it needs us to be in sync with each other."

"Listen, Rene, our marriage has zero significance to anyone else. John and Val don't give a damn about our relationship. It has no bearing on them whatsoever."

"That's ridiculous, and you know it!" From my conversations with them, I knew this wasn't true. I could feel myself becoming angry as he pressed the issue.

"I'm with them—you're not. I'm telling you, our marriage makes absolutely no difference to them."

"Maybe you should ask them outright," I proposed. "I'm not trying to argue about it. I just think talking with them is a good idea."

"Okay, you want me to get them on the line right now?"

I hesitated before I answered. "No, I think this isn't the time. It would be better if you talk to them on your own and in person."

"Well, it doesn't matter. What I need you to do is to stay out of things so I can get this put together. You would only be in my way." There were so many ways he could have communicated the same message without such cruelty.

I let the hurt go and reminded him how he had laid such a beautiful foundation for our marriage in the early days. Now it was up to me to do what I do best, which is see through what he had begun. I explained how I wanted to work on our marriage even while he was preoccupied with the business, hoping that before long he would again give priority to us.

"I like what you are saying about supporting the relationship. Maybe you could turn me around...but not if you are involved in the business. You are a teacher and a writer. You are not a corporate person. I am. I was meant for this. By the way, what's the name of the guy you talked to at the bank? No one knew his name. I have to talk to him. How much will he give us?"

"It's Schulte, and he was considering offering us $500,000 against our Nu Skin income."

"I thought it was three quarters of a million."

"Yes, but that's including the quarter of a million from Comstock that we are borrowing against our house."

"That's not enough. I need more. I'll get it. I would sell every stitch of clothing I own, my musical equipment, my paraglider, every bit of furniture. I would move into a place smaller than Chris's for the next three months just to support this business. I don't care what it takes. I'm going to make this work." The desperation in his voice sounded like an out-of-control zealot. It frightened me.

"What about ATG? Any of their investors coming through?"

"No, it's up to me. I have to do this, and I have two weeks left in which to do it."

"Are we buried if you don't raise the money?"

"No, I'll find it one way or another. But I don't want you to come home right now. I need at least two more weeks to get this thing put together. I don't have time to worry about all of this and you too. You just drain my energy. I really created a monster when I let you get involved in the company."

I had been gone two weeks already, and it hadn't even made a dent in our problems. But I wasn't about to show that it hurt. Instead I simply said, "What made you think I was coming home? I never said anything about that."

"Cyndi said she overheard your mom say something about your packing." Cyndi had been taking care of our house for nearly five years. I suspected it was she who was missing me and wishing I'd come home. "I don't want you to come home yet, not unless you understand I have no time for you. Not for at least two weeks, and then we can talk. But you'd better understand that I know what I want now: I want a wife who will be a wife and let me run the business. That's the only way I could continue with the marriage. When you agree to that, then I'd welcome you home."

His words pierced me like a knife. There was not a word about forgiveness, or regret over what he had said the morning I left. Not a word asking how I am or at least how sorry he was to hear about the sheriff withdrawing his support of ReStart. Not a word about love until his closing remarks: And, oh, by the way, I do love you and care about your feelings."

"That sounds like such an afterthought," I said almost inaudibly.

"I don't want to argue."

"Me neither."

"I'll talk to you on Monday." With that, he hung up.

I was determined not to let myself get discouraged. He was preoccupied. He was feeling the pressure like never before in his life, but I was beginning to wonder how many more times I would have to turn the other cheek. I still wasn't ready to give up. The only thing I knew to do was to continue reaching out to him.

I sat down and composed another letter. I didn't want to hold anything back.

June 25, 1998
Dear Mark,

I have lots of time to think and write, meditate and walk. While here, I've reread the part of my book I wrote more than a year ago on our "marriage and merger." I have absorbed every letter, every poem, and every promise that you shared with me. Because of you, our relationship was founded on some profound and deeply spiritual principles. I responded to them, but it was you who laid them out for us. Our entire courtship was composed and orchestrated by you. And it was the most beautiful symphony any woman could ever hope to have as a prenuptial ritual.

Then it dawned on me. That is what you do so well. You are the visionary that sees something that is not yet and makes it come to life. You've done that over and over again with so many projects and books and plans. The power of you and me together is that, while you create ideas and give them life, I am good at tenaciously feeding and watering them and sustaining their life.

So, if this is what we do well together, after many miles of walking on the beach, I have come to the conclusion that our marriage should be no different. It was you who began it with such zealousness. Now, if I am true to my role, it is I who should be nurturing it now. In one of your letters to me early on, you posed and answered two questions: "Would you please never place outer activities ahead of our love? I won't. And would you promise to work as diligently at perpetuating our love and romance as you do in other endeavors? I will." You were right. And I will.

My letter went on to promise a renewal of my wedding vows and ask if he would take the time to reread his and consider making them again. I reminded him how we had begun by accepting God's role in our marriage and perhaps we needed to bow to Him again during this time.

Once I reread the letter and felt comfortable with it, I tried to fax it but it wouldn't go through. God works in strange ways. Obviously the timing wasn't right yet. I thought it might remain forever in my computer as the letter I never sent.

Monday evening came and went. The entire week passed, and no call from Mark as promised. I talked to Mom about it. She was right there with him every day working downstairs in our home office. She said he kept reassuring her that he didn't want a divorce. After all, I was the one who left. I kept myself busy working on company matters: returning phone calls and emails, training our key leaders, and setting up our voice-on-demand system. This helped protect myself from feeling the hurt, but still I carried the ache in my chest and stomach.

After my Saturday training call, I took my morning walk. I couldn't help but reflect on how once Mark had an abiding and unwavering belief in the fact that we were drawn together by some unseen force of love and that we'd remain together throughout eternity. I was committed to holding on to that belief for both of us. In the meantime, I could only work on my own self-awareness and take each baby step, one by one, to make improvements on myself. I knew I wanted to triumph over this situation before it triumphed over me. I would not let myself be defeated by all the losses and setbacks. What was important was not so much what was happening to me at this moment as how I was dealing with it. Taking the time to make this retreat was the first step in gaining mastery over all that I was facing. I knew that the more attuned I could become to the mysteries of my own soul, the more I would know how to respond to my husband's as well. A life-changing decision needs to be made carefully and thoughtfully with a solid awareness of the extent of its impact on our own life and the lives of those inevitably affected around us. But once made in this vein, no matter what the outcome, our spirit is granted a freedom like we may have never felt before.

CHAPTER 14

REBUILDING TRUST
July 1998

I overheard people at the beach talking about the holiday weekend coming up. I didn't even realize that the Fourth of July was almost here. The long weekend would be like every other day for me, except the beach would be more crowded. I waited for the fog to lift and went out late Friday afternoon for my time at the beach. The sun was out and Doji was as spirited as ever, splashing in the water and chasing the waves. Someone said to me, "It makes me happy just to see him play like that." Boy, I wish I could feel the slightest bit of joy. Today I'm a long way from there.

I was clear about my commitment to our marriage. I also understood that if change was to occur, it had to begin with me. I wanted to stop seeing Mark in such a negative light and open myself to his warmer, more loving side. I made a small bonfire out on the beach, preparing to have a ceremony where I would burn all the mental pictures of Mark of which I wanted to let go: Mark putting me down; Mark elevating himself in business by denigrating me; Mark demanding a new relationship with him as the "man" and me as the subservient wife; Mark's hostility toward me; the lack of intimacy between us; the lack of any kind of meaningful communication between us; the fact that he has no interest or awareness of things going on in my life; Mark's frequent cussing and yelling at things around him...or me. Poof! It was all going up in smoke.

I had been carrying these images around like heavy baggage. Every time I saw him, I would see all of them. I was holding in so much anger. Now I was watching them turn into ashes. I loved it—I felt free. To burn those negative images was not to deny they exist. Rather, it was to take my focus off them and open my heart to the realization that there was so much more to my husband than these behaviors. What I saw in Mark was entirely up to me. By choosing to see him in a positive light, it made it possible for me to begin loving him again.

As I sat staring at the bed of hot ashes, I asked myself what I should do when the lower side of him comes through. Same thing I do when the lower side of me comes through: create awareness without blame. Mark had been most understanding when our co-venture partners couldn't come up with the needed money. He knew they were trying and didn't blame them. He had no expectation that Val and John, our Global Trust partners, would come up with any money at all. He put the burden on himself to find the needed funds. While I didn't agree that this was the best way to conduct business, I fully agreed that this was an excellent approach for a personal relationship.

My thoughts drifted to Valerie and John and our conversation from the day before. Returning to the house, I sent them an e-mail.

>John and Val:
>Thanks for the long, warm talk yesterday. I have
>given more thought to everything we discussed. I
>ask you both once more to consider revisiting our
>contract with ATG and IHI. I feel it. I believe it. From
>both a moral and business perspective, I'm
>convinced that we must correct the problems. If we
>don't have this conversation now, we will end up
>having it later, and it will only get worse. The
>arrangement is inequitable and was not the basis

>for our entering into an equal joint venture. Why is
>it that we are all so afraid to address this issue? It
>is clear to me that we need to put things out on the
>table—now before we confuse the situation with
>other investors.

>In my heart, I believe that Global Trust should own
>a greater share of Global Network because we are
>putting in the greatest amount of work and
>monetary investment. I believe that ATG should
>have a larger percent than IHI, and any new
>investors should be offered stock ownership
>proportionate to their investment.

>I appreciated the honesty of yesterday's
>conversation, especially the part of asking for
>God's support for all of our marriages. I join my
>prayer with all of you on this subject. I can tell you
>that I am committed to continue in mine. But for this
>to happen, I am sure we must resolve the financial
>issues facing our company. So believe me when I
>say that I am doubly motivated. Given Mark's
>preoccupation with our company, I can't begin to
>work things out with him until the finances are resolved.

>I appreciate being able to process my thinking with
>both of you, knowing that I can without being
>judged. Whenever I talk to anyone outside of our
>company, I am made to feel so sane for believing
>that stock ownership is tied to investments.
>Whenever I talk to anyone inside our company, I
>feel like the lone wolf for even suggesting this. I'd
>feel so much better if we could find an outsider
>who was knowledgeable about investments to
>come in and give us counsel. So, I leave all of this
>in His hands and in yours.
>More later, Rene

Just as I got off line, the phone rang. It was Mark. He went out of his way to be pleasant. He began by saying that he had something he wanted to discuss but would like to begin by listening for a change. I carefully summarized the highlights of all that I had been thinking about our relationship. He listened and seemed at ease with what I said. He then talked about our company, the funding challenges, potential investors, and finally said he was bringing in an investment banker who would take the next two to three weeks and try to raise money. I was encouraged. I just knew that someone professional would know what was needed to set things straight.

Mark talked conversationally about his new two-page training outline, the oral surgery he had this week, and asked if I was coming to Seattle for the Upline Masters Seminar. John Fogg, founder of Upline, was counting on us. He offered to wait for me there so we could talk. He sounded optimistic about our marriage, indicating he did not want a divorce. Of all the possibilities this could have meant, only one entered my mind: now that he saw some hope of resolving the finances, he would finally able to focus on our relationship.

As I hung up the phone I realized that the real question was more with me. I was the one who, at this time, was prioritizing our relationship over everything else; but the good of our company and all of the people associated with it mattered to me too. I wanted both to work and felt they were intertwined. Strife between us would inevitably spill over into the company. If there was harmony between us, we would both be more effective in supporting all of the people joining us.

But, in the end, what if we didn't come back together? Could I walk away? I wanted a real marriage, complete with communication, holding, loving, listening, supporting, and growing together. I didn't want to continue in a sham. If I couldn't have an ongoing, loving interchange with Mark, I'd rather live without him and open myself to the possibility of a new life. But I am so much more courageous in my journaling than in my follow-through. Just letting the thought that we might part into my consciousness sent shudders through my body. *Dear God, until I receive a sign that says otherwise, I intend to give everything I have to putting my marriage back together. I put my life and my relationship to my husband in Your hands. Show me the way—what it is You want of me.*

I could feel myself vacillating between my acceptance of our moving on if that is what was meant to be and my determination to make our marriage work. I still couldn't imagine our parting. I didn't *want* to imagine our parting. I could justify this with my sense of loyalty, my Catholic upbringing, even the personal and social responsibility I felt to our distributors. But the reality I couldn't avoid was my fear of being abandoned. I needed to look at this and decide to what degree this was behind my intense determination to work on our marriage. I opened my laptop to my last entry in my journaling file.

> Whenever I face the prospect of being abandoned in my life, I become as a little child. I come from five generations of abandonment, where the men left and the women remained to raise and support the children. My grandfather abandoned my grandmother with four children when my mother was only five and her baby sister was still in the womb. My father was abandoned by both of his parents and left in an orphanage. He and my mother divorced when I was two. For reasons having to do with his own family history, my former husband abandoned me over and over again, always returning only to leave me again. When I married Mark, we spent long hours sharing our deepest vulnerabilities—his, a woman's infidelity, and mine, a man's abandonment. After the complete disclosure of my deepest fear, the one thing I knew beyond any doubt was that Mark would never leave me. He promised to always put our love first and never let outer activities come between us. Damn him for breaking the only promise that ever really mattered to me. I don't want to start life over in my mid-fifties.

> Mark's request was that I would always be faithful and never even put myself in a vulnerable situation. My request of him was that he would never leave me. As reasonable as this all seemed to me back then, I now find myself wondering whether these were requests or demands. Could anyone ever really promise to avoid all vulnerable circumstances? And can anyone ever really guarantee that he will never leave? I would need to do more work on the difference between requests and demands in a relationship. But, somehow, I pray that Mark and I will come out of this renewed and with something much deeper between us.

I was just coming in from my morning walk, when I heard the phone ringing. It was Valerie and John.

"We just wanted to bring you up to date on things happening here."

"Great timing. I just want you to know that my heart is with you both as you face these very difficult challenges around funding. I mean, even though I'm not there, I can't stop thinking about it. In some ways, it helps to have put some distance between myself and the situation."

"We have become more convinced with every passing day that this company is solid," Val said optimistically.

"Yes, we have everything in place now here at the office. We have a great support team in the staff. They are assuming more responsibility for bringing things together. They're not busy enough yet, but we think that time is right around the corner." John was always soft-spoken, but he communicated his thoughts with such conviction.

"I agree with you. The temporary short-term cash-flow problem and the inequitable partnership are what is killing us." *Right! And besides that, Mrs. Lincoln, how did you enjoy the play?* "Beyond that, we have founded this company for all of the right reasons. We have an incredible team of marketing reps joining us, and, God knows, their hearts are in the right place."

"Well, that's what we called to talk to you about, Rene. Bill Puckett has turned Mark onto a friend of his who raises money for companies." Bill was a long-time friend of Mark's and now a member of our presidential team. "His name is Randy Calvert. Rene, this is what you've been asking for. He's an outsider with an accounting and legal background, and he just spent the day looking at our books. He says we're in great shape and he feels sure that he can raise money for us."

"And you'll love this part," Valerie added. "He says in order to bring in outside investors, we first have to put our own house in order. He says you can't run a business with this much inequity, and he will have to get that straightened out first. He has looked at the exact contributions of each partner, but he also wants to know how much the Yarnells have personally guaranteed. He needs that information so he can go down to talk to ATG and IHI."

"Wow, when's he going?" I could hardly believe what I was hearing. A voice of reason in our midst—I felt so validated.

"He has a meeting set up for tomorrow."

"This guy doesn't fool around. But how will he ever get ATG to...?"

"Don't worry. He knows what he's doing. He says to leave it to him."

"How long will it take him to raise the money?"

"He says two to three weeks max."

"I'm so encouraged, I can't even begin to tell you."

"We knew you would be happy. This is the guy you've been wanting to walk through our door."

"How can we hold it together in the meantime? Mark and I can't put in any more money. While we are playing the waiting game, maybe we need to go to our creditors and beg for more time, especially delaying the manufacturing of any pending bottles or binders. I think our vendors will work with us, don't you?"

"What other choice do they have? Besides, two or three weeks isn't much time to ask," John added.

"Yeah, and that will give—what's his name?—Randy the time to find solid investors. In a way—and I don't mean to make light of this, but—that is the easier of the two problems. The more difficult one is the one I was trying to address before I left—equalizing the partnership."

"Randy doesn't seem worried about that at all. He seems to regard that as a given. We really feel good about him, Rene. You will love him."

"I am just so pleased that we finally have an outside arbitrator to help resolve all of this. I'm at peace now, knowing that it is out of our hands to some degree. Maybe Randy is the angel from God I've been praying for.... Where is Mark with all of this?" I asked warily, knowing this is in direct opposition to Mark's viewpoint when I had proposed this.

"He seems fine with it. I think he is relieved that money is finally going to come in. All of us have tremendous confidence in Randy," Valerie declared with absolute conviction.

"Whatever happens, I still believe we should have another business huddle with our partners," I said. "However, if we can resolve this with a mediator going back and forth between us, that is the next best step. I'm pleased that everyone, including Mark, recognizes that we must face this problem head on now. I'm also glad to hear that it will no longer be necessary for us to fight our own battle. One thing is for certain: Whether our financial situation gets better or worse, inequities never go away. This will be a constant problem in the company until we solve it. Hopefully, with Randy in the picture, we're on track now." Promising to stay in touch, I hung up the phone.

With concerns for our finances lessening, I felt even freer to continue the work on myself. I thought back over the things I had seen myself doing, particularly when I was stressed or upset about something. Today I decided to look at the things I do that I want to forgive and release about myself. If change in a relationship is to occur, it must begin with me. Sitting alone on the beach, I began making a mental list of my own shortcomings. I wanted to see how Mark saw me when I wasn't my best self. The scrutiny, though painful, I felt could only bring a healing result.

For one thing, I stay focused tenaciously and won't let go of a point. I don't always realize this is happening at the moment, but I am aware after the fact. At times it is my strength, but it is also an annoying quality that I want to change.

Along the same lines, when I start something, I finish it, whether it's sensible or not. It's almost as if I'm compelled to complete the task simply because it's underway and I have to see it through. I am so determined to finish what I start within the deadline that if anything or anyone gets in the way of that, I get angry. I don't lose my temper very often or very easily, but I did several times over the issue of Mike failing to carry out his responsibilities for product delivery. Consequently, we missed our opening date and then we missed our commitment date to ship the products. I have relived my temper tantrum with Harold Rapp and Larry Brady a hundred times. Even though I was under a lot of stress and going through menopause, I still found it hard to forgive myself for that. I wanted to move past these experiences and do better under similar circumstances the next time.

Still tied into the same issue, I make my point too often and recap too much. In business meetings, I am too controlling on certain issues. In letters, I am too verbose. It is a spin-off of the same principle, namely, not letting go of a point.

In conversations when I am receiving criticism, I will listen and take it in up to a point. Then I turn it back on the other person. I have a nice-nasty way of getting my digs in with a smile and a gentle voice. I especially do this with Mark.

For the third day in a row, the sun didn't shine and I felt depressed. "Flow with it," Nancy told me when I talked to her on the phone. "Sadness leads to introspection, and to awareness, and to understanding, and to change."

Three weeks had passed now, and it was time for Meera and her daughter, Crystal, whose house I had rented, to return home. I had hoped to have things worked out by then, but Mark and I hadn't even talked seriously yet. I found another house in the neighborhood and leased it for a month. The isolation was becoming really difficult to bear, but I couldn't go running back home now just because the going was rough. I reminded myself that my year of silence while living in a religious order had prepared me for this, and writing made it even more worthwhile. If I hadn't created a purpose out of this time, the aloneness would have been intolerable. This "hermit" would have gone berserk.

I appreciated the phone calls from a few friends. That was enough to keep me grounded. Most of my close friends had no idea what was happening. I must have wanted it that way. The rest of my calls and e-mail were from our distributors contacting me about building their businesses.

My alone time brought me to some realizations I hadn't faced before. Mark's addiction and alcoholism had greatly diminished my trust in him. Just about the time I could believe all of that was behind us, something would happen to make me doubt. When he behaved in a bizarre way I wondered: *Is he back on Vicodin? Has he been drinking? Or what is his new addiction?* I found myself having qualms about his sticking with the program. His backsliding often felt like a betrayal, and I hadn't completely gotten over it. And worse, it controlled our relationship. I still measured our life by whether Mark was on drugs, off drugs, or withdrawing from drugs.

While in town, I attended Mass at the parish where I worked nearly 30 years ago as the religious education director. Afterwords, I stopped in a bookstore and picked up a book called *The Marriage Spirit* by Drs. Evelyn and Paul Moschetta. Naturally, I was partial to couples who share a business and married life as well as write books together. They offered a trust test for couples. Using the six areas of trust they outlined, they recommended that I examine whether I feel I come through for my partner in these areas and whether he comes through for me. Then, at the appropriate time, without blaming and conjuring up images of the other in our minds, we should reverently share these, all the while remembering what we love and value about the other. The six areas they suggested were:

1. Trust that you will be sexually faithful.
2. Trust that you will not harm, reject, or control each other.
3. Trust that you will keep each other and your marriage a top priority.
4. Trust that you love each other without ulterior motives.
5. Trust that you will not abandon each other in the face of conflict, anger, or disagreements.
6. Trust in your own capacity to be trustworthy.

Clearly, these points were at the heart of the issues for us.

Over the next few days, I walked for hours on the beach examining my conscience on these points. I may never have analyzed anything in my life as deeply as I did these questions. Later, I summarized my thoughts in my journal:

> 1. Trust in each other's sexual fidelity:
> I have been 100% sexually faithful to Mark. I have never given him cause to doubt this. Even being gone for a month, I don't think it would occur to him that I would not be faithful to him.
> I'm sure Mark has also been faithful to me. This began as a priority for him and has remained so throughout our marriage. In the early days, he was inclined to be obsessive on this point. Over the years, his trust in me seemed to grow.
>
> 2. Trust that we will not harm, reject, or control each other:
> I am not aware that I have ever harmed or rejected Mark in any way, but I am a controller. I oversee the bills and determine how to invest or preserve our money; I overstep this at times by making Mark feel that he has to ask my permission to spend his money.
> When we are speaking together publicly, I sometimes take too long, thereby short-cutting the time left for him.
> When it came to his addiction, I was in a major position of control. I made him choose between the addiction and me. If I had to do it all over

again, I don't know how I would have dealt with this part any differently. While I believe I did the right thing, I think he still carries resentment about the control issue.

Currently, we do not share the same philosophy about our personal financial investments in our company. If, in order to support my husband, I must pour more money into our company to keep it alive, I want to see an equitable agreement reached between the partners. This is a major control issue for us. Mark wants to be free of my having any say in how he spends our money. We are at an impasse on this matter and, I believe, it is the primary reason why we are separated.

As for Mark, he would never physically harm me, but I feel emotionally berated on a regular and steadily increasing basis. I find the verbal attacks to be personally demeaning and seriously damaging to our relationship.

It is Mark's rejection of me that is the most painful of all. For the past several months, we have had no touching, no communication about anything significant, not even eye contacts demonstrating some kind of emotional exchange between us. All we do is argue.

Mark is a controlling person by nature. In the beginning of our marriage, he opened himself and his whole life to me and offered to share it. He asked for a partner in marriage, not just someone who would stand apart and admire his talents. Control was not an issue then. Now he says "I have created a monster." He wants to "be the man" and have me trust him to make all business and financial decisions without input from me. Mark's controlling nature is most noticeable when he wants me to parallel his response to things. When, for example, the marriage was a top priority for him, he wanted the same from me. When it ceased being a priority to him, he seems to resent it being one to me. Mark's most domineering form of control is that he does about 90% of the talking and very little listening, and then concludes the "conversation" by feeling we've reached agreement if I didn't speak up to the contrary.

3. Trust that we'll keep each other and our marriage a top priority:

Since leaving public office, I have treated our marriage as a priority until a couple of years ago when I began to let things slide. I seemed to get out of the practice of making my love for Mark the first thing in my life. In the last few months, since our relationship has degenerated so badly, it jolted me into realizing that we were letting our marriage slip away. I made a concerted effort, though perhaps not my best, to prioritize my love for Mark, but this was often offset by the anger and resentment I felt at the cold war being waged between us. In the month that I have been gone, I have absolutely made our marriage number one. However, it is much easier to do this apart than together. Worst of all, I may have waited too long.

For the first couple of years, our marriage was the highest priority to Mark. Then it began slipping for him. The poetry stopped. The special meaningful exchanges slowed down. Now, for the past several months, our marriage is at the bottom of the list of his priorities. He openly admits he has absolutely no time for it at the moment. The business is the only thing that matters to him. But even before the business, I felt he would enjoy television more frequently and more passionately than he enjoyed being with me.

4. Trust that we love each other without ulterior motives:

I need to be loved by Mark with constancy. I need open and frequent signs of affection long before lovemaking. I need open communication about our life, our business, our personal relationship, our children, and our goals. I need more together time, shared meals, falling asleep in each other's arms, and signs of caring throughout the day. I need to feel that I am heard without him dominating our conversations. I need to feel his respect about the things I do and say. I need to be loved with no fear of abandonment emotionally or otherwise.

I started out loving Mark because he met these needs. I have learned to love Mark when it has been more challenging. So perhaps one ulterior motive is simply this: I'm in this marriage now. We are sharing a life, a highly visible role in our industry, co-authorship of books, joint ownership in a business, and each other's families. I don't want to start over. The next relationship will have its challenges too. I might as well work on the one I have and not fool myself into thinking that the next one will be perfect. Of course, there is the ever-pervading fear of being abandoned. And, lastly, because we are so visible in our industry, I believe we have an added responsibility to try harder to work things out between us. So perhaps another ulterior motive is avoiding the agony of facing our families and the millions of people who have come to hold us up as role models. I don't want to have to say to them, "Mark and Rene Yarnell succeeded in your eyes, but failed each other."

Does Mark have ulterior motives? I believe the boy in Mark experienced love in his life by being successful. So he excelled at nearly everything, and, as a result, felt very loved. I think success and love are still intertwined for him today as an adult. He must be successful first and foremost. Then and only then can he experience loving and being loved again. So Mark may be pushing me away from the business right now with his ulterior motive (hidden even from himself) being that he must succeed alone. Then when he has proven himself "as the man," he will be worthy of love and can become involved in a loving relationship again.

This is why I believe he has put me on hold. The risk I face at the present time is that if a woman were to step in and make him feel respected for his business decisions at this moment in time, without knowing the history or exerting control over his drugs, she will win his affection as well...and I will lose him.

5. Trust that we will not abandon each other in the face of anger, conflict, or disagreements:

I do not see myself ever abandoning Mark in the face of conflict, anger, and disagreements. This is undoubtedly less a virtue on my part and more a Venus thing, as Dr. John Gray would say. As a Martian, Mark tends to drag out a fight. I can't get an argument over with fast enough. It tears me apart to let the sun set on any disagreement.

The only situation in which I could imagine me abandoning Mark would be his flippantly going back on drugs again or if he were to be verbally abusive. It was the latter that played a significant part in my leaving home to come here.

Mark, on the other hand, does abandon me in the face of conflict, anger, or disagreements. He would say he doesn't because, with one exception in our life, he has never physically walked out. But there are worse kinds of abandonment than physical ones. He has abandoned me emotionally, sexually, spiritually, communicatively, and through withdrawal of all forms of touching and closeness. This is very painful for me. This is at the heart of why I am here and not at home with my husband. He has been unwilling to talk about it for months.

6. Trust in each other's ability to be trustworthy:

I feel I am trustworthy in all significant areas of a relationship, and especially now after a month of solitude and reflection. My greatest weakness is in the area of control, and I am committed to working on this in myself.

I find Mark is trustworthy in all areas except two: I can't always believe what he says in regard to his drug habit. And sometimes he only half-listens and gets the facts wrong when he repeats them. But his most common failing in this regard is that he will make up things to prove his point, whether they have any bearing on the truth or not.

As I examined what I had written, my soul-searching helped me look reality square in the eye. From my perspective, we were facing challenges in five out of six areas. Only our sexual fidelity could be trusted.

The second half of the exercise was more upbeat as I looked at the other side: what is it I do love and trust about Mark? And do I believe we can overcome the problems in our marriage?

Beyond question, I was in love with Mark. I loved his positive outlook on the world and his eagerness to make it even better. He loves others through a rare and special spirit of generosity. I used to love the way he loved me. He made me feel so cherished. I loved his poetry. I loved his letters. Now those were gone and I miss them. I loved Mark's free-spirited side because I was more reserved. I loved his benevolence because I was more fiscally conservative. I loved his playfulness and sense of humor because I was more serious and intense. I loved his attitude! The way he believes that all things are possible and makes me believe that too. I loved his wild and crazy ideas for changing the world which, when he was at his best, would come almost daily. I loved the way he spoke from stage. I was always proud of him. I used to love how proud he was of me when I spoke or trained or filled in for him. I loved his body and the fact that he has kept in shape. I loved the fact that we both lived and worked together. Now he resented me in this role. I loved the fact that we had such similar backgrounds and purposes in life, although lately he had chosen to point out the differences between us, little ones, but nevertheless differences. I felt that our differing approaches and perspectives were part of the magnetism between us. I loved the fact that we were opposites and that helped us complement each other, balanced us as a couple, and made us more effective in our service to others.

If we could still come through for each other, showing that we fully understood the other's fear and passion, we could cross the bridge forever from selfishly considering our own position to selflessly respecting what mattered to the other. For me, as described so well in *The Marriage Spirit*, genuine trust implied offering the care of our heart to each other with complete conviction that it will not be broken.

That is all I really wanted from him. For Mark, I believe that real trust meant my demonstrating total belief in his ability to make good business judgments and be successful. That is all he wanted from me. When it comes right down to what really matters, this was little to ask from either of us.

As I came in from a sunset walk on the beach, I felt a calmness settle over me. I felt enveloped by the heat of the sun. It warmed my heart with the strongest determination I have ever known to regenerate renewed love between Mark and me. I felt the kind of love for him that guided me to elevate his spirit as well as my own to a new and higher level. How could I ever know my own inner drive? *Was it fear of abandonment, fear of letting go that kept me clinging to the dream? And if so, do I want to allow fear to make my decisions for me? Or was it a genuine belief that our relationship could survive all of this? It is essential that I know my own intention. What choices would I make if I were fully evolved as a person? At that moment, I could feel myself turning to my own inner voice. I trusted my own wisdom. And it said that I believed with all my heart that I should make the effort to hold our marriage together.*

I made one of my infrequent trips into town to get groceries and replenish my water supply. While I was there, I found a card with the most appropriate words on the front: "No one ever said that love was easy or that there wouldn't be misunderstandings or moments when lovers would need to be apart in order to love better or more completely. I know we've had some difficult moments lately, and sometimes I wonder if we'll ever see eye to eye or if our actions will ever reflect what we really feel inside. But I want you to know my heart still belongs to you, and no matter how difficult this situation is for us, I know we'll get through it. I hope you still believe in me...I still believe in you, and I will always believe in us."

As I wrote the date, July 10, 1998, on the inside of the card, I realized a month had passed since I'd left home. While I felt certain that I was experiencing personal growth, I was concerned about how little progress I was making on improving my relationship with Mark.

He had finally agreed to get together the next weekend. In preparation for it, I wrote this letter to him to include inside the card:

Dear Mark,

You've sounded good on the phone the last two times we've talked. I'm glad you're recovering from the oral surgery and proud of you for your own self-watch on the pain meds.

I've gained so many insights while I've been here—points I want to share with you and am working toward putting into practice. But it is important that I do it right and not rush it. Let's take the time to get to know each other all over again. If you knew me at the center of my soul, you'd like me right now. You might even love me again. I would like for that to happen.

The time we are setting aside next weekend really matters to me. Even the "where" is important. I'd love for it to be someplace where the ambiance is conducive to talking and reflecting. I'd like to be able to be outside and breathe clean air in beautiful surroundings. But I'd also like to feel that I am alone with you. Like you when you were courting me, I've had a lot more time to think about us. I've made the time to envision how I want it to be with us, moving past where we are now.

Before I even open my mouth for words to come out, I am taking deep breaths, inhaling my inner spirit and exhaling my egotistical need-to-be-right side of me. I like my own thoughts and outlook when they come from my spiritual side. I feel I have a lot of wisdom to share and have been writing profusely. It's when I need to be so self-righteous that I narrow my focus and shut out so much good. I've shut you out, and I don't want to do that anymore.

I'm looking forward to my time with you—our time together. I plan to give it everything I have to make this time count.

Love, Rene

The next evening Mark called just I was shutting down my computer. He sounded upbeat for about thirty seconds. Then he dove into talking about the arrangements for this weekend.

"So have we made any decision about where we're going to meet? How about Sacramento—that's about half way between us." Sacramento was hardly my idea of the place I described in my letter. I was trying to think of some place near there that had the right ambiance. Before I could say anything, he said. "I can meet you there Saturday morning."

Saturday? I thought we were getting together Friday. I have to be out of my home on Friday morning. So what do I do? Just hang out waiting for you for 24 hours? "You can't come on Friday?"

"No, I have to be at Amy's play Friday night."

But that's been going for several weeks. Why do you have to be there on the day we planned to meet? "I have to be out of my house on Friday morning."

"Well, where the hell were you going to go? Were you coming home?"

"No, there are some people using this house just for the weekend, and I have to be out. You must not have gotten my letter?"

"No, let me go look for it now. I need a Coke."

Please don't go. Stay and talk to me. "It probably isn't there yet. I only sent it on Friday."

"Well, let me go look. I'll call you right back."

The phone went dead, and I sat there holding the receiver, trying to figure out what just happened. I lived for these phone calls. My whole life is about trying to carve out some time so we could talk to each other. That call lasted less than five minutes, and we said absolutely nothing of substance to each other. I walked out on the deck and watched the ocean waves. I listened to their thunderous breaks as they rolled to shore. I waited there until the phone rang again about an hour later.

"Sorry I'm so distracted. There were about ten phone calls in between. So why don't you handle our lodging arrangements for this weekend? If it is close, I could come after the play Friday night. But I'll come wherever you want." Mark sounded harried.

"Okay, I'll figure something out."

"Well, if you can't handle it, I will. I just thought since you aren't doing anything but fucking around on the beach, you could do that much."

Deep breath...eight, nine, ten. I paused so as not to overreact. "Don't worry. I'll find us something."

"You know, I don't know what you're really doing over there. Are you back in touch with Kavanaugh?"

"No."

"Not even by phone?"

"No."

"Are you seeing any men?"

For god's sake, where is this coming from? Should I be insulted or pleased that there is still some jealously left in him? "No, and I'm not willing to be put through an inquisition. I have been faithful to you throughout our marriage, and have given you no cause to doubt that. I am here waiting as patiently as I know how for you to have the time to sit down and talk about us. All I want from you is some time for us. We've put it off way too long."

"Oh, come off it! I'm not going to take that bullshit! You're the one who left. I've asked you to come back five times now."

This time I couldn't count to ten. "Mark, that is flat out not true. In fact, you *ordered* me to stay away until you could get our financing handled."

"Well, it's a different ball game now. There are lots of people on board. I was always committed to this company, but now I'm even more so. I'm angry, I'm fed up, I'm joyous, I'm exuberant. You name the emotion, and I feel it. Nothing is going to come between me and the success of this company. Either you're on the team, or you're off. I don't have time for anyone who isn't on the team. Do you hear me? I don't have time. If you're willing to come back and do what you're told, you can be part of this. But if you're not, just tell me right now, and we can cut out the bullshit of this weekend. I've wasted six years on you already. I don't have any more time to waste. I need one year to get this business established. I don't have time for anyone else. If my father came back from the grave, I'd say, 'Duane, I don't have time for you. Fuck off.' And I feel the same way about you. You are over there fucking around on the beach, and I am here trying to hold things together. But you have to decide if you are on my team or not. I want to know right now. I want an answer." He paused for a breath. I was holding mine to keep from saying something I would regret.

Before I was forced to respond, he went on. "By the way, I don't want you handling the launch. I don't want you handling the corporate brochure. You contribute nothing. I didn't intend to go into all of that, but now it's your turn to talk."

God, help me. I prayed before I spoke. I was trembling from anger. "I don't want to talk on the stage you've set. I had a different vision of what our communication would be like when we finally did communicate."

"I said *I* didn't want to talk—I'm wiped out—but you said you wanted to. So talk, goddammit."

"I've waited this long for the right moment, and I'm willing to wait longer. I don't want to try to deal with your anger tonight. So I'm ending this conversation and will carry it on when you can be more respectful."

"This weekend I can be 'lovey dovey' about our relationship. But when it comes to the business, I'm telling you how it's going to be. You're either on the team or you are off it. And you need to make up your mind right now."

"Obviously I am on the team, but I don't want to talk about it under these circumstances. I'm going to say goodnight now."

I hung up the phone, still trembling. What could have happened to cause that outburst? My psyche, if not my whole being, felt more severely wounded with each cold telephone exchange. And time wasn't healing anything. We were no better off at this moment than we were the day I left. All my hope and anticipation for this weekend dissipated. If we can't be civil on a short phone conversation, what hope is there for an entire weekend together?

I barely slept. I laid awake looking for answers. The next morning I woke up thinking about the browbeating I had received from Mark the night before. Now I didn't know what to think. *Dear God, please guide me. What do I do? Do I go ahead with the weekend? I don't want to go forward with it if he is going to carry on the way he did last night.* As I continued my meditation standing out on the porch listening to the waves, the phone rang.

It was Mark. His tone was apologetic although he was unable to say the words. "I'm under a lot of stress right now, and maybe I overreacted. I just got your letter and felt bad about last night."

I welled up with tears. Here was Mark talking affably to me. While I was trying to deal with the sob caught in my throat, I could hear him talking on and on about the pain medication he's been taking following the oral surgery.

"...So I went to see this Doctor Lambert, an addiction specialist, who gave me a patch and said he admired me for coming to him. I'd been ten days on the pain medication; but for an addict, that is sometimes all it takes. He said I needed the medication for the complexity of the oral surgery I'd been through, but I was doing the right thing by having him help me detox off them.... Rene, are you there?"

I was sobbing. All I could manage to get out was "Mmhmm."

"Jeez, what did I say? I didn't think I said anything hurtful. Look, if you don't believe me, you can call the doctor yourself. He'll tell you...."

You dodo brain. Don't you get it? My tears have nothing to do with your damned meds. This is five weeks of built-up anguish coming out. I laid awake all night thinking it was completely over between us. I've been trying to decide where to go this weekend... because being with you seemed out of the question. I'm not willing to subject myself to any more of your outrage. Now here you are talking normally to me—this is exactly what I had asked for last night but you were too uptight to give it. Taking a deep breath, I found my voice to respond. "No, I don't need to talk to him. I need to talk to you." I couldn't stop crying.

He went on to tell me about the decisions he's facing, the new reps who want us to expand into Australia and Canada, how he's afraid of showing favoritism to some reps if he does.

"It's a lot easier to see what Blake Roney was up against when Nu Skin went into Hong Kong, isn't it?" I asked, once I had calmed myself down a bit.

"Oh, yeah, I've thought of that. I've talked to Donnie Walker because this group wanting to go international is not under him. I want to know how he feels. Should I do what will stabilize the company or should I...? Are you there? What's wrong?"

My sobs were loud enough for him to notice. I loved hearing him just talk to me. No anger, just his thoughts. Actually, my tears were tears of relief and hope.

"Jeez, I don't understand. I'm trying to keep you in the loop about what's going on here, and all you can do is cry. I don't get it. How 'bout if I call you back tomorrow and give you time to calm yourself down."

"Okay."

"Talk to you tomorrow."

John Gray is right. Men are from Mars. Any woman would understand my tears?

While I was getting myself pulled together, my thoughts turned to the weekend. I would call Robert, our ever-faithful travel agent. He'd be able to think of the perfect get-away place in northern California. The where was the easy part, but what about the process? I needed to set some ground rules. But how? And if I did, what would they be? And would Mark go along with them? I couldn't worry about all of that right now. I started thinking through everything I knew or had recently read on the subject of healing relationships. Then I began writing down the ground rules that made sense to me:

1. Be totally focused on the present moment we are sharing together:
   a. avoiding preoccupations and distractions about other things
   b. without bringing up old, accumulated anger from the past.
2. Treat each other respectfully, seeing the soul mate with whom we fell in love.

3. No verbal attacks (includes yelling and cursing) intended to berate, cause pain, or play mind games.
4. Make a commitment to share honest feelings.
5. Our mutual goal is to understand each other and not to win, persuade, or control.
6. Take turns talking and listening, sharing what we heard the other say.
7. When we feel anger coming, stand outside of ourselves and observe it, focus on it, and watch it pass through us; then continue talking.
8. Without blaming or becoming angry, give examples to each other of
   a. how we've been let down
   b. where we have a conflict of needs
   c. where trust needs to be improved.
9. Have some quiet time together and slowly begin to refocus on what is good between us, remembering the shared purpose that brought us together.
10. Look for solutions for us to work as a loving team rather than as adversaries, with each of us focused on what we need to change about ourselves.
11. Be understanding in the face of inevitable slipups. Apologize and get back on track.
12. Design a plan of how we will proceed from here. What are the next steps?

First thing tomorrow, I would send these to Mark and see if he agrees.

The phone rang. I looked at the clock. It said 6:30 a.m. I was a little groggy but managed to push the talk button.

"Rene, this is Mark." It was the austere voice of a stranger. "I have to talk to you about something very important. Jewelway has gone under. They are bankrupt."

"I know."

"How did you know? It just happened about 4:00 yesterday."

"I am on the phone working with people every day." I thought about a discussion I had had with some Australian leaders who advised me that there were 30,000 distributors in their country alone who would be scrambling for a place to go. Most network marketing leaders always had the hope—and usually with little to no possibility—that they would keep their organization intact under these circumstances. Some of the Australian Jewelway management were offering us a turnkey operation, facility, and distributors if we would just step in and take over. If Mark and I had been in sync and could have talked it through together, that could have been the salvation for Jewelway and for 21st Century Global Network. He obviously had thought this through on his own and had decided not to seize the opportunity. I felt differently, but this was not the time to express my views.

Mark mentioned picking up a few of the American Jewelway leaders and their people who would join us in this country. "Well, anyway, Peggy Long was on a teleconference call I did yesterday with about 1,200 people. She is about 98% ready to join our company and bring her people with her, but she wants to talk to you. She said she is closer to you."

"Okay, I'll be happy to talk to her. I think the world of Peggy."

"She was worried about us. She said she had heard we are separated. I told her that wasn't true—we weren't getting divorced. We just had some challenges over the business right now. I told her you were on a retreat, and I gave her your number. I hope that's okay."

Ogod, I wish what you are saying somehow reassured me. Are you telling her the truth, sweetheart? Is this what you really feel or what you think you need to tell her in order to recruit her? "Mmhmm."

"Don't blow it now. She really wants to join us."

Right! Don't blow it. But the way not to 'blow it' isn't going to be determined by what I say or don't say to Peggy. The way not to 'blow it' is for us to get our act together. At the moment, this shared energy needs to be focused on our company. "Well, that leads us back to what we are trying to accomplish this weekend. Please don't overreact, but I need to tell you that I was really let down when Robert told me that you had shortened our time together."

"Well, I told you that I had the play on Friday and that I would be coming in on Saturday."

"No, actually, you agreed to come after the play late Friday night. So now, after waiting six weeks to see you, our time has reduced from Friday, Saturday, and Sunday nights to only one night."

"Well, I have to be in the office at 7:30 Monday morning. And, besides, Robert is the one who brought up flying me in."

When Robert and I explored the options, we had considered only places within easy driving distance for Mark. "That doesn't make any sense to me. He's not going to fly you into Napa Valley or Lake Tahoe from Reno. You'd drive...but that's not the point. It's the feeling that I keep getting from you that no matter how long I wait, you never have time to set aside for us."

"Look, I have to go. I have to pick someone up from the airport. I'll call you back."

I sat without moving. *Will he ever make time for us again? I believe with all my heart that if Mark and I don't pull together, we will quite possibly, irrevocably destroy the chances of the company's success. But the truth is, I could withstand the loss of the company. I'm just not willing to sit back and watch our marriage go down without giving it my best effort to pull things back together. Dear God, please guide me. Help me to say exactly what I need to say to prepare for this important time together.* I felt certain that our entire marriage rests on the outcome of this weekend.

The phone rang again. It was Mom. I could tell she was worried about me. She said Mark asked her to discuss a proposal with me. He wanted to split our finances down the middle. That way he would feel free to spend his half any way he wanted on the company, and I would be free to preserve mine as I saw fit. It was an interesting thought but a bit late for such an offer. All of our existing funds had already been invested in the company. All we had left was our monthly Nu Skin check.

Even this proposal told me that Mark and I were coming from such different places. I went for my walk on the beach and tried to gain perspective. I wanted to understand his feelings, but I really needed to sense that he cared a little bit about mine. I decided to take the risk—and it clearly was a risk—of letting him know what I was feeling. I sat at my computer, and this letter came pouring out of me.

> July 16, 1998
> Dear Mark:
> I've had nothing but time to reflect on our relationship. You are my number one priority. More than anything, I want to get our marriage back on the track to which we originally committed. Making time to talk has been my entire focus for the past six weeks.
> I have sensed that this weekend is not important to you. By your tone of voice, the postponements of our getting together, shortening the time you can spend—the message is that you really don't want to come. Like the phone call the other night, it is merely an obligation that you feel compelled to carry out. The issue isn't the number of days we have together nearly so much as it is that I need to know you are coming because you truly want to be with me and share the desire to take the first steps toward putting our relationship back together.
> I don't think you have any idea of what I am going through and how very painful this is for me. Not rushing things has been a challenge for me. You know how much I want to solve the problem *now*. Waiting is part of my gift to you.
> I love you more than I can tell you. I am willing to do whatever I must to re-create a life that reflects what we first promised each other. I am unwilling to settle for anything less. I need to know that you are really ready and not just fulfilling some sense of obligation. Please let me know. Love, Rene

I faxed the letter to our office at home knowing that Mom would receive it. I asked her to please put it in an envelope and set it in the middle of his desk where he couldn't miss it.

It was Friday, July 17th, D-Day. No call from Mark in three days. No response to my fax. His insensitivity had hit an all-time new low. With my little beach house rented for the weekend, I had to be out in two hours. Mark and I had a general agreement to meet but no agreed-upon plans as to where. Without an answer to my fax, I didn't want to presume we were getting together.

Okay, Rene, so what are you going to do if he doesn't call? I could drive south toward Big Sur, accepting the reality that his silence means he doesn't give a damn about me anymore. Or I could head back toward Nevada City or Lake Tahoe so I can make it easier for him to get to me, believing that there is some other justification for his silence. If he blows off the weekend and I drive five or six hours to meet him, I'm setting myself up for major disappointment. Can I handle the hurt? Yeah, I've proven that I can handle an extraordinary amount of heartache. It can't possibly hurt anymore than anything else has up until now. But am I crazy to make myself so available to him? Is this being loving...or making myself a doormat? If he really wants to be with me and his genuine problem is time, then it is being loving. If he is agreeing to see me out of obligation and all the excuses and delays are reflective of that, then I am setting myself up to be victimized. God, I wish I knew what he was feeling. So do I or don't I head out to be closer to him? The most I have to lose is time and emotional pain. What I have to gain is the possibility of taking the first step toward getting my relationship back on track. I'll call Robert and ask his help to find us a place.

I began packing a few things to take with me. Just as I was walking out the door, the phone rang.

"I thought I'd call and find out what my plans are this weekend," said Mark.

"So we're on?"

"Yeah, of course." He sounded surprised that I'd asked.

I could feel the tightness in my chest loosen up slightly. I was glad I'd made the decision to go, not knowing whether he would join me. Somehow, it raised my level of loving him to a higher plane—one small step toward loving him without asking anything in return. But I wondered why he wasn't saying more about my letter. "So you got my letter?"

"Yeah, but it was dated June 25. It was quoting our marriage vows and that kind of stuff. What gives?"

"Omigod. That's the letter I tried to fax you three weeks ago. I was actually sending you a different letter yesterday." So, my computer had stored the "fax send" of the old letter; and when I tried to fax the new one out of my computer, it sent the old one. Well, obviously, Mark was supposed to receive the sweeter letter yesterday. All my worry about his real motive for this weekend was wasted energy. As I put down the receiver, I had the feeling that he was looking forward to our time together. It was difficult to keep up with the pendulum swing of his moods, and—given the way he was treating me—my own.

Once I was on the road, Robert called on my cell phone to tell me he had found us a place in Tahoe for the weekend. I called Mark to give him the directions and the phone number. The drive to Tahoe was long and harrowing. An accident on Highway 17, a dangerous four-lane undivided raceway known locally as "Blood Alley," blocked traffic for several hours. Instead of the normal four-and-a-half to five hours, it took me seven hours to get to Tahoe. I checked into the condo on the lake at Chinquapin. It was perfect. I grocery-shopped and filled the refrigerator with all of Mark's favorite things.

I couldn't wait for him to arrive. I wanted him to see the new me. I had made so many self-discoveries that would enable us to make dramatic changes in our relationship. We would again begin to live out the promises we had made to each other in the early days. I fell asleep on the couch with these thoughts whirling in my head.

CHAPTER 15

CONVERSING AT LAST
July 1998

D aydreams drifted into deep sleep. *Mark and I were walking through a field of tall brownish-yellow grass blowing in the breeze. Surrounded by the Swiss Alps, our hands clasped in each other's, we were at peace. He stopped and looked into my eyes and, without a word, his facial expression said it all. He loved me. He would always be grateful that we had worked things out between us. At that moment, I felt gratitude for the pain we'd been through, elevating us to a new state of awareness about each of us, separately and together. Now we knew for certain that we would be together until the end.*

Suddenly I was awakened by the telephone. I groped my way across the room and picked up the phone.

"All right. I give up. I've been all over this fucking parking lot. I can't find your car or anything. Where in the hell are you?" To describe Mark's voice as agitated is putting it mildly.

"Where are you?" I asked unemotionally.

"I'm at the office, which is closed."

"Wait there, and I'll be right down to get you." I walked down about a half a block and saw his black Mercedes. I jumped in the passenger side and guided him to our condo. We parked and walked in together. He was still muttering about how he almost turned around and went back home when he couldn't find me. So much for fantasies. We began our rendezvous weekend in the most basic reality.

He didn't embrace me. We walked out on the deck and listened to the water lapping on the shore. We moved into the living room, where we sat and talked about Amy's play and other safe topics. When he had wound down, we agreed to get a good night's sleep so we could get started talking early in the morning. While he was in the bathroom, I slipped off my clothes and climbed under the covers. One of my favorite things about being married to Mark had been lying near him and smelling his scent. After six weeks of separation, I felt awkward. I was certain that we would not make love, but I didn't know what to expect. By the time Mark undressed and climbed into bed, my heart was racing. For weeks now, I had just wanted to be acknowledged by him. Now I was hoping for some little sign—maybe some sense that he had longed for me. Just a word or a silent touch would be enough.

Before I knew what was happening, we were having sex. It was just sex, no words of longing or love. I felt helpless to stop it. *NO! Not like this, please. I need to know that you still have feelings for me. Tell me that you love me. I think I want to die!* As I turned over and tried to fall asleep, I felt this was the single most degrading moment of my married life.

For Mark it all seemed normal. Afterward, he got the munchies and wanted to drive to Seven-Eleven for some bologna, mayonnaise, and chips. He had already taken a sleeping remedy, so I was afraid for him to drive. After we made a quick run to the store and had our midnight snack, we fell asleep. Mark managed to sleep a little but was up by 4:00. I slept in...until nearly 5:30. We made coffee and settled in comfortably on the deck.

Pre-dawn is a beautiful time at Lake Tahoe. The serenity of the blue water reflecting the snow-capped mountains is almost beyond description. Boats anchored close to shore were all lined up in the same direction. It was stunning.

Conversing at Last

Mark began the conversation. "I've done a lot of searching and reading these past few weeks. And I'm coming to some conclusions that I'm not sure you're going to like. But before I go into my thing, why don't you talk for a change, and I'll listen. I really want to know what you're thinking since you've been gone."

It both surprised and pleased me that he would let me go first. Although I was curious about where he stood and somewhat uncertain about what it was I "wouldn't like," I felt he was making a concession by letting me begin. I talked for an hour and a half, telling him everything that I had gone through these past weeks. I let him know how committed I was to taking our marriage to a new level, once again putting our love first, even though I knew for him our marriage came only after everything else. I went into great detail about my awareness of my own shortcomings and what I was working towards to make myself a better person.

"After weighing everything, sweetheart, I still believe that you are I are soul mates. I've done a lot of reading and reflecting about relationships. What I've come to realize is that marriage today cannot be what it has been in the past. When couples' lives were about raising crops, fighting plagues and famines, or moving west in wagons and staking their claims, married life was in survival mode. There was no time to think about whether they were meeting each other's needs. And, besides, they only lived 'til their thirties. Today, couples have an entirely new set of challenges and, judging from the divorce rate, aren't meeting them very well. The problem you and I are facing isn't unique to us."

"I can't believe you are coming to these conclusions. This is exactly where my head is too. I'm encouraged."

"Well, when life forces us to stop and look at ourselves, it becomes so obvious. You can't possibly meet all of my needs, and I can't meet all of yours. It's unrealistic to think we can. But, because we're caught up in a traditional marriage, we've been trying to fit into that mold. And it isn't working."

"That's exactly where I've come in my thinking. I'm really happy to hear you say this."

"So, much of my thought process has been centered on the kind of relationship we *can* have together. I've gone back and looked at where we started. I've read and reread every letter, every poem, every promise and significant conversation we shared. And, do you know what? I really believe we began our life together on some very solid principles. Putting our love for each other as our number one priority—I still believe in that and I'm totally committed to it. God held a central place in our lives, and we knew that we had come together to share a life purpose. These are the parts of our marriage that I don't want to lose. But somewhere along the way, we lost our focus."

"That's a big problem," Mark said sternly.

"But one that, with awareness and both of us in agreement, we can regain. When I get away from the stress, it is so easy for me to see why I fell in love with you. I want to see the very core of you beyond the angry outbursts. I'm blocking out the negative aspects and focusing on what I love about you: your generous spirit and the openness you once had to make me a part of everything in your life; your humor and, uh, the way you used to love me. You see, what I've come to understand from the reading I've done is that, at first, our personalities fell in love with each other. Not so much you and me, but our most superficial parts fell in love. Then we got married and, after a while, our egos went into battle with each other. Again not the real you or the real me, but the part of each of us that needs to be right was in combat with the other. What I'm making my primary self-work is trying to get my spirit to dominate my words and my actions. That is the true reflection of me."

Mark didn't say anything. This was unusual. It may have been disinterest but I chose to believe it was out of a desire to hear more. So I continued: "You know what I've begun to realize? What I've just described is so easy for me to do when I'm teaching or coaching someone. It's second-nature. In that setting, I don't have to think about it. I am just sharing from the very center of my soul without asking for anything in return. I give all that I have to give and, in the process, receive so much in return. It becomes far more difficult in my day-to-day activities when it comes to business or certain social or political scenes, but most especially when I'm interacting with you. I have a need to be right and for others to confirm that I am right. I don't like that part of myself. I have relived again and again how I wish I had handled my communication with Larry Brady. I still believe in the message I was delivering, but it would have been so much better if someone else had said it. And I wish I could have found a better way to deal with my frustration with Mike. It is so easy for me to see when I step back, like I've been doing, and really look at myself."

"That's good that you can admit that. It sounds like you are doing some really good work on yourself."

"I am." I looked away for a moment. I could feel the lump in my throat. When it subsided, I continued. "Where all this fits, as far as our relationship is concerned, is this. You gave me the most beautiful courtship any woman could hope to have. It couldn't have been more wonderful, and it was you who made it happen. I responded to you, but you took all the initiatives. Like I tried to say in the letter you inadvertently just received, the power of you and me together is that, while you create things and give them life, I am good at tenaciously nurturing and sustaining their life. So, after many miles of walking on the beach, I started asking myself why our relationship should be any different. You loved me enough to begin this marriage right. Now that I understand, I want to give this same intense energy back by paying closer attention to our love when times are tough. I don't know what form it will take—I am open about that—but I want to find a way to continue our marriage, and I'm here to find out if you do too. And if so, can we refocus ourselves on those things that really matter? It isn't the externals that I am concerned about. I want to look within so that we can both rediscover our authentic power. What changes do we want to make in our relationship? And how can we redefine it so that the needs of both of us are respected and we are again able to support each other in pursuing our personal and spiritual growth? What I'm really asking is whether we can pull ourselves back together primarily for us but also for our kids, for our parents, for the sake of those who look up to us, and for the good of our company and everyone joining us? That's where I am. I feel like I should stop there because I really want to know what you're feeling and want to hear what you have to say."

He got up and went to the bathroom, found some matches, and lit a cigarette. Daylight had come, and the lake was beautiful. So blue and clean. Finally, he sat back down and was ready to talk. "Well, I can't argue with anything you said. I mean, frankly, I'm surprised that we are as much in sync as we are, I mean about the part of marriage changing and not being able to meet all of each other's needs. I think I've gone farther in my thinking than you, but we are moving in the same general direction. What I've come to realize is that I loved the newness of our love, and it's gone. I've talked to Bandura about this. I went back and reread C.S. Lewis on the "Four Loves," and I now understand that there is no way to get that back. It's gone, and it will never be again. I don't like that. I deserve to have that. It was a big part of our life for me."

"Falling in love with you was one of the highlights for me too. But just because it changed doesn't mean it wasn't real. We weren't deluded. Maybe we just haven't evolved enough yet to know how to transform new love into the next phase. As wonderful as it was, I think it is nothing in comparison to what we could have long-term. You know, the stable, reliable kind of love that stays together by choice." Although I hadn't read Scott Peck's *The Road Less Traveled* in years, I remember him defining love as "the *will* to extend one's self for the purpose of nurturing one's own or another's spiritual growth." He then went on to explain that falling in love is not really love because it is emotional and not an act of the will. It is not an extension of one's limits because this requires effort; falling in love does not. Real love permanently expands us as persons; falling in love does not. As I recalled this, I resumed expressing my thoughts out loud to Mark. "It almost seems to me that real love may best be experienced once we fall out of the first phase of love and graduate to the second stage, that is, when we act lovingly toward each other because we choose to do so and not just because it feels good. This is our chance to show real love for each other like never before."

"Well, easy for you to say. But I treasured the early stage of our love. While it was there, I didn't need any chemical dependency. And when it started fading, I found myself turning to pills again. I don't think you understand what a major part our newness of love played for me. And when it went away, it went far away. I mean, how can two people spend time in a place like Gstaad and not be happier and more in love than we were? It's sad but true. We just co-existed over there. And there were times when I really went all out and made the effort, but nothing changed. You are not the same person I married. I still am; you even said so. But *you* really aren't." *How would you know, sweetheart? You haven't been around me in more than six weeks? Deep breath. Hold it in, Rene. This is not the time to point out the changes I see in him since the detox program just one year ago.* "I still want you to go see a hormone therapist. Maybe it's chemical. But whatever...you've changed. What I want now is a wife who will respect my decisions in business and trust me to make those decisions. I don't have that in you, and I haven't for a long time. You made a laughingstock of yourself with Larry Brady and Harold. When they received that letter from you—the one you never told me you sent—they called me right away. You really lost credibility with them over that. Everyone comes to me and tells me what they think about some of your business dealings. They seem to be afraid to tell you. When I ask Valerie why she won't tell you, she says it is because you seem so vulnerable and she doesn't want to hurt you. But we all feel that you are out of your element in business. You've pissed off nearly everyone you've dealt with. And your thing about asking Larry and Harold and Graham to give up share of ownership since we put up more of the money was the final straw. That was really stupid. It shows how little you understand about business."

"We really do see that differently. What about what Randy has done, bringing in investors and reapportioning stock ownership? Hasn't he just carried out what I was trying to discuss with the partners?"

"Maybe so, but he had the ability to deliver the message and get a favorable response. You didn't. It's you. It's your delivery. You are inept when it comes to business and negotiations. In fact, I was mortified when I found out that you were checking references on Randy. All I could think of is that you would blow everything. I called my friend, Bill Puckett, and Randy Calvert and talked to them both about it. Apparently you didn't do any irreparable damage. Randy said you were welcome to check his references. That's why he gave them to Valerie and John. He didn't seem bothered but said he was glad he didn't give out the investors' names. That could have caused problems. The point is: I don't want to have to worry every time you open your mouth that you are going to say something that could undo all the work I've done to get things where they are."

"Do I hear you saying that you still don't agree with the formation of the new investment company and the way shares have been adjusted to be more proportionate to dollars invested?"

"No, I don't agree. I just went along with it because everyone else seemed to want it. To me, it was fine the way it was."

"So can we talk about that? That was the crushing blow that finally nearly destroyed us. If we are going to be real with each other, then let's try to learn from this. What if you had come to me and said, 'Rene, we're out of money and the partners can't come up with their share right now. I want to put more of our money into this company because I believe in it.'"

"That's exactly what I did say!" Mark was emphatic. I didn't argue.

"Okay, but what if I had come back and said, 'Mark, I'm willing to go to the mat with you with this company—win, lose, or draw—but if we are going to risk everything we have, I am uncomfortable doing that without a more solid business approach'?"

"That's pretty much what you said!"

"I know, but our actions didn't take each other's feelings into account. What if at that point you would have said: 'Well, why don't we get an outsider to look at this and advise us? If that will make you feel better, and you will go along with me on this, okay.' I mean, there were so many ways we could have tried to be sensitive to each other's fears and concerns. It was you and me risking everything—our life savings and our marriage—over this company. But no one else was going to question what we were doing. Why *shouldn't* they just sit back and let us take all the risk while you allow them to keep the same ownership? No one else was mortgaging their home for our company."

"There wasn't time. We were out of money, and we had to put it in that very moment."

"Or so we all thought. As it turns out, after Randy came on the scene, that wasn't the case. But the point is, in any partnership, and especially one where we are married as well and trying to prioritize each other's concerns and well-being, we needed to go one step further than we did. Mark, I was scared about the way we were pouring everything down this tube."

"'Pouring everything down a tube'. See, that says it all. I have never lost faith in this company. Those words just prove that you did. And that means you lost faith in me. And that's the problem."

I thought about what he was saying. There was truth to his words, at least partial truth. "I don't think I have ever lost faith in our company. I admit to facing the possibility that we could lose everything. I could live with going broke and starting over, but I can't live with that *and* losing you! 'Pouring it down the tube,' for me, meant it was unacceptable business practice to risk everything and not have any verbal or written agreement as to how that would be dealt with by our partners. I never lost faith in you, but I didn't feel we should be running this business the way we run our charitable foundation. Ownership of a company is generally based on the proportion of investment. Graham understood it. But I felt like the lone wolf when I would try to discuss that with you or ATG. And I'm still blown away at the reaction I received when I touched on that subject."

"It's you, Rene. Randy didn't get that reception when he proposed it."

"He was an outsider. He came from more then fifty miles away and carried a briefcase." *He was also a man and not perceived in conflict with a spouse.* Once again, I was a woman in a man's world. This had been one of the most difficult challenges for me over my lifetime. I had almost always worked in a man's world, and faced the same problem again and again. The humility and frustration that go with it are clearly lessons that I was supposed to learn. This time I'd really like to learn them, if for no other reason than not to have to go through them anymore. "But, sweetie, more than all of that, the biggest fear I've had all along is that we were sacrificing our marriage and everything we've built together. Nothing is worth that to me. And that's what I see happening."

"Then get out of the business, and let me run it. If I need to spend money, I don't want to have to worry about you holding me back. I'm not going to let this business fail."

I didn't answer right away. This was a major crossroad for me. This was *the* major crossroad. It wasn't a matter of simply reaching a fork in the road and choosing to separate our business partnership from our personal relationship. It went much deeper. This was at the heart of our trust of each other. For me to agree to back away under these circumstances would change the intrinsic nature of our relationship—or at least what I had always thought was our basis. *Maybe it was never there in the first place and, with no outside pressure to test this before now, it never showed up. Or maybe with the passage of time and our taking differing stands on issues, it gradually eroded.* I felt that my saying *yes* would move us from a relationship based on treating each other with equal respect to my honoring Mark without his honoring me. I would go along with his decisions about our business, our finances, and the spillover effects this would have on our personal lives. He would not be inclined to change his actions even slightly based on my input. I was afraid of loss...the loss of him...of us. That was far more important to me than even the loss of security. I knew that many men and women have made this kind of a relationship work: the man in the position of authority and the woman submissive to his decisions. But this had never been our agreement. *For the sake of preserving our marriage, could I live with that now? In the beginning, he was drawn to the woman who was complete in her own right—the woman who was chairman of the Board of County Commissioners, the woman who had created her own multi-thousand person network marketing organization. He didn't just fall in love with my gentleness and my smile. He fell in love with all of me. So...if I give up part of who I am, what are the chances that he will still love me in the end?* "Sweetheart, this is a really important question. Take all the time you need to answer it, but sometime throughout this weekend, I need to know why you've changed on this point. Why did you start out wanting a business partner and now decide that you need to be in charge all on your own and that I am just an appendage in the way? I'm not looking for the superficial reason—that is pretty obvious. But what is going on inside of you to change things so fundamentally for us?"

"See, there you go again. We've gotten off on business, and I really want to bring it back to what I want to talk about. I didn't interrupt you when you talked. But when you interject, you take me down paths I don't really want to go."

I instinctively felt he was telling the truth. I was taking him down a path he wasn't ready to go. He may not have known the answer, or may not have been ready to look at himself that closely yet. But the answer to this question held the key to our future. "I'm sorry. I can be patient, but at some point we need to face this question. I was feeling that we were just getting to the heart of the issue between us. I wanted to say it before I lost the thought."

"You do that all the time. You plan what you are going to say instead of really listening to what I'm saying. Right now, I just want to get through my points."

"And I am so eager to hear them. I have been waiting for this dialogue for six weeks."

"It isn't that easy for me now...just having you come back as my wife and not my partner. I did a lot of reading. In fact, I went and tried to find everything ever written on romantic love and the passing of the newness phase. There is almost nothing written on this subject. Everyone writes about love during this phase, but no one addresses the fact that it goes away, and why. Most people have something in common to hang onto. You and I don't have that. We like different kinds of movies. You like socializing and I hate it. We like different sports. The reason we have never had a fight about religion is that we never discuss it. You are Catholic, and I am Protestant; and we have very little in common when it comes to religion. The newness wore off, and what do we have left? Graham said something interesting to me the other day. He said one reason he felt his relationship was still so good was because of the geographical distance between them. He essentially just sees her on weekends. And after a year, he is as much in love with her as he was in the beginning.

"Are you wanting spaces in our togetherness?" My thoughts came flooding back to my conversations with Mark about how much I needed a marriage that didn't require this.

"I don't know what I'm saying yet. I'm just trying to figure it all out. I know that the early stage of our relationship was important to me. It's gone, and I miss it. So, if there is a way to move past that, I'm really glad to have heard you say that you understand we can't possibly meet all of each other's needs. I know this isn't going to be easy for you, but let me tell you where you don't meet mine."

I braced myself. I wasn't sure I could handle hearing this. Maybe I just needed a smoother transition, something positive before we got into the negative. I didn't say anything. I couldn't think of how to propose that without being accused of trying to control his communication with me. I watched the feeling rise, crest, and pass through me.

"For starters, you can't meet my intellectual needs. When I want to talk about Socratesian philosophy or the Ebola virus, you can't. You're not interested. I need someone who can fill this need, and there is a guy that I went to school with who could."

I felt a twinge of hurt but let it pass. "So, go for it. I don't have a problem with that. I would love to see you reach out and have more male friends."

"But it isn't always male friends that I am talking about. There is a woman that I went to seminary with who could meet my need for spirituality. Sally is a sixty-year-old black woman, so I can promise you it isn't anything sexual. We are on the same wave-length spiritually."

The lowest blow of all! Why had I never heard of this Sally before now? I wanted to debate this in the worst way but I sat and watched it go through me before I spoke. If a former minister and a former nun, both with degrees in theology, can't find spiritual compatibility, what hope is there? "It hurts to hear you say that I can't meet your spiritual needs. There is a big difference between religious backgrounds and spiritual pursuits. I need to grow spiritually with the person with whom I'm in a primary relationship. That is essential to me."

"But, Rene, let's be real. We made all these promises about putting God first in our lives. We prayed a few times together, and that was it. And if we haven't done it by now, it isn't going to happen. I'm not very big on these phony prayer sessions. We don't share spiritually now, and we're not ever going to."

I was feeling so put down. His style of communicating is to make me wrong about everything. Nothing was being couched in what was good about us, only where we failed. Actually, what I was hearing was where *I* failed. And yet the content of his message was true. Except for family mealtime, we had stopped somewhere after the second year of praying together and sharing spiritual ideas in any depth. "We each pursued our own spiritual reading and personal relationship with God; we just didn't do it together. But now that it has surfaced and we are talking about it, I don't want to let go of this. It is too important to me."

"Yeah, you say that now when you think you are going to lose me. But it wasn't important to you before, or we would have pursued it."

"Mark, I want the chance to grow with you spiritually. If we can't make this a part of our life together, then as far as I am concerned, it is all over between us."

"Well, I don't want to plan on it in some artificial conversation.

If it happens, it happens. But I'm telling you, you haven't met my needs on this level at all."

You mean we haven't met each other's needs. But we can change that...if we both want to. I want to. Why don't you? Why are you giving up on us? "So where *do* I meet your needs? In what areas do you see us doing well?"

"Actually, I'd like to hear you talk about this first."

"No, please, I need to hear what you see because I'm feeling pretty discouraged at this moment."

"Well, I think we do sex well together. That's one area where I have no complaints and could be happy with you, monogamously, for the rest of my life. I wouldn't need anyone else." He talked about this in great detail. I guess I should feel complimented. How many husbands would say this after nearly seven years together? But after the demeaning experience the night before, I felt anything but good about this. For me, our sex life could be better. I'm sure I'm not the only woman for whom it is all tied into the way we treat each other during the day or prior to our lovemaking time. That's what was missing; and without it, sex is hollow, devoid of the substance that drives it. I was afraid to broach this, so I chose to keep my thoughts to myself. "Is there anything else we do well together besides sex, or is that the whole basis of our relationship?" It was too late to take that back. I hoped it wouldn't sound quite so synical. Apparently he didn't pick up on it.

"Yes, I agree with something you said earlier—we travel well together. And I think we entertain well together."

"Entertain?" All I could think of was the parties we gave at the house, and I couldn't believe that would be on his list of good things we do well together.

"Yeah, we do our stage thing well together—me motivating and you teaching. No, I didn't mean our social get-togethers. I hate them. You are going to have to find someone else to meet that need. I'm not doing them anymore unless I really want to."

"So let me see if I understand. You feel the basis of our relationship is sex, travel, and speaking together. And that's pretty much it?"

"You brought it up yourself, and I'm glad you did. You said that couples today can't possibly meet all of each other's needs. There are so many better ways to do that."

"I know. I'm reading a book on that very subject called *The Future of Love* by Daphne Rose Kingma. She explores all the stages of traditional love and the possibilities of where relationships are likely headed in the future."

"Let me see it. I wonder if she is going down the path I'm following." I got the book and handed it to him. He sat and skimmed it for a few minutes. "Well, I'm surprised. She really does cover it. Have you gotten this far yet?" He opened it to the chapter on "Illumined Relationships: the new forms of love."

"No, I'm one chapter behind."

"You need to read this before I tell you what is on my mind. I think it will better prepare you for what I am going to say." I felt myself resist. It appeared to be a stall tactic. He's been referencing some idea he's afraid I'll not like since early this morning, but he won't just come out and say what it is. Again, I watched the resistance rise, peak, and flow out of me. Then I picked up the book and began reading. Mark prepared dinner while I read for about an hour. The book does an excellent job of exploring alternatives to traditional marriage that are likely to be lived out in the coming millennium.

Instead of "saving marriages," the author suggests that many couples will be expanding and elevating their view of matrimony, entering into the most profound vows conceivable and going through a journey of continual metamorphosis together as opposed to enduring each other "'til death do us part." Some will live all the signs of marriage without the vows or the licensing. Others may choose emotionally intimate, but non-sexual, formal marriages or sexually intimate relationships with separate living arrangements. Still others will have a series of marriages due to their growing in different directions, with each relationship offering something of value. There is likely to be an increase in three-party relations which may or may not be sexual, double marriages which complement each other, and, of course, same-sex marriages. More divorced or widowed women in their late forties and fifties will move toward close live-in relationships (sexual and non-sexual) with other women. We are likely to see greater acceptance of age differences in sexual relationships, a single parent living with a single adult child, and more friendships and circles of friends treated as primary relationships. We will see the continuance of significant friendships with those who were formerly involved sexually. Some may consciously choose a celibate life for a time.

I thought back to that period of my life when I pursued a religious life and chose celibacy until I married. Some, the author suggests, may choose to let go of traditional boundaries and replace the exclusivity of marriage with community as their primary relationship. I yellow-highlighted a thought that summarized her viewpoint: "When it comes to love, the form of the family doesn't matter. The soul is asking us to love, whatever the recipe looks like, whoever the family is."

As I laid the book down, I thought, as a society, I believe we will find ourselves less judgmental about those going outside the stereotypes of traditional bonding and more receptive to allowing each other our personal and spiritual search for growth and happiness in relationships. The Internet, even with its numerous pitfalls, has opened up the opportunity for all of humanity to become interactive, crossing over ethnic and geographical boundaries. I realized that we are only limited by our imagination as to the vast number of acceptable lifestyle choices that people are now and will continue making in the coming decade.

I walked into the kitchen to let Mark know that I had finished reading that section. He was sweating profusely from the hot kitchen and the barbecue grill. I tried not to let my mind associate sweating with drugs, but this was a common symptom of methadone use. I took a kitchen towel and wiped his forehead and neck. I tried to just hold him for a minute, but I could tell he wasn't in the mood. Our communication was going reasonably well, but something had changed. I sat on the deck while he flipped the lamb chops. He was sweating even more. "Hey, why don't you let me do that," I offered. "The heat doesn't bother me."

"Huh?"

"Why don't you let me finish fixing dinner? You're so hot. I don't mind, really."

He didn't say anything. What is happening? Did he not hear me either time? Was he being rude or cold? I flashed back to the morning I left. I was pouring out my heart to him, and he kept saying "Huh? Donnie who? Say what?" I welled up with emotion, realizing that this was part of the behavior that triggered this separation in the first place. Seeing a hint of it again, I began to wonder if he was having some kind of brain-block. Where did his mind go while I was talking to him? It frightened me. I sat looking out at the lake deep in these thoughts. This had been a draining day of conversation. It was good. We were making progress, but I realized that so many of my words were coming from my heart and his were coming from his head. He appeared to have no emotional investment in anything we were discussing. We were talking on entirely different planes.

He went back inside and, after a moment, I followed him in. "Anything I can do?" I asked in my most upbeat voice.

"You can set the table." I did. We finished the preparations in silence. The mood had definitely changed.

We sat down to eat, and the potatoes weren't quite ready. That frustrated him. It was a beautiful meal that I had bought and he had prepared—lamb chops, mint jelly, fresh green beans prepared with bacon slices, baked potatoes, and bread freshly baked. We began with a prayer, which I said, although he was the one who usually said the prayer before a meal. We started eating, still in absolute quietude. I wasn't sure what brought it on and what to do to make it go away. Finally, I decided to interrupt the strain of our wordless dinner. "So, do you feel like talking about what's on your mind? I want to know where you see our relationship going. I'd like to hear what it is that you think I might balk at."

"Yeah," then he let out a big sigh. "I just think that no two people can meet all of each other's needs. So we have to consider other options today...." He paused and looked up at the wall behind me. "That's a really pretty picture on the wall." What's with all this diversion? For hours, we had been avoiding the topic he brought up early this morning. I made a half-hearted effort to glance at the picture behind me, searching for some tranquility depicted in its scene to fill that void in our midst. He picked up on my lack of interest and commented about it.

Before either of us knew what hit us, we were in the midst of a full-blown argument. He ended up leaving the table with his plate almost untouched and sitting out on the deck smoking. I stayed at the table staring at the food on my plate, unable to eat either. I didn't know what to do or what I had done. Finally he began talking from the deck. It was an intimate conversation that was being conducted from much too great a distance. And there was a screen door separating us.

"This is the reason I can't live with you. I have to put up with your resistance when I ask you to do something as simple as read a book. I comment on the picture, and you roll your eyes. I don't get respect from you. And I deserve it. I am a great businessman, and you won't trust me. I just can't accept it. I'm fed up with this. We might as well face the truth. We aren't soul mates. And we are never going to fix this thing. You are the way you are, and you always have to be right. You want to control me through every stage. I'll talk when I feel like talking about this whole thing. And I won't let you push me into it."

I am a great businessman, and you won't trust me. I just can't accept it. So here we are again right back to the heart of the issue, I'm the one who brought this up earlier. Now as I listen to him being so brutally frank, I can feel myself backsliding in my courage to deal with this. We were at an impasse on what it truly means to respect each other.

"I'm really sorry. Can we start over? We have a beautiful meal, and we're in this beautiful place. I don't want to be fighting with you." I realized that I was behaving like a martyr to the cause, but I couldn't help myself. My thoughts drifted back to my theological days as I recalled the deacon, St. Lawrence, instructing his persecutors when they cast him into the fire to die: "Turn me over; I'm done on this side."

"That's what you do—just ignore the reality. Pretend this didn't happen. You are so damned insecure that you will try to force this thing to work no matter what. Forget that we aren't right for each other. Forget we don't have anything in common. Well, I'm 48 years old, and I don't plan to endure a marriage that doesn't work for me for the rest of my life. I won't do it. I have certain needs and, by god, they will be met! And right now, you don't meet many of them. You've always got to have things your way. I ask you to get yourself checked to see if you need hormone pills, and you won't do that either. And that reminds me, I don't believe in a lot of things we used to do. I don't believe in public displays of affection. I think it's phony. And I don't want to go to parties I hate just to make you happy. And I don't want you involved in my business doing things you're not good at. I just think we ought to face the real facts."

Our marriage was over. Why was I resisting accepting it so much? Because he was right: I was operating from insecurity and fear of loss. Terrified of addressing the real issue, I shifted our focus. "Mark, I don't know what just happened between us, but it worries me. When I asked you if I could take over for you because you were sweating so much, why didn't you answer?

"I don't know, but what difference does it make? If you wanted to take over, why didn't you just do it? What's the big deal?" He drifted off in thought, staring out at the water. Feeling the sting of another put-down, I sat and watched him for a while, desperately trying to understand him. The only thing more difficult was understanding me.

I stayed inside and cleaned up the kitchen while he sat on the deck. I couldn't imagine how we were going to get past this and survive another entire day together. It was all I could do *not* to argue every point he was making, but I just let them go. I fully expected that at any moment he would come walking through the door and announce that he was heading home. I wanted to do something, but didn't know what. *Is he right? Am I just clinging for the sake of clinging? Or do I believe that we belong together and it is worth the anguish to go through this? How will I know?* With the dishes in the dishwasher, I went out on the deck and sat in the chair next to him, looking out at the lake.

It was he who finally broke the silence. "So, of all the options described in the book, the one that appealed to me the most was the one referred to as 'Intentional Community.'"

"Really!"

"Yeah, I can see myself living that way. Like right now, you thought I would have a hard time with so many people living in our house, but I really like it. In fact, I'm going to miss Stacey's cooking."

"I've lived in community several times in my life, and I've always loved it. But you're right. I thought that would be something more appealing to me than to you. From what you said earlier about your conversation with Graham, I thought you might be tending toward the idea of voluntary separation—you know, living in two separate houses and seeing each other whenever we really have a strong desire."

"Jeez, I thought you'd hate that one after your life with Kavanaugh." Jim and I had tried living in separate houses as one of many attempts to make our marriage work.

"Well, I wouldn't initiate it, but the older I get, the more I could learn to live with it."

"No, actually, that doesn't appeal to me." As much as Mark loves his solitude, this surprised me. But I was glad. I'd had enough spaces in my relationships to last me a lifetime. At this time I wanted to be close to someone who enjoys that too.

There was a lull in our conversation again, each of us lost in our own thoughts. I felt myself vacillating between realizing I should give up and feeling some hope that we might work it out. "What did you mean when you talked about feeling that you deserve to feel the high that comes from the newness of a relationship?" I asked.

"I don't know. I miss it. But I certainly am not suggesting that I run out and have a bunch of relationships to create it. The downside of coming out of them wouldn't be worth it." *He's right.*

The pain of ending a relationship is the most godawful feeling possible. Except for suicide, it is worse than death because leaving you is a choice someone makes—not just the ebb and flow of life's tides. I remembered the anguish I went through each time my former husband left. I recalled something from C. S. Lewis that Mark and I had read together in our early days of marriage: "God whispers to us in our pleasure, speaks to us through our conscience, and shouts to us in our pain." He was shouting to me now.

"So, I'm not sure I am following where you are going with all of this. What is it you are proposing that you think I won't be able to accept?"

"Well, I don't have all the answers," Mark said. "I just know that if we choose to stay together, we have to give up certain things. And we just have to decide if the tradeoff is worth it."

"I wish I knew what you're really feeling. I mean, do you really want to stay with me? You seem so distant in this whole discussion."

"Well, that's why we're here talking isn't it—to figure it out?

"Yes, but I feel like I'm telling you what I'm feeling, and you're giving me the facts and the options like we are in some business negotiation. For example, I'd like to know what you felt the morning I left."

"Well, actually I felt relieved because it meant we wouldn't be fighting. And I could get something done without the distraction of having you constantly nagging me about wanting to talk."

"Didn't you *feel* anything—something pulling at your heartstrings because I'd left?"

"Well, actually, I thought you were running away from your problems. You were going through the demise of ReStart. And you were feeling the rejection of some of the partners. I just thought you were afraid to stay and face your problems."

"The vote against ReStart *was* devastating for me. It felt like the death of my child. I still haven't recovered from it and from the betrayal I felt by people I thought were close friends."

"Yeah, I know it was a hassle." With that, he got up and walked inside the house.

When he returned, I said, "'Hassle' hardly describes what Nancy and I have been through. I feel like there is so much going on in my life that you know nothing about. We don't talk anymore about anything of real value to either of us. But I can't believe that you would think this is the reason. I left because of you. How can you not own that?"

"I never really thought I had much to do with your leaving. After all, I didn't say anything except that I didn't feel like talking."

I wanted to scream. I started thinking about what really happened that morning, but I let it go. "Apart from the reason why I left, I thought you supported what I was doing. But if my leaving was such a cowardly thing to do, why did you ask me to stay away for at least two more weeks while you got the financing handled?"

"Well, once you left, I thought you were turning it into something good. And I needed the time to solve some of the problems we were facing without feeling hassled."

If I ever felt that I needed confirmation about myself, I'd better not be looking for it from my husband. This is one moment in time when I'd better believe in what I was doing. And I did. But I was still fishing for him to say that he missed having me there— for support or nurturing or bouncing ideas off of me.

Mark reminded me that he was not very good at night. He asked if we could pick up again in the morning. As we headed down the hall toward the bedroom, the mood changed again. Only this time, he became more playful and fun-loving. I gave him a full body massage. It was my way of showing him my love without another demeaning sexual encounter. He drifted off in the middle of a foot rub. I didn't sleep much. I came into this weekend feeling such hope and, by the end of the first day, I had almost none. I just wanted to break through his protective shell. But it didn't appear that this was going to happen this weekend—perhaps never.

By 4:00 a.m., I got up. As I came out of the bathroom, Mark was getting up too. We made coffee and headed back to our places on the deck. He seemed well rested and in a good mood. I was just the opposite. I was struggling to remain open to this process. Another pre-dawn morning on Lake Tahoe sent a brief wave of serenity through me. I let it linger, clinging to the feeling as long as possible. Whenever I'm in process of transition and transformation, peacefulness comes only now and then. It is always important to savor such moments.

Mark picked up where he left off the night before. "So, where I was going with all of this is just to say that I think if we are going to try to continue on together, we have to find a new form. We both agree that we can't meet all of each other's needs. It's good that we at least agree on that. I appreciate your willingness to put money into our company. And here's how I propose that we do the business. Randy has taken over the role of finding the funds. That's good because it is not my strong suit. I am going to concentrate on building the field. That's what I do well. I would like to see you focus on training and newsletters. I think you would also be good at working with the new public relations firm that we are considering bringing on. You are good at video production—you've proven that. You can work with them on brochures and catalogs and promoting our image in the public eye. I want to write the ads we run. I have a lot of experience at that. But this launch convention, it is my baby all the way. These are my people I'm bringing into the company."

I found myself heartened by his now talking of including me in the business and cringing when I heard him say the word "my," much like when I would hear him say "my" book and others say "Mark's" book when referring to any of those we had written together. I was gradually coming to accept that Mark receives most of the credit for them. At this time in my life, I wanted to diminish my ego needs and increase my spirit-driven desire to do what is best for the situation at hand. All of this passed through me in the seconds before I responded. "Sometimes I react when I hear you use the word 'my' about those parts of our life that we share."

"I didn't mean 'my' to leave you out, just that these are people I am working with closely and I feel personally responsible for bringing them into our company. In fact, I'm trying to figure out a way to keep you involved."

"I want to make decisions about my involvement in the

company based on how I can truly help make it a better company, not on what I selfishly prefer to do. I think what you've outlined is good. Those are pretty much the areas that John and Val and I had discussed too. Another suggestion I would add is that it might be better and less confusing for everyone if I work from home rather than the office. That would put some separation between us, which I heard you say was needed and would create different role expectations for each of us."

"Wow! I'm surprised to hear that idea come from you. I think that would be good for us and for the company. So, we have the business side of things resolved for now. As far as the personal stuff goes, I think it is too soon for you to come home."

It tore my heart out to hear him say this. I had hoped otherwise. I stuffed my feelings of sadness and disappointment. "I know it is. We are a long way from any resolution."

He talked for a long time about his missing what we had in the beginning and how I was not the same person he married. He felt completely dedicated to our company, and I had no place in it except for training and those things he outlined.

By the time the sun came up, I asked if we could pray. Sunrise services used to be a part of my liturgical experience. He nodded, giving me the okay. "Dear God, as your light shines on us welcoming a new day, shed Your wisdom on Mark and me. Guide us in the direction You want us to go. We started our life together putting everything in Your hands. Once again, we entrust ourselves to You and ask that You show us the way. It's not my goal to force anything, but to stay open to what it is we are supposed to be doing with our lives. Please give us the strength to endure the pain and the openness to explore honestly what is happening to us. Reveal some sign to us that will let us know how this is to take shape over the coming weeks. Help us get past the difficulties that we are facing so that we can again let our love for others come through the love we share for each other. We ask this in Jesus' name. Amen."

Mark made no comment but picked the conversation up where we'd left off. "I think we should keep pursuing the lines we are discussing, trying to find new ways to make our life work. I don't know what that will end up looking like. But I'd like to call you often during these next couple of weeks so we can keep our communication open. Maybe I can work in a visit with you in a couple of weeks just before I do my California tour.

"I'd like that, especially the part of our talking more. This is what I've wanted for weeks, maybe months. The hard part for me, the part I am intensely working on, is to stay open to the possibilities. I don't want to define the rules of our relationship or predetermine the outcome, but this is very scary for me. I feel you searching too. For once, you are not claiming to have thought this through and have all the answers."

"No, I don't have all the answers. I'm just really sure about what isn't working for me."

"What I feel isn't being considered is what we have done well together. We have lived a lifetime in seven years, and we have accomplished so much. I feel like you are overemphasizing the things that are insignificant about our differences—like sports and movies and socializing. But what about all the things we have done well together and the impact we've made on so many lives? What about all the years we loved each other and encouraged each other to become our best selves? I wish you were able to give more weight to those things. I think they count for a lot."

"Yeah, they count, but it's the differences between us that stand out right now. They weren't carrying us, like with Bandura and his wife, when the newness wore off. All I can think about is what's missing between us and the areas where you no longer meet my needs."

"I believe we have an awful lot going for us. And we have a lot of people who look up to us and depend on us. Before we just brush this off, I feel we have more responsibility than the average couple to try to work these things out. Would you consider turning to a third party and getting some counseling before we give up?"

"No, I'm not willing to do that, but I do feel good about this weekend and the direction we're heading. In fact, I think we have accomplished about all that we can for one weekend. I may head on back this morning and do a little paragliding this afternoon before I have to go into meetings this evening."

I looked at my watch. It was 7:30 in the morning. We had talked for nearly three hours. A feeling began in the pit of my stomach and continued swelling up through me. It rested as a mammoth lump in my throat. We had planned to spend the day together. If we were finished the heavy talk, how I wish we could just play together—go down to the beach or rent a boat and enjoy the lake for a while. I just didn't want this moment to end so abruptly. More than that, after six weeks apart, I wanted to feel him wanting to be with me, that of all the places he could be this day and all the things he could be doing, that his desire was to do something with me. If he wanted to go paragliding, then he could invite me to come watch him. But that was my fantasy. His was getting out of here and heading back to safer grounds.

By now the tears were streaming down my face. How could I share with him what was going on inside of me? He came to negotiate a deal, and the deal was done. It was time to leave. I came to be with him, to love him, and to stay open to the possibilities of new directions in the life we were sharing. At this moment, more than ever, I wanted to cling to the past. I yearned for my old life and my old husband back. He had vowed that we would be together "'til death do us part." Only now was I coming to understand that no one can make an absolute promise to give himself to another forever. We can request it and even hope for it, but we have no right to expect or demand it. But now, for him, our relationship was over. I knew it was over. What lay ahead was beyond anything I could imagine as I learned to come to terms with accepting this.

CHAPTER 16

CONFRONTED WITH DIVORCE
July - August 1998

Mark saw my pain, but it was always difficult for him to deal with my tears. He ran to the store to get cigarettes, and when he returned he had gotten an extended check-out until 1:00 p.m. I appreciated the thoughtfulness. It was the most caring that he had shown to me all weekend—actually in months. It didn't slip by unnoticed. We went for an invigorating walk around the lake and, surprisingly, it lifted my spirits for the moment. The debilitating pain in my chest and knot in my stomach were replaced by deep breaths of refreshing Tahoe air. He made a heroic effort to prolong his stay, but Mark is an elusive butterfly. Once his mind has departed, he might as well take his body with him. We parted on a high note about 11:00 as he headed back to Reno. As we stood next to his Mercedes with the top down and his CD set with his favorite music, he seemed like a teenager to me. Mark was vivacious as we hugged goodbye and spoke of getting together soon. "Depending upon my sexual needs, maybe even this week before I begin my eastern tour for the Company." I let the comment go.

I sat out on the deck after he left and regrouped my thoughts. Never once this entire weekend did Mark act as if he needed me or longed for me or missed me. Never once did he apologize or take responsibility for any aspect of our separation. Never did he initiate a simple "I love you," except as a response to me once during sex. The fact that he could not spend a leisurely day with me spoke volumes. The newness of our relationship was gone, and for my husband, without the bells and whistles, "the endorphins and unblocked opiate receptors" as he would say, something significant died and would never be again. Mark was mourning the death of our passionate love affair, while I was lamenting the absence of long-term stable love. He wanted the former and I the latter.

Being this close to Reno, I wanted to see my family. I stayed overnight with Mom and my stepfather, Lin, and Chris stopped by so we could catch up. The next morning, while everyone was at the office, I stopped by the house, my house, to pick up a couple of books and things I wanted. During the hour I was there, I didn't feel sad about coming back to Windara or leaving again. I was completely detached from the material possession of this mansion. I met Nancy over cappuccinos at Deux Gros Nez. She showed ten times the exuberant emotion of seeing me that my husband had shown. As usual we were soon heavily engaged in meaningful conversation.

"Relationships are no different than drugs or alcohol," she pointed out. "They too can be an addiction. We are chemically attracted to people. So just as alcoholics or addicts have to say no sometimes to a drink that they know is bad for them, in the same way, some people have to say no to certain relationships. You may have to learn to create an entirely different behavior with Mark."

"I have to stop trying so hard to hold on to the past, Nance. You are right. I have to open myself up to something entirely new with him. I just wished I felt more courageous right now. The truth is I'm petrified of what all of this means, but I have to begin preparing myself for the likelihood that things are over between us."

After hugging her goodbye, I ran a few errands and just before leaving, called Amy. We hesitated about what was "right" about our getting together. I left the decision to her. She said she'd meet me at Deux Gros Nez in five minutes. It was my rendezvous spot of the day. Again, the hug and interchange with Amy displayed more emotion and feeling than anything I had with Mark all weekend. What was that about? Is it just something women express better than men? No, I remember Mark in the early days. I know the peak of emotion of which he is capable. It was gone. And I had to take some of the responsibility for having killed it. I could feel Amy's love and concern for my well-being. I could also see the stress of the whole situation in her eyes. We said very little about any of it. Knowing we cared about each other was enough.

At the last minute, Chris chose to drive back to the beach house with me. We both felt it would be a chance for us to have some time together to talk about his personal challenges and explore his professional options. We spent some time strolling on the beach, talking about his life and mine. We were both at crossroads. At the age of twenty-five, he was supposed to be. At the age of fifty-four, I was not. My expectation about life was that I should be settled into a stable family existence with my husband, and our focus would be on finding new ways to love and serve others together. The days of the week passed with no call from Mark. No letter. No surprise visit. No word through anyone. Just the sounds of silence as I listened to the lapping of the waves outside my house. I was left with empty promises of how we would have more frequent talks after our weekend, but they never came.

I checked his schedule on the Internet—the modern-day means for knowing the whereabouts of my husband. Tomorrow he was off to Atlanta. I thought back to the memorable time we spent there. It was one of the highlights of our early courtship. I waged a mental battle with myself. One side said that I should distance myself from Mark for self-protection. The other side recognized that he was stressed and covering it up to everyone but me. This person who is so thoughtless right now is not the real Mark Yarnell—certainly not the man I married. The latter side won the battle. No doormat. No more sex. But I could be kind and supportive. I faxed this note to his hotel in Atlanta and arranged to have it waiting for him when he arrived. The opening words were a take-off of one of his favorite talks:

It took hundreds
And thousands of years
For the universe to evolve...
For planets and comets
And countries and kingdoms
And time and history
And every piece of the puzzle
To fit just right...

And it must have taken
A little faith
And hope
And dreaming too,
To think that
out of all the places
And people,
Improbabilities
And possibilities
And plans
The whole world over...

You and I
Found each other...
And it all came together
In Atlanta.

This City has been magical
For us in the past.
And you will make it magical again
By your presence there.

I wish you everything good
On our first company tour.
You are in my thoughts....
Love, Rene

Mom called to give me my messages from home. She couldn't believe that Mark hadn't called after all this time. She said he was so "up" about our weekend together. I told her one thing I could count on was that when he finally did call, he would tell me how busy he'd been and how he was too "wiped" to talk.

Confronted with Divorce

Susan Silva from Prima had called. She wanted to coordinate a book tour with Mark to coincide with his road trip. *Your First Year* had hit number thirteen on the business bestseller list for *Business Week*. As an afterthought, she mentioned that Ben was not interested in the book I had discussed. They only wanted trade books, not anything quite so personal as this one. I was devastated. Writing this book was what had kept me going. Now it too had been rejected at the very moment that I became a "best-selling" author.

With Chris there with me, I tried to project an upbeat attitude. But no matter how hard I tried to hide it, these next few days were dark nights of the soul for me. I spent the entire time crying, sobbing, struggling just to breathe. Still no word from Mark. I thought about Lin's philosophy of what makes life worth living: someone to love, something to do, and something to look forward to. With no call from Mark and the publisher having turned this book down, I was striking out on all three at this moment. For a long time I sat mesmerized by the lapping of the waves until I was picturing myself trapped on the ocean floor—helpless, unable to grasp air, no strength to push off and propel myself back toward the top, a lingering desire to stay there and not try to resurface. I felt overwhelmed with self-pity. The previous weekend, I had given away all my power to Mark, leaving myself with no inner strength. It was Samson and Delilah in reverse. I was left with no personal efficacy of my own. It was a blessing for me to have my son with me for a few days. As I put him on the plane to send him back home, even that felt like finality to me.

By the time I arrived back home, I was at my lowest point. I didn't think I could make it through the night without some human contact or reassuring voice. I picked up the phone and called home. Our partners had their own homes in Canada, so they stayed at our home when they were in Reno. Valerie's daughter Christine answered and fortunately her mom was right near by—just the person I needed. It was probably better than had I reached Mark.

"Val, are you free to talk for a few minutes? I'm having a really hard time."

She let me talk while I tried to make some sense of my life with Mark. She waited with me while I cried and regained my composure so I could go on. She listened and, when she spoke, she offered words of encouragement about how strong I am. I was falling apart in front of her. How could she speak of my strength?

"Last weekend, I gave away my strength. It was a mistake."

"But you don't have to leave it there. Remember the Pacific Institute philosophy. Think about your ability to control this."

She was right. I did have the power to take mastery over my own emotions. I just lost it for a few days. I could get it back. I knew I could. "Val, say something—anything that comes to your mind that you think I need to hear as we hang up."

"Give me a minute. Let me think.... I know. You have the power to choose."

"Thanks, I'm glad you were there tonight. I'll be okay now."

"Let's talk again over the weekend," she said as we said goodbye.

Finally, late Saturday night Mark called. There was warmth in his voice. More importantly, he apologized for not calling all week. He'd been very busy. He thanked me for my note and told me how well the meeting went in Atlanta. He was too wiped to talk tonight. So far, this conversation went just as I had expected. Then he surprised me by proposing that we get together the following weekend. He wanted to come see me and actually sounded eager—upbeat about the tour and more like himself than he had in a long time. His promise to call and silence that followed had broken my spirit. Now, in the midst of hopelessness, I felt a tinge of hope.

Before I could pull myself completely out of the doldrums, I was hit with a dose of reality from Valerie and, to a lesser degree, John. At first, it showed up as pressure when our distributors needed answers from us or support materials that weren't forthcoming. I was the liaison with the field distributors and they needed decisions made, questions asnwered, brochures released—all of which were caught up in the bureacracy of our own system. Further, there was a misunderstanding about a payment to Stacey, our consultant. Maybe it was stress on all our parts; maybe it was Val and John's inability to understand why I was still here and not there standing side by side with them, facing the innumerable day-to-day challenges within our company. But for the first time since we began working together, there was tension that displayed itself in our phone calls and e-mails. I'm sure it was coming from me as much as from them. I desperately wanted to clear up this strain on my relationship with John and Valerie right away. I couldn't handle all the problems with Mark and have discord with them too. *Why was my relationship to Val taking a downturn just when my relationship with Mark seemed to be coming together?*

The next day I called the office, determined to try to get things moving for our reps. I could no longer justify in my own mind how every request from the field was hung up with my partners. I reached Val on the first try.

"I'm in a meeting and can't talk to you right now." Her voice was cold and angry.

"Val, we need to talk. We can't let things fester like this."

"I'm busy right now."

"Val, I can tell you're angry. How do you suggest I communicate the needs of the field? Is there a better way than how I'm doing it?"

"E-mail is fine."

"Yeah, but it isn't working. Everything gets bogged down."

"You make it sound like we're just sitting here doing nothing. You act like you're the only one who does anything. We're trying to solve the funding problems, and that's taking a lot of our time. And quite frankly, I don't like your accusatory tone."

"Val, what are you talking about? I'm frustrated that we can't work together like we did before we opened. We set deadlines and we got things done in a timely way. Now, since Randy has come on the scene, nothing is getting done. How can I help you understand that keeping the office efficient is great, but responding to the needs of the field is everything in network marketing? As the liaison between them and corporate, I feel totally ineffective. I've got all I can handle with the situation with Mark. I can't deal with having you mad at me too."

"You should have thought of that before you sent a letter like the one you just e-mailed. I'm insulted by it. How dare you accuse me of doing something inappropriate under a single signature!"

"Val, I never said...."

"Rene, I have to go. I'm in a meeting and can't talk."

I held the receiver to my ear until I realized I was listening to the dial tone. How did we get to this low point? And why now? I sat down and immediately typed back an e-mail to Val and John. I addressed the issue of the single signature that seemed to be the core of Val's upset.

>Subject: Talking is greatly needed
>Date: Wed, 29 Jul 1998 20:57:42 -0700
>From: Rene Reid Yarnell <yarnell@ibm.net>
>To: jradford@globalserve.net, vperkio@ibm.net

>Dear Val and John:
>I never meant to be accusatory of you, Val. I
>believed that you thought our consultant was being
>paid in arrears and you weren't aware that she was
>paid in advance. Had I signed the check with you, I
>would have known since I am the one who initiated
>the contract. As a result, we have overpaid her.
>The only thing I was "accusing" you of was the
>possibility that you were not aware of payments
>being made in advance. That's all. Beyond my
>marital challenges, nothing could be more painful
>to me than to be out of harmony with the two of
>you. Please let us take the time as soon as
>possible to clear this up. Perhaps we need to look
>at the possibility that there are issues deeper than
>the points listed on the memo. I am counting very
>much on hearing from you. I find this exchange as
>painful as anything I've / we've gone through.
>I'm sorry. I'm truly sorry. Being isolated out here
>is really difficult. I believe we are all trying hard.
>We need to get back to some kind of regular
>communication. I look forward to hearing what
>you recommend.
>Please call soon, Rene

I didn't hear from my partners the rest of the day, and barely slept that night. I woke up early and felt the only comfort I could derive was writing in my journal.

> Hearing Val's anger tore my heart out. I didn't see it coming at all. I reread what I wrote, and I don't think what I said warranted her reaction. I attribute it more to stress than to what I said. It is not like Valerie to lash out at me like this. What else could be causing this?
>
> I am really concerned about the business. John and Val are busy, but seem to be more caught up in the internal affairs than they are in being the "field support team," as they chose to call themselves. Most everything I submit that is needed by the field gets hung up for weeks. I need them to suggest a better way than what I'm doing. Otherwise, they are upset because they must face the fact that they are not following through. I'm really concerned that this company can withstand the distance between Mark and me. For the sake of everyone, Mark and I must pull things together between us. I attribute every problem we are facing to the fact that we are not together in our thinking and in our support of each other. We must resolve this.

Later in the morning Mom called to relay a message from Mark. He was in his hotel room for about twenty minutes and said I should call him there. He might be able to come in early for our weekend. I felt a ray of hope, and hung up and dialed the phone.

"Hi!"

"Well, I don't believe it! I've been trying to reach you for days. I've called nine times this morning. You're either never there or your line is busy. Apparently, even your mom couldn't reach you. It's been forty-five minutes since she started trying." His voice was angry. I couldn't believe I was being berated for my phone being busy. *Why didn't you try my cell phone?*

"So, how was the meeting last night?" I asked, changing the subject.

"Great. Each one of the tours just keeps getting bigger. Really great people. I couldn't be happier."

Then why are you always so angry around me? "I'm glad it's going well."

"Now listen, you've got to get off this thing about wanting everything in a contract. The other partners don't have contracts. Why should Randy? You're just being ridiculous."

Do we have to talk about business? Can't we just talk? Please. "Well, of course, we are the founding partners. When we add a new partner, though, and give away a percentage of our company, I believe we should have an understanding in writing of what we are each giving. I don't think that's unreasonable."

"Look, Rene, you just have to stay out of this business. You don't fit. You're way off base and everyone knows it. Last weekend, you promised that you would stay out of it, and you're right back in it again. I can't believe you."

You promised me a few things on that weekend too, like you'd call regularly and we'd begin to work on us. "Can't believe what?"

"You know what I mean. John read me your e-mail. You have no business looking at the books and checking up on payments and things like that." That didn't sound like John to go behind my back and read Mark my e-mail. I would have to talk to John.

"Mark, I'm a partner. All partners should be looking at the books. And the item I pointed out to them was a payment I was involved in making."

"Well, you're totally wrong. And you have no business getting involved in that."

"Mark, those payments to the consultant were made in advance, not in arrears. I wasn't trying to accuse anyone of anything. I truly believe that they didn't know. Val and John both indicated that our consultant had extended her stay but was working on her own time. John was quite insistent in telling me that we hadn't paid her. But in reality we had because we were disbursing her checks in advance. As long as we kept doing that, of course she would continue working. If her check had had a double signature like we agreed to, I would have been able to sign off that it was the final payment. Since I wrote the first few checks myself, I was more aware of this.... Mark, this is really upsetting me. Is this the reason that you called nine times? I had the mistaken hope that you wanted to come see me and talk about our relationship."

"You always do this to me. I intended to save this for when we get together this weekend."

"Then, I'm glad you got it off your chest now because I don't want to talk any business this weekend. This one is reserved for discussions about you and me."

"No, I've got some things about business that I have to talk to you about." *What business? What warning signal was I missing?*

"Mark, I can't handle it. If you're coming here to belittle me and lecture me about the business, I'd just as soon not...."

"We've got to get some things worked out. That's the whole point."

"The point is that we are supposed to be rediscovering each other. Just once, I'd like to hear that you love me, and you miss me, and you're wondering how I'm doing." I realized when I got to the last word that I was yelling.

"Goddamn it, you know I love you!" he screamed back at me.

How? How would I know? The kindness you've shown? Our time together? Your cards and letters? Your concern for my well-being over being here alone? There's been none of this. "Geez, you sound like your father— you know, the guy who could never say 'I love you.' I don't want to have to read in the margins of your writing to find out what you feel about me. I've waited seven weeks for you to have time to resolve things with us. I deserve to have that time set aside for nothing else. I want to know how you feel about me."

"And you think you're going to get that by yelling?" He was right. If it weren't so serious, this conversation would be a comedy—a tragic comedy.

I sighed. "I'm sorry. This is the first time I've lost it with you since I've been gone."

"Humph, that's not how I remember it."

"I've waited patiently. I've tried not to push you. But you treat me like dirt. Do you know what it made me feel like when we were sexually intimate for a night after months of no involvement, and then you go off and don't call for the next eight days?" *How could he not understand that for a woman, having close intimacy with a man followed by little or no communication is one of the worst degradations possible?*

"The phone works both ways, you know."

"Not for me, it doesn't. You're always too busy or too wiped out. That's why I write to you instead."

"Just once."

I took a deep breath. Even my letters were forgotten. Nothing I did was good enough. "I've written several times. The last one I faxed you in Atlanta." *I've e-mailed you a get-well note. I faxed you at least three letters and hand-wrote three more. They were loving and sweet and supportive of our getting back together. I can't do anything that will elicit kindness from you.*

"Yeah, well, I thanked you for that. You know, Amy calls me three times a day."

"Well, obviously, I don't have the same relationship with you. Maybe you have time for her. All you've ever said to me is that you don't have time or you're too tired to talk." For the first time ever, I felt jealous of Amy. That wasn't like me.

"Listen, I didn't call for this. My taxi's waiting downstairs. I've got to go."

"Mom said something about your coming in early?"

"Yeah, well, I don't have time to do anything about it now. I've wasted all this time...."

"Please try. We need time together."

"Okay, got to go." The phone clicked.

I spent the entire day in tears, of anger and frustration and depression. I didn't hear from Val and John. I felt cut off from everyone. I couldn't remember how long it had been since I had felt a nurturing word from Mark. I went for a long walk on the beach, trying to understand the lesson in all of this. I came back feeling that I'd hit bottom again. That was happening consistently these past two weeks. I felt sure I could blame some of my emotional outbursts on menopause. But it was more than that. I couldn't see any hope. I checked my e-mail. There was one message from our daughter replying to my last message to her. It gave me hope.

> <Date: Thu, 30 Jul 1998 15:46:13 -0700
> <From: Amy Yarnell <yarnell@powernet.net>
> <To: yarnell@ibm.net
> <i love you too.

I reached John at his home in Vancouver.

"John, this whole misunderstanding is tearing me apart. But I just have to ask you one question. Knowing you as I do, it doesn't sound like you to have run behind my back and shown my e-mail to Mark. Why would you do that?"

"Rene, I didn't do that. What makes you think I did?"

"Mark said you did."

"Well, let me look into it with him. It isn't true. I wouldn't do that."

I hung up more confused. *Then who did...and why? And who is Mark covering up for?* Only later would I learn that it was Valerie who had shared this information with him. Why would he falsely name John instead of just saying it was she who told him?

I had another sleepless night and got up early to write in my journal:

> Let me look long and hard at the reflection of myself. There is a huge gap between my intentions and my delivery. There must be. I have everyone in Global Network angry with me. I feel ostracized, misunderstood, and truly hated. If anyone says anything about me that is negative, Mark is always ready and eager to jump in and join them. We have no marriage, no relationship, no hope. It is over

between us. I don't understand why he wants to come this weekend—except that it is another chance to beat up on me while I'm down. The thought of having him come is terrifying me. I don't want him to come. I'm not strong enough today to take more of his berating and belittling. I just wish this horrible, godawful nightmare would end. Please, Mark, don't come. Stay away from me and stop hurting me. I can't take it anymore.

I closed down my computer and headed for the beach. As I walked, I realized I was braver in writing than in person. The question was, did I really have the courage to tell him this? The bigger question was: did I have the courage to get on with my life? I had no life with Mark, but I was petrified of a life without him. I didn't know where I belonged.

After my walk, I was determined to face a new day with a new uplifted attitude. After speaking with my friend, Duncan Anderson, who lived in New York, I made contact with the publishing house that he had recommended. Much to my surprise, while I expected Duncan to refer me to a New York publisher, this house was located in Novato, California, just north of San Francisco. I called the publisher, Marc Allen, also an author, to let him know that I was submitting my partially completed work. When I reached his voice mail, my ears perked up when I heard, "For those of you in the South Bay, I will be giving a lecture this evening, July 31st, at 7:00 at the East West Bookstore in Mountain View." What a coincidence! I was coming into the San Jose Airport to pick Mark up late that evening, and Mountain View is only about ten minutes north of there. With my packet in hand addressed to this very publisher, I headed out to hear his lecture, and walked in late. Marc Allen, a laid-back man of about forty, average build with shoulder-length blondish, brown hair, was seated comfortably on a stool, talking casually to a small audience about his principles for a *Visionary Life*, the title of his newest book. One of his examples was especially germane to me.

"Sometimes do you ever find yourself heading down one track and you just keep running into walls. Instead of beating your head against that one, why not turn in a different direction and try walking down a new path instead? Watch where it leads. If things flow smoothly, continue down that path for a while and see if your options don't open up."

Isn't that exactly what had just happened to me? That's how I ended up at this particular lecture. After the meeting, I waited my turn to get his autograph in the book he'd previously written, *Visionary Business*, that led me to him.

"And what's your name?" he inquired politely.

"Rene."

"Oh, didn't you call me this afternoon?"

"Yes. I was actually calling to introduce myself and let you know that I wanted to submit a book for your consideration." I went on to tell him how I came to be here. What a fortuitous meeting.

"Do you have the manuscript with you?"

"Just happen to have it, complete with a cover letter to your publishing house. I was going to put it in the mail until I learned of your lecture this evening. Since I had the time before my husband's plane lands in San Jose, here I am, hand-carrying it to you."

"Great, let me take it back with me. I look forward to reading it."

Just one week ago, I had been turned down by my current publisher, and here I was hand-delivering the first draft of my personal story to another, and one who specialized in this type of book. Whether this turned out to be the right publishing house or not, I felt clearly on track again with my writing. The very act of submitting it and knowing that it would be read made all the difference in my attitude.

Mark's plane was due in at 11:00 p.m. I headed for the airport, carrying a gigantic mixed bag of emotions. He was one of the first off the plane. His hair was going grayer, even more than the last time I'd seen him. Then I saw his face. He was near exhaustion, having just come from a week-long tour. All of a sudden my guard was down. I could hardly wait to put my arms around him. After all my ranting, at that moment I wanted to take care of him, really baby him. I could feel myself clinging to the tiniest thread of hope that we might still pull things back together.

Driving from San Jose to Santa Cruz necessitated taking "Blood Alley" again. Mark wanted to sleep on the way down but was unnerved by the dangerous curves and the speed of the cars. After an hour, we pulled into my little cottage on Sunset Beach. Mark made himself a midnight snack, and after a few minutes of talking we both collapsed into bed. He made overtures to have sex, but I stuck with my conviction not to allow it this time.

He was up before dawn walking on the beach. By the time I awoke, he was dressed and had been into town already, exploring Capitola Beach. I made a pot of coffee, and we welcomed the morning sitting out on the deck with a sweeping view of the Pacific.

"Well, do you want to start or do you want me to?" Mark inquired eagerly.

I knew we had a lot to talk about since the last real conversation two weeks earlier. "If you've got something on your mind, why don't you begin? I'll go after you," I said.

"I've done a lot of thinking since we were together, and I've come to a decision. I've really thought this thing through, and what I believe is that we would both be better off going our separate ways. We just don't like the same things. We don't listen to the same music or enjoy the same sports. You know the list, we've talked about it before. I would like for us to get a divorce. I'm convinced that if we can do it amicably, we will end up being much better friends."

I was stunned. I hadn't prepared myself for our conversation to take this direction this weekend. I believed we were here to pick up on the general theme we had developed two weeks earlier at Tahoe. My entire focus for weeks now had been around ways I could improve my part in our marriage. Despite my premonition, I wasn't ready for the "D" word. What had happened between the time he seemed so "up," as Mom described it, and now? Grasping for something to say, I uttered, "How does that work—the friendship part?" sincerely trying to understand the spirit of what he was saying.

"Right now, we are always arguing. It doesn't take much to set off a fight between us. But with all this behind us, I honestly believe that we can have fun together. I just think we will be even better friends. But the thing I'm worried about is the fight over property. I came ready to offer you a settlement, which I hope you'll accept. What I don't want is for each of us to have separate attorneys and give away a third of everything we've built to these guys." Referring to a copy of our monthly statement, which he'd gotten from Mom, Mark then proceeded to lay out a plan.

I found myself observing him even more than I listened to the details of his proposal. Mark Yarnell is completely unattached when it comes to money: giving it away seems to boost his ego. And he was consistent. It didn't matter whether he was giving away money from our foundation, giving away ownership to partners who had made little or no investment in our business, or settling up with his wife to end a marriage. Money grows on trees, and as long as he has enough to take care of his basic life needs, you are welcome to whatever else he has.

Every couple should experience the process of a property settlement *before* getting married. The truth about one's basic core values and insecurities definitely comes out. Paradoxically, it was at the moment my husband was proposing a divorce settlement that my respect for him and his carefree attitude about money reached an all-time high point.

Mark was throwing out numbers: I would have 75% of this and 60% of that if I would just be willing to back away from the business ownership completely. When someone is that giving, it engenders a similar reciprocity of behavior. I had no faith in the business with Mark and me split. So had I just wanted to watch out for myself, I would have accepted his deal. But I felt so much appreciation for his fairness that I spontaneously responded, "Why don't we just split everything down the middle? I think you should stay in the house, and you can't possibly live on that little if you have to keep it up." We were two people settling a divorce by putting forth what we thought was in the best interest of the other. I commented on this.

"I want to love you in the way C.S. Lewis describes it—loving you enough to let you go so you can be loved in the way you deserve. I know now I can't give you what you need. But I love you, and I want you to have it. You are a good person, and you have earned the right to have someone who can sustain the kind of love you long for."

I believed him. But more than anything, I wanted to know what had led him to this conclusion. I craved to know every tiny detail how he reached this decision. No, not just decision, but philosophy. What he was saying was a reasonably profound, well-thought-out belief system. Was it just trumped up for the sake of letting me down more easily? Somehow, I didn't think so. "So what about you? What is it that you want from life and from a relationship?"

"Remember when we were in Hawaii with Don and Sara Schmanski?" He was referring to Dean's parents and a trip we took with them the previous year.

"Of course."

"Well, Sara and I were sitting out on the porch smoking together and talking when Don came out. He hates to see Sara smoke and unleashed the full throttle of his ammunition on her. After he had stomped back into the house in a huff, I said to her, 'Doesn't that embarrass you? I mean, I'm embarrassed for you. And I feel kind of guilty, because you wouldn't be out here smoking if it weren't for me.' And you know what she said? She held out her fingers, studded with some beautiful rings, and said, 'As long as he keeps me in these, I can handle it. I don't even hear the anger; and by this afternoon, we will be making mad, passionate love and both have forgotten it.' You see, Rene, what I need is my Sara Schmanski."

"I know I could never and would never be Sara. That isn't who I am."

"I know you couldn't. And that's why we're going apart."

"Please know that anything I am about to say isn't to argue. I just want to learn from this. I really want to understand. Okay?"

"Deal."

"When you plucked me off of the Board of County Commissioners, I was the Chairman that year. Surely you must have known that I had a strong-enough side that enabled me to get to that position. You don't get there with candy kisses."

"True, and I was drawn to your power. There is no question that that was part of the attraction. But your demeanor was so sweet and gentle, and I was also attracted to that. What I thought was that you would exert your authority in training and speaking and working *with me* to fight our mutual crusades together; I never expected to see it used *against me*. I thought you would show your softness in your dealings with me. That's what I idealized, and I carried that ideation through our courtship and honeymoon. But it was about two weeks after we returned from New Zealand that my bubble burst. It was when we were preparing to go to Denver and Colorado Springs to do a Nu Skin meeting, and some of the people in your downline were running ads in anticipation of our going there. Remember?"

"I remember that whole scene really well. And you're right— I felt torn between my people and you. They wanted to believe that when we married, they weren't losing me as their upline but gaining your support as well. But the truth is that I didn't heed your request to press them to stop running the ads. I tried, but I was torn between feeling empathy for their needs and for the awkward place it put you with your people."

"That was a big turning point for me. It changed everything. Up until then, I believed that the way I loved you, that feeling, would never go away. I think we could have sustained it. I had never ever felt like that with such genuine feeling in my whole life."

"But how could you really believe that kind of love would last?"

"I did believe it. I thought ours was so special that we could have *made* it last."

"And you're saying that it was my controlling, my stubbornness, that killed it?"

"Yeah, and believe me, I tried to overlook that part of you; but it was there, and it didn't go away. And after that, other things compounded it."

Mark got up and looked through the binoculars at the ocean. He spotted a school of dolphin and was entranced. I sat there reflecting back to that moment nearly six-and-a-half years earlier. Would that we could go back in time. Would that I could relive that scenario. Feeling what I felt at that instant, and knowing what I had come to know about loving another person, I would have handled that so differently. I could have made things a win for everyone. I wasn't at all sensitive to the seriousness of the problem for Mark. With the benefit of hindsight, I see how I could have explained it to my distributors. I could have promised them Mark's support on conference calls, and he would have worked with them to convert their prospects into distributors. Just please don't compete with his downline in their own city. They would have understood, and, out of respect for me, I think they would have backed off. At the very least, I could have tried harder. Now here we were making plans to go our separate ways.

"If you believed that the emotional high of first love would last forever, then I never had a chance. No one could make it last."

"I talked to Bandura about this." Mark was continuing to develop a close personal relationship with this wonderful professor and author after we had spent time with him earlier this year. "He agrees with you that new love can't last. He feels he and his wife just got lucky. After it wore off, they still had a lot of things in common. That's what held them together all of these years. But, see, you are I are so different."

I was convinced that Mark was making too much of the little things. We shared so many parts of our lives in the bigger picture, and did them well! We taught together. How many couples could co-author a book and agree on what to say? Roslyn Carter said that when she and Jimmy were writing their memoirs on their days in the White House, they almost got a divorce. We were strong enough as a couple that we were not only able to write a book together, but it had just jumped from number 13 to number 11 on the business bestseller list. And now we had started a business together.

"What about the business? How do you see that working with us? Would you rather I back off entirely?"

"No, I want you to go on training. You're good at it, and our people need it. And I want you to speak at convention. In fact, we need to decide how to roll this thing out to everyone."

"I don't want to put any black cloud over our convention."

"Why don't we let people know our decision in two phases," he proposed. "We can tell our family and business partners right away, and just keep it quiet. Then let's tell everyone else after the September convention. By then, they will have seen us together and know that everything is going to be okay."

I knew I was in shock and asking questions out of sheer knee-jerk reaction. "So how do you want to handle things in the interim? I mean, I want you to have the house, and it will take me some time to find a house for myself. Let's decide what I will do while that is all coming together."

"Well, I think you should come home. Let's do just what we talked about last time. You work out of our house and write, return calls, and do the training. I'll go into the office every morning and do my thing. I think we'll be fine."

"Are you okay with that? With me coming home?" I asked.

"Yeah, I want you to. It's your home too. And Valerie and Christine are moving into an apartment this weekend. I didn't know they were even thinking of it. Actually, I was a little hurt that they didn't tell me. Christine has become my buddy; we've had some interesting talks. She is doing a great job as receptionist for us. I'm going to miss having them both around. So the house is virtually empty. John will still stay with us a couple of days each week, and Amy is moving back at the end of August. So we will be a small household again. I guess the only question is whether you're okay with it. I don't want to give you any false hope that we're going to work things out. I really believe what we're doing is for the best."

I didn't. This was bizarre to me. How could we possibly split up at a time when our new company was so vulnerable? "I hope you know that I'm going along with this because it is what you want. If living with you under these circumstances becomes too painful for me, I'll let you know. In the meantime, if I'm going to get on with my life, and it's going to be in Reno, I have to live somewhere while I'm looking for a house, and I'd rather be in my own home, our home, than anyplace else."

"And remember, honey, this is our life," Mark said. "It's nobody else's business what we do with it or how we choose to live it. It's completely up to us."

We took a break. Mark made breakfast while I did my Saturday morning training call. I tried to keep my spirits up with our people. There was a large group, more than a hundred people on the call, with lots of new people under Peggy Long. I had to be strong for them. *Please excuse me from today's call. My heart isn't in it. I'm grasping at the tiniest straw to hold onto my marriage. My Catholic tradition, my innate loyalty, and my utter fear of abandonment are driving me to cling to my vows: 'til death do us part.* But they were counting on me for support, and I had to put their needs of that moment before my own. I could do it. I did do it. When I hung up, Mark came walking through the front door.

"How did it go?"

"Good questions today. We have the beginnings of a great company. I love our people." As always, I came away from the training invigorated. Even after all these years, I would begin the call with the mistaken belief that I was there to give to them. But I always came away feeling that it was they who gave to me.

The sun was out, and we went for a long walk on the beach. Mark found a piece of kelp and jumped rope with it. I found some new shells and carried them back to the house. For the moment, we were playful with each other. Finally we settled back into our places on the porch overlooking the ocean. We were both lost in the sound of the waves and our own thoughts.

"Sweetheart, I want to pick up where we left off on this whole topic of control—my unwillingness to let go and the way I deal with people when I think they're not living up to their end of things. I am trying to accept that it's too late for us. I don't really believe that, but I accept that that is where you are. And I don't want to try to 'control' that too."

"You don't do well with alpha men, Rene. Behind that soft voice and gentle, almost vulnerable, exterior is a person who can castrate a man and not even blink an eye. Very few men are strong enough to stand up to you. I may be one of the few who is not intimidated by you. It doesn't make you bad. But what you need to know about yourself is that you can push the button of an alpha male and make him react in a way that he would never behave otherwise. You destroyed our formulator after he failed to provide us with our products. You were right—and you probably saved this company because we were going nowhere with him. But the way you delivered your message to him left him without even a tail to drag. You pushed Larry Brady's button, and he is still apologizing to me for the way he reacted to you on the conference call that day. But your style of delivery is so needling that you trigger that reaction in certain types of men. It is too late for you to change; but I think if you understood the effects you have on certain people better, you might soften at times before making your point."

How many times had I heard this about myself—my former husband tried to tell me something similar. My son has told me, and several people in my dealings in public office. How many more times would I have to hear this before I learned the lesson? But, how could it ever be too late? I wasn't willing to accept that. I believed I could still learn, and grow, and change those parts of me that did not bring out my higher self. I would never stop working at becoming a better person and, most especially, at loving others without making so many demands or unrealistic expectations. I could hear the voice of every person who had ever tried to tell me this talking to me through Mark. But it was he who was finally getting through. Timing is everything. I was ready to hear. I had spent nearly two months opening myself to the truth and asking for divine guidance to allow me to let in those things that I needed to hear. There was no point in telling him I was hearing, really hearing. Only my actions would prove it so.

I recognized that I was able to talk about my shortcomings, but why is it that we never got around to the topic of his? I knew I should be feeling some anger, but I wasn't. Why? I was too scared about what was happening in my life. It was taking all the energy I had to breathe, to get through one minute and begin another. If I let my thoughts wander too far out...to the next day, or week, or month, I panicked over the feeling of being utterly alone. So, instead of venting anger at his unwillingness to work through the issues in our relationship, I thanked him for his honesty and turned the topic of conversation back to him. "So what do you want to do for you. I mean, how do you see your life without me?"

"Well, first of all, I don't want to go on without you. As I said earlier, I see us becoming better friends without all the expectations of marriage. I think we'll spend quality time and have fun together." *You really think that is going to happen?* "You are still the only woman who turns me on. And, after nearly seven years, you should feel good about that. There isn't another woman who does that to me."

"Are you saying that that is a sign of love?"

"Absolutely. For a young man, it is just lust. But for men of my age, after years of marriage, I believe it is an unmistakable sign of deep love."

"I don't get it. I mean, I hear you, but it is so different for me and I think for most women. It would never occur to me to feel loved because a man saw my naked body and became sexually stimulated—even if that man had been married to me for years."

"Well, it ought to make you feel good. Why do you think Viagra is such a big deal right now? Men are no longer in love with their wives. They aren't turned on, and they have to rely on a drug to create and sustain it for them. I don't need that. I love you. And why should I have to tell you when I'm demonstrating it in a way that I absolutely could not fake it?"

"See, I need you to tell me. I can't hear it enough. I need to have you come downstairs to my office, lean over me and kiss my neck. I need you to put your arms around me while I'm standing in the kitchen. I need a note left on my dresser. I need all of that build-up before we make love. Then lovemaking becomes something so extraordinary. It is the culmination of the day or the week of kindness and loving acts that you've shown me. That's what was missing for me two weeks ago."

"What do you mean? Are you trying to say that our lovemaking wasn't good for you?" *Ogod. Men* are *from Mars!*

"I know this is hard for you to hear, but we're both trying to be honest. It absolutely was not good for me. In fact, it nearly broke me. Why? Because for five weeks prior to that weekend, we barely spoke. And when we did, it was to fight. I felt demeaned and belittled. All you ever wanted to tell me was what I had done wrong. Then you got to our place at Tahoe and jumped into bed with me. No warm-up. No 'I love you.' No 'I'm sorry for what I said.' Just sex. I rationalized that it was okay by convincing myself that to say 'no' to my husband would have only made the situation worse. I wanted you to know, regardless of how you felt, that I loved you. So I believed that I was making love to you while you were having sex with me. I held onto the hope that the acts of kindness would follow, but they didn't. Then the weekend ended without any sign. You said you would call and we would begin to work on our relationship by phone, so I held on to that hope. But after a week of not hearing from you, my spirit was broken. I was crushed. I felt used. I had prostituted myself and felt cheapened. I felt like any woman would feel who had sex with someone who dropped out of her life immediately afterward. Only this someone was my husband. I fell apart, Mark. I cried so hard I couldn't get my breath. I finally called Valerie for support. I was so devastated I didn't think I could go on. I'm not telling you all of this to make you feel bad. I'm telling you so we can begin to understand how different we truly are. And maybe we will start to have real empathy for each other. If we can't put ourselves in each other's place, we will never be able to really love." I had finally worked myself up into a state of anger. Just thinking back on it made me furious all over again.

"That just doesn't make any sense to me. I can't believe you didn't feel good about how we were together," Mark said.

"I would have been fine had there just been something either before or after to corroborate our lovemaking. But with no words or actions or phone calls, I felt used, that I didn't really matter to you."

Mark got up again and lit a cigarette. He looked through the binoculars, saw more dolphin, and invited me to come look. Usually I could see them close to shore, but these were far out to sea. They were playing, diving in and out of the water. "I'd like to have fun like that with you again," he said softly. "But I don't want to cause you pain. I guess you're going to have to decide whether you can handle lovemaking with me or not."

"You mean you're serious? You would really want to continue that part of our relationship?" I asked incredulously.

"Yes, I still love you. I'm attracted to you. I just can't handle the rest of it."

I felt speechless. After a moment, I asked, "Well, how do you see your life going after our 'divorce'? I don't quite understand how all of this plays out in your mind."

"I don't think marriage is for me. I want to stay more open, more like that community deal we talked about—you know, expanding my world to gather in many individuals who share things in common. Right now, I want to dedicate my life to the business. In my free time, I want to paraglide, hanglide, and race sports cars."

"Race sports cars?" *Is this mid-life crisis or just the Pinocchio syndrome, the boy who will never grow up?*

"Yeah, I just met this guy who used to race and he's going to teach me how. I want to win the Indianapolis 500. I'm going to do it. In fact, that guy who just won it is in his 40s and his first name is Mark. I'm halfway there." Mark was smirking and his eyes twinkled as he spoke.

I couldn't tell if he was kidding or not, but I didn't think he was. He full well intended to take up sports car racing…and win. Now that the adrenaline rush of new love wore off, he was determined to replace it with the endorphin release of major business risk and adventure sports. This was the addict personality at its best, always in search of the eternal high.

Mark pulled some papers out of his suitcase and said he needed my signature to okay the new stock splits that Randy had negotiated. My husband seemed comfortable with this arrangement as long as the proposal came from anyone but me. I wasn't surprised that Graham had gone along with his proposal but I was flabbergasted that Larry Brady had agreed. Randy made it part of the deal that he be the managing partner until the investors were all paid back. John had been sending me the various drafts of this document. I was familiar with it and signed without giving it much thought. Business was the last thing on my mind. Mark's demeanor seemed anxious but, as I handed him the signed paperwork without discussion, he relaxed.

We took a drive and picked up a video that Mark wanted me to see: *Fly Away Home.* We lay beside each other with my head on his shoulder in a low lounge chair and watched it together. I was very aware that the little girl in me just wanted to cling to this moment and be protected from any more hurt.

I quickly understood why he wanted me to see this movie. It's the story of an off-the-wall dad who loved to fly hangliders and other contraptions. His ex-wife dies and he is left to care for their daughter, Amy. Yes, her name in the movie is Amy. She's unhappy after the loss of her mom, and reluctantly comes to live with her dad. She finds some abandoned goose eggs in the barn and wants to preserve them. She moves them to a dresser drawer and puts a heat lamp near them for warmth. The eggs hatch, and she becomes the proud mother of a flock of geese. It's hectic at first trying to feed and nurture them, but the real trauma comes when it's time to teach them to fly. They apparently learn by modeling, not by instinct. The story reaches its climax when the father teaches Amy how to fly an ultralite, which they decorate to look like a goose. And then the father and daughter, each in their own ultralite, set out to lead the geese south for the winter. It's a beautiful, uplifting story. By the end of the movie, when the geese found their way back to her the following season, tears were streaming down my face. Even Mark had gotten a little teary.

"It makes me feel bad when you show more emotion over a movie than over our real life situation," I whispered.

"I've had more time to think it through. I'm really convinced that we are going to be happier and more loving without the encumbrances of marriage. You'll see." *God, I wished I believed that.*

"But, honey, you talked about my finding someone else who will meet my needs for how I want to be loved. I don't get it. How does this play out when I'm living across town in my own house, and one day I call to tell you I've met him? This is the one."

"Like I said, I'd like to check him out for you. If he is the one, I'll love you enough to let you go. I'll be happy for you."

"Knowing that that would put an end to the Mark-and-Rene union—our working and playing together?"

"Yeah, because I would believe that it would be in your best interest."

Does he actually believe this? Or think I will? Who is he kidding? I couldn't conceive of reversing the situation. I've loved deeply and passionately twice in my life. Both marriages have led to divorce, although I didn't want either to end. I couldn't have encouraged the closure of either relationship with the open invitation to find someone else. Was it that my love for them was too centered in myself? Had I not reached the higher plane of love? Or is this going beyond what the human heart can endure? These were questions I would ponder over the next few weeks as we transitioned into our new relationship.

As I came out of the shower, cleaning up after our walk on the beach, Mark was lying on the bed. He was calling to me, begging me to come be with him. No, I promised myself I wouldn't. How could he want to divorce me and make love to me all at the same time? If I could dig deep enough to find the answer, I would uncover the mystery of Mark's attraction to me in the first place. I would be able to understand why he fell in and out of love with me. The incongruity made me begin to laugh. And as I did, he got sillier in his pleading to me to come lie next to him. I can't explain why I did, but I'm glad I did. It was beautiful lovemaking— and it was our last time. I would remember it always.

"Well, I'll see you in four days," Mark said as I kissed him goodbye in the airport. "Are you okay with things?" he asked with genuine concern.

"No, I'm feeling extremely anxious, but I'm eager to come home."

"It's going to be better than ever. I promise you that. You'll see." Mark seemed so sincere. *I want to believe this. But his responses are so erratic. If I wait an hour, his behavior could change.*

"We may not have done so well at marriage, sweetheart, but we may go down in history as having had the most romantic courtship and the most loving divorce of any two people in modern times." I philosophized that we had come full circle in our relationship, linking the ending back to its beginning stage. More than ever, I wanted to believe that our ending would have some of the sweetness of our initial phase. I knew I was stretching, trying to make some sense of what was happening, still not really believing that we must go our separate ways, but if we did, that our separation would be all that loving.

As I watched him board the plane, I wondered what the transitional period of living together while divorcing would be like. Right now, I just wanted to go home—to my family, my familiar surroundings, and my adrenaline junkie.

On my last day, I took one final walk on this beach I had come to love. I watched the tide come in, leaving behind piles of seaweed and lone seashells. On this last walk, I found a perfect, unbroken sand dollar. I had found countless cracked and shattered shells over the weeks there, but only this one was whole and perfect. A poem came flowing out of me. I planned to frame both the sand dollar and the poem for Mark. Finding it on this last day felt so symbolic.

> *Amidst the chipped and broken sand dollars*
> *Scattered aimlessly about the beach.*
> *Only rarely does a perfectly intact one*
> *Emerge within our reach.*
> *Treasure it—you may not find another.*
>
> *With the passing of time flaws may appear*
> *Yet its shape is molded to the form of your hand.*
> *Its scent and crevices have blended with your own*
> *Prepared to toss it aside, you begin to understand.*
> *Treasure it—you may not find another.*

CHAPTER 17

FACING THE REALITY
August 1998

On my way home, I stopped in San Francisco and spent a couple of days with my friend Kathryn Blue, a woman of strong conviction—exactly what I needed at this moment. It felt good to be back in my old stomping grounds. I enjoyed walking through the Mission district recalling happy memories of the time I lived there in the '70s. After dinner we continued talking late into the night about the total life spectrum of my situation. We explored my options, looking for the best way to deal with my return home from a position of personal strength.

"Are you sure you're ready to go home?" Kathryn asked with justifiable concern.

"I have to. Mark needs me home to help host a barbecue for about fifty people tomorrow night."

"That doesn't mean you *have* to be there!"

"Hmmm. You're right. Maybe I just feel a sense of responsibility to all these new people who are joining our company. I feel I should be there."

"Okay, but how are you going to present yourself?"

"What do you mean?"

"Well, where will you put your things when you get home? Where are you going to sleep? Where is he going to sleep?"

"I have enough to deal with without worrying about every move I make. I'm really scared."

"None of it matters except that you feel good about yourself. I worry about you feeling victimized."

"I feel like I don't have a lot of options at the moment."

"Oh, my! You've got unlimited options. You can come waltzing into the house just in time for the party to begin and make a grand entrance. You can leave whenever you want, announcing that you have decided to stay in a hotel for the time being. You can move back into your bedroom and let him know that he should sleep in one of the other ones. You can do whatever you damned well please. You don't owe anyone anything. You need to do what is healthy for you. That's the only thing that matters."

"I can't even imagine me choosing one of those options. I don't relate to Mark like that. If I'm honest, the problem is, I love him and really want to sleep next to him."

"And that may be okay...if it doesn't give you false hope or make you feel demeaned."

"You are so good for me, forcing me to open my mind to more possibilities. I *am* scared, Kathryn. I'm petrified about what lies ahead of me. I don't feel very strong as I think about getting through our convention, moving, holding everything together, and getting on with the divorce. Ogod, I just want to bury my head. I don't think I can even begin to anticipate every step. I'm going to have to play some of this by ear."

"Well, I just want to see you prepared to do the right thing for you—whatever that turns out to be."

"You have helped me. You have helped me a lot."

On my way out of town, I spent the afternoon with Sister Josephine. Fighting against feeling like a victim was tough, but talking with friends helped as I tried to anticipate what lay ahead and brace myself for how I would deal with it.

I will always remember August 6 as one of the most courageous days of my life. Preparing to make my way home, I was ever faithful to my journal writing.

I am going home today. Kathryn and Jody have been wonderful. With their help, I feel clearer and very supported. I couldn't have made it through this without the support and nurturing of friends.

My issue is abandonment. It has been all of my life. And here I am again, at this stage of my life, looking it square in the face. Mark has chosen to abandon me. I have to put that in writing to let it sink in. There is no softening of the words. That's what it is. I cannot conceive at this moment of abandoning someone I love. *Abandon*, according to Webster, means to leave completely and finally; to forsake utterly; to give up the control of; to discontinue any further interest because of discouragement, weariness, or distaste. The etymology of the word *divorce* does not mean to terminate; it suggests the tendency to take the parties in different directions. Webster says it means to formally separate or to disunite. I can separate the two in my head; but, given my background, my heart tells me that to divorce is to abandon. This association, even if only in my mind, completely devastates me at this moment.

In my lifetime, I have grown on so many levels. I am a strong, mature, assertive woman who can take charge of my life and support others in their quest to do the same. This side of me must take the lead right now. It is she who must help me disassociate the concept of abandonment from divorce. But there is another part of me that is still underdeveloped. When the abandoned feeling surfaces, I feel like I am about two years old and, if left on my own, will die.

I feel a tremendous surge of anger that Mark has put me in this position. It is hard for me to let it out. I wasn't exposed to anger in my growing up years. I seem to have a belief instilled in me that to become

really enraged is to lower myself in my own eyes
and those of others. Intellectually, I know better now.
There is a time and place for letting out the anger.
However, now is not the time. I let the feeling rise,
peak, and pass through me. I didn't want to return
home exuding anything but personal strength and
confidence. I have the strength to be loving toward
Mark without expectations during this period. I am
supportive of him in becoming his best self as I am
working to accomplish the same. By being
empathetic and truthful with him, I will turn his heart
toward being a loving and caring person...toward me
and especially toward those he is supposed to be
serving. These are affirmations I will add to my list.

As I drove up to the house, my heart skipped a beat. *What was
in store for me? How would I handle it?* I repeated several of my
affirmations just to give me strength to get out of the car and walk
into the house. *I am a strong, dynamic woman as I stand by my
husband and love him through this challenging period of our lives. I
am an important and valuable person, and worthy of the respect of
people who are important to me.*

Fortunately, no one was at home. Somewhere deep inside,
though, I wished that Mark had cared enough to be there for my
arrival. I unpacked the car and put my things away. He arrived a
couple of hours later and we met in the hallway, exchanging a
perfunctory hug. He had some "important" calls to make. I made
my way downstairs to my desk to begin catching up on my mail.
An hour or so later, he joined me and sat down across from me in
my office. He began talking, and suddenly worked himself up
into a frenzy. I was shocked. I hadn't been home long enough to
have caused this. What happened to the loving divorce and the
promises of how great things would be when I came home?

It was time for our guests to arrive and I was expected to
play the lady of the house to all of our new people. "You have
a beautiful home. You and Mark are such a wonderful couple.

Now that we see you in your environment, it makes it so much easier to know that this company is for real." I heard comments like this all evening. I felt like a hypocrite, but I saw no way out of the situation. Valerie and I exchanged a token hug. I topped the evening off with a long conversation with John DeHart, who was the top marketing rep for this group. As we stood outside beneath the master bedroom, he told me how glad he was to see me at home. He said he felt that I added a balance and stability to Mark that was very much needed. Mark, who was upstairs in our bedroom with the windows opened, overheard the comment.

After the last person left, I sat on the patio overlooking downtown Reno. This had always been my favorite place in our home. Mark had apparently made a run to the store. He was nowhere in the house, and I felt uncomfortable going upstairs and climbing into bed after two months of being gone. I waited there for him, not certain where to go or what to do in my own home. The long hours of conversation with Kathryn still didn't prepare me fully for this moment. I now understood why he wanted me home at this time. He needed the Mark and Rene Yarnell image to bolster the image of our company. I knew I was being used.

Soon he came through the door and joined me on the patio. He let me know how angry John's comment had made him. I said very little as we sat looking out over the city. Finally, he suggested that we get some sleep. We had a big day ahead of us. We did just that—sleep.

I spent the next two days working with John DeHart and helping train his new people. It was good for me and for them to work closely together. I always come out of my own self-pity when I am serving in the role of educator. Teaching is the best profession in the world. It changes lives in a dramatic way, but the teacher somehow ends up more replenished, receiving more than she gives.

On August 8, two days after my return home, I sat down at my desk early in the morning to write in my journal:

Now that I am home, I don't want to stop working on my own growth. Last night, Mark said something that really cut deep: he compared me to Valerie, whom he had dubbed "the ice queen," and said I was just like her—cold and impersonal. He again reminded me that the person he most admires is Sara Schmanski. She is warm and loving and has this whole man/woman thing figured out. I don't, and I know I don't. I'll spend the rest of my life trying to understand the relationship between men and women.

I think I am ready to face divorce, although it takes a lot of spirit out of me. It saddens me that Mark is so unwilling to try or to own any responsibility in what has gone wrong with us. If we worked at it together, fully committed, we could get through this and have a good life together. I am going to do the work no matter what happens. I want to become a better person: a better lover, woman, friend, businessperson, teacher, and writer. I believe I can do all of them without one superseding the other. The business side doesn't have to dominate the lover and woman in me. I can be a strong woman, a loving woman, a sensitive woman all at the same time.

Mark and I are missing so many moments to be loving toward each other. And once they are gone, they will never come again. I still love Mark. I want to own up to whatever I've done to make him act so hatefully toward me. I ask his forgiveness for this part of what has gone so wrong between us.

These past two months I have been through overwhelming emotional upheaval. I have gone from being completely focused on wanting to prioritize my love for Mark and renew our marriage to being faced with the reality that Mark doesn't share this desire and wants a divorce. Just in the past week, I have run the full gamut of feeling so many conflicting emotions:

- accepting his decision to divorce, though I don't want it;
- agreeing to come home and live with him, putting up a front until after the convention;

- knowing that I would have expectations, living together while divorcing is just too painful;
- recognizing my fear of abandonment was staring me in the face again;
- confronting this fear and making progress toward conquering it;
- confident that I can live without Mark and have a full and successful life;
- deciding to move out and find a place on my own next week;
- spending the last two days with distributors and realizing how very much they will be affected by our decision to part;
- wondering why Mark won't consider counseling or otherwise working on our relationship with me;
- wishing that we could turn over this last stone before we opt for a divorce that would be so detrimental to so many people;
- feeling intermittently that my desire to stay with Mark is not out of fear of abandonment but out of love for him and love for the people in our lives;
- wanting Mark to see me as I am today, not as the image he is holding of me;
- believing that my love for him will elicit loving response from him;
- asking that he respect me for my talents and what I truly can contribute through my teaching, writing, and participation in the business.

Mark and I agreed to talk this morning. But some things just don't change: once again, he has chosen TV, important phone calls, and meetings over me. *Dear God, please guide me and help me stay centered. What is the lesson in all of this for me? What is it I am supposed to do? How do I treat him? Lovingly. That is the only way I will treat him. The prayer of St. Francis, so much a part of my childhood, came to mind: where there is hatred, let me sow love; where there is injury, pardon.... I must find that balance to love him while still loving myself. I have to realize that Mark's behavior is not targeted against me. It is for him. He is protecting himself the best way he knows how. Neither one of us is stable right now. Like me, he is doing the best he can do to take care of his own needs. It just happens that his needs involve shutting me out. My God! I just want this horrible nightmare to end! What is my goal today? How will I get through just today and live it to its fullest?* I repeated all of my affirmations, concluding with "I am a warm and compassionate woman, expressing this sensitivity first to my husband and also to others who need my understanding."

I let Mark know how much I needed to talk. I couldn't keep asking. It was the same pattern that drove me to leave in the first place. He seemed more determined than ever to decide not only what *he* was going to do and what *we* were going to do, but what *I* was going to do. If our plan was to try to work things out and stay together, then, of course, I would compromise and work things out with him because I believe marriage is about doing just that. Making concessions is a necessary part of intertwining two lives into one. But if we divorce, particularly when it is he who has chosen this course, he must relinquish all his rights to giving any direction to my life. If he doesn't figure this out soon, I will help him with the process. I feel anger. God, I wish I could let it out.

Early morning writing was my form of caffeine. I put on the pot of coffee out of ritual, but it was writing that got my day kick-started. I sat down at my computer to make this August 10 entry into my journal:

> I have reached another breakthrough today, and it feels wonderful. Mark and I finally talked. That always relieves some of the pressure. Little by little, I am coming to understand why he wants a divorce. I represent the restrictions of marriage as he and I have come to know the meaning of this concept. He wants his freedom; he wants not to have to answer to a partner. He wants to spend his money any way he chooses, run off mountains with a paraglider or race sports cars in the Indianapolis 500.
>
> There are only two choices: either change the parameters of the marriage or escape from its restrictive boundaries. The first weekend we explored the former option. The second weekend, he came

with the predetermined decision to opt for the latter. I still wonder what happened during that two-week interval that changed things so radically.

Understanding this helps me immeasurably. I keep telling myself over and over that this has nothing to do with abandonment except in the archaic repository of my mind, that place where I store old emotions for safekeeping. Letting this sink in is one of my more difficult challenges. I have spent a lifetime and before building up a belief system about being abandoned. I want to see this simply as a matter of our having differing ways of addressing the challenges we are facing. And because of the disparity, we are no longer growing together and are now going our separate ways. My preference would be to alter the parameters of marriage and find a new form that fits us. His preference is to close out the form called marriage as we now know it, believing that by divorcing we will be better friends. With the marriage restrictions eradicated, our relationship will be more joy-filled and more genuine with fewer expectations. I know he believes this, but I wish I were convinced. He will always come up with some new reason, some justification, some behavior on my part as to why it doesn't work out that way in the end.

But for now, I take one day at a time. Mark and I are divorcing. I have to keep reminding myself of that reality. I have no illusions about where Mark stands on this issue. I will make every effort to do this in the most loving way possible. I know that there is inherent value as I face going on with my life alone: it forces me to rise to a new level within myself. It compels me to ask penetrating questions, like "what are my gifts and how am I to use them to fulfill my life purpose?"— questions I might otherwise not be asking if the circumstance wasn't forcing me to look more introspectively. Today I am grateful for this opportunity. Affirmation for the day: As I prepare a life on my own, I welcome the opportunity to look inward and uncover new ways that I might give of myself and impact the lives of others.

Talking during this period was difficult and the opportunities rare. I was still going through menopause and Mark was trying to quit smoking, all of which added to the tension. Even though I'd come home to him, I was still living alone. It is better to be lonely alone than to be lonely together. I tried to cope by writing a note to him, hoping that I could say in a letter what he was unable to hear when we talked.

> Dear Mark,
> Whatever directions each of our lives takes, I am grateful that you and I found each other. I will always be able to say that my life is better today for having known you. I hope, as you examine the changes in your own life, you will also be glad for my having come into yours.
> Every morning I do journal writing. I started this daily practice in Santa Cruz. I am enclosing this morning's in an effort for you to know exactly where I am today in my vision. I hope you will eventually make time to read the entire book I've been writing for the past two years. I want you to know me at the very core of who I am. I especially would like to share the insights I gained while I was apart from you.
> I hope your health improves and you are able to make this tour all that it needs to be. I'll be with you in spirit and supporting you from a distance, I can honestly say, as we close out this phase of our life together, that I love you and appreciate the goodness in you and all that you have given me. Take care of yourself always. Rene

Leaving the letter on his desk, I headed down to my office. A few hours later, Mark called down and asked if I could meet with the attorney today at 2:00. No mention of the letter. I indicated that it was fine and, about fifteen minutes before the hour, he asked me to follow him in my car. Somehow that put me off. If we are going to see the same attorney, I felt that we should ride over together. He reluctantly agreed.

About five minutes into the drive, Mark said that we were going to sign, seal, and deliver the papers today. I was stunned! I refused to sign anything today. What happened after that is a blur. I know that I ended up shrieking at the top of my lungs, "I hate you for putting me in this position. I hate you. I hate you." I finally let the anger out but, for me, it was one of the most horrendous moments of our life together. I avoid anger at all cost, and when I finally do feel the emotion, I have little capacity for harboring it. It's good I wasn't the one driving. Mark pulled over to the side of the road giving us both time to reagain our composure. Of course, rather than let the anger sit there, I immediately retracted my words and told him that I didn't mean it. I was scared, frustrated, and hurt beyond words. I didn't want this divorce, and I certainly wasn't going to be coerced into signing divorce papers without someone else reading them over on my behalf. The tension was thicker than any early-morning San Francisco fog. We were both visibly shaken by the experience. We collected the paperwork from the attorney and returned home with the unsigned documents. I sobbed most of the day and collapsed into bed, physically exhausted. Up until that day, we had been sleeping in the same bed. Mark took a different room in the house, but neither of us was able to sleep that night at all.

The next morning, I was sitting at my desk when the phone rang. It was Dr. Brewer, Mark's doctor from the detox center in London, returning my call. I told him that I was searching for answers. Could he help me understand the personality change in Mark? Did the treatment have anything to do with my marriage falling apart? Did he have any advice for me? Will time eventually bring this full circle, or is this the real Mark—clean and sober?

Every case is different, Dr. Brewer explained. But, yes, total withdrawal from drugs definitely alters the personality. Certainly this could play a part in my relationship to Mark. No, there was nothing I could do about it. After approximately six months, his system was completely drug-free. And, yes, more than likely, the person I was seeing now was the real Mark, without artificial stimulus. What he needed was to learn new coping mechanisms for dealing with life and, particularly, stressful situations. If I was seeking hope, this conversation didn't bring it.

Dr. Brewer asked to speak to Mark, so I had to admit to having made contact with his physician. Mark was enraged. How dare I? It was one more reason to blow up at me. Our convention was two weeks away, and we had a thousand things to do together to get ready. We couldn't afford this kind of distancing between us at this time. All attempts at verbal exchange ended in a monstrous fight, so, once again, I tried communicating by letter.

Dear Mark,
    I'm sorry my very presence causes you so much upset. Even though you have decided to shut me out of your life, I am not willing to do the same to you. I love you and will continue to care about you in spite of yourself.

    I'm concerned for your health and for your well-being overall. The continued sleep deprivation is not good. Your constant state of anger is not conducive to accomplishing the things you want to do with your life. We have shared seven years together. I'm unable and unwilling to stop caring about you. I want your life to work for you, just as much as I want that for myself.

    We have much to do to get ready for the launch and to get our own act together so that we can direct our energy towards our reps, who will be here looking to us for support. We owe it to them to give them our best. And I will always believe that we have more to give together than either of us alone. Whatever personal differences exist, can we please put that aside for the good of all those people who are counting on us?

    I need to work with you today—getting scripts approved, recordings set up, etc. Can we please do this and put others ahead of our personal problems?

    Feeling you pull away has been one of the most painful experiences of my life. The past several months have been anguishing. If the steps I take to try to deal with this cause you any upset, I'm truly sorry. I am continually trying to find ways to understand what is happening and to heal the hurt between us and within myself. I am in unbearable pain over the loss of you. There is almost no limit to how far I would go to try to put things back together. So far, you have rejected my every offer.

I accept that we are separating our personal lives, but we are still going to be involved in business, and I don't want to experience your anger anymore. Let's take a step toward healing things between us. Neither of us can take much more of this.

Rene

I left the letter on his desk, but he was too filled with anger to respond beyond a few perfunctory words. Once again, I asked if he would read the book I was writing. "I don't have time to do your editing now. I'm too busy with this company."

"It isn't editing I need from you; it's having you know what's in my heart and soul."

"Not now, for god's sake."

"If not now, when?" I pleaded. No response.

Two days later, he moved out, leaving me a letter much as I left him the morning I walked away.

Rene, I suppose turnabout is fair play...you left me with a note, so I'll do the same. As you know, I go cold turkey this weekend (beginning tomorrow) and give up my cigarettes entirely. I won't subject either of us to that. I'll be checking in with you regularly as I'll be here in Reno at some hotel while also looking at small apartments. I just took a few clothes so I'll be back for other things periodically over the next few days. I'll call you this evening.

Mark

I was crushed, and even more shocked that he would move out just before convention. The timing couldn't be more detrimental to our company. I needed to talk to someone and called Nancy.

"When you're at your best, sometimes that is threatening to your partner because you're too good to be true," she advised. "He'd be a lot more comfortable if you'd just yell back at him and get the anger out. Being so 'perfect', you become an irritant to your partner. When you have normal give-and-take, it makes you human and gives him an out to be human. When you're too understanding, the partner thinks, 'damn, now I have to live up to this.'"

"I'm such a dichotomy even to myself. Partly I behave this way because I'm practical. We've got a job to do and we need to get on with doing it. But another part of me is programmed to avoid anger because it isn't a pretty picture. It looks ugly to me and, besides, people might not like me if I let it out."

"If being liked is the goal, it's having the opposite effect."

"You're right. It sounds like I can't win. We're launching our company and our people are arriving for convention in less than two weeks. This is a nightmare."

"Maybe the message is that it is time to let go, Rene. You can't control what is happening, and you are tearing yourself up over trying to hold on to him."

"I know. I accept it in my head, but it's just so hard for me to accept in my heart. Despite the way he acts toward me—am I crazy?—I believe him when he says he still loves me."

"Perhaps. But, obviously, it takes more than love to make it possible for two people to live together. What you are experiencing is the pain of loss right now. That's understandable."

"Losing someone because he chooses not to be with you is a thousand times more painful than losing someone through death. I get so caught up in the rejection, the abandonment, the feeling of being left completely alone that I can hardly stand it. I just want this pain to stop. When will it be over?"

"I know. It is so natural to look for ways to escape. The only escape I can think of that may legitimately help is laughter, if you can watch a funny movie or listen to a humorous tape."

"And keep remembering good things about the relationship. That seems to help me. Sometimes, when I'm being selfish, I want to believe that Mark can't make it without me. It's my need to have him need me. It's so much about me, and not about him. Just when I think I'm being loving, maybe I'm really not."

"Maybe you're being too hard on yourself right now. You're going through the mourning process. Losing someone you love, especially after your lives have been so entangled with each other—that is the deepest kind of grief."

"But you know what I'm coming to realize? He was never mine to lose. Mark, the real Mark, is an elusive butterfly. He will never be with anyone for a lifetime. He has to feel the adrenaline or he doesn't feel fully alive. Our love did that for him when it was new, but when it leveled out...." I choked and couldn't finish.

"When relationships end, far more often than not, there is always someone else...in some form or another. They may not be having a relationship yet. They may just have seen someone else who attracts them, but when that happens, they begin asking themselves: what is it that makes me attracted to that person and no longer attracted to this person? Trying to understand what causes that shift can be confusing."

"I don't think that's happening with Mark. That is the one thing I'm pretty sure about."

"Maybe not, but when you fall in love, the other person is so beautiful. And when you fall out of love, he or she suddenly grew giant warts."

"Well, I see his beauty marks and his warts, and I still care about him. But he definitely can't see anything but my warts."

"Do you have any regrets?"

"I regret that we didn't seek counseling. I regret that we didn't get Mark on a program after going through detox. But, if this is the end, I will thank God the rest of my life for having loaned him to me for these seven years. My life is better because of him. I have found both personal and professional strengths within myself—particularly my writing and speaking—I may never have pursued. I have more to give to others because of him. He taught me a spirit of generosity like I have never seen in another human being. These are things I will carry in my heart and choose to remember about him."

"You've come a long way, sweetie. You're going to be just fine. I think you're ready to move on with your life."

I couldn't have made it through this time without the support of family and friends. Mom stayed close to me through this period. She didn't say much, but I felt her concern and her love. I checked my e-mail, and there was a message from my San Francisco friend, Kathryn Blue, waiting:

>From: "Kathryn Blue" kblue@earthlink.net
>To: yarnell@ibm.net
>Subject: The Crux of Creativity
>Date: Thu, 20 Aug 1998 22:00:38 –0700

>Rene: Just to 'light up your message board' I'm
>going to quote from Joan Rivers: The first rule of
>survival is: make your own rules. The hell with what
>anyone thinks about the way you're acting; listen
>only to yourself. And while listening, remember the
>words of Nietzsche: "Whatever doesn't kill me
>makes me stronger."

>Joan's second paragraph is even better: "Since
>your loss didn't kill you, it has made you stronger
>and has also given you the right to respond to it in any
>way you damn please. The loss may have been a
>universal one, but your circumstances are unique,
>so don't let anyone tell you how you should feel or
>behave. Keep fighting in your own way—with
>courage, with humor, and without shame...."

>The crux of creativity: Make your solution work for
>you. It's not only okay—it's imperative. Now if that
>isn't more tonic than orange juice in the morning, I
>don't know what is. Try it—you may even like it.
>Love, Kathryn

With Mark gone, I felt like I rattled around in that 8,600 square feet of house. I sobbed from morning until night. Menopause, loss, rejection all rolled into one. I couldn't get hold of myself. I ambled into his office and sat down at the desk. If this was to be my home, maybe I needed to clean out this room and turn it into my office. It was far nicer than the space I now occupied.

I made this my project for the day. I opened the windows to get rid of the odor of smoke imbedded in the curtains and wood paneling. I began arranging the bookshelf. I took some of my things out of my desk drawers and moved them upstairs to this office. As I began cleaning off his desk, I found a note in his handwriting sitting under the desk mat. He had titled it "Deception Management." What a strange name! I began reading his words, slowly letting into my consciousness what they really meant. They were obviously written during my extended absence.

He described sitting in the library in the dark talking to someone. He didn't say her name, but it was obviously someone close to us. Apparently, it had been a heartfelt conversation steeped in emotion and honest exchange. Nothing happened. He kept stressing that. Nothing happened. Suddenly headlights appeared coming up the driveway. It was Amy coming home. He described feeling guilty. But why should he? Nothing happened. They were sitting close together in the dark. He struggled to decide if he should put space between them, turn on lights, or stay the way they were. No matter what he did, he felt "caught." Apparently, he chose to stay the way they were. Amy came in and sized up the situation. She gave him a knowing glance before heading to her room. He concluded his writing with some thoughts on the significance of what he termed "deception management."

I felt a deep pang cut through my heart. Thoughts of Nancy's recent words came flooding into my head, along with sporadic and unrelated thoughts of Jimmy Carter asking the world's forgiveness for "lusting in his heart." Thoughts that the one unwavering aspect of our marriage was mutual fidelity. Thoughts of his insistence that I never put myself in a vulnerable position by even opening the door to a possible infidelity. I wondered if this scene occurred before or during the interval between our two meetings; if it was the latter, one more piece of the puzzle just fell into place. I didn't know who she was, but suddenly I understood. It didn't matter who she was. What mattered was that it happened.

While I sat on the beach in Santa Cruz attempting to put our marriage back together, he was becoming emotionally involved with someone else. I know how Mark works because it happened with me. He grew into lust or love with me long before he ever made a move. No wonder he was not open to counseling. No wonder he was so detached when he announced he wanted a divorce. No wonder he was so ready to move on. He had already moved on emotionally. "Nothing happened." Oh yes, something most definitely did happen. A one-night stand could be overcome. An emotional attachment is much more enduring. Sitting there with his notes in my hand, I was holding the last tangible evidence to the fact that my marriage was over.

It was Wednesday morning. I was sitting at my downstairs desk working when Mom asked me to look over the bills that had come in today's mail. The top one was from Neiman Marcus, Mark's favorite store. I opened it up, intending only to scan it, when I felt riveted to the itemized description: evening gown, $781.19, and a Louis Vuitton purse, $969.75, both purchased on August 21, just twelve days earlier. With the other purchases, the bill came to $2,152.85. I sat there staring at the bill until tears began streaming down my face. This could only mean one thing. The thought of Mark buying such elegant things for another woman broke my heart.

I heard Amy walking down the stairs. I didn't want her to see me falling apart like this, so I wiped my eyes and attempted to hide my emotions.

"What's up?" Amy asked as she came bouncing into the room.

"Just paying bills. What are you up to?"

"I just needed to get some things together for my photo shoot Friday. Then I'm going to look for a place to live." Amy had temporarily moved back home but, under the circumstances, was staying with a friend.

"You know, you don't have to move out." I really wanted her to stay. I needed family around me at this time, and I felt so close to Amy.

"I know, but….I just don't want to get caught in the middle between you and my dad. I'm not going to live with him either for the same reason. It's just too hard."

"Well, think of it this way: we both want you to come live with us; so you have to feel wanted."

"Gosh, that makes me feel really good. I hadn't thought of it that way."

As my eyes fell on the Neiman's invoice, the sobs started to well up in me again. Amy came over to hug me, thinking I was upset over her moving out. I was, but it was more than that.

As we held each other for a minute, I saw Amy's eyes fall on the statement. "If your dad would just have his bills sent to an address other than mine, it would spare me a lot of anguish," I choked out.

Amy didn't say anything but gave me one more hug, and was up the stairs and out the door.

Mom and I were left in the room. "Is there anything I can do?" she asked.

"I wish you could make it all better like you did when I was little. But, no, I just have to face reality. It's over between Mark and me. I have to move on. You watch, though. He'll try to say that dress and purse were for Amy or something equally hair-brained."

I was going to have lunch with two of my oldest friends in Reno, Bev Harvey and Ann Kemmerle. Just as I was pulling into the restaurant we had chosen, my cell phone rang. It was Mom.

"Mark called. Amy must have told him. He said he meant to tell me that that bill was coming. He said he bought the dress for Amy for the convention, and the purse was for Stacey for her birthday."

"Right! What does he take me for? Like he'd really buy a thousand-dollar purse for a birthday present for our consultant while we're worried about how we're going to pay our bills each week for this damned company?"

As I walked in to the restaurant to meet my friends, I was

shaking I was so upset. They had both joined the company as marketing reps, so I felt I couldn't say anything about it, not yet. Somehow I'd make it through the lunch without crying.

After lunch, I stopped at the attorney's office to pick up the final draft of paperwork for the property settlement. By the time I got back to our office, I was livid. It was the first time I'd really gotten mad. Full-blown, pissed off, out-of-my-mind enraged! I stomped down the hall to Mark's office and slid his copy of the settlement under the door. I didn't want to talk to him. I didn't want to see his face. I 'd finally had enough! I went straight to my office and closed the door. I wanted to shut him out of my life.

Minutes later, Mark was standing in the doorway. "Why didn't you knock on my door?" he asked.

"Because I don't want to talk to you. I closed my door for a reason. Just leave."

"Rene, this is crazy. We have to talk. I bought that dress for Amy."

"Mark, don't. Don't even go there. Don't insult my intelligence." *Deception management! So this is how you do it. It's called lying, Mark.*

"No, I really did. She looked like Cinderella in it. I know our money is a little tight, but I just wanted to get it for her."

"Mark, stop it! I don't want to hear it. I just want to be left alone. But one thing—if you've got that kind of money to throw around, while we're doing our property settlement, you can damn sure pay for her Nissan all on your own. You tried to sweet talk me into paying half because you were so worried about money, remember? Well, I'm not falling for that anymore."

He left. Minutes later he was back in my office. "And the purse was for Stacey. I just thought it was a way of saying thanks for all she has done for our company. So I spent a little too much."

"Mark, please leave. And don't add lying to the godawful pain you have already caused."

"You think I'm lying? I'll go get Amy."

"Amy already had her chance to acknowledge the dress, but she missed her cue. Now please, I want to be alone. Just leave."

Mark left, and I didn't see him any more the rest of the day. I went home and cried myself to sleep. All I could think about was the white skirt and sequined jacket he bought me from Neiman's when we were first dating. I wondered who she was, and whether I could ever get over the hurt.

I was up at the crack of dawn, working at my desk at home. Stacey was in New York, so, with the time difference, I could talk to her in my wee hours. We had a lot of work to do on the convention together. While we were talking, the private line rang.

I put Stacey on hold and took the call. It was Mark. "Good morning. I thought I'd catch you up."

"I'm on the other line," I said curtly.

"Okay, how long do you think you'll be?"

"A while."

"Look, I think we need to talk. I'll call you back in twenty minutes."

"I really don't have anything I want to talk to you about."

"I need to talk to you. I'll call you back."

I switched back to Stacey and managed to slip in a question around the gift. "So Mark tells me we bought you a birthday gift, but I don't know what it was." So subtle.

"Oh, Rene, I'm still so uncomfortable about it. I mean, it's too awesome. I have it sitting as the centerpiece on my dining-room table just so I can look at it."

"So what is it?" I asked knowing now what it *wasn't*.

"It's a purse—one of the most special Louis Vuitton's I've ever seen!"

I was speechless. He really *had* bought Stacey that purse. Omigod! Could that mean that he bought Amy the dress? How would I know?

A few minutes later the phone rang again, and it was Mark. He asked very nicely if he could come over. Feeling a little sheepish, I said yes. Within twenty minutes he arrived at the house. We sat in the living room and talked.

"Rene, I don't want to hurt you. And I know I did, but I didn't mean to. I really did buy that dress for Amy. I know I shouldn't have with our money situation, but she looked so pretty in it. You have to believe me."

"Can you understand what I thought?"

"Absolutely! That's where I took you shopping. You were right to feel angry. Anybody would have. I should have told your mom the bill was coming. I just didn't realize it would come so soon. I'm really sorry that the whole thing caused you so much pain. Look, here's the reason I came over: I really want to work together. We have a company to run and a convention coming up. We don't have time for this nonsense. Although the maddest I've ever been at you was over your calling Dr. Brewer, it turned out really well. I needed to talk to him, and we actually spoke twice. He said something that turned my thinking when he said, 'You know, Mark, getting off of methadone doesn't give you the right to be an asshole. You may have been unconscious through most of your hospital stay, but I wasn't. I saw your wife stand by you through one of the most challenging periods of your life. She slept in a chair and never left your side. She held your head while you vomited and helped clean you up when you had diarrhea. I think you should go see her and apologize. Whatever else is going on between you, she doesn't deserve to be treated so badly. You could at least start giving her the respect she deserves.'"

I hadn't heard Mark speak this honestly to me in so long. He was soft and caring and genuine. I know I should have been on my guard, but I wasn't. Tears ran down my face. We hugged and prolonged it while I cried. I thought I felt his body trembling. It was an emotional crest for both of us. *Was it possible to go forward now with kindness. Even though we were going apart, was it possible to do it without causing each other more hurt?* I was trying to convince myself that we were going to be able to work together now. Something heavy had been lifted from our shoulders.

On Thursday, though deciding to stay married for the present, we went to see the attorney to finalize the property settlement. Dorothy Nash Holmes had looked over the paperwork for me, and had no probems with it. Mark had been fair. We split everything down the middle—all our assets and our gigantic liabilities surrounding the company. Tears ran down my face as I signed the papers. My emotions were out of control. The whole thing was unbearable. I heard Mark asking the attorney questions completely contradictory to the direction he had set for us.

"Now, if we decide to stay married, then what happens?" Mark inquired.

"Nothing, you already are married," the attorney explained.

"Yeah, but what if we want to cancel this whole property thing?"

"That's the easy part. We just undo everything we did."

That's the first time Mark had asked about such a possibility. I tried to stifle the glimmer of hope. I was afraid to even think about it.

As we walked down the stairs out to the parking lot, Mark asked, "Why are you so upset? I don't get it. We're not getting divorced. We just settled the property. What's the big deal?"

Mars and Venus at work here again. "It's hard for me to understand how you could not understand. It's that the separation is confirmed now. I dread living apart."

"You know, I don't know what lies ahead. I don't know what I want. I'm confused. I just feel that I need some distance for a while. It will do us both good. I want to date other people and compare them to you." *You want to date other people? This can only mean one thing. You have someone waiting in the wings—the mystery woman from the library scene. A man's cure for covering up pain. Whatever you once felt for me is gone. You want to find that feeling again with someone new!* "I want to see how things go in the business this next year and how we work together. I don't know where all of this will lead. I don't really need sex with other people." *You're going to date other women and not have sex? Right!* "As far as I am concerned, we had that down perfect."

I stood there in front of him, feeling all of three feet tall...a two-year-old child, praying that Daddy wouldn't leave me. *Please don't go. And if you do, tell me that you miss me and you'll come back. Please come back.* "Do you miss making love together?"

"Of course, but I'm afraid to pursue it because I don't want to confuse you. It wouldn't be fair. I do love you; I just don't think I can be married to a powerful woman anymore. I know, I know, it was your power that I fell in love with. But now I want a demure woman, and you could never be that. I was rereading C.S. Lewis again this past week, and the part that I really want to emulate is where he talks about loving someone enough to let them go. If I love you, I will want your happiness—not just to have you happy only if you're with me. I will really want you to be happy, whatever that entails, even if it means you will be with someone else."

I believed him. I truly believed Mark meant every word of this. Standing up on my toes, to reach my full child's height, I leaned up and kissed him on the lips. "Kiss me, really kiss me." Our lips held, and our tongues met and lingered for a few moments. I was clinging. I didn't want him to leave me. Daddy, Jim, Mark—I felt the excruciating pain of abandonment from all of them at that moment.

"I'm off to paraglide in Mexico for the Labor Day weekend. I'll be back either Sunday night or Monday, and I'll call you about the script. I know we have to get that handled for convention." Then he climbed into his car and gave me one last glance.

As we each got into our cars and drove symbolically in separate directions, I tried to prepare myself for the next phase of my life. Still married but with our property officially settled, we got what is for most couples the toughest part out of the way first. But formally separating our lives and assets just before the official launch of our new company? I didn't understand.

CHAPTER 18

DISMISSED FROM THE COMPANY
September – November 1998

I returned to the office and tried to prepare the training and corresponding materials for convention. When I discovered that the audio script had proprietary rights attached to it, I called the originator of the script and negotiated a royalty so that we could have the use of it for the short time until we could write one of our own. As I sat working on the script one last time before having Mark record it, the phone rang.

"This is Randy. I understand that you cut a deal for the audio script."

"Yes, there are no strings attached. The minute we want to write our own, we are no longer obligated. But this way, we have something that we like and will be ready in time for us to sell the business package at convention."

"Rene, that isn't your place to negotiate. It is mine now. Fourteen cents per tape is outrageous. I won't do it."

"Randy, I am as fiscally conservative as anyone on this team. But there are times when serving the field becomes more important than a few lost pennies. We need a package ready for convention, and we are going to let everyone down big time if we don't have it. We already have to face the fact that we promised new products and can't deliver. Let's don't add more disappointment if we don't have to. "

"Well, the fact is, that is not your call. I'll get back to you later."

Randy and my partners rejected my action and decided that a new script would be written. Though a setback, I was still determined to have it written, recorded, and duplicated in time for convention. John DeHart took the first run at it, and I followed up after him. I then turned it over to Mark to add his thoughts. Despite the impossible task, we made an appointment to record the audio three days before convention. With overnight mail and an overnight trucking company, we believed we could still have copies for sale by the second day of convention.

Mark took the script with him on his paragliding weekend to continue reworking it. I still worried about him every time his feet left the ground and, if anything happened to him, would anyone know where he was?

No call from Mark on Sunday or Monday as promised. The appointment at the recording studio was set for Tuesday morning at 9:00 a.m. I called the recording studio to make sure everything was going as planned. Mark wasn't there. By 10:00 he still hadn't shown up at the office or the studio. It wasn't like Mark to miss important meetings or at least not to let the office know where he was. I was sure he was lying dead on some mountain in Mexico. I found Amy, but she didn't know where he was either. For the next hour I couldn't function. None of us had a clue where to begin looking for him. By 11:00 I was sure he was dead. I sat staring out of my office window when Christine's voice came over the loudspeaker: "Amy, Mark is on hold for you." He's alive. I waited. Instead of calling me, Amy went flying down the hall.

"Amy," I shouted, "what's going on? This is killing me."

"Dad's been in an accident. I'm going to pick him up."

"Is he okay?"

"Yeah, but apparently his Mercedes isn't. He wrecked it pretty bad."

"When did it happen?"

"Just now." And she was off.

So the accident had nothing to do with the missed

appointment. I wondered what had happened to make him miss something so important to us.

Mark returned with Amy about a half hour later. He walked past my office but didn't stop. I waited a few minutes and walked down to his office. I felt more comfortable doing this since we had called a truce. He was on the phone, so I sat down and waited. When he hung up, he turned to me and said harshly, "What right do you have to be calling my people and giving them assignments?" *Why can't the peacefulness last, just for a little while?*

"Assignments?" *Damn you!* "It's my job, and besides, you even *asked* me to do it. I thought having a roster of speakers in the welcome package would add a professional touch."

"Well, you've got them all confused. Joan Rudloff thinks you assigned her a topic to speak on." *I find it hard to believe that she feels confused.*

"I'll call her and straighten it out."

"Don't bother. I'll handle it," Mark retorted.

What happened to our commitment to work together pleasantly and cooperatively? And why didn't you have the courtesy to call on Sunday or Monday like you said? And why were you so irresponsible as to stand Mike up at the studio this morning? And why did you crash into another car? I'm afraid this can only mean one thing. "Are you still up to recording if I reschedule this afternoon?" I asked, withholding all the questions I really wanted to ask.

"Yeah, sure. What time?"

"John DeHart and I need a couple of hours to go over your changes to the script. How about 2:00 this afternoon?"

"Okay."

He handed me the script and I spent the next two hours on the phone with John carefully going over every word. When I came out of my office, I hurried down to Mark's so we could run over to the studio together. There was no Mark. I went next door to Amy's office, and she helped me look for him for the next hour. No luck. We couldn't find him.

Once again, I called the recording studio, but Mark wasn't

there either. I apologized and said these were very stressful times for us. I asked if they would hold our time indicating I was on my way. Amy said she would keep trying to find her dad and would send him right over.

By 3:30, I decided to record the first side myself. Mark and I had done a bazillion tapes together; it would not seem strange to anyone that we did this now. When I finished, there was still no Mark. Just as I sat down in the booth to begin the second side, Mark walked through the door. I didn't ask any questions. I just showed him where to pick up on the script and offered him my chair in front of the microphone. I closed the door and sat down outside the booth. Feeling more worried than judgmental about what was going on, I just thanked God he had shown up.

When he finished, he hung around for a few minutes but decided to leave the editing to me. He called Amy to come pick him up, and went outside to have a smoke and wait for her. *So much for his quitting smoking.* I had hoped after our conversation a few days ago that our work life together would be as rewarding as it once was, but obviously this was not to be.

It took me longer than usual to edit the tape. We both made mistakes, Mark many more than usual. I was concerned about him: the missed appointments, constant disappearances, the wrecked car, so many blunders on the recording. *Omigod, he can't relapse now—just before convention.* I finished just in time to run the master over to Southwest Airlines and put it on a counter-to-counter delivery to the duplication facility in southern California. I was exhausted but exuberant to have gotten the task completed—and still in time for convention. I drove home and collapsed into bed.

I felt somewhat uplifted as I rose to start the new day, until I got a call from Mark saying that he felt we made a mistake having me record the first part. In a recruiting audio of this nature, it should be a male voice, he explained. Whether he was right or wrong was not the issue. It was the circumstance that led to my doing the recording that made my blood boil when he suggested this. And if I dared ask where he was and why he missed the appointments, we would have begun fighting, so I let it go. I just responded, "What is done is done. For the sake of having this ready for convention, please let's just live with it. We can always redo this tape anytime we want." He hung up but apparently still carrying his concern.

There was so much to do in the couple of days before convention. I was sitting in my office when John Radford called to ask if we could have a teleconference call with the partners in about thirty minutes. Valerie and I continued working on other aspects of our preparation for convention. When the conference call came through, we took it in my office.

Randy and John were on the call, but no one could find Mark; so the four of us proceeded. We covered basic topics and then Val opened up the subject. "Rene, we'd like to talk to you about 'The Little Red Tape,'" the name given the new audio we had just recorded. "It was our understanding that Mark was going to record that. Why did you take it upon yourself to record the first side?" I was furious, at first too irate to respond.....*eight, nine, ten.* Finally I found words.

"Val, you've been with me in the office all morning. Why didn't you just ask me?"

"Things are different now, Rene. We do things more formally than we did before the launch."

I didn't plan to tell anyone about Mark's behavior the day before. Only Amy knew. They could think whatever they wanted. I didn't care. *Where was Mark? Why wasn't he here to stand up for me? He would tell them how I held that taping schedule together.* But of course he couldn't defend me. He was the only one who could have told them that I recorded the first side. *What explanation did he offer them? Did he tell them he missed the appointment twice and that I covered for him? I doubt it.*

I made some half-hearted explanation, and then simply said, "If you had been there, you would have done what I did. Mark and I have recorded lots of tapes together. It will seem normal to the outside world."

"We are hearing some rumblings about the field thinking that Mark is on drugs. Are you spreading that rumor?" Randy asked.

Pull your righteous heads out of the sand. Why can't you ever find him? Why isn't he on this call? And if, by chance, he is back on drugs, assume some of the responsibility. It is all of you, putting every damned financial and recruiting burden of this company square on his shoulders, who may be driving him to it. The pressure you have put him under is horrendous. "I think you should take this up with Mark. I can't be held accountable for him, but I will admit that I am very, very concerned. There is so much you don't know. But I don't feel comfortable discussing this further with any of you."

"Have you discussed this with John DeHart?" Randy pressed.

"I believe it was the other way around. I suggest you pursue that matter with John." For a minute no one spoke.

Randy broke the silence. "Well, in any event, we don't think a woman's voice will do for this tape."

I am not just "a woman." I am Mark's wife and business partner. I am a founder, investor, and a partner; I have sacrificed everything precious in my life for this damned company. And when did this "unholy trinity" suddenly become such marketing experts? I could hardly contain my anger. But I simply said, "I am my own worst critic. You all haven't heard the tape, and I have. It is good and will serve our people well. I beg you all to let this tape go into reproduction. If you aren't satisfied with it, we can always redo it. Please, trust me on this one decision. We need this tape for convention. We will destroy our credibility with our representatives if we go into convention without the promised products *and* without this prospecting tape for the business package. I promise you: you will not be unhappy with it."

After much discussion, my partners pulled the tape without ever hearing it. Mark rerecorded it the next day. Although we weren't able to have it reproduced in time for convention, we did manage to distribute one copy to each convention participant.

I felt I deserved an Oscar for my performance at our convention held in Reno September 11, 12, and 13. With the help of a little

Valium, I was enabled to speak from the stage, present awards, train, and be a social butterfly as I posed for pictures (some with Mark), played hostess, and danced with everyone. My best friend from grade school, Ann Marchak, and her husband Roy were there. Aware of what was happening, she stood close by me.

Under the circumstances, my convention talk was the most important talk of my life. I wanted to address every representative, my partners, and most especially, my husband. My talk was entitled: "The Spirit of Global Network." I wasn't nervous, but I was fighting tears as I heard Mark announce my name. As he left the stage and I came on, he stopped, as he often did, and kissed me. Given all that had happened and the most recent occurrence over the audio recording, it felt like the kiss of Judas.

I walked over to the podium, where I had put my outlined notes ahead of time. I took a deep breath, prayed for guidance and wisdom, and most of all, that Mark would hear me. After a few opening comments, I shared how I had been captivated by a book I had come upon this past summer written by a married couple, Drs. Evelyn and Paul Moschetta, called *The Marriage Spirit.*

"In the early phase of exploring a new relationship, most of us go through three stages.

"The first stage is personality, or what we understand to be our own unique human nature. It is the sum of all our attributes, attitudes, habits, and experiences that have shaped us through our heredity and environment.

"The second is ego, which is our preoccupation with our outer self-image. It is our need to be right and in control. Life is a constant struggle to balance the need for a strong ego with the ability to recognize the strength and contributions of others. But, in reality, as the Moschettas point out, ego is a 'survival mentality', more concerned with physical safety and emotional security, often more 'me' than 'you'. It clings to the past with remorse or looks to the future with anxiety but, more often than not, finds it difficult to leave room for living in the spiritual now. It is a delicate balance because we need a stable, secure ego to function in the everyday world.

"Spirit is the immaterial, intelligent, sentient, aware, conscious and alive element of the human species. It is that part of us that stands outside of our ego and guides everything we do. Our spirit can bring balance to our egotistical side, pulling it up or down as the need arises. 'It is the sacred presence in us, the invisible light that animates our body, mind, and senses. The same transcendent energy that powers the entire universe pulses in and through us,' says *The Marriage Spirit.* It is our inner source of soul-centered love and the absolute key to interpersonal relationships." As I looked out at the audience, I doubted that they knew where I was going with this but I could tell that I was reaching them.

"In personal relationships, couples typically will go through this process determining first if their personalities mesh, then whether their egos can co-exist with mutual respect, and finally if they are free to meet and discover each other's spirit. Many couples get stuck in the first or second stage. They may break off the relationship when they discover that their personalities don't click. Some move comfortably into the second stage but get stuck trying to entwine their egos. The challenging part of most relationships is getting past the power struggle as we discover ways to make our self-images conform. But it isn't until a relationship reaches this third level, allowing our ego to follow the lead of our spiritual self, that two individuals ever truly meet each other. When my spirit meets, discovers, and falls in love with your spirit, then and only then can we hope for a long-term, enduring, trustworthy love relationship." I paused and searched the audience to catch Mark's eye, but he was nowhere in sight. I prayed that he was backstage listening. I focused all of my energy on him as I continued: "Any relationship that is serious about having a future together must make it to this third phase and owes it to itself to make this spiritual discovery of each other before giving up.

"So where am I going with all of this? You see, each one of you will inevitably go through these same stages with Global Network. You will want to check out our personality. Are the founders solid? Does the corporate office look like it will be here tomorrow? Do you like the products? If we pass that test, then many of you will, perhaps unconsciously, move on to the next stage and match egos with us. You want a measuring cap for the laundry liquid or samples to give to your customers? You don't think those white labels on our personal care line are the most beautiful presentation you've ever seen? You dare to suggest that we might improve this?" I was jokingly referring to the fact that, in order to open on time, we used glued-on paper labels instead of the silk-screening process for the first batch. I also apologized for the fact that we had promised new products for convention and couldn't deliver. We trusted the word of our manufacturers who let us down.

"We want to be able to offer each other honest exchanges at all times. We sometimes will need your understanding as you will sometimes need ours. In this light, it is only when we're both ready to have our spirits meet that we can expect a genuine coming together of a relationship guided by our higher selves. It is our hope that this is your last stop—that you have found a lasting home in Global Network." Applause resounded throughout the room. I paused until they quieted down. "For that to happen, we must do something different than many of us have ever done before. Let's come to know and trust each other on the level of spirit.

"Remember our vision statement: 'We are made up of one network of high-integrity people committed to restoring ecological balance, the ethical distribution of scientifically validated natural products, self-efficacy principles and values-based financial freedom…one such network, in which those ideals are lived and duplicated, eventually spreading to every village, state, and country, will help usher in a new millennium of human attainment and global balance as never before imagined by history's boldest visionaries."

To understand the real spirit of our company, I broke the word "spirit" down into each letter. "'S' is for Soul—that we are being guided to live out our ideals with one another. 'P' is for Philanthropic Prosperity—that we may truly transform human potential. 'I' is for Integrity—to be integral or whole. 'R' is for

Relationship—a quality that connects two or more parts as belonging or working together. Our approach allows you to forge lifetime relationships with people you know and love, working more intimately with each of them." I caught Ann's eye as I said this. "'I' is for Inspiration—the power to move the intellect or emotions through storytelling." I then read the following poem to the audience:

The Most Beautiful Flower
The park bench was deserted as I sat down to read
Beneath the long, straggly branches of an old willow tree.
Disillusioned by life with good reason to frown,
For the world was intent on dragging me down.

And if that weren't enough to ruin my day,
A young boy out of breath approached me, all tired from play.
He stood right before me with his head tilted down,
And said with great excitement, "Look what I found!"

In his hand was a flower, and what a pitiful sight,
With its petals all worn - not enough rain, or too little light.
Wanting him to take his dead flower and go off to play,
I faked a small smile and then shifted away.

But instead of retreating he sat next to my side
And placed the flower to his nose
and declared with overacted surprise
"It sure smells pretty and it's beautiful, too.
That's why I picked it; here, it's for you."

The weed before me was dying or dead.
Not vibrant of colors, orange, yellow, or red.
But I knew I must take it, or he might never leave.
So I reached for the flower, and replied, "Just what I need."

Dismissed from the Company

But instead of him placing the flower in my hand,
He held it midair without reason or plan.
It was then that I noticed for the very first time
That the weed-toting boy could not see; he was blind.

I heard my voice quiver, tears shone like the sun
As I thanked him for picking the very best one.
"You're welcome," he smiled, and then ran off to play,
Unaware of the impact he'd had on my day.

I sat there and wondered how he managed to see
A self-pitying woman beneath an old willow tree.
How did he know of my self-indulged plight?
Perhaps from his heart, he'd been blessed with true sight.

Through the eyes of a blind child, at last I could see
The problem was not with the world; the problem was me.
And for all of those times I myself had been blind,
I vowed to see beauty in life,
       and appreciate every second that's mine.

And then I held that wilted flower up to my nose
And breathed in the fragrance of a beautiful rose
And smiled as I watched that young boy,
       another weed in his hand,
About to change the life of an unsuspecting old man.

"That is the kind of effect that all of us in Global Network can have in changing people's lives. And, finally, 'T' is for Training—to teach is to change lives forever.

"All my life I have admired people who have done something great with their lives. One Man gave up his life that others may have life abundantly. Countless soldiers have died for their country that others may live in peace. Perhaps in some small way, this is our contribution. For me personally, this company is the pearl of great price. It has changed my life more dramatically than I ever anticipated. As with childbearing, there has been a great deal of agony associated with giving birth to this company. It has forced us to sacrifice some aspects of our lives that I considered to be of the highest importance. This is the final reason I am convinced that Global Network is destined for greatness—measuring it by the magnitude of what we've given up and believing with all my heart that something even more valuable to this world awaits us.

"Join us at Global Network in creating a spirit for a new millennium. Check us out and get to know us at a deeper level, beyond labels, and images, and audio-visual media. Get to know our spirit and make that part of the story you share with others as you build your organizations. Most importantly, get in touch with your own spirit and that of your spouse or partner if you have one. Treasure that bond above all else. When you discover that the union of your spirits blends harmoniously with ours, that is the moment that we will soar to new heights and experience explosive growth. We can make that happen beginning right this moment and carry it out the doors of this convention hall into our own midst and watch it spread like wildfire into the world that we each are privileged to touch. I love you all and am so glad our lives have been brought together. Thank you."

I received a standing ovation from the audience. As I mingled among the distributors afterwards, we exchanged hugs. Some were teary. Others just expressed their gratitude, pointing to the copious notes they had taken.

But not everyone was pleased. I knew the moment that Mark came back on stage that he was angry. I wasn't sure why, but I could sense his vibes. I hardly saw him after that, and he left dinner early that Saturday evening. On Sunday morning, I took a large group out to the balloon races for the dawn patrol. We all celebrated the official launch of 21st Century Global Network as our balloon rose into the sky. Mark did not join us for this event either.

I had lunch at the convention with one of the presidential team members, Ranya, a medical doctor, and his wife, Kamara, from

East India. We had become close friends over the early months of launching the company and I knew that we could talk openly.

"Rene, your talk was beautiful."

"Awe-inspiring," Kamara added.

"But both of us recognize that there is something amiss here. You don't have to be real astute to figure it out. What's going on?" Ranya asked.

I burst into tears. I had held myself together as long as no one asked, but I lost it completely at that moment. Maybe I felt free enough with the two of them. They are both such gentle souls with deeply imbued healing philosophies. Briefly, I told them the truth—that Mark and I were separated. They were shocked. At that moment, I heard my name being called. It was time for me to be back on stage to acknowledge our top two leaders: John DeHart and Donnie Walker. The instant transformation from the gushing tears to my stage personality was my finest moment in my brief acting career.

The only noticeable downer of the entire convention happened just before the closing event. Randy went back up for an unscheduled presentation on the newly revised rates within the company. This included shipping, handling, product pickkup, rep support services, and the like. We had everyone feeling up but his announcement of new service charges left them feeling disheartened and demoralized. We spent the first days after convention cleaning up the repercussions of his presentation.

"Rene, it's John. We'd like to set up a teleconference call this morning and just wanted to see if you're available." The partners always had John call me.

He was phoning from our downtown office, and I was at home working. "Sure. Val and I are going over the brochure and business briefing one more time, so we're both nearby."

A few minutes after the agreed-upon time, we began our call. Once again, Mark couldn't be located, so it was just John, Val, Randy, and myself on the line. We began by doing an assessment of the convention—what went well and what could be improved. The biggest complaint they had was that my talk had gone on too long. No word of appreciation for its message or reception from our representatives. No concern was expressed about Randy's faux pas— only the length of my talk. Mark was in charge of the awards and recognition (a major feature of any convention), which, with no explanation, was dropped at the last minute. No mention of that oversight either—only the length of my talk. And how I go off on my own and don't play with the team. From my perspective, had I not done my part, there would have been a lot of gaping holes in the convention. I handled the orientation on Friday and the balloon launch on Sunday morning, and organized all of the training throughout Sunday. Not one word of thanks for that—only comments that people were confused as a result of the training. I understood Randy's attitude toward me. Mark and the partners never questioned him. Only *I* continued to press him for some accountability. But I couldn't understand why Valerie's demeanor toward me had changed; and as always, John went along with the others.

We moved on to the specific tasks each of us would undertake. I proposed that I begin working immediately on a post-convention package that would include audiocassettes of each of the main speakers and that I begin updating our company video to include parts of the convention and balloon launch. I made several suggestions about new ways of handling training and sales aids that would better support our marketing reps.

Randy was the first to respond. "You'll have to check with Mark on all that. He's overseeing all the training." *Why isn't Mark on this call. Why isn't he ever on calls?*

"I don't understand. That is my area of responsibility."

"No, you are to report to Mark on this."

"Randy, we divided up our responsibilities among ourselves before you joined us. Building and supporting the presidential team are Mark's primary areas. Public relations and training are mine. What is this about my 'reporting' to Mark?"

"Well, Mark is on the managing board, and you are not."

"What do you mean? When did this happen? Randy, I thought you alone were on the managing board."

"When we signed the new operating agreement. Your attorney should have pointed this out to you."

"My attorney? We all have the same attorney, Bob DeLett."

"Well, it was his job to tell you this."

"Who else is on the managing board?"

"Valerie, John, Larry, Graham, and myself."

"In other words, everyone but me!"

Val responded, "Ron is not included."

"But, Val, your husband has a full-time job and was contributing part-time to Global Network when he could. I have been full-time from the very beginning. What is really going on here?"

Again Randy spoke up. "Rene, you are better off working on your own. You're just not a team player. You go off and do things without consulting with the rest of us. That just doesn't work in this kind of a setting."

"Randy, we never had any problems working together in the pre-launch." Most of our team problems have come since you came on board. Is that just a coincidence? Or is it that you are bothered by the fact that I keep asking, *show me the money* that you were supposed to bring to the table? Or for the contracts that never quite get drawn up with Network Capital? Mark and I have more than six-hundred-thousand dollars riding on this company, and another couple of million in personal guarantees. You have fifty thousand personally and have raised another hundred and fifty thousand. The rest is either ours or Mark's friends, Bill and Ann Puckett's. I do question that, for so little delivered and risked, you should be given the privilege of calling the shots. In fact, during pre-launch, I never would have had to ask an attorney to tell me what was going on. My partners would have discussed things with me."

"Things have changed, Rene. It isn't pre-launch anymore," Randy stated emphatically.

"Obviously. Well, if I'm hearing you correctly, I guess I need legal advice now to figure out what else really happened here that I haven't been informed about. You know that, given the strain between Mark and me, it is impossible for me to report to Mark.

We've never been set up like that before. Previously, we each had areas of responsibility and reported back to the team as the situation warranted. Working this way has never been a problem for us, and we got things done. The kind of partnership we had before involved open communication with all of us. I don't understand why changes are being made so secretively now and why I have to go to an attorney to find out what has happened."

"Like it or not, I'm in charge of the finances now," Randy stated firmly. "I will be in this role until my investors are paid back."

"Well, as one of your 'investors,' I would like to have a contract. We need to pay off the 'loan' and transfer this money to the investment fund. What is the problem in getting this done? There is too much money involved not to have this in a written agreement," I responded, matching his tone.

"I'll get to it. I just have more important and pressing things to handle now," he retorted.

I didn't say anything more. John Radford was quiet throughout most of the exchange, and I wondered what he was thinking. I missed the old days of Valerie and John and Mark and me working so well together. The call ended with little fanfare.

I felt cut off from everyone. I lived alone and worked alone at the house. My communication was with our reps. That relationship was wonderful and is what kept me going. Since dealing with the reps is the most critical of all liaisons in our type of industry, I wondered why I hadn't been cut off from them as well. I suspected it was because my partners had little understanding how much the representatives are the lifeblood of a network marketing company. I had to force myself to face each new day. I was depressed, hurt, and uncertain how to deal with this runaway company. I was a founder, owner, the biggest investor along with Mark, and, with my Global Trust partners, held the top distributor position in the company in lieu of being paid a salary. But I had absolutely no say in how the company was run. The decision makers were the managing board, two of whom had not one penny in the company, one of whom had a miniscule investment, and one who could rarely be found. I was rapidly losing hope. They had me standing on a trap door, their hands just waiting to pull the lever. I knew that my next step would have to be a major one. I needed time to think it through.

Through IHI, John and Laurie Metzger were investors in our company and also served on the presidential team. Sensitive to my situation, they invited me to spend a weekend at their ranch about three hours from Reno. It was a welcomed relief from the loneliness. Chuck McGee, a local district judge, and his wife also joined us. I knew Chuck from my days in politics.

I hadn't been on a horse in years, but with their smooth gait, their Tennessee walkers were a dream to ride. I didn't even feel saddle-sore. Chuck's brother, Don, also a representative in our company, was aware of some of our internal challenges and had apparently shared this with Chuck. It was comforting to be able to talk freely with all of them in this relaxed environment. As we prepared to leave, Chuck handed me a poem he had just written, one intended to give me hope and encouragement that I would get through this.

> *If a soul evolves the same way a sparrow builds a nest...*
> > *A twig at a time*
> > *Fiercely, tenacious, persevering*
> *So that when the wind blows*
> > *the partially constructed nest apart,*
> *She instinctively picks up the pieces*
> *And emerges safe in the morning's light.*

Back home, my first call on Monday jolted me back to reality. "Hi, it's Mark. I just want you to know that, thanks to you, Don McGee is having serious doubts about the solidity of our company."

"Mark, he isn't alone. With you and me apart, and a managing board made up of people with little or no monetary investment or experience in network marketing, God himself would question us."

"Well, I'm not going to stand by and let you bad-mouth our

company. But that isn't why I called. How about meeting me for breakfast? There is something else I want to talk to you about."

I hesitated. Only because I wanted to hear his explanation of my being left off the managing board did I agree to meet him. "Okay."

"Peg's at 7:30. Is that good?" It was a breakfast spot located downstairs in our office building.

"I'll see you there."

I was sipping my coffee, waiting for him, when he arrived. When his coffee was poured, he opened the conversation.

"Rene, you need to really listen to me. If you never listened to me before, you need to now. I want you to get out of the business. You just aren't a businesswoman. You can write and do your network marketing thing, but you just don't belong in business. Trust me on this."

There was no one I could trust within the company anymore; but because of our seven years together, I clung to the hope that Mark would level with me. "Mark, what happened to 'you and me against the world'? Why didn't you come to my defense on 'The Little Red Tape' or tell me that I was being left out as a managing partner?" He didn't answer. I should have let the silence prevail, but instead I continued: "If we had only stuck together on the financing, we wouldn't be in this mess."

"I don't want to go back over that again. A deal is a deal, and I believe in keeping it." *Could any deal even compare to the solemn vows we exchanged? Wasn't that a deal worth keeping?*

"So do I. And you and the partners are not keeping your deal with me. Had our partners held up their end of the deal, we'd be facing about ten percent of the financial stress we're in. You and I are upside down in the trees because of them; and if and when we face the worst, I don't believe any one of them will stand by us. They'll all tell us how sorry they are, but...."

"Rene, I just don't want to go back over all of that. You and I will never see eye to eye on this. What will it take to get you out of the business?"

"Two-hundred-thousand dollars returned to me." My answer was a knee-jerk reaction. I had briefly discussed with Randy finding another investor to take my place. That is the figure he said he could get.

"That's it—two hundred thousand?"

"Yes, that will take me out of my half of the investment account with Network Capital. I know I can't get out of the personal guarantees, and I will still have money in Global Trust. So I will remain an owner and will continue to hold my place in our distributorship, but we can start to phase me out as an investor in the holding company. I've talked this over with Randy, and he says it is an option. He can easily find an investor or two to take my place."

"So what do we have to do next?" Mark asked eagerly.

"You understand that I would prefer to stay in the company and see this through? But if I can't be part of the managing board, I don't have much faith in the future of this company."

"I know you don't trust my judgment. That's why we're going apart. I have to have someone who believes in me. The partners trust me. Amy trusts me. Only you don't."

"Mark, it is so much more complicated than that. They don't know everything I know. They know you can't be found a lot these days. They know you totaled your car. They don't even want to know what caused you to miss the recording session. Do you think maybe it is time that you told me what happened that day?"

"It's none of your business anymore. I just want to know what we have to do to make this business transition happen."

"I need to see the final contracts. I want to know what else was done behind my back."

Without ever ordering breakfast, Mark jumped up and said, "Okay, let's go upstairs and find them."

We stopped at Valerie's office and asked her if she knew where the contracts were. She said she didn't know but thought it was worth trying Bob DeLett's office. Mark asked me to follow up on that. Bob's secretary said they were there, so I drove over immediately and picked them up. Back at the office, I plowed through the documents, comparing the one I'd been e-mailed as the final version with the actual signed document. I could see that the redline version given to me was clearly not the final draft.

In the version sent to me, Randy Calvert was named as the manager, which didn't raise any red flag to me. It had been proposed and crossed out that Mark, Val, and John be named to the managing board. Someone—I can only guess who—had removed the cross-outs after the document was sent to me.

> ...~~"Board of Managers" means initially John Radford, Valerie Perkio and Mark Yarnell, jointly representing Global Trust, Randall Calvert, representing Network Capital, LLC, Lawrence Brady, representing American Technology Group, Inc., and Graham Simpson, representing Integral Health, Inc., or any other person or persons that succeed him or her in that capacity or are elected to act as additional managers of the Company as provided herein.~~ "Manager" means RANDALL K. CALVERT, or any other Person or Persons that succeed him in that capacity or are elected to act as additional managers of the Company as provided herein. "Managers" means all such Persons collectively in their capacity as managers of the Company.

I thought back to Mark's visit with me in Santa Cruz, and remembered now how fidgety he was waiting for me to sign the contract. *That* was the purpose of his visit. That is why working out some business matter was so all-important to him. Letting me know about our divorce was a well-timed convenience. The partners sent Mark to do their dirty work, and he went along with it. Mark would never have initiated anything this underhanded on his own. Randy was clearly the mastermind of this. While I'm sure my partners could all rationalize that omitting me was in the best interest of the company, I didn't know the meaning of the word "betrayal" until this moment.

How could I be so naïve? And how could a company founded with so much good will and high integrity be reduced to such subterfuge? I could no longer wonder if I was being paranoid. This was unmistakable deception. The partners whom I took on and loved, the ones I began this venture with, would have discussed this matter with me. But then what could they say? "Oh, by the way, Rene, we are forming a managing board and putting all of us on it except you. We hope you don't mind. Since you and Mark are separating, we have to choose between you. You're not a team player. Mark is willing to go on supporting this venture and you aren't. We prefer his optimistic message to the negativity of yours." I worked as hard as anyone to establish this company and get it up and running. It was the dishonesty, the lack of integrity, that was tearing me apart. *Who do I turn to? It is no longer Mark and me against the world. I don't have a husband and partner on whom I can count. I could turn to Bob DeLett...but I would only be putting him on the spot. He represents all of my partners, not just me.* The more I contemplated my situation, the more alone I felt.

I called my friend, Dorothy Nash Holmes, who had left the DA's office and was now a Deputy Attorney General. I explained what had happened and asked for her unbiased opinion. She expressed concern for me and said I needed legal counsel. She asked me to give her an hour while she thought about the best law firm to represent my interests.

When she got back to me, she reported, "I called Leo Bergin and Spike Wilson at the McDonald-Carano-etc. etc. firm. They are waiting to hear from you. I really think you need to talk to someone. This is a serious matter. Partners don't do this sort of thing to partners."

"I'm really shaken, Dorothy. I don't want to do anything I will regret, and I don't want to misread this, but...."

"Rene, you've been screwed. You need someone in your corner. Phone Leo right now."

"Thanks, I hope I can be there for you when you need me. Wish me well."

"You got it."

Leo Bergin took my call immediately and suggested I come right over. I brought copies of the documents to his office and briefly explained the situation. As I finished my story, Spike stuck his head in the door.

"What's up? I got a call from Dorothy. She said you've got some trouble."

"It doesn't look good."

"Come on down to my office. Let's talk."

The consensus was that I had a big problem. By being taken off the managing board, I had no say over my investment in this company. Mark and I had divided and settled our property, so, even though we were married, I no longer had him as my defender and protector.

A meeting was called with Bob DeLett to provide background on how we reached this point in the amended operating agreement. Bob was uncomfortable coming to meet with my attorney alone, so it was suggested that he bring one of the partners with him. He chose Valerie. They arrived together and announced that Randy would like to be present by speakerphone conference call. As the meeting progressed, it was Randy rather than Bob who provided the background history.

"Because the Yarnells contributed the majority of the capital without any adjustment to the stock ownership, problems arose. I was able to get the agreement changed to reflect a more proportionate share of investments. What made the deal come together was giving Global Trust an incentive to hit projected targets. This made all the partners happy."

"What percentage do the Yarnells now own?" Spike asked.

"The Yarnells own 28.34% of Global Trust and 40% of the investment company, Network Capital. If targets are hit, that breaks down to their owning 17.7% of Global Network."

"Why did you create the managing board?"

"The co-venture partners were concerned about the management and wanted it to operate like a real company. They requested a clear delineation of who is responsible for what."

"Mr. Calvert, where do you fit into all of this?"

"I was admitted into Global Trust as a 15 percent partner. This organization is member-managed. There is no board of managers."

"And Network Capital?"

"It is simply a flow-through entity. It bears no expenses. I manage the finances."

"And what is your position with Global Network?"

"Significant changes were made here to clean up the disproportion of investments. We did not want to see Global Trust take an equity cut since sales depended on their management skills, so we worked out an agreement whereby they would have an incentive if they hit sales projections. We revised the role description of the president, and, until the investors are paid back, I am the executive director of this company."

"Given the property settlement drawn up between Mark and Rene, perhaps this is a simple matter of splitting their voting power down the middle as well. By the way, should you be using corporate titles in an LLC?"

"Well, that is discretionary. That really isn't the problem. And as far as her splitting her voting power, that won't work. The way it is divided, Global Trust (Mark, Val, and John) gets 27% voting power; Network Capital gets 27% voting power; ATG gets 27% voting power; and IHI gets 17% voting power. The real problem is that the partners feel that Rene did things without authority or accountability. She pursued what she wanted to do and not what the partners had agreed upon."

"Can you be more specific?"

"Sure, one example was when she cancelled the contract with the bottling company and moved it over to another company, which in the end has caused us immense problems and set us back financially."

I turned to Val who was sitting across the table from me. "That just isn't true. Val can attest to the truth. And Randy wasn't even in the picture then, so he would have no first-hand knowledge. I am the one who found another company when the first one started reneging on their commitment. But then I brought this back to all the partners and introduced them to the new company. Our decision to go forward with them was unanimous. It was in no way just mine. The problem set in when ATG's representative signed a contract with them on his own on behalf of Global Network." I paused giving Val a chance to jump in, but she didn't say a word. I was crushed that she didn't come to my rescue, so I continued in my own defense. "Like everyone, in hindsight, I was not pleased with our choice of bottling companies. But Val even went down, personally met with them, and came to the conclusion that, given the two companies, this was the right choice. We all thought so at the time." Val still didn't make eye contact with me as I spoke.

"I have one last question, Mr. Calvert. Do ATG and IHI want Rene out?" Spike asked.

"No, we don't have the votes to make that happen. It all comes down to a personal decision on Rene's part. Can she work under Mark's jurisdiction rather than operating like a freelance consultant? We just can't have her going off on her own anymore."

By this time, I was really practicing the art of letting my anger pass through me and having my spirit govern my ego. The series of events to which he was referring ran through my mind: my confrontation with Larry Brady over the partners matching our funding, my distress over the ATG employee who could never quite see a project through, my repeated requests of Randy to produce a contract for our investment in Network Capital and evidence of his share of the contributions, my negotiating an agreement over the proprietary rights on the audio, my filling in for Mark and cutting the audio tape the day he didn't show, my talk going too long at convention.

My transgressions almost always involved sins of *commission* designed to move us forward. My partners' offenses usually involved sins of *omission*, not taking action and thereby holding us up. For reasons I may never understand, *failing* to take action seemed to be easier to overlook than *taking* action as far as my partners were concerned. Before launch, we moved quickly. But now, my concern for our company was how slowly we were getting things accomplished. Whether it was forms that needed to be created or corrected, new product development, small requests

from the field that would make the marketing reps' job easier—
we were taking weeks to get on them. The only real sin of
commission that I noticed from any of my partners was Randy's
closing comments at convention. He managed single-handedly
to send everyone away on a down note.

I lost all hope for communicating with Randy, but I still
believed I could talk with Valerie and John. I sent them messages
by e-mail and stopped by Val's office, but they didn't respond.
Now I had committed the ultimate crime: I had hired an attorney.

Attempting to carry on with routine business at home, Mom
handed me bills to okay. I glanced through them and one jumped
out at me. It was an invoice from Chinquapin at Lake Tahoe for
September, a few weeks after Mark and I had stayed there together.
It was in Mark's name and billed for a party of *two*.

Late that afternoon, I was alone sitting at my desk when the
doorbell rang. It was our secretary delivering a manila envelope to
me from the office. We chatted briefly, and as I turned and closed
the door, I instinctively knew this was not good news. I sat down
in the living room, took a deep breath, and slowly began opening
the sealed mailer. It contained a letter signed by John Radford on
behalf of all the partners, informing me that I was no longer wanted
in any capacity in our company. Enclosed was a public
announcement that they planned to release to all of our
representatives. I read and reread the notice, not quite believing
that they would really send this:

> Organizations in the startup phase often
> experience change. 21st Century Global Network is
> no exception. In a unanimous vote, the Board of
> Managers of 21st Century Global Network has
> decided to conclude Rene Yarnell's association with
> the company. The training responsibilities will be
> divided among Valerie Perkio, Amy Yarnell, John
> Radford and Mark Yarnell. We wish Rene all the best
> in her numerous endeavors, and thank her for her
> assistance with the formation of Global Network.

We thank her for sacrificing her life, her marriage, her home, and family. We thank her for investing her life's savings when the rest of us were unable or unwilling to do so. Whatever happens, we will always be grateful for her benevolent financial and personal contributions for the good of all at Global Network. I was in shock—a mixture of hurt and anger. A few days later, that announcement went out to more than two thousand of our marketing reps. On the call with our presidential team and top leaders, Mark's response was that his gut was wrenched over this. I believed it truly was. Having abstained from voting on this matter (which meant it wasn't unanimous), I pictured him in the role of Pontius Pilot. There was no doubt with *Whom* I identified in this crucifixion scene.

For the next week, calls came in from dozens of people in our company. I prepared an outline so that I delivered the same positive message to each person. "I appreciate your support. Starting this company put unbearable strain on Mark and me. We have separated and, under the circumstances, I think the partners did what they thought was the best thing. Maybe now Mark will be able to give you all his undivided attention without the distraction of our personal challenges. You'll have Mark on the inside supporting you. And you'll have me on the outside working to build up the industry. I have just entered into a contract with our publisher to write my next book. This one is on network marketing as the rising new profession. I'll be writing it with Dr. Charles King. So you'll have the best of Mark and the best of Rene now." With a couple of exceptions, nearly everyone responded well to my congenial message without question. Setting my own feelings aside, I was determined to reassure our people that everything would turn out just fine.

"Everything really will turn out just fine," said Lynn Carasali. Write this down somewhere so that you can read it a year from now. 'I thank God all of this has happened. My life is so much better now.'"

I couldn't have made it through this period without the support of friends. My tennis friends kept me on the court three and sometimes four times a week. My friends from political days and several Global

Network reps took me to lunch or had me over for dinner. My phone rang more than usual with people just checking up on me. It was the lowest point of my life.

Nancy and her husband, Deno Paolini, introduced me to a program called Rapport International, and I signed up for a weekend workshop that would be a major turning point for me. I was ready to take charge of my life and accept all that had happened as part of a plan leading me to the next significant level of my life. God had a plan. I knew it. I just couldn't see how it would unfold. There was a high point during the weekend when I was able to feel that I was no longer abandoned by either my partners or my husband. I had been *released* to get on to fulfill my real purpose in life. If someone could look into the center of my husband's soul, I believed that one would find he was as motivated by his conviction that he was holding me back as much as he felt I was constraining him. When I came home from the Rapport weekend, I felt an inner-strength and an ability to focus like never before. It was on this weekend that I determined I would do whatever it took to launch my writing career.

Two weeks later, Missy McQuattie introduced me to a Catholic retreat, where the emphasis was on forgiveness and healing. I had much to forgive and be forgiven for. Father Tom Donnelly, an Irishman through and through, anointed us with holy oils and performed numerous Catholic rituals that brought me back to my roots. I used this time to address an unsent letter to Mark and my business partners, forgiving them for the way they cast me aside and asking their forgiveness for my part in all of this. Only Randy could I not forgive. It wasn't so much his unfulfilled promises to save our company, nor his deceitful delay tactics to formally transfer our $300,000 loan to the newly formed holding company, nor even his orchestrating my dismissal from my own company. Only his manipulation of a kind and gentle man who, without his influence, could never have acted in such a heartless manner—only his villainous control over my husband—could I not yet forgive.

Feeling more a part of the fold and without the usual travel schedule that kept me from commitments at home, I signed up to serve as a Eucharistic minister in my parish after this retreat. And while attending one of the Monday Night Football events at the Flanigans, I met Fr. Frank Murphy. He e-mailed me shortly afterwards and offered his support if I just needed someone to listen. A month or so later, we met for coffee and began what was to become an important friendship in my new life.

With the help of Realtors Kathy List and Marna Griffin, wife of Reno's mayor, I found a rental home. During my final days in Windara, I felt some pangs of nostalgia. It wasn't the house. It was my life in this house—our family togetherness, the Christmases, the dinners, the friends and parties, but it was mostly Mark, memories of him and the life we once had. The programs I had recently experienced truly helped me to let go of anger and blame, and opened me to be filled with love.

I felt an overwhelming sense of passion come over me, a feeling so strong I could not contain it. I climbed out of bed and walked across the room to the stereo. Our song, "Somewhere in Time," was already in the CD holder. Had he been listening to it, or was it there from the last time we made love here in our bedroom? No, that would have been too long ago. He must have been listening to it. Pushing the play button, I turned up the volume and returned to bed, to our bed. I felt that first swell of notes and chords run through my body. I rolled over to lie on Mark's side of the bed. I closed my eyes and let myself drift off "somewhere in time" to a hotel room in Atlanta. The time was November 1991. Mark and I were lying on the bed holding each other. Mark led us in prayer.

"Oh Lord, look down upon us, two of your children, longing to love and serve You. It is You who have brought us together to merge our lives and share in some special work that You would have us do. Allow us to deeply touch the lives of others and to make an impact that will bring just a little more good into the world. Never, never let us lose sight of the love we share. Without that love, we cannot hope to enkindle this love in others. It will be from our love for each other bonded in You that we will be empowered to reach out to countless people whose paths cross ours. We feel that we are destined to be together, not selfishly just for our own happiness, but to love and serve You in a more far-reaching way. Guide us to the work You want us to do. Teach us how to put You first in our lives, then each other. By so doing, all else will naturally follow. The love we have for each other at this moment is so powerful that we feel we could move mountains. Allow our love to grow to the point where it can embrace everyone who comes to us needing our love and support. We vow our commitment to You and to each other to have and to hold, to love and to honor, from this day forward, for better or for worse, in sickness and in health, until death takes us from each other. We ask this in the name of Christ, our Lord. Amen."

I remembered sealing our commitment with the most beautiful lovemaking. As far as we were concerned, we were married at that moment. We didn't need to wait for the more formal ceremony that followed. It was so profound a moment that no legal decree could ever undo it.

I could now feel Mark lying close to me in our bedroom. The music swelled up inside of me and swirled throughout the room. I could feel love penetrating every corner of this extraordinary chamber we had shared together. We even designed it to look like the Victorian era from "Somewhere in Time." I concentrated as deeply as is humanly possible and, at that moment, I felt that I was in Mark's body. I loved him more deeply than I ever thought possible. My spirit of love was infused into every pore of his body. It lasted only a moment, but it was real. And then I found myself back in my own body, lying in a pool of sweat. The crescendo of the music rose and fell, softening to utter stillness. I lay there in the silence regaining my strength. In that single act, I had forgiven Mark for all the hurt, shared my love with him in the most penetrating manner, and given him his release from me to go on with his life. Our spirits were forever entangled with each other, but our lives would now be separate.

I dressed and began my day, though I was terribly disoriented. I missed a luncheon appointment with a friend, thinking it was Wednesday when it was actually Thursday. At the time I should have been at the restaurant, I found myself wandering through the mall for no particular reason. As I looked up, I saw Mark walking towards me. He spotted me at the same time. There were only seconds before we would be face to face. *Would he turn away? Would he be able to face me?* He reached out, and we walked into each other's arms.

Ogod, how I love you. Don't let go. Hold me for just another second. There now, I'm okay. I'm ready to let you go.

It all happened in a split second. "So what are you doing wandering around the mall?" he asked.

"I have time now," I retorted. "What are *you* doing wandering around the mall?"

He looked sheepish. "I just took a break to look for a religious CD I want. I think we have it at home, but I really wanted to get it."

"Well, if it is at home, then you won't need to find it. Your attorney called this morning, and I want to accept your offer about your moving back into the house."

"Great, when do you want to make the switch?"

"As soon as possible, whenever you're ready."

"Do you have a place to go?"

"Yes, I found a furnished place that I can have month to month."

"Okay, I have to be out of town this weekend. But I'll be home Sunday morning. I'd like to be back in before Wednesday to have an opportunity meeting there for some of our reps."

"Sounds good."

"Will you be home this afternoon?" I nodded. "I have to get back to the office, but I'll call you around 3:00....By the way, you look really good."

I watched him walk away in his usual half-running gait. Out of the nearly 300,000 county residents and half as many again who visit Reno at any given time, what were the odds of running into my husband? They were one-out-of-one—because a Higher Power was orchestrating things now. This was clearly out of my control.

CHAPTER 19

CREATING A NEW CAREER
AND NEW LIFE
November 1998 – May 1999

With the last few things packed, I moved only the bare essentials—a few clothes, my computer, and office items—into my new little house. Otherwise it was fully furnished, complete with linens and towels, pots and dishes. I took one last walk around the old house and sat out on the back patio overlooking downtown. As I gazed out at the setting sun, casting its pink shadows across a Nevada sky, I felt a calmness overtake me. One part of my life was going down with the sun, but a new phase was commencing with the next day's sunrise.

My life changed dramatically over the next few weeks. Although I was technically married, I was no longer living lavishly with my husband in our Windara mansion. I was no longer serving as vice-president of Global Network. I was no longer Mark's life partner—co-writer, co-teacher, co-creator, co-owner of everything we had built together. I was an extremely frightened woman who, for the moment, was living in a small rental house where I owned nothing but the one carload I brought with me. I was single, for all practical purposes, and liable for two or three million dollars of debt if our company went under. The proposed buyout of my investment didn't happen. Apparently Randy, the venture capitalist extraordinaire, didn't find it that easy to find another investor after all. Everything I had been doing for the past nearly seven years was stripped from me.

Desperately searching for a reason to get up in the mornings, I carefully chose my new career because it was the only activity for which I felt the inner stirrings of passion. Writing my next book became an obsession. It gave me a sense of purpose, the only one I could grab onto. My new home was the right environment for this project, small and cheerful, with a breathtaking view of the city. I brought a half a dozen CDs with me and played them all day long. I surrounded myself with soft piano classics and various instrumentals. I seemed to require extensive alone time.

After our years of teaching the University Certificate Seminar, I found comfort in knowing that Dr. Charles King was writing the book with me, and that he believed in me. Charles and I had a lengthy teleconference call with Ben Dominitz, the publisher of Prima, who had published the last book Mark and I had written. *Your First Year in Network Marketing* was still holding its own on the bestseller list, having now moved up to number seven. Led by Ben, we came up with a name for the new book. It was to be called *The New Professionals: the Rise of Network Marketing as the Next Major Profession.* I liked it. We were on our way.

I felt that getting this book written and published was the key to my professional future. This could lead to speaking engagements and seminars on many expanding topics within the network marketing industry. With brief breaks, I wrote from 4:00 or 5:00 in the morning until 9:00 or 10:00 at night. *Could I write a book without Mark? Networkers around the world had a warm place in their hearts for Mark and Rene Yarnell, but would they accept Rene alone?* I knew I would have to prove myself.

Writing came before everything else. I screened my phone calls and returned them later so I wouldn't lose my concentration. The one exception was my taking calls from our distributors. I wanted them to keep their faith in the company even with me gone. I loved them and cared about so many of them; I knew it was mutual.

Over the course of the week, I had several calls from our marketing reps concerned about the future of the company. Randy had been their favorite target, but now something new was sending a shockwave through the field.

"I didn't know if you knew. But it has caused a lot of upheaval in the field," the caller said.

"What has? What are you talking about?"

"You mean you really don't know?"

"Know what?"

"Well, I don't know how to say this except to say it: Mark is dipping his pen into the company ink well."

"For heaven's sake. Stop talking in riddles and just tell me?"

"Rene, think about it. I just told you."

I thought about what he'd just said. I had never heard that expression before—then it dawned on me. I took a shallow breath to ease the pain in my heart. "Who?" I asked.

"Honestly, don't you know?"

"No. Honestly, I don't."

"Well, she's not a distributor."

I excused myself and hung up the phone. My stomach was in knots; my whole body began shivering. Within minutes, I had a full-blown case of diarrhea. *Valerie and Mark. Omigod. The thought never crossed my mind. I could barely let it in. My friend and my husband. My two partners. I wondered where her husband, Ron, was with all of this. The library scene. Of course. With Valerie as a guest in my home, I should have known. Her sudden anger toward me followed by her coldness. It all finally added up.*

Over the next couple of weeks, I heard various versions of the story. I'm not sure how much of what I was told was true, but the general picture was that Valerie and Ron were also going through divorce and that Valerie and Mark were like two giggling teenagers experiencing first love. They were also in complete denial to everyone that it was happening.

My priest friend, Frank, called later in the day and I told him I really needed to talk. He was pastor of the campus parish at the University of Nevada, Reno, and this was his day off. We took a drive to Lake Tahoe while I poured out my heart. "Why is it that most men only leave a relationship when they have someone else in the wings? Can't they stand on their own damned feet for ten minutes?"

"Most aren't strong enough to go it alone. When it comes to relationships, women are much stronger than men." I loved his Irish wit coupled with a New York accent. *Women are stronga than men.* Frank was becoming such a good friend. We talked every single day. With his kind, rounded face and nearly six-foot frame, he was like my guardian angel sent to watch over me.

"You know, it's really true. In nearly every breakup, the woman stays by herself for a time, often a long time. More often than not, the man already has one foot in a new relationship before he has the other foot out of the old one. And only with that in place does he seem to have the courage to move on with his life," I said.

"Are you surprised by this with Mark?"

"Ogod, yes, but I shouldn't be. It doesn't seem like something he would do. And yet it is the very thing he did with me. He had just come through living with someone else when he reached out to me. I thought it was completely over between them. I guess it was for him; but from a brief conversation I had with her, it definitely wasn't over. It is his pattern. Mark has not spent a great deal of his life living alone. He has almost always had a woman with him. I don't know if he could go it alone for very long."

"Are you angry at them?"

"I'm more stunned than angry. I feel foolish...all those times I kept trying to put things back on track between Val and me. At least subconsciously, she had to find reason to be angry with me. How else could she..."

"Betray you? I mean, you must feel some betrayal?"

"My heart feels betrayed. With no financial investment, it took some kind of gall for her to vote me out and take over my company *and* my husband. But my head understands what happened. Understandably, Mark is a man who needs to be deeply respected by his woman. I know Valerie pretty well. We shared a lot with each other about our personal lives. She wasn't happily married and hadn't been for a long time. Brought into close proximity with Mark, I'm sure she viewed his handling of our business affairs as that of a bold and courageous man, and in her own way, probably expressed this to him. With things obviously falling apart for us, she may have been somewhat of an opportunist, but, nevertheless, she could give him the one thing I couldn't—unquestioning loyalty and support. Of course, she doesn't have the history I have with him."

"I feel a kind of jealousy when you describe the life you had with Mark. Your time in Switzerland sounds like nirvana. It is what I think, teach, and preach about when I discuss healthy, life-giving relationships.

I thought about what he said for a while before I asked my next question: "Do you think we'll see married priests in our lifetime?"

"You can count on it! It must happen not long after we have a new Pope, or we'll all become Presbyterians." I laughed and thought about my previous husband. He had such strong feelings on this subject and wrote about it in a well-publicized book, *A Modern Priest Looks at His Outdated Church*. With more than thirty years since he wrote it, very little has changed.

"I always felt that Jim Kavanaugh would have been a good married priest," I said.

"Have you heard from him recently?"

"No, but I'm sure I will when the time is right. If it were up to me, I'd like to have a friendship with both Mark and Jim."

"I think I told you that Jim and I were in grad school together at Catholic U. He was just a few years ahead of me in the priesthood. We both served on a religious education panel once."

"I bet that was interesting."

"Not really. Jim liked to do all the talking. I could hardly get in a word," he laughed.

"Did you know him when that article came out in the *Saturday Evening Post?*"

"You mean 'I am a Priest and I want to Marry'?" Frank asked.

"Yeah. No one was supposed to know who wrote it. He signed it 'Fr. Stephen Nash.'"

"Oh, let me tell you, he had such a distinct writing style that it took the Catholic U. librarian about ten minutes to figure out who authored it. He was popular among the students but a pain in the ass to the old-guard priests."

We arrived at a restaurant and chose a spot on the deck overlooking Lake Tahoe. It was a beautiful afternoon, and I could feel the sun on my face. I needed all the solar healing power I could take in. Breathing in the mountain air, we talked quietly while we waited for our food to be served.

He said a prayer once our meal had been placed in front of us. "It's good to see you eating. You haven't been doing enough of that. Is it polite to ask how much weight you've lost?"

"Probably about twenty pounds. The divorce diet is one of the most effective ones I know," I said jokingly. It was the closest I'd come to humor in quite a while.

"If you don't mind my saying so, you need to put just a little back on. You're really thin."

"I know. I will get my appetite back. There just have been so many changes in my life. And this latest bit of information—well, I just have to let it in."

"So where are you with it? I mean, what are you feeling?"

"After all the emphasis Mark placed on fidelity and never placing ourselves in a vulnerable situation, I am surprised he would have let that happen. I *am* angry, more toward him than her. While I was in Santa Cruz trying to make myself a better wife for him, he's at home playing goo-goo eyes with Val in the library. Then, when my heart is breaking and I call home for moral support, who do I turn to? Her! How could I be so naïve?

"You tend to trust people, Rene, perhaps without any foundation."

"Yeah, I guess. Whatever I feel, I do understand why, and that helps ease my pain. I mean, even if it only lasts for a little while, they might be good for each other right now. They're both good people. I doubt that either one of them set out for this to happen.

"Where are the Global Network distributors with it?"

"The ones who have talked to me about it are taking it pretty hard."

"Well, I gather that Mark and Rene Yarnell were beloved in your industry. God help the person who is perceived to break that up."

"The truth is, she didn't. Not really. She just happened to be there when it all fell apart. And she didn't have the history with him that I did. He needed to be reaffirmed and she was there to offer that." We sat looking out at the water for a few minutes. I felt the warmth and support of this dear new friend. "For his own sake, I wish Mark could just be by himself for a little while. You know, go it alone and develop strength within himself without needing someone else to reinforce it."

"But you know how we men are..." he teased.

"Yeah, and I'm starting to get clearer on what I want in my next relationship. Not that I'm ready for that yet, but I will be sometime."

"Do you think you'll marry again?" Frank asked me.

"No, I don't think so, but not because I feel this one failed. My marriage to Mark was anything but that. I am losing my belief in marriage, the way it is set up today. It isn't a viable system.

"So what then?"

"I want someone I can love and who will love me. I want the intimacy. And I want to grow on all levels and help my partner do the same. But I don't see myself getting tied down with legal or financial entanglements. That's the part that makes so many people feel they've *failed* at marriage. The expectations are unrealistic. So instead of marriage, I guess I am looking for a kind of spiritual relationship. I think that would work better for me."

"Spiritual relationship, hmm. I'd like to talk to you more about that idea sometime...after you've had time to work through your present situation. You know I want to be your friend and help in whatever way I can."

"I know, and I really thank you for that." He squeezed my hand.

It was beginning to cool down quickly as the sun lowered on the water. " Are you done eating?"

"Yes, I did pretty well." There was still about half of my meal left. I seemed to be able to make two meals out of just about any one I ordered these days. With my doggie bag in my hand, we headed back to the car and down the hill toward home.

I woke up on the couch. The dawn was just breaking. I seemed to be making a habit of falling asleep there at night. I wasn't able to sleep alone in my bed yet. The king-size bed emphasized my aloneness. The couch with the pillowed back was narrow and enveloped me. My sadness was still lingering. I cried some everyday. I just knew I had to get through it. Eventually, it would pass. I knew it would...eventually and when I was ready.

I broke my writing isolation to join Nancy and Kathy Wishart for lunch. The three of us had lived through political upheavals together, and the ups and downs of Project ReStart. Through it all we had become good friends. I ordered my meal but could barely eat any of it. Before I knew it, I was blubbering over my Caesar salad.

"Have you thought of going to see your family physcian and getting some meds to help you through this?" Nancy suggested.

"No, you know me. I don't even take aspirin."

"Rene, why not see your doctor. Get something to help you through this just for a little while," Nancy said with noticeable alarm.

"We're worried about you," Kathy added. "You've been through a lot, and it wouldn't hurt to get a little medical help until you can pull yourself together."

Hugging them both and thanking them for putting up with me, I called my doctor's office from my cell phone and headed there right from the restaurant.

Dr. Lovett diagnosed me as moderately depressed.

"I didn't think you termed it depression when there was justifiable cause," I said half serious and half jesting.

Since Dr. Lovett was also the medical advisor for the

methadone clinic where Mark had been a client, he was well aware of my situation—all sides of it.

"Paxil—that's what I'd recommend. Let's start you on a small dosage and see if that doesn't take the edge off. I don't think you'll need to be on this for long, but you definitely could use something right now to help you get through this."

I noticed a difference after taking the very first half tablet. After six months of constant tears, I felt somewhat normal again. Maybe I finally understood Mark's explanation of "normal."

I was sitting at my computer writing, with a lighted candle beside me on the table and "Somewhere in Time" playing softly in the background. The phone rang. Instinctively, I picked it up without thinking.

"Hi, it's Mark." He sounded pleasant, and we chatted for a while. If he had a reason for calling, it wasn't apparent at first. "Is that what I think is playing in the background?"

"Umhmm. I love to write to it."

"Is that what you are doing—writing?"

"That's what I do every day."

"Good for you.... Listen, the reason I called was about the house. I want to refinance it and get some more money out of it for the company." *So why isn't dear Randy handling this? Why is it up to you?* "I can't do that without you since you're on the note too." Before I could say anything, he went on. "I know you probably won't want to do this. So here's my proposal. Why don't I try to refinance it in my own name and, if I can, I will take the house back and take you off the note."

We already had a million and a quarter in first and second mortgages on the house. We had tried unsuccessfully to sell it. Getting out from under that debt sounded like the only sensible thing to do from my perspective.

"Yes, why don't you see if you can qualify. I will sign the house over to you if you can."

There was a pause in the conversation. Then from out of nowhere he asked, "So have you heard from Kavanaugh?"

"No, what made you ask?"

"I just thought you would have by now."

Turnabout is fair play. "So how are you and Valerie?"

After a pause, he cleared his throat. "You mean John and Valerie?"

"No, I mean *you* and Valerie."

"Hold on a minute." I could hear him lay down the phone and scurry off. When he came back, he tried to sound unaffected by my question. "So where were we? Oh yeah, don't tell me you've been listening to those silly rumors. That's all bullshit."

I let it go. "So how is the business doing?"

"We're doing fine. We have more investors interested in us. I'm not worried at all." *So why are you trying to find more money for the company?* "One thing you can count on: I will get you your money back. This company is going to be around for a long time to come."

"That's reassuring." I lingered for a moment. So did he.

"My attorney recommends we finalize the divorce before the end of the year. There are tax advantages if we each close out the year single rather than married." *How strange. Seven years of sharing our lives on so many levels. In the end, it all comes down to tax advantages.*

The spiritual bond had long been terminated. Now we had only to deal with the legal part. From that perspective, taxes were as good a reason as any. "Okay, whatever you think." I was resigned to it. But setting a definite time to close out our life left me feeling empty inside.

"Good luck with your writing. I have to get busy on my book too. John is going to write some of it, and Valerie is picking up parts of it."

"That's good. Are you still calling it *Self-Wealth?*"

"Yes, I'm trying to patent the name. We hope to give Self-Wealth workshops and use the name in a variety of ways."

"Sounds good." There was so much I wanted to say. And yet there was nothing left to say. So we said goodbye.

Over the next several weeks, with one small tablet a day of Paxil, I could feel my emotions leveling out and my energy picking up. I kept hearing from distributors who were, one by one, bailing from our company. It was breaking my heart to see everything we had built in such jeopardy. Surely there was something I could do.

I lingered over the decision for days and finally picked up the phone and called a business associate, Graham Anthony, who was with *Upline* magazine. I had gotten to know him from the Upline Master's Seminars, and I knew he had been in the mortgage brokering business before getting involved with our industry and the magazine.

"Rene, how nice to hear from you." Graham always sounded so proper.

After some light exchange, I told him why I was calling. "I'm worried about our company. I'm still an owner and, with Mark, the largest investor. I don't want to see it go down—for Mark's sake and for the distributors'. More money doesn't seem to be forthcoming, so the only other alternative I can think of is a buyout. I thought you might have your finger on the pulse of companies looking to buy."

"Actually, I am no longer at Upline. We had a parting of the ways." I listened as he explained the details of his leaving, but he concluded by saying, "I may still be able to help you. I do have some connections. Let me make a few phone calls and see what I can come up with."

A few days later, he called back. "I've got someone who is interested. He'd like to discuss it with you further. I've had him sign a confidentiality agreement, and I know we can trust him to respect it. He has been around the industry for a long time. He got his start in Amway. Are you available now?"

"For this, you bet."

Graham put me on hold while he linked the three of us together. "Rene are you there?"

"Yes, I'm here."

"I'd like you to meet Ted Elias. He's the president of Legacy USA."

Ted and I talked long enough to determine that we were both interested in pursuing the matter. He lived on the East

Coast and I on the West; but he was on his way to the Direct Sales Association convention in Dallas, which we agreed would make a good meeting place.

I flew to my hometown with some excitement about the possibility of finding a solution for our company. I knew I could not let my former partners and, especially, Mark know of my involvement; that would be a deal-killer. Ted was a 6-foot distinguished-looking man with grayish thinning hair. He looked physically fit and represented his product line well.

As we ordered coffee, he began to explain the background of his company. "It all originally began with two major Fortune 500 companies, Dupont and Conagra. Together they set up a research company that they named Dupont Conagra Vision, or DCV. The outcome of years of research was an immune builder that is derived from chicken eggs. DCV then created a co-transfer factor that allowed the immune builder to be transferred to and become effective in the human body. It is an incredible product. With the backing of such notable companies, the product gained a great deal of interest and DCV was eventually bought out. Today the research company is owned by Legacy. Although I am the president, we have an active board of directors. I would need to involve them in anything we do."

"And, Ted, I want to make it clear that I don't have the authority to act either. There are partners who will ultimately make this decision." I proceeded to explain how our company came to be formed and how I was ultimately asked to leave.

"I've been divorced before myself, so I understand the pain you are going through. I am happily married again now, so have hope."

"Thanks. My reason for meeting with you is to quietly, behind the scenes, give my husband and our company a boost. But it's important to me that none of the partners know of my involvement."

"I certainly am willing to respect that, but...why?"

"First, because my partners probably wouldn't follow up on this if they knew. And secondly, this is my parting gift to Mark. I care about him and want to see his dream come to fruition. The success of this company is all that really matters to him at this moment. I also care about the distributors. They put their faith in Mark and me, and I want to see them be part of a company that is going to thrive. That isn't going to happen unless we raise more money. And, lastly, it is the only hope that Mark and I and the other investors have of getting our investment back."

We talked for a couple of hours, answering each other's questions until we were satisfied that we had the makings of a healthy merger. Legacy had the money and the corporate structure. 21st Century Global Network had several thousand distributors, some proven leaders, and, of course, MarkYarnell. We also had a product line that would complement Legacy's mission. It seemed like a good match.

"So where do we go from here?"

"I think we let Graham make the next call. He is a friend of our daughter, Amy. So I suggest that he call her and tell her what he has in mind. Then Amy will put Graham in touch with her dad. That way there is no need for him to mention my involvement."

"How soon do you think this can take place?"

"Can you move quickly on your side?" I asked.

"There's nothing stopping us."

"Our distributors are restless. We need to have this in place by the first of the year."

"That suits us just fine." Ted and I parted, agreeing to stay in touch by phone.

Christmas was a blur. I received an ornament from a luncheon and hung it on the ficus tree. That was the extent of holiday decorations this year. Although I didn't have the Christmas spirit, I was feeling much better emotionally. I stopped taking my medication only to discover on Christmas Day that I had what is known as "Paxil brain," a feeling that your brains are swishing around loose in your head. The drug was a wonderful cure for my depression; but being on it such a short time, I didn't realize how difficult it would be to stop using it. The effect of getting off Paxil paralleled the feelings of winding down my marriage—swooshing in my head, vertigo, upset stomach. By trial and error, I learned that one gets off Paxil only one way— very slowly and incrementally, one baby step downward in dosage at a time. How much like ending a marriage.

My divorce was final on December 30. Knowing how I was feeling, Frank invited me out for another of our special lunches. We went to his favorite hangout, Portofino's.

"So how are you?"

"Sad.... Maybe glad that it's over. I need some kind of finality to this so I can get on with my life."

"You seem to be doing fine as long as you're writing. It's when you stop and think about your loss that you start to feel bad."

"Yeah, there is no way around it. I just have to feel the feelings, the emptiness, the sadness, you know, what used to be there and isn't anymore. Recovery, whether it is from addiction or loss, is a two-step forward one-back process. Sometimes it feels like those feelings will never go away, but I know from experience that they will...eventually."

"You're right to take it at your own pace. If you don't stay with the feelings, you will never complete the grieving process. But some of those feelings will always be with you." Reaching into his portfolio that he carried with him into the restaurant, he pulled out a card. "I got this from the Carmelite Monastery while I was there saying Mass this morning. It seemed so right for you at this time."

As my eyes scanned the card, I found it was so very descriptive of my own experience. I noticed it was a quote from the theologian Dietrich Bonhoeffer, whom I had studied back in the sixties. I cleared my throat and began reading it out loud: "Nothing can make up for the absence of someone we love, and it would be wrong to try to find a substitute. We must simply hold out and see it through. That sounds very hard at first, but at the same time it is a great consolation. For the gap, as long as it remains unfilled, preserves the bond between us. It is nonsense to say that God fills the gap. God does not fill it, but on the contrary, keeps it empty and so helps us to keep alive our forever communion with each other even at the cost of pain." The words said it all.

The start of a new year, the last one of the second millennium! This had to be a momentous year. I knew from several of the distributors that discussions were underway about a company merger, but I was getting concerned that it was not being finalized. Distributors were dropping like flies. I couldn't understand what was holding it up. I spoke with Ted, who said a lawyer/accountant from our side named Randy, a difficult guy to deal with, was slowing up the process. I should have known. All of January passed and no closure on the buyout. Finally, in February I received a call.

"Rene, it's Mark. How are you?" he asked perfunctorily. I could tell from his voice that this wasn't going to be a pleasant call.

"I'm good. What's up?" I tried to match his matter-of-fact tone.

"I've found a buyer for the company. It's a company based out of Florida."

"That's great. That's really great news."

"Well, let me tell you how this is going to work. If we do everything right, we can make a lot of money over the next...well, we've got a five-year window. But we're going to have to hit 75 million in sales to do it. Now, here's the bottom line. The whole way it's broken down is the first amount goes to the investors to pay them back. We're going to get our money back—you and I and Puckett and Randy. IHI and ATG are getting nothing.

"That doesn't sound right to me. I didn't believe that they deserved equal partnership when they didn't contribute equal funding; but on the other hand, they don't deserve to be entirely cut out if we get money back."

"Look, Rene, it took a lot of negotiation. Graham Simpson basically walked from it because he hadn't contributed anything. ATG admitted that if it weren't for the website and the fact that we were deceived, we would have probably built a dynasty." I knew he was referring to some negative press ATG received a few weeks after we got underway that was being flaunted around the Internet. "So they feel bad about it. They just want their product back. The only people who want their money back are you and me, Puckett, Randy, and the two doctors who invested. So the first money that comes back goes to us. After that, the rest of the money is based on services rendered. It's got nothing to do with investors.

"So who gets the rest of the money?"

"Well, those of us who built the downline."

"And who is that?"

"Me and Val and John and Randy—the partnership."

"And I'm no longer a partner?"

"Well," he laughed nervously, "you haven't been for a long time. You've been an investor. We're the ones doing the work. We're the ones building the downline.

"You see, Mark, what is wrong to me about your thinking—whether it is ATG or IHI or me—we all deserve our money back. But I also have a place in the downline. And that just can't be wiped out...."

"No, you don't have a place in the downline."

"Yes I do." I was emphatic.

"You're not building anything. You haven't built anything. And you're not going to build anything."

"Do you remember all that advice that you used to give to people in our downline when one partner wanted out because the other partner was not doing his fair share? You would tell them: 'That's the way it works, guys. You have to live with what you started.' I put in long days, sometimes 20-hour days, into forming this company and working with our distributors. I am part of Global Trust, and Global Trust holds the top distributor position with our company."

"It's not going to be Global Trust. It's going to be a different company."

"Mark, think about it. This isn't you. It's just plain unethical. It doesn't matter what name you give it. It is still the organization of distributors we built that you are taking with you to the new company."

"No, what's unethical is to pay you to do nothing."

"Mark, it's wrong and you know it."

"Well, sue me.... Do you want your money back or not? I thought you would be very, very pleased. You almost lost everything...had I not busted my ass to negotiate this deal and create this merger." *Keep you're cool, Rene. Don't lose it, babe. Eight, nine, ten.* Deep breath.

"I'm really pleased with the way you've negotiated this deal, but that doesn't give you the right to toss me aside now."

"Do you get it? We are going into a brand-new venture, Rene. We don't have ownership in the venture."

"A brand new deal means brand new people. You are taking all the people that we brought into this company with you. That is not a brand-new deal."

"You and I are not going to solve this today over the phone. I thought you'd be happy."

"I definitely see the good in this, Mark. And you are to be commended for what you've accomplished. You really are....The Mark Yarnell that I know has always bent over backwards with generosity to the point of fault. In fact, one of our arguments was about accountability with our partners. But now it seems like you are going the other way. Like ATG doesn't deserve anything. Well, they do. And like I don't deserve anything for my position in the downline for the year that I devoted to this project as a member of Global Trust. Well, I do."

"No, you're missing the point, Rene, totally. Listen to me carefully. ATG is exceptionally happy with the deal that they're getting."

"I don't believe that."

"Holy shit," he whispered almost inaudibly. Then louder, "Well, okay. I never thought this would come up."

"Mark, I'm not willing to give up my position in the downline. That's just wrong for you to even suggest it. That's a lifetime income. And we worked hard, putting in long hours for that. Our position in the downline was to be our payback. It's a lifetime deal, and you can't just dump me."

"Look, Rene, if you get your money back and I get my money back, then we've got what we deserve."

"But you are taking the downline that I helped build, that I helped attract into our company, and are removing me from my position. And that's wrong!"

"That is future revenue based on future sales of a totally different deal...."

"...with the company that I helped build and I helped train and I helped form. Mark it's wrong! Think about it. Just think about it."

"I am thinking about it. The reason our company almost went under is because no one was doing anything. The reason that they hired me at the new company is to work with their five-thousand people and bring on another twenty thousand because our company isn't doing shit. So if you think what you did and what we did entitles us to future income, you're all wrong. It's all going to be brand-new people. I'll just tell you that right now. It was our people who almost put us under. It was people pushing plug-and-play systems that don't work...and Donny quitting."

"And why did Donny quit?" I asked quietly.

"I don't know."

"Yes, you do."

"No, I don't because, goddamnit, he wouldn't tell me."

Neither of us said a word. Donny Walker was special to both of us. He was our first distributor. Having him leave, for me, signaled the death of our company.

I took a few more seconds to formulate my words. "If a new company is going to succeed, the one thing that you and Val and John and I believed (and I'm leaving Randy out of this because I don't think he ever held this value) is that things had to be founded on very, very high principles. We built this company on truth and ethics."

"That's right."

"Donny left because he could no longer believe things being said by the corporate team. And if the new company is going to get off the ground, it can't be that you, John, Val, and Randy take care of yourselves and forget everybody else's well-being. Right or wrong, good or bad, ATG had a place in the company, IHI had a place, Rene Yarnell had a place in the company *and* in the downline. And unless you honor that, you are going to screw up the new deal."

"Yeah, well, we'll see. If we're fortunate, we'll get our money back. If not, I'll lose the house and everything else."

"*We'll* lose the house and everything else." Mark had not yet succeeded in getting the house refinanced. My name was still on the note. I still owed half of all our debts.

We hung up agreeing that he would get back to me on this later. I sat looking out of my window overlooking the city. How could two people who loved each other as much as we had come to this low point in our dealings with each other? Was it desperation driving Mark to this? Undoubtedly, the influence of Randy, now the High Priest of Global Network, was clearly at work.

I called Ted Elias for reassurance. He indicated that Randy was still dragging out the negotiations. He had no control over the downline situation. It was all being handled by the Legacy attorneys. In early November when I'd first met with Ted, I had such hope. I believed that this merger or acquisition would solve innumerable challenges facing us. It would save our company, preserve Mark's pride, offer our distributors a home, and give all the investors, including us, a return on our investment. I never needed any thanks for the part I played. But neither did I expect to be shoved aside.

It was time that I face some realities. My financial situation was a disaster. Between our house and our company debts, we owed several million dollars. We were so deeply indebted that if this venture failed, I didn't know how we would ever pay back our creditors. And based on this conversation, my hope for the future of our company was deteriorating quickly. It was a house built on sand.

I was determined not to let myself be beaten down by this new turn of events. The next day, I refocused my attention on my book. Thinking about company issues could only tie me to the past. Working on the book was leading me into the future. I had set up interviews with dozens of people within the industry. I recorded them over the phone and, with the help of Antonette, my former secretary who did all the transcribing, I began editing them and finding just the right place where each interview fit in the book. The only thing concerning me was that Charles wasn't coming through with his part. He was being called in as an expert witness in the Amway vs. Proctor and Gamble case, and it was taking hours of his time day after day and week after week.

By the time I saw Charles in February when I arrived to teach our UIC Certificate Seminar, I had finished my half of the book. I was prepared to keep going but knew that I needed to resolve this with him while we were together. This was my first public appearance since Mark and I had ended our marriage. That would be challenging enough. But Mark was also coming in to deliver the keynote address for the opening night. I wasn't sure I was up for it.

The night of the dinner, we were placed at opposite ends of the head table, like two rooks on a chessboard. I don't think any of the participants knew about our divorce, so we both flowed with it. Minutes before Mark was to deliver his talk, he got up from his seat, made his way behind the length of the head table, and bent down on his knees in a near proposal posture. I couldn't imagine what he was going to say.

"Hey, do you mind if I borrow the story about having only 'five months to live'?"

"No, go for it. I'm not using that one anywhere in the course."

"You look great, by the way," he said with his boyish grin. He seemed hyper, but he was often that way. For just that moment, it was the old Mark. What was new and somewhat surprising to me was his sharing openly with the class, "One thing I have learned is that I am *not* a businessman."

As the Amway court case continued, Charles and I kept reaching new agreements about the extent of his contribution to our book project. From writing half the book, to a quarter, to two chapters, we finally settled on his doing the foreword. Although I felt let down by him, with each gradation, I kept Prima informed. None of this seemed to concern anyone there until Charles's decision to do only the foreword. Three weeks before I was to submit the entire first draft, I received a call from Susan Silva, my primary connection at the publishing company.

"Rene, I have some bad news. This isn't the manuscript we were expecting, and we have decided to 'can' the book."

I felt traumatized. I didn't know what to say. As far as I knew, our current book was their second bestseller, having only been outsold by Richard Poe's *Wave Three,* which had been out a couple of years longer. Why would they want to abort my book?

"Susan, you have only seen the first three chapters. There are sixteen chapters in all, and the first fourteen are ready for submission. Why would you make this decision before seeing the rest of what I have?"

"We don't make decisions like this easily. But our committee has met, and the decision is final."

Writing this book is what had kept me going these past five months. Every rug in my life had been pulled out from under me. Now this one too? There I was facing that feeling of abandonment again—first from Charles and now from the publisher. *I will learn this lesson this time. I'm sick of letting myself feel forsaken by everyone. There is a reason this is happening. There is something better just waiting. All I have to do is take the next step toward making it happen.*

The phone rang. It was Frank. Ah, my guardian angel. He dropped what he was doing and came right over. We poured ourselves each a glass of wine and sat watching the sun go down as we talked about what might have led to this.

"Why would they do that? Do they think you didn't really write the other book or that you didn't contribute your share?"

"No, that can't be it. Susan, especially, knows the full extent of my involvement. During the second and final month that we were working on *Your First Year,* Susan didn't know where Mark was, but she knew he wasn't accessible. And despite his being in recovery all during August, I submitted a chapter a week. She knows I kept it going during a highly stressful time."

"Is this publisher a chauvinist?"

"I think he could be."

"So that's it. It's not your writing ability. It's that you don't have a male co-author. Without a Mark or a Charles, they think you can't cut it."

I thought about what he was saying. That is the only explanation that made any sense. People find motivation from a lot of different causes. Once I thought I understood the reason for dumping my book, it made me just mad enough to kindle a fire in my belly. I was three weeks from submitting it for editing. No way was I going to let the bastards get me down. It was Friday night. There was one publisher I could turn to over the weekend.

I called my friend, Werner Reifling, who owned his own publishing company. He had made millions publishing Art Bell's books. His friend, Jennifer, was the daughter of one of my friends. I told him what had happened.

"Who the hell has ever heard of Charles King? He wouldn't be the one I'd want. If I were branching into the world of network marketing, I would want a known commodity, preferably someone who had already successfully published and proven herself. Rene, they have to be crazy not to want you."

He made me feel good regardless of where we went with this. "Thanks, Werner. I seem to be going through a phase these past six months where I'm not feeling really wanted by a lot of people. You know, husbands, partners, publishers, co-authors. I just seem to be striking out."

"So what do I have to do to get you?"

"Just tell me that you love me," I faked in a sexy voice. "Seriously, what I really need to know is that you have the time to move on this right away. I can publish. I know how. I just don't want to. I want to be the writer and work with a publisher who will oversee the mundane tasks and keep the project moving in a timely fashion. I have my whole professional future riding on this book. I need it to come out this year."

"This is great timing for me. I have just finished another project. As you know, Mark's book was supposed to be done by now, but it still isn't ready. So if you come in with a finished product, you will be my first priority."

I hadn't thought about Mark's book until he mentioned it. "Do you foresee that as a problem? Representing both of us on our respective books?"

"No, I will just treat you both as professionals. Why should there be a problem?" He was right. Why should there be? Werner and I worked out our terms. We agreed that I would have the first draft to him by April 9, and he would release the book in July. That was a month earlier than Prima had projected. I loved it. It took all of 24 hours to put the aborted project back on track. On Monday morning, I called Prima to inform them that I was going forward with the book. At their request, I agreed to let them keep the title. That was a good title, but not the only good one. Certainly we could come up with a new title. Selecting a title is usually more the publisher's job than the author's, anyway.

Charles called. He sounded remorseful to have caused this. He promised that he would still write the foreword and said if I needed any help regarding problems over the title, just let him know.

My attorney began receiving communication from Randy Calvert about the transfer of our company over to the new company, Legacy USA. By waiting so long, the number of our distributor force had dropped at least in half. If this merger was going to take place, it needed to have happened by early January at the latest. My last conversation with Mark had taken my spirit out of what was left in the company and its future. After sound legal advice, I offered my so-called partners the freedom to remove me from the distributorship I shared with them if, in turn, they would formally take my name off all remaining debts left owing in the company. If 21st Century Global Network succeeded under the new flag, it was probably the worst decision I could make. If the company failed, it was, by far, the best decision. I had lost faith, so, for me, it was the right decision.

By March I had completed almost all of the interviews. I just needed time to pull everything together. Missy and I and another friend had planned a celebration trip to Hawaii this month. I had expected to be finished with the book, but as it turned out, I was in my final stage.

"You need this time away, Rene. You've been under terrible stress. And what better setting to work on your book!"

"You've not exactly been lying in a bed of rose petals

yourself. This will be good for both of us to have a change of environment," I rationalized. "And it will be good to be able to spend time with you."

We rented a cute little two-bedroom condo right on the beach. For the next week, I developed my routine, much the same as if I were home. I crawled out of bed trying not to wake Missy, and began my day around 4:00 in the morning. I worked non-stop until night, shutting down only to join my roommates for lunch and dinner. Once I even made it out to the beach with them for a relaxing afternoon. I saw a huge school of dolphin and a whale heading south to deliver her young. I was extremely happy writing in this setting. The weather was beautiful. I was with friends, and could enjoy the ocean all day long. Shortly after I returned home, the book was done. I turned it over to Werner and felt immense satisfaction.

Werner got together with the sales team who would be distributing the book and together they suggested the new title be: *The New Entrepreneurs: Network Marketing as the Emerging Profession for the 21st Century.* I liked it. That fit what I had written. It would cause Prima some concern—it was awfully close to my previous title—but titles were issues between publishers.

As I hung up the phone from talking to Werner, it rang again.

"Rene, it's Ted Elias."

"Ted, how's it going?" I noticed he bypassed my question.

"I'm here with my wife staying...with Mark at your house." He was referring to Windara. "What are you doing this evening? Can you join us for dinner?"

"I'd love to. I presume it's the three of us?"

"Yes," he chuckled. "I don't think Mark's quite ready for a foursome yet. How about meeting at the Silver Legacy?"

"You're just partial to the name," I teased. "You'll go anyplace with the name 'Legacy' in it."

Over dinner I learned that Mark had had another one of those—what for lack of a better term I call—brain-blocks. The difficulty was that it occurred in the middle of a meeting with Ted and the presidential team members present.

"Was Valerie there?" I asked, hoping there would be someone there for him.

"Yes, but she didn't budge from her seat. Actually, the only person who had the presence of mind to do anything was David Avery, Mark's protégé. The meeting broke up just before I called you, and we decided to come spend the evening here in town. Mark had plans this evening up in Incline." I doubted that, but I didn't say so. "So what's the story?" Ted probed. "Obviously, he has some kind of drug problem. But what is it?"

"Well, it's a long story but here's the short version. Mark became addicted to a prescription drug after a hang-gliding accident in the late 70s and has battled the problem ever since. For the past several years he was on a government-approved program that countered the craving but, to our surprise, turned out to be more harmful and more addictive than any prescribed pain medication he had previously been hooked on. Nearly two years ago, Mark chose to go through major treatment to terminate even this program but getting off *this* drug was nearly an impossible feat. He's up there with Betty Ford in my mind and has taken all the right steps to conquer this disease."

"I always admired Mark but hearing this makes me think even more of him."

"So what you're describing seems to be the aftermath of all of this. For that matter, I feel even our divorce is part of the aftermath. I've experienced a couple of similar incidents since he went through this last detox, but nothing quite like what you described. I don't know, Ted. I've been out of his life for some time now. But I believe Mark has made a valiant recovery from his drug habit and, to the best of my knowledge, he has it under control."

"Ted isn't likely to pass judgment on anyone," his wife spoke up. "If you think this was one of those rare occurrences resulting from all that he has been through, he'll just let it go."

"Yeah, I've been through enough of my own stuff that I wouldn't begin to judge someone else. I really like Mark. We get along well. More than anything, I was concerned about him," Ted explained.

"The couple of times I've witnessed one of these brain-blocks, I didn't understand it. I wished I had. But I don't think they are common occurrences. If it doesn't happen again, I'd let it go. If it does, maybe your relationship will be such that you can be there for him. You are lucky to have Mark as part of your team. He is a good person and an incredible motivator and recruiter."

We discussed the growth of the company and how things were going generally. After dinner, I drove them back to Windara. As we neared the top of the narrow road leading up to the house, we saw lights on downstairs. I let them off without going any further. As they walked to the door, someone opened it from the inside. At some risk, I began backing down the long winding driveway. It wasn't the time for me to be seen driving up to our house with the president of Mark's new company.

It had been six months since I moved out of this home. With my book in the hands of my publisher, I was feeling more self-assured. I was ready for the next step. I just didn't know what it should be. As has happened so often in my life, the answer came before I even asked the question. After seven years of leasing my home, my tenants phoned to announce they were moving out of state. My own home would be available to me next month. What timing! This dwelling was my rock of Gibraltar. It has been my residence off and on since 1982. It always came back to me just when I was in dire need of a home.

I recalled how my former husband, Jim Kavanaugh, and I bought this home 17 years ago as part of an agreement between us. We had had a tumultuous love affair in which he ended up leaving again and again. It wasn't the lack of loving each other that caused us anguish. It was his inability to commit. Consequently, we married each other three times: once in a civil union, then a pact on a high hill "ratified centuries ago by the sun that we would walk together through sunshine days and foggy nights," and finally a full sacramental wedding with his family and mine present.

Given our history, this third time around, I asked for only one thing: a home, in the event that if he ever left again, I would have a place to raise my son. He agreed and we bought and renovated our Reno home during the latter half of 1982. We lived there happily until '84, when Jim had the opportunity to pursue a professional dream, which required us moving to Santa Barbara to work there together. Seven months after getting down there, our new partnership fell through and our marriage was once again in jeopardy. But, worse, the promised home had been sold. I was devastated. Instead of having this home as a fallback, I found myself in a town where I knew no one, had just lost my job, would soon have no home there, had no plans for where to go, and was responsible for my eleven-year-old son. I felt lost and alone.

I remember walking out on our deck looking out over the ocean and praying: *Please, dear God, give me a sign. I need a really clear one that won't leave me wondering. Just let me know what it is I am supposed to do next. For my son's sake, don't let me flounder. I need to make a good decision and put our life on a track that will give both of us a sense of stability.*

It was about ten minutes later that the phone rang.

"Rene, I don't know if you remember me. I bought your home here in Nevada City five years ago."

"Yes, of course, I had almost forgotten that your balloon note is due about now." Just before moving to Reno, I had sold the home on nothing-down terms, a style that had become popularized in the late '70s.

"Well, I don't know how to tell you this..." *Ogod, more bad news! I don't know if I can handle anymore.* "...but I can't come up with the funds. I've been thinking about what to do for some time now, and all I could come up with is this: If it would be acceptable to you, I would just like to return your home to you. Under the circumstances, that seems the fair thing to do."

"Just give it back to me, I take over the payments again, and you walk away?" I reflected back to him, making sure that I grasped what he was proposing.

"That's what I was thinking."

"Give me a few minutes. I will call you right back."

I walked back out on the deck and looked up. I waited for the clouds to part and the voice to speak from the heavens, but it didn't happen. Looking out across the ocean again I prayed: *Okay, is this the sign? Dear God, is this IT? I can't afford to mess up this time. I have a little boy and can't just drag him all over the country. He needs a home and school and friends. He needs stability...and so do I. Please tell me now if this is not the sign. But if this is it, I am about to move us back to Nevada City. Oh, and thank you for responding so quickly.* I stood there in reflection for a few more minutes. A peacefulness came over me. Yes, it must be the right decision.

I phoned back and accepted the offer. Within a week, Chris and I were back in our former home in Nevada City. We were just in time to celebrate Halloween, one of his favorite holidays. He was thrilled to go trick-or-treating with all of his old buddies. But, best of all, Jim came with us. I knew for sure there was a God who loved us and was watching over us. Life was very, very good.

I should have been prepared for this after all the times it had happened, but somehow I never was. By Christmas, Jim left again. I was crushed. We were self-publishing his books, so with him went my job and source of income. After he drove away, I can remember walking out into the woods behind our home and, standing all alone, far from where I could be heard, I began crying out at the top of my lungs. *I trusted You. I put all of my faith in You, and look where it has gotten me. I moved here believing that I could bring stability into our lives. Now what? Where do I turn? What do I do? Oh God, what do I do? Whatever it is, this time I am doing it on my own.*

With little faith but strong determination, I left Chris with friends and headed for Reno. It was a bigger city, and I stood a much better chance of finding work and a life there. I stayed with friends while I once again searched for work, home, and a school for Chris. I was a guest in the home of my friend, Phyllis Blake, and we had stopped at the grocery store to pick up a few needed items.

"Rene. Rene Kavanaugh."

I heard my name called out. I looked around and there was Tom Reed, the man who had bought our Reno home, with his wife.

"What are you doing back in town? Where's Jim?"

"I just can't seem to stay away from Reno too long. I'm thinking of moving back...just Chris and me."

He gave me an empathetic look, but chose to let Jim's absence go. "That's incredible. We're in the process of moving back to California. We're going to have to put the house up for sale. Why don't you just buy it back?" I calculated the two nickels I had to rub together and knew they wouldn't buy my old home back. But just knowing that it was available tore my heart out. I could barely speak. Phyllis stayed on to visit with them. I excused myself. My heart was in my throat and words just wouldn't come.

A few minutes later Phyllis joined me out in the car. She had been the Realtor who had handled the sale two years earlier. So I assumed she was discussing the possibility of listing the house for them again. Instead she came back laughing.

"Okay, dry up. Stop blubbering. You need to really listen to me."

"Okay, I'm listening," I said meekly.

"They are moving to California, okay—to *Nevada City*, California." I could hardly believe what I was hearing.

I went for a walk outside of Phyllis's home when we got back. *Dear God, forgive me for not trusting You. I'll never doubt You again. I promise.* Had we not first moved to Nevada City, I would never have had the means to trade for my home in Reno.

It took only a month to transact the most unusual real estate deal in the history of trades. In 1985, the Reeds moved into my Nevada City dwelling, and Chris and I moved back into our Reno residence. We had come home and were settled in the place that had been promised me in 1982. And we did it without exchanging a dime.

Both times my marriage ended, this house appeared. So why should I have been surprised when in the spring of 1999 it should once again welcome me home? It was a sign of hope and my readiness for new beginnings.

I hired a moving service and began the dreaded task of moving out of the home I shared with Mark. The movers were late, and it was a tense time for both Mark and me. He seemed to be watching me as if I was about to steal some precious jewels. About every 15 minutes, I ran outside to cry. Sitting on top of a desk that had been plopped on our driveway, I was trying to get hold of my emotions when my cell phone rang.

"Ms. Yarnell, how in the world are you?"

I recognized the voice. John Fogg, founder of *Upline* magazine and soon-to-come *Network Marketing Lifestyles*, is the only person I know who addresses me that way. "John, I talk to you so rarely. You have an uncanny way of making those rare conversations come through at the most critical moments of my life."

"Well, my dear, what have I caught you doing?"

"Oh, just one of those typical days in the life of Rene Yarnell. I'm closing down my old life and getting ready to begin a new one. Today is moving day."

"Ah, I can see the headlines now: "Rene Yarnell moves from her palatial mountaintop estate overlooking the city of Reno to the simple neighborhood life." I started laughing through my tears.

"Good, I've got you in good spirits. I've done my job. By the way, tell Yarnell that he's letting the good one get away." I heard the click of the receiver. I knew I would be fine. Leaving the elegance of this home was the easy part. Leaving the memories was tearing me apart.

While the movers took a break, I walked around to the patio off the VIP guestroom overlooking the city one last time. I sat in one of the chairs and pulled my knees up to my chin as if holding myself together. I let my tears flow.

I could no longer think of this as a loss, for truly he was never mine to lose. "'Til Death Do Us Part" is really accurate, reflecting not so much physical death as the death of the relationship itself. At that moment, I wanted to scream out that I finally understood.

A new and exciting, but somewhat unsettling, view of relationships was emerging for me. We were merely on loan so that we could help raise each other to new heights. Our purpose was fulfilled—he had begun down a road of newfound freedom because of me, and I had so much more to give because of him. Perhaps, with the healing of time, we would find a new level of friendship. But, for now, it was time to let go of the hopes of what could no longer be.

Real love is transforming those selfish yearnings to desiring what is best for the other. Not "I long for you to stay because I need you," but "I am willing to let you go because I love you." Mark was teaching me this lesson. It's easy for me to get so hurt by his words and actions that I lose his message. Of course I understood that Mark had his own internal battles. And sometimes the war being waged within him spilled over onto me. But I was now able to look past that. Beyond the lifelong disease that inflicted him is a man filled with wisdom and love and generosity.

When he spoke of the kind of love of which C.S. Lewis has written, I believe that Mark was truly exercising such love in asking me for a divorce. I had no doubt that, like me, Mark had a wide assortment of reasons for wanting an end to our time together. Among his reasons, I could envision him facing the fact that his treatment in London had only brought him so far in his own quest for freedom from the addiction. Perhaps he had come to accept that he must go the rest of the way on his own. And, in that moment of choice, he released me to go the rest of the way on my own as I continue my own growth process. It is in coming to acknowledge our partners with the highest possible intentions that our own pain and sadness will finally go away. Choosing to remember the good and letting the rest go, I said my farewell. *Goodbye, sweetheart. You have meant more to me than you will ever know. You have given me so much that a part of you will always be with me. I have work to do, spiritual growth to realize, and lessons to share with others. It is time that I stand on my own now. With each passing day, I am feeling more whole and complete within myself. Thank you for sharing so much of yourself with me for these seven years. I love you.*

Chapter 20

SAYING GOODBYE
June 1999 – July 1999

P art of the process of bringing structure to our lives is getting the outer pieces of the puzzle in place first. Then, properly framed, we can begin to fill in the middle sections. My book represented the *foundation* that would lay the way for the future. Being back in my cozy home nestled in the trees on Rancho Manor Drive was literally the *roof* over my head that gave me a sense of belonging. With both of these in place, I was ready to create the structure of the life I envisioned, not walls that confined but flexible partitions that could be adjusted and serve as guideposts to keep me on track.

I had been asked to speak at a regional gathering in St. Louis that was being put on by a group of field leaders in the Excel Corporation, the network marketing company that sold long-distance phone service. Beyond teaching my University Seminar several months earlier, I had not been speaking, teaching, or making public appearances. I hadn't felt ready, but now I was eager to get back out on the circuit and introduce new information gathered from my research for the book. It was a good experience. I enjoyed seeing old friends: Brett Dabe, an Excel leader; Doug Firebaugh, a motivator in the industry; and, of course, my old friend John Fogg. So many people came up to talk and inevitably ask about Mark. I held up reasonably well in front of the crowds, but I still fell apart back in my room. *When would this ever end? What did I have to do to finally put Mark behind me?* When John was speaking from stage, he still referenced "Mark and Rene." *Will I always be linked to him in everyone's mind? How can I make the break and stand on my own?* I cautioned myself not to rush it. After all, this was the first time I was speaking publicly where people knew we were apart.

I stayed close to John during the social events because I felt shaky inside. We were driven by limo out to the home of Chris and Lorraine Gallagher, who were hosting a festive celebration after the full day of speakers.

"Thanks for sticking by me, John. I thought I was ready for this, but I'm not as ready as I thought."

"You're doing fine, lady. You're much more conscious of your being here without Mark than anyone else, believe me. You were always the better-looking half of the team anyway. What are you worried about?" he teased.

"It has been nearly a year now, and I am still falling apart over the mention of his name."

"It's your choice. You can change your mind and stop that whenever you want." *If I'm not choosing to get over it, what will it take?*

"It's as if I still haven't put closure to it. I think I've come such a long way this past year, and then someone like Doug says, 'How's Mark doing? How's he really doing?' and I become an emotional marshmallow."

"Do whatever you need to do so that you can get on with your life. You won't stay single long."

"Oh yes I will! At least from a legal perspective. I don't want to be in a relationship based on shared finances and legal bonds. But I do want to have someone in my life—someone I can be close to, someone who wants some of the same things I want, someone who wants to grow together. I do miss that."

"Well, he has to be someone who is worthy of you. And he's

going to have to answer to me if he doesn't treat you right." John loved playing the protector role with me.

"I am starting to feel ready for that again. But then I get out in one of these events, and I realize something is still incomplete. It's as if there is some missing step I haven't taken."

"So what is it? I'm sure you know."

"Well, I don't know for sure. But I'm here in Missouri, Mark's home state. His mom and sister live here, and I haven't talked to either of them since all of this happened. I just couldn't bring myself to face them. And even if I did, I didn't think I'd be able to find the words…without choking up."

"So, you choke up. Big deal."

"You're right. So what? I'm just feeling that it is time I contact them."

"Then do it."

The next day, I called Patsi's home. Mark answered the phone. Hearing his voice at the other end of the line literally rendered me speechless. I didn't expect to find him there. So I did something silly. I hung up. It had taken courage to make the call, and I didn't feel I could explain to Mark why I was calling his mother. But I needed to do this. I waited a couple of hours and called back, prepared to deal with the consequences. This time Mark's sister answered.

"Melissa, it's Rene."

"Omigod. How are you?"

"That's a loaded question, but overall, I'm doing much better. Thanks."

"Mark's here."

"I know. Why is he there?"

"Mom is in the hospital."

"Oh, I'm sorry. I didn't know."

"It's serious. She's in intensive care. She may not make it this time."

"Melissa, I had no idea. I was calling because…well, because I thought it was time. I felt I owed her some explanation."

"Mom really wants to talk to you too. She has picked up the phone to call you a dozen times, but she hangs up fearing she would look like the interfering mother-in-law."

"She'd never be that with me. Is she coherent?"

"In and out. She's been in the hospital for a week. You just never know what stage she is going to be in."

"Let me figure things out, and I will get back to you." Melissa gave me the name of the hospital, and we hung up.

I hadn't counted on this. I lay there thinking about what I should do. Something told me this was a consequential moment. I called Frank and told him the circumstances.

"Were you close to her?"

"Not in the sense that we saw each other that often, but we were close in those moments when we did communicate. Once a long time ago when Mark left me, he stayed with her. And she and I stayed in touch with each other."

"Trust your feelings about this being a necessary step in the process. It may be important for both of you."

"Something about the way Melissa sounded made me feel I should go there. It wasn't so much what she said as how she said it."

"Stay in touch. Let me know if there is anything I can do."

The next morning, I checked out of the hotel, rented a car, and headed for Branson. For a change, I was glad I was driving. It gave me time to think about what I wanted to say.

At the hospital, I parked and made my way to the information desk to find out her room number.

As I walked through her door, I found Patsi sitting up in a wheel chair on the far side of the room close to the window. Though only in her seventies, she looked older and frail. Her hair was even whiter than the last time I'd seen her.

"Sweetheart," she greeted me. "I knew you'd come." I was surprised and pleased to see her so alert. I leaned over and we prolonged our hug.

"Where's Mark?" I asked hesitantly.

"He went back this morning." What a relief. He had been

one reason I was reluctant to come. I knew he wouldn't approve or even understand. "We have a lot to talk about. I've been holding my questions in for a long time. I'm so glad you're here. Come sit down." She pointed to a chair nearby. "Honey, what happened?" With the last question, she had that same furl on her brow that I have seen so many times on Mark's.

I began to explain about starting the company, the pressures, the partners, not enough funding, and our different perspectives about it all. Patsi listened intently before she finally spoke.

"When Mark called to tell me you were splitting, it crushed me more than I wanted to admit. I knew at a heart level that you were good for him."

"We were good for each other, Patsi. And we did some good for other people, especially in our industry. We made a good team, he and I."

"I took your separation hard—harder than I probably should have—but I felt so much hope for Mark since you came into his life. He and I were out of sorts over it. And that rarely happens. When he started telling me about all of your faults and how you had caused this breakup, I shut him out. All of his life, it has been someone else's fault."

"I hope you've both gotten past that."

"Yes, we did during this visit. He seemed a lot less frenetic. I sensed almost a calmness about him."

"I'm glad. That hasn't been a state Mark has ever achieved easily."

"We had a good visit yesterday and another this morning before he left. We made our peace with each other." Patsi began telling me stories about Mark as a little boy and how he had never really changed. "I couldn't control him then, and I still can't today. He marches to his own drummer, for sure. But he has always been so excited about whatever was happening in his life."

"I loved him, Patsi. And I grew to love that excited little boy part of him even more over the years."

"I know you did, honey. I could see it in your eyes. But even more, I could see that he loved you too. More than all the rest." I felt that was true, but it meant so much coming from her.

"He won't ever grow up, Patsi, but that's part of his charm. We faced some demons in his life together and made some headway dealing with them."

"Yes, you did, and I can see the difference it has made in him."

"What I most want you to know is that your son was a good husband to me. We had a few challenges, but who doesn't? Although, the last year was hellacious, there were reasons for it. But for six of the seven years we had together, we were pretty happy. We were loving and supportive to each other. We touched the lives of literally hundreds of thousands of people in the network marketing world. Mark helped me grow as a person. He encouraged me to write and pushed me out on stage to speak. Writing and speaking are my life work now, and I owe all of that to him."

"Thank you for telling me that. He has given me a lot of heartburn over the years. But he has filled my life with joy and surprises too. He has been a good son. I wouldn't be honest, though, if I didn't tell you that I would feel better for him if you were still together—maybe better for him than for you."

"I understand. I felt that way too until just recently. But I have accepted what is. Maybe more than accepting. I feel I am supposed to move on from Mark."

"I'm sure I can't understand it all. But I understand at least one part of why you are saying that. Mark is a promise-maker, but he's not a promise-keeper. That has been his lifelong struggle. Until he comes to grips with that part of himself, his life will always be in turmoil. This has caused a lot of pain to a lot of people." She didn't say this judgmentally but with such passion that I wondered what was behind her words.

"One thing I believe about him, when he makes those promises, he means them from the depths of his soul. I know with absolute certainty that Mark meant our wedding vows. He intended to keep every single word of what he promised."

"So what do you think happened?"

"I probably don't have to tell you how much time I've spent thinking about that. I've looked at it from both sides. As much as I can understand, Mark lives in a world of his own making, a world that can be arbitrarily enhanced or diminished with a variety of different highs: Flying, running off mountains with only a paraglider for protection, taking financial risks—all of that keeps his adrenaline pumping. He seems to be on a mission to sustain life as an all-time permanent high. But remember when he went through the treatment program in London?"

"Yes, of course. We talked on the phone when you got back to your home in Switzerland. He could barely talk."

"He could barely function for the first month. I believe going through such extreme detox was the hardest thing Mark has ever done. But it changed him, and it changed us forever."

"How, sweetheart? I mean how did it cause your marriage to fail?"

"It ended, but I don't believe it failed.... You see, in the beginning I was one of his addictions. He loved me more than life itself. I'm sure he loved me. I was almost an obsession. It was different for me. My love for him started out slower; then it grew and deepened over the years. All things considered, we did pretty well. But after so many years, our initial 'high' of new love gradually lost its momentum and became a 'low.' And when the lows hit, that was a signal to his brain that it was time to pop another pill or find a new mountain to run off or a bigger thermal to ride...or take the risk of starting a new company. But once all traces of drugs were completely cleansed from his body, he had no resource to fall back on, no way to get back up to another high when life took a downturn."

"You know, he was like that as a little boy too. He was always looking for ways to stay 'up' especially when things weren't so great at home. And when he couldn't, he would sort of bury his head in the sand. Mark's life has always gone from one exciting adventure to the next," said Patsi.

"Sometimes I think when Mark sees real things, he tends to

see them as downers. Dealing with life the way he does, he chooses to focus mostly on the highs, and, overall, this trait seems to have served him well. It has given him a special gift to help others believe in themselves and realize that anything is possible."

"I just wish for him that he could stay the long haul with something...or someone." She looked at me with a knowing glance and emphasized her last two words.

"But like you said, even when he was younger he saw things the way he chose to see them. The fact that sometimes life changes from the way he originally experienced it or wanted to see it means that it doesn't warrant his continuing with it because people or circumstances let him down.

"Not that *he* let them down?" she inquired.

"No, life is supposed to be always 'up' in his world. He believes people and projects are supposed to be bigger than life. At least, that's how I see his mind working."

"So when he doesn't stick with something or follow through on what he said he would do, it is because the conditions changed," she reasoned. "And if *they* change, then he feels he is no longer obligated."

"I think so." My thoughts drifted back to how this applied to our co-venture partners. "The part that I had the most difficulty understanding was his determination to keep his promise to our partners when, in fact, the conditions really *did* change. They didn't deliver on their promises. And yet Mark stayed with his commitment regardless of their inability to come through."

"Well, that fits his pattern, doesn't it, sweetheart?"

"How? I'm having trouble seeing that part."

"Well, he couldn't let the company fail. So to keep his positive attitude about it, he had to see everything as stable—his commitment to the partners as well as their commitment to him. Seeing the conditions as changing implied the company could go down, and that simply wasn't an option," Patsi reasoned.

"Hmm. I never saw that before. I think I get it. I do understand that succeeding and being loveable are linked together for Mark. When I stopped sharing his belief that he and he alone could make our company successful, to him that meant that I didn't love him anymore. But I wonder if I had understood what you just said at the time...well, if there was anything I could have done about it."

"Probably not, honey. But you could still do something about it now."

"No, that isn't possible, Patsi. It really is over between us. I appreciate all that we had together and I always will. But going back isn't an option for either of us. He is already on his quest to find the next high in life so he can ride it. I'm just afraid he will always believe that the newness of the high is supposed to last, and he will always be let down and surprised when it doesn't."

"You know, honey, I think you're right. I know my son pretty well. But you've helped me see him from a new angle."

"I'm glad. You've helped me too. You see, what is so lovable about Mark is that his desire for the highest of everything isn't just for himself. He sees the world and everyone in it as having 'unprecedented magnitude.'" I imitated Mark's body language when I said this. "What you've helped me see is that his promises are always within the context of his reality and as long as that reality holds, he will keep his word. It is only when that reality dissipates...."

"Can I get you anything, Mrs. Yarnell?" a nurse asked from the door.

"Yes, I would like a sleeping pill." Patsi turned back to me.

"Honey, I'm glad that you came. I feel so much better about it all now. Why don't you find Melissa and catch up with her? When I wake up, the three of us will have some girl talk."

I helped Patsi get back into bed and pulled the sheet over her. We chatted until she drifted off. Sadly, that was the last coherent conversation we were able to have. Her communication gradually dwindled to a few syllables: pill, doctor, water. I felt blessed to have had this time with her. I was clearly led here by a Power outside of myself.

I sat watching her for a while. It wasn't long before Melissa appeared at the door. "They told me downstairs that her daughter was here. I knew it wasn't me, so it had to be you," she laughed. We hugged, and stood back and looked at each other.

"You look better than I expected you to look. But pretty thin," she exclaimed.

"You know, the old divorce diet."

"Did you get to talk to Mom? How is she?" she asked with concern.

I described how I found her and briefly touched on our conversation.

"Mom needed that, more than you will know. It had been bothering her that she hadn't talked to you."

"Obviously it had been bothering me too. But I accomplished one of my goals. I got through the whole conversation without tears. I really wanted to be strong when I spoke to Patsi. I don't mind blubbering in front of you, but I wanted to be composed for her."

"How long has Mom been asleep?"

"She just drifted off a few minutes ago. She'll be a while."

"Let's go grab a cup of coffee down in the waiting room." Stopping first to tell the nurse's station where we were, Melissa poured our coffee and we sat down on the couch.

"I'm not sure where to begin—maybe with congratulating you and Pat on your marriage."

"Thanks. We were planning to come out to Reno last fall and I tried to get a hold of you or Mark, but I couldn't find you."

"That's about the time we were in the worst of our trauma. First he was in the house, then we were, then I was, then he was. We were playing musical house for a while trying to find a less stressful way to deal with all that we had to face." I filled her in on the story from my perspective, just as I had done with Patsi.

"What a disaster!"

"You know Mark," I sighed. "You can see why he would want to be the one to save the day."

"Oh, yeah. That's my brother. Once he sets his sight on something, it's not within his consciousness to accept that he can't conquer it." *How well I knew.* "At the same time that you were going through your trauma, I was having my own back here. It was all coming down on me just as Pat and I had decided to get married. It couldn't have happened at a worse time." We refilled our coffee as she continued. "When you guys were sending me money every month so that I could take care of Mom, I didn't realize it was considered income and that I was the one responsible for paying taxes on it. To make a long story short, the IRS made a big stink about it and started sending me threatening letters. I contacted Mark in a bit of a panic and he, of course, said not to worry. He promised to take care of it." *How many times had I heard that? "Don't worry, Rene and I will take care of it" to Larry and Graham. "Don't worry, Rene and I will cover you" to Val and John.* "But," Melissa continued, "I wouldn't hear from him. Then more threatening letters from Internal Revenue, finally saying that I was going to go to jail if I didn't begin to make some kind of payment."

I thought back to my conversation earlier with Patsi. I understood better now where she was coming from in reference to Mark not keeping his promises. "I didn't know about any of that. It must have been going on while I was down in Santa Cruz. But I will tell you this—if there were any way that Mark could have pulled that money out of a hat for you, he would have. And, absolutely, he believed that he would *eventually* find a way. So rather than admit to you that he was living one of the worst nightmares of his life, he kept up the bigger-than-life big brother routine. What you couldn't have known is that we had partners who needed him to pull money out of another hat, and he was feeling enormous pressure to save you and save our company."

Melissa's eyes opened wide as if for the first time seeing her brother in a new light. "Pat and I had set our wedding date but we put our relationship to the ultimate test before we got married. I turned to him for help, and he bailed me out days before the final date set by the IRS."

"So, you got married instead of going to jail? Not your everyday fairytale ending, but it works." We laughed and gave each other a hug.

"Let's go check on Mom," she said as she began to stand up.

We headed back into the room and chatted about her condition. "Mom wants to die. Now I have this ongoing battle with Mark, like it is my job to keep her alive." *There is Mark again seeing life as he wants to see it in its highest and best form.* "One of the reasons he was out here just now is that I insisted on it. I told him he needed to deal with this directly and not vicariously through me."

"How did it go?"

"Well, actually, really well. He and Mom got things worked out between them. I think he left feeling peaceful about her and about himself in relation to her."

"Wow! Then that was worthwhile." As she nodded in agreement, I noticed the fatigue in her eyes.... Hey, you really look tired, Melissa."

"I am. I have been here every night for the past week."

"Can I give you a break? Why don't you go home to your family tonight and I'll stay here."

"Oh, Rene, I would really appreciate that." We chatted for a while and then, after checking and rechecking on her mom, Melissa hugged me and thanked me as she left for home.

I settled into a recliner chair with a blanket and pillow. It reminded me of my stay with Mark when he was in the hospital in London. I was up and down during the night when Patsi would call out for something: water, pill, nurse. We developed sign language when she was too groggy to speak.

When morning came, I was working on my laptop, writing, of course. The phone rang. I expected it to be Melissa so I answered it quickly before it woke Patsi.

"Ms. Yarnell," I heard a familiar male voice say.

"Yes."

There was an awkward pause and then he said, "Mom?" It was Mark on the other end of the line, and there was no way out of this for me. So I decided to play it lightly. "No, this is the other Ms. Yarnell."

After a moment for him to take that in, he asked quietly, "What are you doing there?"

"It's a long story, but I was nearby giving a talk. When I called and learned that your mom was in the hospital, I came."

"Can I talk to her?"

"She's sleeping. She's been sleeping pretty steadily since late yesterday afternoon. But I'll try to wake her...."

"No, that's okay. Where's Melissa?"

"She should be here any moment I would think. But you can try to catch her at home if you want."

"No, just tell her I called. I'll call back." He didn't say anything more about being glad or mad I was there. I didn't know what he was feeling, but I'm sure what was on his mind was his mother's impending death.

Melissa arrived soon after, and I caught her up on how Patsi was during the night and that Mark had called.

Patsi woke up. She was dazed and not very communicative, but we visited with her as best we could. There was a flurry of nurses and room checks and bath activities. I took a drive into downtown Branson and left Melissa alone with Patsi so they could have some personal time. When I returned, Melissa seemed anxious to talk.

"Well, it's done. Mom couldn't talk much, but she asked me if I was okay. Then she said she wanted to know so that she could let go. I'm waiting for the doctor to come, and we'll pull everything allowable this afternoon." Her throat was quivering but she didn't break down. She is a Yarnell. Yarnells don't cry easily.

"Have you talked it over with Mark?"

"Not yet. I'm dreading that part."

"It will be hard for him," I said more to myself than to her. I had lived with Mark through the death of his father and now, soon, his mother. He lived with me through the death of my father. The milestones of life. "Will Mark agree to pulling the plugs as your Mom has requested?"

"He agrees in theory. It's just hard to really do it."

Soon the doctor arrived and the order was given. For a long while, Melissa stood on one side of her bed and I on the other. We stroked her, held her hand, and gave her sips of water. She looked up and smiled once in recognition.

We walked over and stood looking out the window together.

"I'm really glad you came...regardless of how Mark feels."

"I'm glad I did too. It was almost as if Patsi waited for me. I'm beginning to feel some closure about the Yarnell part of my life now. That was missing before I came. I wasn't ready to move on yet. Something was still holding me back."

"Do you think you'll ever marry again?"

"A friend asked me that recently. No, I don't think so. Not unless we could totally redefine marriage, but that's going to take a while. Don't misunderstand. I want someone in my life. But I don't want the confinements of marriage. I think the way it is set up in society today, marriage tends to make cripples out of women and burdens men with responsibilities that tie them down their whole lives. Both partners would gain so much more from their relationship if they came into it respecting what each has to offer and supporting each other's growth. Instead of him being responsible for their source of income and she being dependent on him for it, each one becomes accountable for his or her own support."

"So the distinction you are making is mainly financial."

"That's only part of it. It seems to me that financial self-sufficiency or dependency has a lot to do with a person's self-efficacy. Did Mark ever mention a man by the name of Albert Bandura to you?"

"No."

"About a year or so after your dad passed away, Mark attached himself to this man much like a father figure. He wrote a book, a very deep, scholarly work, called *Self-Efficacy*. The word refers to people's effectiveness, how they value themselves, and how their success is based on their own competence and belief in themselves. Well, I've come to believe that financial self-sufficiency is the first step toward self-belief and self-confidence. Keep finances and legalities out of marriage. If there is a want or need for that kind of support, make it a separate agreement but not part of the reason for the relationship. That would free the couple up so they could come together as two equals who want to share their lives, achieve some things independently or together, and support each other's growth on all levels—personally, professionally, but most of all, spiritually."

"You've done a lot of thinking about this," Melissa mused.

"I hope to do a lot more thinking about it. This whole question of marriage is the subject of my next book. I'm tired of seeing the ending of a relationship equated to its failure. Mark and I didn't have a failed marriage. As far as I'm concerned, along with the usual ups and downs, we had a wonderful relationship for six of the seven years we were together. This is what I came here to share with your mom. I wanted her to know that Mark was a good husband to me. Despite whatever he is saying right now, I know he loved me and I him, and nothing will ever change that. Circumstances arose that led to us going our separate ways. Our life together is over now; but, believe me, it was anything but a failure."

"I can see my brother's growth in the time he has been with you. He was different this visit. I enjoyed being with him more than I have in past times."

"Melissa, that is the best thing you could possibly say to me right now. I needed someone who really knows him to confirm that. I believe it, but hearing it from you and your mom makes it all worthwhile. I know exactly the areas where Mark has enhanced my life. But it also helps to hear how I have improved his. He may not have whipped all of his addictions. He may even substitute something else, hopefully less harmful, but I would be surprised if he ever fell back to a dependency on prescription drugs or alcohol again. He will never know how much I admire him for his victory over this."

"Mark seemed clean when he was just here. And I would know."

"This may sound crazy, Melissa, but being here has made me realize something. Closure is really important. In the same way a funeral or wake is needed for the family after the death of a loved one, I think that something similar is needed after the ending of a relationship. I mean, why not? We have a ceremony to begin it. Why not one to end it? This time of being with you and Patsi has served that need for me. It has definitely brought closure to my Yarnell life. I am not going to leave here the same as when I came." Tears were running down my cheeks. But I didn't feel sad—I felt uplifted. Melissa, a few inches taller than me, put her arm around my shoulder and I put mine around her waist. We stood looking out the window together.

The phone rang. It was Pat, Melissa's husband. "He'll be over soon. I'm anxious for you to meet him. And you won't recognize Travis. He has grown a foot since you saw him last."

Pat and Melissa's son, Travis, arrived together. Patsi slept through it. I asked Travis how he was dealing with his grandmother's illness. He let me know that he had come to accept death as part of the process of life, but that it hurt. *That seems like a fairly sophisticated response for a teenage boy who had never faced death before.*

Again the phone rang, and this time it was Mark. While he was talking to Pat, a Catholic priest showed up at the door. He was looking for someone else and seemed to have come to the wrong room. Of course, I knew he had come to the right room when out of nowhere, he asked, "So does anyone need me here?"

"Yes," I said without hesitating. "My mother-in-law is in her final stage."

He stepped into Patsi's room. With the phone call to Mark continuing and the soft din of conversation in the background, he began reading the ritual for the Sacrament of the Sick. I answered on Patsi's behalf and mine. Father concluded with the words, "May the God of all consolation bless you in every way. May the compassionate Lord fill your heart with peace and lead you to eternal life. Amen." It took only a few minutes, but I felt complete closure...for her sake and for my own.

Mark told Pat that he wanted to return to Branson with Amy and expressed frustration over my presence here. Given the circumstances, it seemed best that I leave. My reasons for coming had been accomplished. I said my goodbyes to all of them and, leaning over, kissed Patsi on the cheek and whispered my farewell to her. Late that night, I headed back for St. Louis.

Back in Reno again, it seemed that I was coming home to begin a new life. I was really ready now. Frank stopped by and, sitting on my back deck, I caught him up on all that happened during my visit with Mark's family.

"You seem different. It shows in your body language and in your eyes."

"I've *neva, neva* felt more at peace than I do right now," I said mimicking him. "Something important happened there. I do feel that I ended a chapter of my life and am now able to open myself to the next one."

"Remember that conversation we had months ago when we drove to Incline Village and had lunch?"

"Yeah, we talked about what kind of a relationship I wanted next, something more akin to a spiritual partnership."

"That was an enthralling concept. I'm just wondering where you are with that today."

"Melissa and I talked about this too. I know that I don't want to be married in the traditional sense again. God knows I've tried that enough. Like so many, I was raised with the belief and the dream of a one-man, one-woman relationship wherein each would fulfill the other in all aspects of their lives until death separates them. That is no longer my fantasy."

"So if not that, then what?" he asked. I thought about the question and sipped my wine before answering.

"I'd like to believe that I am becoming a strong, wise, sensitive, and mature woman who has finally discovered some things about life. I have stopped asking the question: What is wrong with me that I can't have a long-lasting relationship? Certainly I no longer equate the ending of my marriage with failure. I have ceased finding fault with myself in my lifelong quest to find love. I am replacing the old questions with new ones: What is it that life is directing me to do? Where am I being led next, and who will be with me on this new journey? Most of us, I especially, have lived our lives as if the outcome was all that mattered. Everything short of a 'happily-ever-after' fairytale ending is written off as failure. What I am coming to understand is that life *is* the journey. The hardest lesson I have ever had to learn, and one I am still learning, is to appreciate the moment-to-moment happenings and live fully in the now. What I so often do in a relationship is focus my energy on the end result—how I want it to come out—and I miss out on some of the joy of the process. Whatever lies ahead for me now, I know I am being guided to do my life's work and to live the life I was meant to live."

"I see you growing...getting in touch with your true self. It seems to appear and express itself in just about everything you say and do, but especially your teaching and your writing. You know, Rene, you *are* living your life purpose now."

"Yes, I know I am. I realize that life is not about breaking any record or climbing a higher mountain. It is simply about being better than we were before. And I am conscious that the people I attract into my life will be those who are striving for this too. Those friendships that are based on helping each other through our search for growth and personal enhancement are the ones that I see becoming primary relationships in my life now."

"It sounds like your vision is a communal one. I can see how that might work for me, but you? And what about intimacy? Where does this fit in?"

"No matter who we are, we all need intimacy. Even those living a solitary, monastic life need it. I believe that intimacy is the deepest form of relationship possible—two people who are profoundly connected and, beyond their own directive, seem to have come together as if by divine ordinance to help each other touch the innermost core of their being. I used to believe that one and only one person was meant to be our soul mate in life. I have come to understand that those truly blessed with this rare form of intimacy need not feel limited to one person or even one form in a lifetime. Soul mates can come one after another or even two or more at the same time."

"There is nothing more precious in life than a spiritual bonding between soul mates. I read an article recently that describes intimacy as a sacred experience. It is the mystery of encountering another person," Frank explained.

"I like that. And one does not necessarily need to be sexual in order to be intimate. They are two clearly distinct characteristics of a relationship. I think you and I have an intimate relationship."

"I'm glad you feel that way. I know I do. You are very, very special in my life."

"I don't know what I would have done without you in mine this past year. You saw me through a really painful transition. As excruciating as ending a long-term relationship can be, I will always opt to have loved intimately and to the fullest during the time we were given."

"That's what the Gospel message is all about. You know, marriage began as a pagan event. It may have been to further validate women's subservient role to their husbands. Your idea of spiritual partnership as celebrating equality and commitment to each other's growth is magnificent, if not mind boggling with its implications. At the Vatican Council, marriage was presented as a commitment, not so much to physical security as to spiritual growth between two equals."

"Exactly. Gary Zukav touches on this in his book *Seat of the Soul*. He has developed some strong beliefs that I have just begun to discover on my own over the past year now."

"That's the book you shared with me on spiritual partnerships, isn't it?"

"Yes. He points out that marriage places emphasis on the couple's shared financial and physical union, while those in a spiritual partnership are more committed to their own and one another's spiritual growth. He often talks about how spiritual partners are assisting each other in the discovery of what he calls "their authentic power," which he describes as "the alignment of the human personality with the soul." When you think about it, every hour of every day, we are confronted with choices, and each one is an impulse to follow one avenue and not another. Gary points out that our authentic power is created choice by choice, and our growth can almost be measured by our awareness that we are making more responsible choices along the way. As we pay more attention to the consequences of our choices, they provide a glimpse into our own creative power. Doing the inner work on ourselves in the presence of someone doing the same leads us beyond ourselves to co-creation between spiritual partners."

"So how does he distinguish between married partners and spiritual partners?"

"Spiritual partners bring a different consciousness to the relationship. The couple mutually respects each other as equals and understands that their primary reason for being together is to enhance the development of each other's souls. I especially like the emphasis he places on trust, which he indicates is essential in a spiritual bonding—with the partners trusting most in their ability to grow together. Gary writes that this kind of intimacy can only work between two reasonably well-rounded, self-assured individuals who value each other's needs as much as their own. Because spiritual growth is their primary focus, they understand that they put the relationship more at risk if they don't express painful and sometimes difficult emotions to each other."

"That puts a major responsibility on each of them, doesn't it?"

"Absolutely. In fact, he goes so far as to say that spiritual partners are so committed to growing that they create a safe space to say the things that really need to be said but they can't be afraid to say those things that they most fear would destroy the relationship. Spiritual partnership is all about helping each of them become conscious of the unconscious parts of themselves. Sharing these feelings with the intention of healing is part of building that sense of trust between the partners."

"That's fascinating. But where does all of that fit for *you*, love? What are you looking for in your life now?"

"I'm still trying to figure that out. I long for closeness but I want to make certain that I remain fully responsible for myself. I am on a mission seeking to reach way beyond those comfortable places I've settled into in the past. I find myself examining my intentions more carefully, really striving to be clear with myself about the purity of my motives before I speak or take action. I want to surround myself with people who have a shared desire to reach their creative pinnacles, whether it is appreciating the beauty of our surroundings; making an impact on our world; reaching out to love those who come into our lives with a genuine desire to help them reach their highest potentials. And I believe I am capable and perhaps even have the need of experiencing this kind of spiritual partnership with more than one person."

"And what if one of your intimate relationships or spiritual partnerships should become sexual? And by that I'm referring to the real meaning of the word: a body, psyche, spirit reality."

"Hmm, I guess I would embrace that expansion cautiously and extremely selectively. To me, human sexuality is a mystery in so many ways. Why are we drawn to one and not another? And how do we attach a definition to it when, in reality, a glance can be sexual? Holding hands and touching in a soft and gentle way can be sexual. Embracing, dancing, even thoughts can be sexual, while the act of intercourse itself can be a mechanical, programmed response. I don't have all the answers, but given this wide range of understanding, I can see myself becoming close to people on more than one level but reserving my deepest, most intimate sexuality for one other person."

"At our very core, the whole build up and release of the human sexual nature is symbolic. It is nothing more than the pull of our bodies wanting to become one with our spirit," Frank philosophized. "There is an article I will share with you that describes this beautifully." Frank was always bringing me readings and tapes. I was conscious at that moment how much I loved him; how much I loved his mind and our ability to have these kinds of discussions.

"When I think about what it is I want in this next phase, I feel the influence of Teilhard de Chardin, who wrote and taught so beautifully about life as a series of concentric circles. The innermost core consists of the intimate spiritual bonding in my life. Traditionally, this has always been limited to one person, and probably will be for most people. But for me, at this stage of my life, I see this inner core made up of more than one person with whom I am in soul-mate relationships." I was deeply engrossed in this thought process as I attempted to describe it to him. "Just beyond that circle, still very close in," I continued, "are those relationships with a carefully chosen group of family and special friends. Beyond that, I have circles made up of more casual friends who share in my life on a variety of levels. Beyond that, I have the larger circle of the world of acquaintances, mentors, students, teachers, readers, and all those who touch my life as I touch theirs."

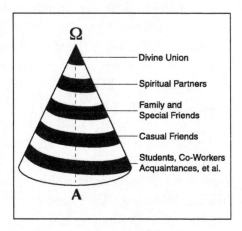

"That is beautiful. You weren't that clear the first time you brought this subject up several months ago."

"No, I wasn't. My vision is evolving...still is. The question that keeps coming up for me is, when all is said and done, how do we measure our life? I believe mine will be evaluated from the outside in with each extension of circles. As I consciously begin my journey— the alpha point **A**—my life will be measured by the lives I've touched and the seeds I've planted in that outer sphere; the kindness I've shown during those informal and relaxed moments spent with casual friends; the support and love shared with my family and a few special friends; and, most especially, the depth of my close spiritual relationships. At the end of my life—the omega point Ω—all of this will ultimately lead to the evolution of my soul becoming one with God."

"I read something recently about the soul's connection to spirituality. It is the transcendence of the mind and heart to that which is greater than ourselves, whether it be God, nature, or the community. That seems to be where you are headed in your thinking. It certainly fits for me too. I feel proud to be a part of that inner spiritual circle of yours." Frank and I hugged goodnight, knowing that we truly were in each other's lives at this time to enhance our personal and spiritual growth.

Saying Goodbye

It was nearing time for the release of my book, but we were running into obstacles. My former publisher and my present one were having a standoff regarding the similarity of titles. Neither one would back off from ownership of their version. Charles was asked by Prima to be the co-author of our old title now with Jim Robinson (instead of me). As friends and business associates, the similarity of titles put the two of us in an uncomfortable place. I prevailed upon him to convince Ben to relent, but to no avail. No matter what position I took, the battle continued.

Further, despite his conviction that he would not face a conflict, my present publisher found himself caught in the middle between representing both Mark and me. Mark was concerned about our books coming out at the same time. In order to satisfy him, Werner began dragging his feet on getting mine out. Given the importance of this book to my career, that didn't please me. Finally, weighing all the facts and after much consideration, I took the book back and decided that I should walk my own talk. I wrote about entrepreneurship in the book, and yet was proceeding with mainstream publishing. If I bought into my own party line, then I concluded that I should have the courage to create my own publishing house. It was a bold decision and I was conscious of the risk. It was not only going to cost me time and money but also credibility. There would be those who would question the value of the book based on my not being with a mainstream publisher, much less a New York house. It was a chance I had to take and I would live with the consequences. All the work fell to me: finding a cover artist, a proofreader, a graphic artist, an indexer, a printer, a distributor, a publicist. But the integrity of the book would be preserved. And in the end I would fully own it. This also put me in a position to change my book title and end the cold war. It would now be called: *The New Entrepreneurs: Making a Living – Making a Life through Network Marketing*. In the final days of preparation for this book to go to press, I knew that I had accomplished a milestone. I had proven to myself that I could not only write a book but also publish it all on my own. I could look forward to speaking and touring and all that lay ahead in the aftermath of the book's release.

I was working at my computer when the phone rang. It was Mark. It had been about a month since his mom passed away. "Are you in town?" I asked. He had taken an apartment in San Francisco several months ago.

"Yes, just for a while.... So how are you?"

I don't think he had asked that question in a very long time. It made me feel good to hear him raise concern, and I genuinely sensed he wanted to know. I was especially glad to be able to answer honestly and know that I meant it. "I'm fine. I'm really fine. How about you? You've been through a lot with your mom and all the company pressure on your shoulders."

"Yeah, that was tough. Melissa and I were with her when she died. We had a nice little service there in Branson and all of her friends were there...and Amy."

"Did you speak at the funeral?"

"No, I couldn't. It would have been too hard. I've really been getting into the religious thing again. You may be surprised, but guess where I've been going to church."

"I can't imagine."

"The Catholic Church."

"You're right. I'm blown away! How did that happen?"

He paused and then said, "Valerie."

"It is strange that we had to part for you to discover Catholicism."

As he described how it came about, he concluded by saying he fell in love with the music and liturgy at St. Francis of Assisi parish in San Francisco.

"I am also more involved than before. I serve as one of the Eucharistic ministers in my parish."

"I'm glad. With all the time you've spent in parish work in the past, you should be doing that.... What are you doing right now?" he asked cautiously.

"Just catching up on my e-mail."

"Would you like to come up to the house. The refinancing on it came through. We could celebrate that and...it would be nice to visit."

This would be a double reason to rejoice. With the house no longer in my name and the company liabilities no longer mine, I was out from under the weight that had been heavy on my shoulders. I was debt-free, ready to start building a new life from the ground up, without feeling overburdened by financial obligations. But beyond that, I had prayed that one day Mark and I could be friends again. I just didn't expect it to come so quietly like this. "Sure."

"Great. See you in a bit."

I got to the house and stood at the door waiting for him to answer it. Of course, I thought back to 1991 when I stood on this same spot, and how we ended up lying side-by-side in the hammock and talking about our dreams and hopes.

The door opened and Mark was dressed as he often was at home—in shorts. He looked older. Otherwise, he seemed like himself. He led me into the living room and offered me some juice to drink. We sat and talked for a while. It was like so many conversations we'd had in this room. It felt natural.

He began reminiscing again about his mom. I understood his need to talk about her. "I brought some family albums back with me. Do you want to see them?"

"Yeah, that would be fun."

He carried in a couple of boxes filled with photo albums, scrapbooks, and loose odds and ends. We sat on the floor near the fireplace, leaning against the couch, and for the next couple of hours went through them. There were a few photos I recognized; but for the most part, these were snapshots I had never seen before. There was Mark as a little boy with birthday cake on his face and Patsi holding him. There he was in high school, president of his class and looking like a stud. Here was his wedding day to Jill, Amy's mom. And another where he was a new father holding Amy in his lap. I couldn't help but notice that I didn't see any of the Yarnells as a family.

Holding his cigarette over the fireplace, Mark flicked the ashes and let the smoke go up the flue as we talked. He jumped up and down a lot—same old Mark. He must have come in and out of the room twenty times over the course of the evening.

While we were still rummaging through the boxes, I opened up the conversation on a more personal level. "So are you happy?" I stopped short of addressing him by name. I would normally have called him by some term of endearment. I wasn't yet in the habit of addressing him as "Mark."

"Yes, I think so. But I need to move beyond network marketing. I want to write and work in other areas."

"I can relate to that. I really have to expand my own horizons too. You're already ahead of me. Your next book has already done that while I'm still writing about the industry."

"I know that isn't what you meant. You wanted to know if I was happy within myself. In the end, it is all up to us, isn't it?" I nodded. "Valerie and I have moved on in our relationship." Since I thought I was supposed to believe they never had one, I just listened. "She called it off."

"Are you okay with that?" I thought I noticed some pain showing through his eyes. Maybe it was the combination of everything in his life of late.

"I think so. We figured out we are good business partners and we meet each other's needs spiritually and intellectually. But that's where it stops." I thought back to Mark's frequent references to her as the "ice queen" in past times. As if he read my mind, he continued, "She wasn't okay with the sexual part. I think she went so long without physical closeness in her marriage." I thought back to conversations Valerie and I had had on this subject when we were baring our souls to each other. What he was saying fit with what I had understood. He seemed deep in thought before he spoke again. "I want you to know I never kissed her in this house." *Hmm. What a strange thing to say. I wonder how he expects me to feel about that.* I was at a loss to know how to respond.

He didn't say anything for a while; neither did I. My thoughts wandered back to the scene he depicted in the library in his scribbled notes. At that moment, I surmised that the exchange when *nothing happened* between them took place between Mark's first and second visit with me at my beach house. If that was so, it explained some unanswered mystery to me. "I'm over the pain of us, sweetheart." *Oops, I slipped.* "It isn't important how you define your relationship to Valerie. What matters is that, with the unraveling of her marriage and ours, you were there for each other when you both needed nurturing. Maybe you are what I call 'spiritual partners.' You will probably always have a special bond."

"She's a good person."

"I agree. We got to know each other pretty well. The whole thing between you caused me some pain at first but now, with some distance from it all, I can see that it was good you were there for each other. You needed someone and I couldn't be that someone anymore. I had the support of my mom and Nancy and other close friends. We all need that during the kind of trama you and I went through."

Mark indicated agreement as he again stood to leave the room. When he returned he sat on the ottoman and made reference to the lateness of the hour.

"Yes, I should be heading home. I would just like to say one thing before I leave. No matter what, I will always see our marriage as one based on profound love and, because of it, we were able to reach out and touch the hearts of countless people all over the world. I don't think you and I have any idea of the number of people we have affected or to what extent."

"That's twue. It's twue," he mimicked as he often did.

"I just believe that we're both better for having known each other. I would never be writing and speaking if it weren't for you. And I hope you will one day appreciate me for what I was able to give you. I've let go of the painful parts. I choose to remember the good, especially our speaking and travel time. Gstaad and New Zealand will always be memories I will treasure." My whole body welled up with emotions as I spoke these words. I felt the feelings, but they didn't emerge as tears. I was glad. I didn't want to cry at this moment.

I would have liked to hear him reciprocate my comments. He didn't, but it was okay. He said more than I could have ever expected by the very act of reaching out and inviting me up to the house. It was a meaningful gesture on his part.

As we walked to the door, we had our arms around each other's waists. "I just want you to know that being with your mother helped me bring closure to the 'Mark and Rene' phase of my life. Tonight is the finishing touch. I'm really glad you called and asked me to come over."

"Me too," he said almost whispering. I'm sure he was feeling some emotion at that moment.

We kissed gently, and I walked outside. Glancing back, I watched the door close on a momentous chapter of my life. I knew finally I was ready to move on to the next phase. I felt complete within myself and could now eagerly look forward to what lay ahead.

EPILOGUE-
AFTERWORD

November 1999 - September 2000

EPILOGUE

NEW BEGINNINGS
November 1999—January 2000

I was boarding Qantas Airline heading for Melbourne, Australia, on my way to teach the University Certificate Seminar with Charles King. My friend, John Fogg, was going to be joining us as the keynote speaker along with a Nu Skin associate and friend, Tim Sales.

I reclined my chair, adjusted my pillow, wrapped my blanket around me, and settled in for the fourteen-hour flight from LA, keenly aware that this was my first time to take an international flight alone. This wouldn't be my choice. Given the option, I would prefer the companionship of a close friend travelling this far away.

As the plane headed upward 30,000 feet, I let my thoughts drift back to where I was exactly one year ago, November 1998. I had moved out of my home, the place where I had lived happily with my husband and children, and was living in a rented home where the only things I owned were my computer and a few clothes I'd brought with me. I often fell asleep on the couch at night because I wasn't ready to sleep alone in my bed. I was taking Paxil to regulate my uncontrollable tears. I was just beginning to write my next book, hoping against hope that I could write a book— alone. I couldn't see ahead more than a day at a time. My life purpose had been stripped from me, or so it felt. I didn't know if I could stand on my own professionally, or if I would be accepted. I was a blubbering basket case and couldn't stand in front of anyone at that moment. All I knew was that, like it or not, my safe world was gone. I was being shoved out of the comfortable nest we'd built and forced to begin a whole new life.

What I had finally come to understand was that the heartrending sadness resulting from a relationship ending need not signal failure, but can be the portal to an even deeper experience of personal growth, guiding us to a renewal of our present situation in a new form or forging out to create an entirely new spiritual bonding. We can allow that pain to bog us down in self-pity and prolonged misery, or we can choose to emerge with full appreciation for the precious time we were given to share moments of our lives with another person. Once ended, it doesn't matter whether our love is reciprocated or not. It doesn't matter if the warm memories are mutual or not. It doesn't matter if the time is for a moment or a week or a year or a decade or a lifetime. What does matter is that we shared part of ourselves with each other, and the experience is raising one or preferably both of us to an elevated capacity to love.

I let warm memories sit lingering like morning dew on the surface of my psyche, determined that all of this would eventually seep in. I couldn't allow myself to forget, ever, what I had come through during this traumatic period. But now I knew with certainty that I was ready for the next phase, for a deeper level of spiritual bonding and shared intimacy that I welcomed openly into my life.

I had used every power within me to envision the life I wanted next. But even I found it hard to believe where I was just one year later. I could only look ahead in tiny, fragmented glimpses. There were dark, thunderous clouds everywhere around me. But for a millisecond of time, I would part them in my mind, and see instead a blue sky with billowy vapors floating on a bright summer day. Then the next time, I would see this picture for two milliseconds. Soon, I could hold the thought for a whole second, then several seconds, then a whole minute, then several minutes. Before long, I actually began believing in my vision, knowing that I had the power within me to make it happen.

I pictured myself settled in a home that was warm and cozy. I saw myself holding my completed book in my hands, feeling proud to have written it on my own. I envisioned myself speaking to audiences all over the world impacting their minds, influencing their thinking, touching their hearts, and making a difference in their lives. These were bold mental images considering where I was in reality. But as I sat pondering these thoughts and feeling these feelings, I knew beyond any doubt that I could make them happen in my life.

Now, it was November 1999 and I was settled and happy in my own home. *The New Entrepreneurs* was out and would be available to the participants in this coming seminar. And I was on my way to teach in a foreign country where I had the opportunity to influence the minds and hearts of our students and make a difference in their lives. There were no overwhelming miraculous events—only the marvel of healing that happens slowly, hour by hour and day by day: the tenant who moved out, my dogged determination and persistence to get a book to press, a phone call from Charles asking me to join him in this event. No big deals. Just several small events all strung together.

Dear God, I don't want a day to go by that I take anything for granted. My life "is" because You have given it to me. It is "what it is" because of what I am making of it. I knew I had come a long way in a year. Growth doesn't seem to spread itself out. It comes in spurts, and this was a major growth phase. I didn't want it to wind down. I loved the newness of life and felt driven to continue developing myself. I was a woman on a mission with such discovery ahead, so much to learn and to share. I looked forward to the unfolding of each step along the way.

I declined dinner when the stewardess offered it. I pulled out my laptop and, with fourteen hours before landing, decided to use some of this time to do a little journaling.

November 25, 1999

As I see the end of a millennium coming and face the awesome realization that I am living at one of the most significant moments in history, I find myself seeking answers to the basic questions of life. Who am I? Where am I going? What am I supposed to be doing? What do I want to do differently as we turn the corner of a new era? It isn't as if I haven't asked these questions many times before, of myself and of countless students and colleagues. But at this momentous time in history, and in my own life, it is fitting for me to ask them now.

Professionally, I see myself doing much of what I am doing now—writing, speaking, and teaching. I am at an age where wisdom is beginning to solidify itself for me in a way that I understand more and have the ability to communicate that understanding to others. Most of my knowledge comes from experience—usually painful experience. I am living and continue to explore the mystery of being a woman in search of life's meaning. I feel at ease with my own form of spirituality. I have experienced loving and being loved. And I have faced the ecstasy of beginning and the agony of ending relationships with people I love. These are the topics in which, through my writings and teachings, I see myself expanding, delving into, and sharing my insights with humanity.

I see my passion growing for addressing women's issues in greater depth. For centuries, men have been ingrained in the practice of meeting their own basic needs, but have fallen short of reaching the higher plane of Maslow's hierarchy of human needs. For centuries, women have been satisfied to have their basic needs met for them, but have given more attention to their personal development and others-centered love. Unless we build on this by developing more self-sufficiency and assuming responsibility for meeting our basic economic needs, women will forever be held back in our natural intended evolution. Unless *we* see ourselves as powerful—as able to offer vital contributions—the world will never see us that way.

While men are inclined to compartmentalize their lives, we women integrate ours. Their ability to categorize their lives would seem to be what has made men more successful in business but less successful overall in the rest of their lives. Our integral nature, on the other hand, has hurt us as businesswomen but helped us to become more self-actualized. A question to ponder: how can we use our feminine qualities to become more successful in business while preserving the integration of our lives? How can we create businesses that conform to our self-actualization needs? I see myself awakening women to a new self-awareness as we set forth a new role model for our daughters and all future generations.

I see myself dedicated to working with individuals interested in raising marriage to a higher plane, transforming it from a financial and legal institution as it is primarily understood today to a joining together of two interdependent human beings for as long as they have something of value to contribute to the other as they form a kind of spiritual bond. Their primary purpose in sharing their lives is the personal and spiritual enhancement they have to offer each other. In this vision of marriage, any other entanglements, whether legal or financial, would become optional and secondary. If children are involved or anticipated, the couple might consider a parental agreement made in advance. I believe children will be better cared for if raised in an environment of spiritual relationships, regardless of whether the parents stay together or grow apart. Separating the legal and financial issues could well serve to prolong the duration of marriage. But if a couple chooses to part, I see myself helping to change the paradigm when a marriage ends: no longer a "failed marriage" but a relationship that enhanced two people for the time they were together and prepared them to become more aware and more responsible with an increased capacity to love. How much better our world would be if significant relationships ended with open communication, a sincere desire to understand the changes that occurred in their relationship, and a mutual support of one another to continue growing in the next phase of their lives.

I read over what I had written and realized how much of my life philosophy was still unfolding. I knew these were the subjects I wanted to pursue in my next book and future books over the coming years. Curling up in my chair, I slept through the night and woke up as breakfast was being served. A day was skipped as we had crossed the international dateline during the night. It would be the 27th when we landed in Melbourne.

I flew from there directly up to Brisbane and transferred to a single-engine puddle jumper that took me onto Hamilton Island and from there caught a ferry over to Long Island. My bungalow was right on the beach with wallabies running like squirrels outside my door. It was a perfect place for continuing to write this book. My words flowed. They always do when I can hear the surf and watch the waves roll in. If I had any vision of meeting that someone new and special, this was not the place. Surrounded by families and honeymooners, I was vividly reminded that I was alone...but reasonably content in this romantic setting. I took long walks on the beach as I reflected on my life, my book, and my future.

I used this time to do some reflection about myself and the two men who had been primary in my life over the past quarter of a century. They are both bigger-than-life personalities. *What qualities do they share that attracts me? They were each powerful in their own right. So what does that say about me? I hate to get back to childhood, but I have to ask myself: What was missing in my life growing up? A father. And what does a father represent to a child? Power. He is big and I am little. He will protect me.* No matter how far I come, fear of abandonment continues to loom in my relationships. Apparently, I keep attracting men who have bigness and power, subconsciously hoping that they will fill this father-protector role I seek in my life. But so far, the powerful men I've attracted have had their own confrontive issues, which made it impossible for them to fill my needs on a long-term basis. So in the end, the pattern of abandonment keeps repeating itself. This may always be my pattern. But I can't stop yearning for that intimate relationship that will be lifelong. Even knowing intellectually that relationships are likely to end, our hearts will always long to seek one that will be forever.

What I was coming to understand in my own growth process was the importance of fostering the development of that two-year-old child in me—the one who craves protection and fears abandonment. Allowing her to grow up into a mature, self-sufficient woman would make it possible for me to preserve my emotional autonomy. Self-reliance is the only way anyone can ever be truly free, and it is what will ultimately allow us to join with partners in focusing on our spiritual growth. In the beginning, I achieved this with Mark. Our persona as two individuals and as a couple was very strong and very powerful. But in the end, when our shared life fell apart, it was so obvious to me that I gave too much of my inner strength away. I promised myself that, no matter what, I would preserve my authentic power in my next relationship. I vowed to radiate out the emotions that I most want to impart into my world and to put my greatest energy into those activities and people I want to attract into my life.

The four days passed all too quickly. It was time to head for Melbourne to begin preparation for our University program. The night I arrived, John had also just come in from Malaysia where he had been speaking. He and I along with our hosts for the event had dinner together frequently during this time. It was over a meal of pesto pasta, and a specially chosen bottle of wine as only John can choose, that we talked about our respective books. He seemed surprised and pleased that I was branching beyond the world of network marketing in the book I was now writing. As he listened, he casually mentioned a mutual acquaintance whom he'd just seen in Malaysia, someone who had recently gone through the ending of his marriage as well. When we arrived back at our hotel, John gave me his e-mail address and one other, believing that these two men might be instrumental in sharing their personal insights on the subject of relationships and their endings.

With a few minutes to spare the next day before our closing ceremony, I sent each of them a message explaining the book I was presently writing. I finished the first one and began the second.

>E-mail is such a wonderful medium for
>communication. I am in Melbourne teaching a
>seminar on network marketing with John Fogg and
>others. Your name came up and I learned that we
>have both gone through similar experiences
>recently. Our lifestyles have changed since the last
>time I saw you at an Upline Masters seminar
>several years ago.

>I am working on my next book...on relationships. I
>would love to visit with you for no particular
>reason—except to share experiences and expand
>my thinking. I will be traveling home today.

>Crossing the Int. date line, I am due to get home
>about 4 minutes before I left. If you would like to
>give me a call, I'm listed in Reno, Nevada. Or
>send me your number, and I will give you a call
>when I get home.

>Hope you are doing well. I am far better as I face
>this holiday season than I was during the last one.
>Warmly, Rene Yarnell

I finished just in time to scurry downstairs and participate in the closing panel discussion. It was our largest class ever and we knew, even without the evaluations, that we had conducted a successful program. I was stimulated rather than fatigued, as I often am after a successful teaching experience. With demonstrative hugs goodbye to old and new friends, I boarded my plane for the nearly daylong flight back to the States.

Home, there is no place like it. My own bed, my own office, my desk, my music, my computer. Ah, my computer. I couldn't wait to get online and check my e-mail. With more than 24 hours of not checking my messages, I was in withdrawal. It had become a means of conducting business as well as staying in touch and bonding with so many friends.

As I watched 38 messages pop up on the screen, I began deleting the junk mail. Oops, not that one. It was a message from John's friend.

Epilogue

We had met only once—at a speaking engagement more than four years ago—and hadn't seen or spoken with each other since. I tried to remember the city but couldn't. He was the keynote speaker and Mark and I were each giving a workshop. I was lured by his message.

>Dear Rene:
>I know you may not believe me, but I am being
>honest in telling you that I have thought about you
>many times.

>You made a lasting impression as I sat quietly
>watching and listening to your program, and then
>during the brief time that we had to talk afterwards.
>When I discovered that you and Mark were no
>longer together, I thought immediately that of all the
>people I had ever met, you would be one that
>should be treasured for a lifetime. And then, I was
>stunned to learn that my marriage was ending
>suddenly with no warning.

>I would very much like to spend time with you and
>get to know you. We have much in common, but
>more importantly, I have thousands of
>acquaintances but very few intimate friends.

>Quality of life, beauty, integrity, sensitivity and
>sharing are everything to me. I want to spend time
>experiencing those virtues and I feel that you are
>one of those rare individuals who have those qualities.

>I tried to call you today, December 7, immediately
>upon my return from Taiwan. I am flying to Orlando
>today to do a seminar, but will return Thursday evening.

>My numbers are listed below. Please call anytime
>day or night. I would love to talk to you.

As I reread his words, I was drawn by his open, have-no-fear attitude. He seemed confident to say whatever was on his mind. His self-assurance with words was evident, but they seemed to come straight from his heart. I sat staring at the screen for a few moments.

"Of all the people I had ever met, you would be one that should be treasured for a lifetime." Was I ready for this encounter? Go slowly, Rene.

My life was full. For several weeks, I had been developing a new audio program that would serve as a companion to *The New Entrepreneurs*. I was consulting with a new startup company and acting as a spokesperson for another technological group that was planning to offer their program to network marketing companies. I had become involved in my parish again as a Eucharistic minister; my spiritual life was intact and I felt the power of God so very present in my life. I was back playing tennis on a regular basis with my long-time women friends. I had built close friendships new and old with some wonderful people. The balance wheel of my life was as well-rounded as it had ever been.

I took care of so much of my personal and professional activities through e-mail that I checked it at least twice a day just to keep up. I answered an uplifting message from Frank who often said something wonderful to get my day off to a good beginning. There was one from Missy who had just come home from a trip. Nancy was still travelling and teaching, and now getting ready to join her husband on a bike trip. Biking was her newfound passion.

There was another message from him. I scrolled down past several others eager to read that one next. I enjoyed reading about where he was living, the transitions he had just gone through, and his hopes for the future.

> >...Of all the people in the world, I never would have
> >dreamed that I would be single at this point in my
> >life. My career positioning couldn't be much better
> >and I am enjoying new global opportunities which,
> >like you, enable me to travel when and where I
> >want to go. My absolute mission is to be happy for
> >the rest of my life and leave a legacy my kids and
> >grandkids can be proud of.
> >I look forward to communicating with you soon.

It was Thursday night—the night that Heritage Bank was hosting a book-signing reception for me. I saw my whole life in

Reno pass before me. So many people whom I'd come to know and care about in my nearly twenty years of living there came out for the event. I felt truly blessed to have such good, supportive friends. As the evening wore on and the crowd was dwindling, my cell phone rang. It was a voice out of my future....

As he introduced himself on the phone while I stood in the midst of dear friends who were celebrating this auspicious occasion with me, my thoughts wandered. The Jewish religion has a word for what I was feeling at this moment. It is expressed in a prayer reading that begins with the events of creation and goes something like this:

"If Yahweh only created the stars—that would be enough for us to love and serve him." Then it continues: "But if Yahweh only created the moon, ...that would be enough." Dayennu. Enough. The word represents a magnificent love song to God for the tremendous unsurpassable gifts of creation. *If I had only completed the book and gotten it published, then "dayennu." If I had such wonderful friends to celebrate with me, then "dayennu." But to receive this call at this moment, then, my God, "dayennu, dayennu, dayennu."*

We made plans to connect later that evening, and spoke for a long time—maybe an hour, maybe more. It seemed like only minutes. It was easy to be open with him, and so pleasant to listen. He probed gently into my life and what had happened to Mark and me. He shared so much of himself and the surprise ending of his twenty-year marriage. As we hung up the phone, I felt as if I knew him.

I found myself checking my e-mail more often. "You have mail" took on a whole new meaning. As I watched the messages pop up one by one, my heart skipped a beat as I spotted his.

>Dear Rene:
>Talking to you was like pure oxygen to a mountain
>climber. I look forward to growing our friendship.

I immediately hit the reply button. I thought about our phone conversation where we both acknowledged that we had recently been on foreign soil, walking alone on some of the most beautiful beaches in the world. Thinking of this, I wrote:

>You write like a poet. We've both had the recent
>experience of that walk along the ocean by
>ourselves. I look forward to a walk along the ocean
>with you...and more talking. Warmly, Rene

E-mails became the measure of my days. Each message was a bridge linking one day to the next. I could hardly wait to cross into another. He wrote back the next day:

>Dear Rene:
>The essence of my life is this:
>A baby's smile, a loved one's kiss
>A book, a tree, a fire, a friend,
>And just a little time to spend.
>I hope we can spend some time
>Together....

From out of nowhere a poem flowed out of me. I was torn between my attraction to him and my desire to go slowly, sensitive to the newness of his situation. I hit the reply button and captured it as my words fell onto the monitor.

>You touch my soul in some unexplored place
>As I learn what brings a smile to your face
>A book, a tree, a fire, a friend,
>And just a little time to spend
>Perhaps too soon to invade your space?

>Anticipating moments to be shared
>Eager to allow my soul to be bared
>Hurry up, slow down, push-pull within
>Now, then, sooner, later, when?
>Hesitancy dissipates sensing you cared.

Several days passed and I didn't hear anything from him. I kept myself busy but my thoughts kept wandering back to him. *Maybe I said too much too soon. Why am I feeling so vulnerable?*

Epilogue

On December 16, a Blue Mountain Art Card was waiting in my e-mail inbox. "You have every reason this season to feel that you are special." It was a beautiful card with so much of his sensitivity showing through in his message. I busied myself getting ready for Christmas, but still unable to move my thoughts beyond him for very long. More silence followed after the card. *What does this silence mean? Does his withdrawal have anything to do with me? I doubt it but I'm feeling my strength slip away somewhat. I have come so far out of the depths of agony. I don't want to slide backwards. Please, God, help me. I am a strong, centered woman. I have a full life without the "need" of anyone to fill some empty space inside of me. My feelings for him are developing so quickly...too quickly, I suppose. All this has happened by e-mail and phone. However, it isn't vulnerability that scares me. It is neediness that frightens me. This is an area of myself I must continue to work on. It is important that my longing to hear from him again is based more on "want" than "need." This is such a fine line. Who can ever really know the difference?*

It was just days before Christmas when I next heard from him.

>Forgive the silence, after all my hoopla. I have been
>in court and also doing some last minute planning
>for my kids to stay with me for Christmas.
>Tomorrow night, December 22nd, the moon will be
>the biggest and brightest it has ever been in our
>lifetime. It has not been as big as it will be (14%
>larger) since 1866 and will not appear the same
>again for another hundred years.
>I hope it is a clear night in Nevada tomorrow night.
>Look at the moon, make a wish, and I'll do the
>same. Maybe we can share the experience when
>we take that walk.

>Hope you have a warm and wonderful Christmas
>with those you care for.

With visions that so filled my heart, I imagined taking that walk with him. The waves splashing at our feet, the sound of the surf so overpowering, that we could not help but be reminded of our smallness in this planetary system. And yet each one of us is so significant. We have a purpose to fulfill while we walk on this earth. It isn't where we walk, but how we walk the distance that matters. And those with whom we choose to walk can have such influence on the forks in the road toward our destination. I knew that this was someone with whom I wanted to explore walking on my journey at this time.

Understanding my innate tendency to throw caution to the wind and go too fast too soon, I held back my feelings. And with far greater reserve than I had previously known in those rare instances like this, I simply wrote back:

> >I made my wish. Given the circumstances, it has to
> >have very special meaning. Rene

And he responded:

> >That special moon shone through my bedroom
> >window all night and illuminated my room as if a
> >hundred candles were burning. It was very difficult
> >to sleep.
> >I too made my wish.

Instead of Christmas cards, I sent out a millennium greeting to my friends and network marketing associates. Through light-hearted poetry, I felt I could best explain the changes in my life and why they hadn't heard from me in more than a year:

As I sit at my desk with the fireside flickering
The shadows of candlelight dancing on the ceiling
And in the background the carols softly playing
I search for words to describe the past two years
The changes, the sadness, the countless fears
Friends bearing with me through the tears
At last I see light as the dark clouds part
Back in my old home, a mended heart
A newly released book signifies a brand new start
Putting the past behind and looking ahead

Epilogue

Touring, speaking, writing, no longer wed
New relationships, another book, a new life created
To good friends always there, my heart outpours
My own crises make me more sensitive to yours
As some windows close, there are new open doors
Not one new year, not even one hundred will do
To put the past behind and the new day through
It will take a thousand to start anew
Toasting a new millennium as we lift our glasses in unison
Our lives are not nearly done, and I'm no longer a nun
Whatever is in store for us, the best has just begun

Christmas came and went. It was a loving time with my family and that close inner circle of friends. It was a happy season for me, but my thoughts kept drifting back to him. I wondered how his Christmas was with his family—and if I was in his thoughts. The starting and stopping of our communication was torture for me. Of course, I longed to experience only the feelings that filled my heart with that overpowering exhilaration that comes with the new possibility of loving and being loved. There is no other emotion in the human realm quite like it. But pain is an inevitable part of loving someone. People tell me it can be otherwise, but I have never experienced profound loving without it.

I can remember when I was four or five years old: my parents had been divorced since I was two. I was living with a family, Mr. And Mrs. Ayers and their daughter, while my mother traveled directing road shows in various communities. When she was home, the Ayers would drive me to her apartment so I could spend the weekend with her. I was small enough that I could lie in the back windowsill of the old nineteen-forty-something Ford and feel the sun beating down on me. All the way to Mom's, I was stifling sobs. My excitement at seeing her was overshadowed by my sadness at leaving this wonderful family. Then I would get there and have the most perfect weekend with Mom. We spent time reading stories and doing things together that were special. On Sunday night, the Ayers would return to pick me up. It was usually dark as we drove home and, lying across the floor of the backseat, I would smother more sobs, devastated that I had to leave Mom.

I know that, from earliest childhood, I carry a kind of emptiness inside of me, a sad spot left by those whom I have loved and who are no longer in my day-to-day life. I thought of Bonhoeffer's words that Frank gave me. I had framed them and kept it standing on my dresser: "Nothing can make up for the absence of someone we love.... For the gap, as long as it remains unfilled, preserves the bond between us.... God does not fill it, but... keeps it empty and so helps us to keep alive our forever communion with each other even at the cost of pain."

Opening myself up to this new relationship was not going to be without pain. I was already sensing an ache in my heart and I had yet to be with him. But, on the other hand, I was *feeling* these feelings again. Even a year ago, I couldn't imagine that it was possible. When one relationship is dying, it is so easy to believe that even the *possibility* of ever loving again will end with it. But was I really ready for this? Was it too soon after the ending of my marriage? I intuitively knew the answers. Yes, I was ready. No, it had been a year and half since I faced the collapse of my marriage. Being vulnerable is part of loving someone, I mean, really loving someone. The only way to greater intimacy is to be vulnerable and open ourselves up to the endless possibilities that love may bring. Avoiding the risk of pain stifles intimacy like nothing else I know. Frank's concern for me was, given the newness of his divorce, that this would be a transitional relationship. I weighed that but....

No, I would not hold back out of fear of being hurt. Doing so would only cause me to miss out on the chance to experience loving someone. As Garth Brooks has said in one of his songs: "Life is often left to chance. I could have missed the pain, but I would also have had to miss the dance." The key for me was to enjoy the journey and not focus on the destination. Where this relationship would lead was far less important than what might happen to us both along the way. I was blessed with some close personal relationships that would continue to play a major role in my life. My writing and teaching would consume another significant part. And this new friendship, if it was meant to unfold, would find its rightful place amidst the concentric circles of those who influenced my life.

Two days before the end of the millennium, he wrote again:

> >Thought about you as I saw the green afterglow
> >from a Kona sunset at the reef, listening to a live
> >harpist. My daughter was at the Spa, so I watched
> >it solo. It would have been nice to share that with you.

> >I have decided to go up to the volcano (which is
> >flowing) on the big island of Hawaii and toast the
> >new millennium by tossing a champagne glass into
> >the crater. It will symbolize the ending of an era and
> >the beginning of a new life.

Like everyone, I felt the momentous aura of this time in history. And...dayennu...I personally felt it tenfold. I knew my life was never going to be the same at the turn of this millennium. I had put closure to one phase. No bitterness. No anger. No blaming. No guilt. On the contrary, with tremendous awareness for the life I'd formerly shared, I now felt ready to open myself to whatever lay ahead. I felt thankful beyond words that I had experienced that time with my former husband and now I had been released. Ah, yes, released—not abandoned—to move on to the next phase of my life. I was ready to give birth to new relationships and nurture existing ones, with full awareness that each passage carried far more significance than the outcome. I would strive to make loving foremost in all my relationships, more emphasis on loving than being loved.

With this in mind, I hit the reply button:

> >Going to the big crater sounds memorable and
> >symbolic. For myself, I have decided to spend the
> >evening at a small formal dinner party here in town.
> >There will be a dozen or so people there, two of

>whom are very close friends. Part of the evening
>will be taping a memory video with each of the
>guests reflecting on where we've come and where
>we see ourselves heading—a little something to
>preserve for posterity.
>Wishing you the happiest of new beginnings. And
>in this coming millennium, may our wishes come true.

Beginning with New Zealand where I had such fond memories with Mark, we watched the entire world welcome in a new millennium. Country by country, we were inter-connected as each hour celebrated the turn of this momentous event and the world watched mesmerized as each ethnicity expressed itself each in its own style. While the whole world was exulting during this historical occurrence, I was somewhat lamenting our lack of communication. It had been days since I had heard from him. I teach visualization, self-talk, affirmations. Surely I could control the angst building up in my heart. *This is absurd,* I would say to myself. It has been less than a month since he *e-rrived* into my life. *Just go back to the way things were before his first message appeared in your inbox. Right! There is no going back once someone has touched your heart. I can't open my e-mail without scrolling the list in search of a message from him.*

The continued silence was tearing me apart. It brought up the old feelings of the painstaking silences I experienced with Mark at the end of our time together. I turned to poetry to expel the emotions building in me. It would be one I would never send— just my need to write it.

> *A budding friendship so fragile at first*
> *Like a blossoming bud it needs care*
> > *Open communication its food*
> > *Consistent flow of sharing its water*
> *With such nurturing its blossoms can burst*
> > *Into a beautiful flower.*

> *A budding friendship so delicately built*
> *Like a blossoming bud it craves sustenance*

Epilogue

It won't be the heat that causes it to wither
Not even the cold will shrivel its petals
Without such nurturing it will soon wilt
And die from the silence.

Where are those people who say love can be without pain? I needed to be reminded that this could happen. Maybe pure joy-filled love, the kind without heartache, will come to me in this second half of life. It most assuredly did not in the first half. Another few days came and went and still no word. I was distracted from my daily routine. It was impossible to keep my mind on business. Even my writing was affected. Poetry was the only release I could find.

It's too soon to feel pain
We haven't even met yet
I know...I should try to feign
Indifference to your silence
Of course love has no right
Either to expect or demand
Whisper this to my heart
It doesn't quite understand.

With each passing day, I began having doubts about the future of this relationship. If the e-mails weren't still sitting in my computer, I would have thought I made up the whole exchange between us. But there they were.

Preparing myself for the inevitable, I wrote one last poem as I reflected back on what had transpired and prepared myself to move on from it.

I made my wish
On a moon so close to the earth
Shining down on my deck peering through the trees
As the steam from my hot tub vanished in the gentle breeze
Imagining myself walking on a deserted beach
And you within my reach...

You made your wish
On that same special moon
That illuminated your room
It shone through your bedroom window
As if a hundred candles were burning
    Foolishly, I thought I felt your yearning...

You made your wish...and I made mine
On a moon that seemed bigger than life
And will never be seen again in this century
I wonder what will come of them
    Your wish and mine
Will they loom like the light in your room
Or drift away like the steam above my roof's beam
    Dear God, I do wonder what will come of them....

As I prepared to shut down my computer, I heard the familiar ding of an e-mail arriving. There at last was a message from him. He shared with me the recentness of his divorce, the settlement not yet resolved, financial concerns, health issues, family obligations—all of which he felt were obstacles to pursuing a relationship. He let me know that he cared enough for me already not to want to impose these matters into our growing friendship.

>I realize how suddenly silent I have become after
>our initial phone conversations.

>I cannot describe how much of an impact the early
>communications with you have had on me. If I were
>to attempt to define the kind of woman I most
>desire as a soul mate, you would be a near-perfect
>match. Although many soothsayers swear that
>opposites attract, it could be that they are wrong,
>at least in the sense that I feel two people must
>have the same values, integrity, caring spirits,
>tastes for beauty, etc.

>I love your spirituality. Your intrinsic goodness is
>further enhanced by your relationship with God. I

>respect that in you, especially with you sharing His
>grace with me.

>I know, if and when I see you, that my natural
>instinct would be to court you and lavish you with
>the kind of attention and affection that I reserve for
>only one person in a millennium. And, were I to
>spoil our initial walk with heavy discussions it would
>seem a shame to waste that special moment with
>such talk.
>You have no idea how I have lain awake and
>thought about you these past several weeks and
>wondered how someone like me, who has always
>given his best in everything, would be in a position
>to have to qualify himself to someone he could
>easily love.

I have lived long enough to know that getting involved with someone recently divorced has almost no chance of survival. Anyone, man or woman, needs time after the divorce to discover, to explore, to become the person he or she is meant to be. And following that transition, time is needed to redefine the foundation for the kind of relationship he or she may want to have next. Even if I were ready, he might not be. How wise was it for me to begin something now? *Should we wait until he has had more transition time? Should I back away before we meet? Before a more serious relationship could develop?* My head said yes, yes, yes; my heart said no. I didn't let the battle wage for long. I let my heart rule, knowing that I already cared about this gentle, sensitive man. He met my vision of the kind of person with whom I felt I could develop a spiritual partnership. We both proceeded with our correspondence, not yet clear whether we were developing a friendship or something more. But something more seemed to be strongly present in the cyber-sphere of our communication. Still not understanding the extensive silence, I wrote back letting him know once again that making a habit of prolonged silence did not have a positive effect on my soul. In response, he wrote:

>Dear Rene:
>Now that you are in my life, I have every intention
>of keeping you there, regardless of the relationship
>that develops.

>My silence has not resulted from the inner turmoil
>normally associated with a sudden breakup. My
>silence has come from wanting to get to know you;
>sensing that you move me at the very heart and
>core of who I am; and accepting the reality that it
>may be best not to take that first walk together.
>Silence is not my way of coping, nor a normal flight
>response for me. And, no, I would never again be
>silent and cause you hurt or doubt. I never want to
>lay my head on my pillow wondering where I stand
>or what I did or didn't do. My silence was confusion
>as to how and what to say to you.

>Rene, I don't normally beat around the bush and am
>usually pretty good at presenting understandable
>thoughts. I care about what you think. I do want to
>get to know you better. I do feel that we deserve to
>spend time exploring. I love e-mail, but I prefer
>hearing your voice or looking at you.

Our communication was going back and forth like a chat room. We wrote several messages all the same evening. Beyond the multiple concerns he expressed, he indicated that there were no other hidden issues. I wrote back in response.

>I feel much happier with our communication opened
>up again. You have been so honest with me.
>I can't think of anything to share with you about me
>that should concern you. The baggage I have
>carried throughout my life has been on the
>emotional level. I have lived most of my life fearing
>abandonment. My father left me. My former
>husband, Jim Kavanaugh, left again and again and
>again. Mark promised that he would never leave
>me... and he did. I come from five generations of

>women whose husbands ran off, or died, or
>otherwise left the women to hold the family together.
>I've come to grips with this issue more in the past
>year and a half than I have ever before.

>Abandonment may always loom in the shadows of
>my life as an issue to be dealt with, but ever since I
>processed this after my recent divorce, I haven't
>been feeling the struggle with this personal demon
>as deeply as in the past.

As I signed off on the e-mail and hit the send/receive button, there came a reply from John Fogg. I had recently written to him thanking him for making this connection between us. I was open with John in telling him how I felt:

>I feel myself already caring about him a lot, but he
>is a complex man. I seem to have a knack for
>picking them that way.

To which John responded:

>Yeah, you do. How about just loving the hell out of
>him and letting the chips fall wherever...? In the
>wake of that "being loved" I find I am free to "be love"
>and "be loving." I think all complex people yearn for
>simple. And simply loving them makes it possible.
>Love to you—John

He was right. If my primary focus is to love without putting forth demands or expecting anything back, then I will be a loving person. That is really all that matters. Being loved is not the primary objective. It shouldn't be. That will happen in its own course. If I'm not afraid to love—like I'd never been hurt—with nothing held back, I will have the opportunity to become a more giving and loving person. That is the purpose of our life on this earth and really *is* all that matters.

A bouquet of virtual roses arrived in my inbox. Actually,

there were three buds with a note: "one for your past and one for mine; the third rose represents not our separate pasts but our present together."

As we began to take steps toward our first meeting, we discussed the setting. Of course, it had to be near a beach where "we would not build memories but previews."

To: Rene Reid Yarnell
Subject: Looking forward to the weekend

>Rene:
>Come with me, with sails unfurled;
>The wind at your back, with eyes on the far horizon.

>Come with me, beyond the jagged reef,
>past the storm clouds, far from the noisy ports of call,
>teeming with greedy merchants and
>cruise ships searching for nirvana.

>Come with me, where the sun never sets,
>where gentle currents beckon us to feast our souls
>in childlike wonder on a banquet of our own dreams.

>Come with me, where the only certainty
>is the safe harbor of arms
>we trust.

The joy of anticipation filled my heart. Passion pervaded my entire being. With full realization of the risk, I felt ready for new beginnings. And what better place than a walk on the beach!

AFTERWORD

ENDINGS AND
MORE BEGINNINGS
July – September 2000

B ehind every ending awaits a new beginning. As painful and devastating as the shutting down of a relationship can be, if looked at honestly and courageously, it often serves as the threshold to an entirely new and uplifting transformation of our lives. It can be the next step in our lifelong search for getting in touch with that authentic power within us.

Endings take different forms. Some couples may go down into the depths of the dark cavity and come up renewed and still together—their relationship simply embracing a new life and a new dimension. Others may go through the same soul-searching and choose to go separate ways. More likely, one chooses to move on while the other clings to the security of what once was and the hope that love can be renewed. Still other endings come unexpectedly, through death or physical disabilities or emotional disorders, neither party *choosing* the end.

The challenge is that each of us encounters these transitions differently. One feels called to proceed in a new direction while the other experiences abandonment. One partner dies or finds someone else, and the other is left alone and overwhelmed by the loss. Rarely do two people reach the same conclusion at the same time and part with mutual understanding.

When a relationship ends, it is easy to fall into reaction mode. More than ever, this is a time to stay rooted in ourselves and not react to our partner's behavior. He or she, of course, has the power and the right to close down the bond as we once knew it. But our response to the situation must be independent of our partner's actions. We can't always control *what* happens to us, but we have complete charge over *how* we choose to deal with it.

So much of the sadness we feel at the end of a relationship has to do with being forced to face a new beginning. In his book *Soul Mates,* Thomas Moore suggests that endings are a natural outgrowth of a relationship, and, as such, both sides of the emotional spectrum need to be experienced by both parties. If we only feel the need to move on, or if we only live through the abandonment, we will be bogged down in the constraints, missing the natural tension of the yin and the yang. To truly be ready to transform an ending into a new beginning, each party must experience all sides of the emotional prism. We are drawn into the sense of loss. Something has ended and will never be again in quite the same way. We feel alone, missing what once drew us to that person in the first place. We are compelled to rediscover ourselves and determine our purpose separate from the other. With enough time and enough tears (or however we express our pain), we eventually find that we are ready to begin again. This can happen in any order, but we want to run the gamut of those feelings of sadness, numbness, being unloved, anger, fear, forgiveness, renewed passion, feeling loveable, building confidence, finding inner strength. And when the full spectrum of human emotion is felt, then, and only then, are we ready to begin again.

"Starting over," as we so often say, shouldn't have to mean going back to where we were before the union occurred. If allowed to unfold naturally, moving on from a relationship can be an awakening—not a failure but an upward movement toward a new level of maturity. This consciousness has the capacity to lead us into a new kind of relationship, a commitment with a partner for whom we have mutual respect. We are as concerned about the spiritual growth of the other as for our own; we are as sensitive to the other's needs as we are to our own. This kind of relationship may best be described as a spiritual partnership. Recognizing, however, that no one can adequately fulfill all the needs of another person, spiritual partners encourage other relationships that foster and enhance the growth of each of them. These broader relationships make up the circle of love in our lives. This movement from one relationship to the next, however, even when done in a positive light, is not without pain. The void that we feel at the closing down of a relationship is part of appreciating the bond that held us for the time we shared in each other's lives.

From start to publication, this book will have been nearly a five-year project. Each part was written as it was being lived. I wrote the happy times during the happy times and the sad times during the sad times. By some twist of Providence, something I don't even question as anything but divine intervention, another significant happening occurred just as I am completing this book. Seven months after it began, my newest relationship ended. Given its rather dramatic but precarious start, the reader may not find this surprising. Lest you be saddened by hearing this, let me share with you the good that came from it. I grew as a person. My involvement with him lead me to discover, after my marriage, that I could love again. After the initial and inevitable loss of confidence and worthiness, I emerged with far greater self-efficacy. Though a transitional relationship for both of us, through the experience, I continued to discover my Achilles' heel when in a relationship and learn from that as well. Most importantly, had this ending not occurred when it did, this closing chapter may never have been written.

Though the relationship only lasted these few months, that doesn't lessen the pain of its ending. How fitting that, like the rest of this story, I should be feeling the feelings of the very subject of this book, ending a relationship, in the moment. With every word written in complete authenticity, why would I think I could get away with the finale being written out of my head and not from my heart? I have taken three months to complete this afterword to allow myself to go through the grieving-renewal process, and share this in some detail with my readers.

Similar to the experience of losing someone through death, the ending of a relationship also goes through a process. I have experienced this in stages: sadness, anger, seeing reality, seeking understanding, rediscovering self-worth, forgiveness, and risking new beginnings.

Facing the sadness and coping with the pain

For me, the best therapy has always been to flow with my pain and keep the wound exposed, allowing it to heal naturally. I have found that band-aid treatments only prolong the healing process. Tears, journaling, music, and the support of friends are what get me through the grieving.

Most of us fear our tears, as if they are a sign of weakness. But tears, even convulsing sobs, are nothing more than a healthy release acknowledging the loss of someone who was very real and core to our lives. Contrary to the myth, the release of tears makes us stronger. There is a time to cry: the death of a loved one and the ending of a relationship are such instances.

About two weeks after my most recent relationship had ended, a friend held me very close, and the physical proximity led to the outpouring of tears that came from someplace deep inside, some previously untouched place that obviously the relationship and he alone had tapped. My sobs were gut-wrenching but cleansing. Of all the tears I'd cried over this loss, this was the most integral and healthy release of my sadness. By experiencing really painful emotions, we are able to eliminate those aspects of ourselves and move past them. It was a turning point in the process.

Grieving over the loss of someone we love consumes so much energy. We all need an avenue for channeling those feelings. For me, journaling is such a release, giving me an outlet to say it all with nothing held back. It is the right place to let out every feeling, analyze, ask questions and attempt to answer them. And music…there's nothing quite like listening to soothing music to help me heal the loss of someone I love.

My inclination has always been to focus on those who leave, not on those who remain. "As you experience the angst of loss and loneliness, don't forget to image yourself surrounded by all of us who love you," my friend Frank reminded me a few weeks ago. "You are blessed with countless people in your life who care about you. As you feel the emptiness inside, also let in the warmth of that circle of love that enwraps you." As I gradually turned the spotlight away from the stage left empty to the countless loved ones still surrounding me, my healing accelerated.

"I can do that," I whispered between the sobs. For that moment, I could feel the protectiveness of that innermost circle of loving spiritual partners, along with my family and all the close friends who make up the concentric circles of my life. If we think of ourselves as alone, we will continue to exude weakness. But if we can see ourselves connected, our authentic power will once again begin to emanate. The more we can allow ourselves to feel the warmth and loyalty of those who continue to stand by us, along with feeling the loss of those who leave, the healthier we become.

About three weeks after this relationship ended, I spent a week at Lake Tahoe with a group of my tennis friends. My depression was still quite evident and they addressed their concern over dinner: "You need to exercise, move about, get outside and breathe the fresh air; you need to be out with friends during this time." My feeble protest that I didn't want to impose my sadness and tears on them was brushed aside. "That's what friends are for," they reminded me. The next day, the five of us spent a glorious day boating, picnicking, and dining on Lake Tahoe. There were moments when, for the first time since the ending, I could take in a full, deep breath. Tahoe is noted for being one of the coldest lakes in the world. I didn't care. I dove off the side of the boat and swam. For those few minutes, I was revived. I felt invigorated. And even though I have an aversion to the cold, I never noticed the freezing temperature.

Time really does allow for movement. Slowly we regain our appetite. Sleep returns: first only three or four hours, then five or six, until we eventually sleep through the night. And then we find laughter again: a light-hearted movie, a funny joke, something silly that happened. Laughter too can be so healing.

The healing power of anger

I have always fallen in love with men who are good with words. And I have let their words lead the relationship. Once again, for the third time, I repeated that pattern. In this most recent encounter, I developed strong feelings for the man behind the beautiful words. Had I paid more attention to the painful gap that continued between his captivating words and unfulfilled actions, I would have become justifiably angry and spoken up early on to protect myself: "This relationship isn't working for me. Your intervals of silence, creating wide gaps in our communication, are excruciating. And it makes me sad when you don't keep your promises. I want to stop this now before things go any farther between us and before the pain gets any worse."

Why didn't I do that? Because the pain of losing the relationship in my mind outweighed the pain of being in it. I allowed the fear of loss to hold me back from standing up for myself. As I recall the verbal onslaughts I suffered from Mark during the last year, even now I wince at my passive martyr-like behavior. I should have become furious. But out of fear, I clung to a dying relationship. In both instances, they would have had greater respect for me, and I for myself, had I spoken up at the moment it was happening.

This time around, I am feeling the anger as I recall one phone conversation when I raised the issue of why he promised to call and sometimes didn't. He explained that when he was a child, his parents never kept their promises. And that led him to develop a relationship with his grandmother who taught him to build a life of emotional self-sufficiency that didn't depend on others. He concluded the conversation by describing how she had always taught him "to pull out the weeds, while reveling in and savoring the splendor and the fragrance of the flowers"—a principle by which he has lived his life ever since.

What was the point of this lovely story? *Therefore, Rene, you should learn to do that too and not build your hopes around what I or anyone else might promise you?* I could imagine him saying. Propelled *now* by the force of my anger, I realize that his explanation was self-excusing nonsense. In a relationship, you live by your word. You don't promise things that you don't intend to fulfill. By not addressing that issue at the time, I missed the opportunity both to stand up for myself and to share with him an invaluable lesson in what it means to love someone. Not expressing warranted anger delays and thwarts the grieving-renewal process.

Recently, I made a retreat—an intense five-days with Gary Zukav and nearly one hundred other searchers—for the purpose of discovering how to live in spiritual partnership. Along with revealing our wholesome and powerful parts, much of our time was spent in a circle format sharing our feelings as we revealed the unhealed parts of ourselves in an effort to heal them. We were given these simple guidelines: (1) be aware of our intentions, (2) speak from the heart, and (3) detach from the outcome. My intention in being there was to heal the part of me that relinquishes my authentic power when I become deeply involved in a relationship.

One of my greatest awakenings came when I was asked what parts of the circle experience "pushed my buttons" the most. Undoubtedly, it was the interruptions. I found myself getting increasingly upset each time members within the circle would interrupt the speaker reminding that person that he or she was off track, speaking more from head than heart, or otherwise wasting everyone's time. And the demeanor of the one interrupting most often seemed to come from a place of frustration and anger. *If you must break in,* I thought, *can't you at least do so with more compassion, gently nudging the speakers back on track rather than making them feel shut down right in the midst of such painful self-exposure?*

"It is those things that we react to the strongest," reminded our facilitator, "that we should carefully examine within ourselves."

I have long understood that it is not just what attracts us but also what repels us in others that is a mirror of ourselves. But I couldn't see how this had any reflection on me. After all, I don't interrupt others. I can barely get angry without apologizing before I've even gotten the words out of my mouth.

The person with whom I was paired had an insight into her own reactions. She saw the behavior to which she was reacting within the circle as potentially positive— something that, if applied in the right moment, could be beneficial. Ah! The light bulb went off. Of course! Interrupting could be a good thing. In fact, there were times *I* should be the one to question the flow of my relationships—and not necessarily with compassion but from anger—because the interaction between us was no longer helping my growth or respectful of my needs. Some of the prolonged pain of my own relationships came from my lack of courage to be the one to speak up. The very thing that caused me the most reaction in this setting is the very thing I needed most to be my authentic self in relationships. That insight alone was worth the whole retreat.

I felt the anger about my recent relationship dissipate as I reflected back on an e-mail he sent toward the end when he described himself going through "intimate relationship withdrawal" and concluded by saying, "For me, this means, as it has always meant, that I neglect nurturing the flowers while pulling out the weeds." The contradiction was too apparent. My upset turned to concern for him, sensing that, with the pressures he was under, he was not functioning at his best. Had I made this retreat sooner, when he expressed these views, I may have found the courage to speak up and question him, leading us both a step closer to discovering our authentic selves.

Seeing reality as it is and not as we want it to be

I didn't spot the red flags with Mark until shortly after we were married and I received the letter from him letting me know I was not meeting his expectations as a wife. But they were present in my recent relationship only ten days into our exchanging e-mails when silence became an issue. And despite his reassurances that it would not be a recurring event, the starts and stops in our communication never let up throughout the entire time. At first, I addressed it but when intermittent silences persisted, I chose to overlook reality and see the situation as I wanted it to be.

Warning signs usually show up early. Instead of making the decision to ignore them because we've already determined that we are going to go forward—damn the torpedoes, full speed ahead—what we may learn is that there are some red flags worth exploring right away. And if we do, we might overcome them, making our relationship stronger from the onset, or we might decide that the warning signs are significant and unchangeable and it is not in our best interest to go forward. Admittedly, making the latter decision takes self-discipline of the highest form.

Despite the warning signs, during the first days of e-mail exchanges and phone conversations, my new friend met my image of the kind of spiritual partner whom I could love deeply and enduringly. But wasn't it I who said: "The key is to enjoy the journey and not focus on the destination; where this relationship would lead is far less important than what might happen to us both along the way?" Despite every good intention to enjoy the journey for however long it was to be, my heart still longed for a certain outcome. My yearning, which undoubtedly translated more as demanding, drove him into his shell. So much so that we referred to him as the turtle and my pet name for him was turtledove. Once he wrote: "If you need a bit of armor around you for self-protection, I understand completely. We could be a fairytale—the Princess in armor and the Prince who had turned into a turtle under a sorcerer's spell. Will the Prince's kiss melt the armor? Will the Princess's patience and inimitable charms turn him back into a man? These questions are the essence of longing, and fairly I need to understand how painful it can be."

While I sent out vibes that kept him in his shell, he, on the other hand, prevented my enjoyment of the journey by the very fact that he lapsed into periods of silences and broken promises. By not finding security or peacefulness in the journey, I was driven to place more hope in the outcome. Surely, I thought, the agony of the present situation would eventually get better as we grew closer toward some convergence in our relationship. What we were doing to each other was inadvertently a self-replicating pattern.

It is critical to begin each new journey with an agreed upon understanding of what is needed on both sides. And if that agreement is sidetracked, we must have the courage to face it head on. If we're fortunate enough to get it back on track, and if there is real substance and depth to the relationship, I truly believe we will be able to *enjoy* the journey—to grow with it, to give to it, and to receive from it. Begun in this way, based in reality, we lay th foundation for a journey that will carry us upward and forward for however long it may last and wherever it may lead us.

Seeking understanding after the relationship ends

Often at the end of a relationship all contact is stopped because one party is feeling the pain of loss and the other is experiencing some guilt for having caused the hurt. So communication breaks down. I find this ceasing of communication one of the most difficult aspects of the whole experience. It prevents us from ever getting to the point of being able to ask the pressing questions and offer valuable insights that would bring genuine closure to that phase of the relationship.

For the sake of mutual self-discovery, I believe it would be healthiest, after some time has passed, for former lovers to just talk from their hearts about the cross-currents that created the undertow in the relationship. Of course it takes a lot of courage to be this honest with each other. We would want to have gotten through most of the grieving process before attempting such an in-depth conversation or even letter or e-mail exchanges. Otherwise, we might be too vulnerable to hear the truth. Clearly, this level of communication can only occur where there was a great deal of caring on both sides.

Chances are, the bond broke down because one or both parties grew too afraid to tell the other the truth of what was happening inside of them. Had a more honest exchange occurred, however difficult to say, the relationship might have changed, but the spiritual bond could also have deepened. It would be most regrettable if that opportunity were missed a second time.

This conversation, of course, can only take place once both parties are certain that the relationship is over, at least in the form that it once had. The partner who left is not likely to respond openly if he/she thinks that the one who was left is really asking questions for the purpose of getting back together. It must be clear to all that the motivation is purely one of desire to grow personally from what we learn, and to make ourselves more ready for our future.

If this understanding can be achieved, it is only natural to want to raise questions—deep, penetrating ones—when a relationship ends. In my situation, I reflected back to the poem my previous husband, Jim, wrote as part of his marriage vows to me: *It is not love I now fear, but a life without it.... More than anything else, I want to hold you in my arms, gently, beyond sex and security, prestige and triumph, to say once and for all, "I love you," and mean it from the top of my head to the depths of my soul.* I thought about Mark's wedding vows: *I am prepared to give up all that I hold dear in this world for your presence in my life. You are the "pearl of great price" whom I have sought for 41 years—the very completion of my destiny and nothing short of death can drag me ever from your side....* I thought about my most recent relationship when we were first e-mailing: *You move me at the very heart and core of who I am.*

Was there something that gradually revealed itself in me that caused these feelings to change? Or perhaps what they discovered triggered unwanted introspection within themselves and challenged their own personal development. The very act of asking these questions raises self-doubt. What we want is to move beyond self-effacing to examine, as objectively as possible, what really happened. We want to look at ourselves in a positive way while asking pertinent, probing, dig-deep questions. "Can you tell me for my own personal growth at what point you knew that I wasn't right for you in the relationship? When did you sense that the flame was dying? What quality did you find more attractive in someone else? Tell me whatever you can tell me in detail so that I can get past this and move on." When we go on to be with someone else, the relationship will be different, but *we* will still be the same. So that we can learn about ourselves, we want to know the part about *us*—at what point the chemistry changed and the spiritual bond was breaking down.

If we are committed to growing as persons, we don't want to sweep this experience under the rug. If there is something in ourselves that we have the power to change and that will cause us to be more loving and more lovable from this point forward, then most of us would want to seize that opportunity. So, if there was genuine depth to a relationship, these are appropriate discussions that merit being shared.

I have been through the ending of a number of significant relationships over the past nearly forty years: with my high school sweetheart, my religious community, my son's father, Jim again and again, Mark, and now my most recent one. While I have always come away with an understanding of what I gave to and received from these experiences, I have not always let them know. With the right moment for open conversation, I would want that opportunity to share what growth occurred for each of us as a result of our time together.

Obviously, the chance for caring communication with our former partners may not always be possible. In that event, we can think about employing alternative approaches to achieve the same purpose, perhaps seeking professional counseling or spiritual direction or turning to close friends who were present during the relationship. My friend Nancy observed that I was making positive strides in my choice of partners. "I saw something different in you this time," she commented. "In your relationship to Mark, you gradually lost you. You changed to become someone you thought you should become to make the relationship with him work. This time, you grew. You remained yourself and better: you matured into a stronger and more total person." It was good to hear from someone close to me that my self-esteem returned with a vengeance.

Rediscovering our self-worth

It is only natural that we lose confidence when a relationship ends. This is a crucial period for honest probing: *how in the world did I wind up here—and alone?* Confronting this issue sets into motion the rebuilding of our self-worth.

This kind of soul-searching naturally leads us to assess the partners we've had and to revisit our values that are in keeping with our authentic selves. What elements in the relationship fostered our true nature and enhanced our worth as persons? What did I give to and what did I receive from the relationship? A deeper ability to love, a better grasp of life, experiences we would never have had otherwise, a child? And, conversely, what needs were unmet for me in my past relationships? What values were suppressed? What contributed to my sadness *during* the relationship? In my own life, I have always needed communication, even if hurtful. But when my partners' prolonged silence displaced this, it caused me agonizing pain. The answers to these questions will identify the weak and strong links in the chain of our values within relationships.

The greatest fear most of us have at the end of a relationship is that we will be alone, that we will never again experience the kind of intimacy we once knew or desire to have again. The love given and received in my relationships with Jim and Mark, even though they ended, made it increasingly possible for me to know that I am capable of such love again. My first and greatest joy since the ending of my marriage to Mark is to discover that my capacity to feel those feelings was still inside of me and, in fact, had never left me. This provides me with some understanding as to why I so willingly entered into this latest relationship. During our intense though brief involvement, he reinforced my own self-worth as he continually reminded me of the beauty of my soulful nature. "Your intensity and totalness are among the loveliest things about you," he wrote once. His experience of love in previous relationships, as he had described them, was based on pragmatism and responsibility. I feel that I was able to demonstrate for him the power of loving freely and openly without constraints, and perhaps liberating him from the guilt-ridden, accountable kind of love to which he had become accustomed. It is the acknowledgement and appreciation of these types of gifts shared with another human being that would cause one to shout out: I am alive and capable of loving again!

Looking back and reflecting on what I've carried from previous relationships, I see a wealth of values and skills that I either questioned or didn't realize I possessed. Thanks to the honest appraisal of my former partners, after going down into the depths of self-doubt, I emerged from my relationships with a greatly heightened self-esteem. Without Mark, I wouldn't have had the nerve to go beyond writing technical training manuals. Without this last relationship, I could not have envisioned myself addressing and motivating women throughout the world. If we can identify and celebrate our gifts to each other and can acknowledge that we have grown for having had these experiences, then the relationship will have enhanced our lifelong process of personal growth. But its real value is in the rediscovery of our self-worth and what each of us carries away and retains as a part of ourselves forever.

Healing through forgiveness

It is the cumulative effect of all of these experiences that can lay the foundation for the kind of healing that comes only through forgiveness. I recently attended a talk given by Archbishop Desmond Tutu from South Africa. His message was a simple one: There are three ways that couples, communities, or nations go about healing major rifts: retribution, amnesia, or reconciliation. The first method demands that each strike back, setting off an inexorable spiral of revenge, of reprisal provoking counter reprisal. The second suggests that they let "bygones be bygones," turning a blind eye to the past. But we are often reminded that "those who forget the past are doomed to repeat it." When we don't deal effectively with our past, when we pretend it hasn't happened, predictably it will return to haunt us. The third way, reconciling love, teaches us that there is no future without forgiveness. Whether we are speaking of healing the grievances between countries or the fall-out between two individuals, the options are the same. Neither getting even nor seeking to forget the past will solve anything. There simply is no healing without expressed forgiveness on both sides.

If we truly want to be healed from our past or recent relationships, it is vital that we create an opportunity to let our partner know that we have forgiven him or her and, at the same time, to ask for forgiveness. Rarely does anyone set out to hurt the other. Certainly Mark and I didn't. Nor did my recent relationship. While it may appear on the surface that I am the one whose spirit is more broken, both of them also experienced pain over our relationships ending. Never should I be afraid to be the first to forgive and to realize those things for which I need to be forgiven. As Mark Twain said so beautifully, forgiveness is the fragrance the violet sheds on the heel that crushed it.

Were this to happen, the question of continued friendship would naturally arise. It takes two very secure people with a strong sense of their self-worth to transform their formerly romantic relationship into an evolving friendship. Sadly, this isn't for everyone. It is one of the deepest sorrows of my life when I am not in communication with cherished former partners. Nevertheless, for such an extraordinary event to occur, it needs to unfold gradually over time energized by the ongoing healing and forgiveness of each other. If this can be accomplished, the new friendship can often be an even greater bonding than what it was before. Because we know each other so well, we have even more to offer one another in our pursuit for spiritual growth.

A word of caution is needed here: Sometimes the one choosing to end the relationship pledges friendship as a means of letting the other one down more easily. So how are we to know if friendship is being offered sincerely? This is the time, more than ever, to listen to the other's *actions,* not just the words. If the departing partner pursues a friendship, and we decide that we want that and are able to handle it, then we can respond. But, in the early stages, it is important to discern the leaver's intentions; it is not up to the one left to initiate the friendship. When two people do succeed in having friendship be the outgrowth of a close personal relationship, it can lead to one that holds a special place in that intimate circle of spiritual partners in our lives. And its healing power can also free us even more for the next phase of our lives. But, like everything else, this too will unfold in its own way and time. You and I cannot mandate it.

Risking new beginnings in the name of love

Loving thoughts of Jim have consumed me for more than a quarter of a century, of Mark for the past decade, and of my newest friend for the past several months. There are moments with each of them that I will treasure for a lifetime.

The week I spent in this latest relationship on Heron Island, twenty miles off the coast of Australia on the Great Barrier Reef, was one such time. On my last day there, with Tony O'Connor's "Mariner" playing in the background, and in response to his earlier "come with me" invitation, I wrote a birthday poem for him reflecting my philosophy of spiritual partnership.

> *Come with me you ask, with sails unfurled*
> *You may not see me, yet I am there*
> *Docked and waiting for you with spinnakers open wide*
> *Ready to embark on a sacred journey side by side*
> *   Oh yes, far from any town*
> *   Out beyond the pier that ties ships down.*

Afterword

Come with me you ask, beyond the jagged reef
Always present even when hidden beneath the rising tide
Yet you and I—we know it looms
Soon to be exposed again by recurring magnetic moons
We'll find the channel that can lead us—you and me
To a passage of our hearts onto the open sea.

Come with me you ask, where the sun never sets
But what of those glorious sunsets we watched
As they slipped behind the horizon of the waters edge
Orange and golden hues lighting up the earth's ledge
A reminder that there's always another tomorrow
Where true joy evolves out of yesterday's sorrow.

Beyond the storm clouds and far from the noisy ports of call
We share secrets of the heart meant only for you and me
A voyage of our spirits devoid of outside acclaim
Knowing with certainty our lives will never be the same
Brought together by some celestial Sovereignty
Bound soulfully in spirit, not entrapped by decree.

Come with me as I would come with you
To a faraway place where even the tortoise and the heron
Find safe haven to breed their young
Sharing painful emotions knowing that healing will come
Where caring far transcends even the ocean's rhythmic rhyme
Trusting at last in a love that does not fade with time.

To experience love, even if only for a brief time, is to be fully and genuinely alive. No one who has loved another person comes away less for it—even if it seems weighted to one side or comes to an abrupt end. As difficult as it may seem, I now know that the measure of a relationship is not in its duration but in the quality and depth of love and the personal growth it engendered. Without taking a risk in the name of love, I would have missed out on these life-enriching experiences.

I will not even attempt to understate the anguish that comes with the shutting down of a significant relationship. But the reality is: *that pain always passes.* "Love comes to slay what needs to be slain in us, in order for something new to emerge," Marianne Williamson writes. "It is hard to go through this, to surrender deeply to the waters of intimate romance, to wield its power and endure its pain, without a sense of God's love moving through us in the process." Withdrawing into oneself for fear of being hurt is to shut out the possibility of ever loving again; it is to shut out the possibility of God's love moving through us in this manner. Holding back will almost certainly ensure our worst fear—that we will be alone, that we will never again experience the kind of genuine intimacy that allows us to share every aspect of ourselves with another person without fear of rejection.

No, it isn't fear of being hurt that should concern us. It is a life without experiencing the joy of loving and being loved that should terrify us. The only real tragedy is never to have loved at all. Life *is* relationships and the personal growth that emerges from them. Understanding how they fit into our lives is the key to experiencing lifelong joy and peace. It is worth the pain and the soul-searching to discover how they shape our lives. The anguish that accompanies the ending of a relationship is merely the release of our soul's outer covering, like the shedding of placenta after birth, exposing its true essence. The process serves as a reminder that our spirit is letting go of something that had become a vital part of us and preparing itself for the experience of new life.

Fear of love translates into fear of living. Embrace each new spiritual bond without hesitation, allowing the spirit of loving another to fill our bodies and souls that it may spread throughout every fiber of our beings. We want to treasure each moment with special persons in our lives. If we are only blessed with being loved, then "dayennu," it is enough. But, if we have the joy of loving in return, then "dayennu, dayennu."

None of my experiences in relationships has caused me to lose my idealism. On the contrary, I am still awed by a marriage of two people who have lived together and grown deeper in love for thirty, forty, fifty years. I am also relieved that I am not one of the marriages still together that long *without* love. But I am also a realist. Remaining happily married to one person for fifty years requires perseverance, shared values, mutual growth, and a lot of good fortune. Some marriages last that probably shouldn't. Others go apart that, perhaps with a little mutual effort, could have endured. But "'til death do us part" is no longer a realistic and achievable standard for the majority of couples entering into relationships today—unless we mean by this the "death" of the relationship. And as lives are extended through the advancement of science, it becomes even less probable that a marriage begun at the age of 25 or 30 will last for 70 or more years. It is conceivable that some men and women will experience two or three 15-, 20-, 25-year treasured relationships over their lifetime. Others will take roads less traveled in the past. Each one will take them further along life's journey. But eventually they are likely to go through the anguish of endings…in order to move on to new beginnings.

The death of a relationship is as enigmatic as its first signs of life. We are as startled by its initial development as we are by its shutting down. Even if the downward spiral was evident, relationship endings generally catch us by surprise. And we are quick to place blame. Even when it ends in death, such blaming occurs. But what if we were to enter our relationships realizing that they have a life expectancy—some longer, some shorter, some "'til death do us part"? We may try to prolong them—that's only natural—but all too often they define their own boundaries, identifying their own culmination and breakdown, not so unlike the feebleness of old age signifies impending death.

I began and now end this book with one thought: The heartrending sadness resulting from a relationship ending need not signal failure but can be the portal to an even deeper experience of personal growth, guiding us to a renewal of our present situation in a new form or forging out to create an entirely new spiritual bonding. It would be most unfortunate if, at the ending of such shared closeness, we found nothing to appreciate. The merit of a relationship is not necessarily in its lasting forever. Its value lies in the journey two people shared while together and the heightened awareness that each carries forward.

It is that forward thrust that gives life its meaning, in which each conclusion is only the beginning of yet another level of personal growth, a new transition of life experience. Despite how difficult this lesson of appreciating the journey has been for me, little by little I am learning it. I doubt that I am alone in this struggle. It may be one of the most fundamental lessons of life. Once we have fully experienced the emptiness, we will then be ready to open ourselves again. Once we have related the ending of our relationship back to its beginning— remembering the joyfulness and spirit of loving exchanges—are we able to move beyond blaming. Only to the extent that we feel both the yin and yang, closing down while we go through the deep sense of loss, experiencing forgiveness, and then gradually opening up to the possibility of a new spiritual bonding, will we be ready to explore a fresh passage of the heart.

But why, you ask. Why can't it just all work out? Because. Just because. Renewal in our lives manifests itself only after crisis. Growth occurs during times of discomfort. We cannot know the ecstasies of loving without having suffered its agonies. Without experiencing death, we cannot know the meaning of resurrection. Without fear we cannot know courage. Without sadness, we cannot know the true meaning of joy. Before we can soar through the clouds like an eagle, we must know what it is to be vulnerable, despondent, and left abandoned on the earth.

Nature itself teaches us the significance and the euphoria of new life as we watch each bud emerge and each season recycle itself from planting to harvesting. Without letting go of the dream, we cannot face the reality. And without facing the reality, we cannot put closure to our old life. Without endings there can be no new beginnings. As we experience the closing of each phase of our lives, around the corner waiting for us is another new beginning. After we have looked our past squarely in the eye, then we can be ready for our future. We need only reach out and take hold of it.